D0744303

The Persisting
Osler—III

The Persisting Osler—III

Selected Transactions of the American Osler Society 1991–2000

Edited by

Jeremiah A. Barondess, M.D.
Charles G. Roland, M.D.

Krieger Publishing Company
Malabar, Florida
2002

Original Edition 2002

Printed and Published by
KRIEGER PUBLISHING COMPANY
KRIEGER DRIVE
MALABAR, FL 32950

Copyright ©2002 by Krieger Publishing Company

All rights reserved. No part of this book may be reproduced in any form or
by any means, electronic or mechanical, including right of transmission and
information storage and retrieval systems without permission in writing from
the publisher.
No liability is assumed with respect to the use of the information contained herein.
Printed in the United States of America.

FROM A DECLARATION OF PRINCIPLES JOINTLY ADOPTED BY
A COMMITTEE OF THE AMERICAN BAR ASSOCIATION AND A
COMMITTEE OF PUBLISHERS:

This publication is designed to provide accurate and authoritative
information in regard to the subject matter covered. It is sold with the
understanding that the publisher is not engaged in rendering legal,
accounting, or other professional service. If legal advice or other expert
assistance is required, the services of a competent professional person
should be sought.

Library of Congress Cataloging-in-Publication Data

The persisting Osler, III : selected transactions of the American Osler
Society, 1991–2000 / edited by Jeremiah A. Barondess, Charles G. Roland.
    p. ; cm.
   Includes index.
   ISBN 1-57524-191-9 (cloth : alk. paper)
    1. Physicians—Canada—Biography—Congresses. I. Title: Persisting
Osler, three. II. Title: Persisting Osler, 3. III. Barondess, Jeremiah A.,
1924– IV. Roland, Charles G. V. American Osler Society. Meeting.
    [DNLM: 1. Osler, William, Sir, 1849–1919. 2. American Osler Society.
3. Physicians—Biography. 4. Physicians—Congresses. WZ 100 O82p 2002]
R464.O8 P4723 2002
610′.92—dc21
   [B]   2001038852

   10 9 8 7 6 5 4 3 2

To those who value the timeless precepts
exemplified by the life and work of
William Osler as guideposts for the physician.

Contents

SECTION III   Clinical Matters   157

SECTION IV   Societies   187

SECTION V   Varia   239

 # Contributors

Stephen Ashwal, M.D.
Head, Division of Child Neurology,
Departmnet of Pediatrics, Loma Linda School
of Medicine, Loma Linda, California

Jeremiah A. Barondess, M.D.
President, New York Academy of Medicine,
New York City

Michael Bliss, M.D.
Professor of History and History of Medicine,
University of Toronto, Toronto, Ontario

Charles S. Bryan, M.D.
Heywood Gibbes Distinguished Professor of
Internal Medicine and Chair, Department of
Medicine, University of South Carolina School
of Medicine, Columbia, South Carolina

Dee J. Canale, M.D.
Associate Clinical Professor, Department of
Neurosurgery, University of Tennessee,
Memphis, Tennessee

G. S. T. Cavanagh
Bookseller, Emeritus Books, Athens, Georgia

Marilyn Fransiszyn, M.L.S.
Librarian, Humanities and Social Science
Library, McGill University, Montreal, Quebec

W. Bruce Fye, M.D., M.A.
Professor of Medicine and the History of Medi-
cine, Mayo Medical School, Rochester,
Minnesota

Christopher G. Goetz, M.D.
Professor, Neurological Science,
Rush University, Chicago, Illinois

Richard L. Golden, M.D.
Curator, The Osler Library; Assistant Professor
of Clinical Medicine, SUNY/Stony Brook,
Centerport, New York

Shigeaki Hinohara, M.D.
Chairman of the Board, St Luke's
International Hospital, Tokyo, Japan

Patricia G. Kahn, M.L.S.
Librarian, Penobscot Bay Medical Center,
Rockland, Maine

Richard J. Kahn, M.D.
Staff Internist and Chairman, Education
Committee, Penobscot Bay Medical Center,
Rockland, Maine

Jack D. Key, M.A., M.S.
Emeritus Librarian, Mayo Clinic and Mayo
Medical School, Sandia Park, New Mexico

Joseph W. Lella, Ph.D.
Professor of Sociology, King's College, and
Professor of History of Medicine, University of
Western Ontario, London, Ontario

Lawrence D. Longo, M.D.
Director, Center for Perinatal Biology, Depart-
ment of Physiology and Obstetrics and
Gynecology, Loma Linda School of Medicine,
Loma Linda, California

Janet K. Murray, M.D.
Medical Humanities Program, Dalhousie
Medical School, Halifax, Nova Scotia

T. Jock Murray, M.D.
Professor of Medical Humanities, Dalhousie
Medical School, Halifax, Nova Scotia

David S. Musto, M.D.
Professor of Child Psychiatry and the
History of Medicine, Yale School of Medicine,
New Haven, Connecticut

Alvin E. Rodin, M.D.
Professor of Pathology, Wright State University,
Dayton, Ohio
Deceased

Charles G. Roland, M.D.
Jason A. Hannah Professor Emeritus,
Medical History, McMaster University,
Hamiliton, Ontario

Mark E. Silverman, M.D., M.A.C.P., F.A.C.C.
Professor of Medicine (Cardiology), Emory
University School of Medicine, Atlana, Georgia

Marvin J. Stone, M.D.
Chief of Oncology and Director, Sammons
Cancer Center, Baylor University Medical
Center, Dallas, Texas

Herbert M. Swick, M.D.
Executive Director, Institute of Medicine and
Humanities, and Professor, University of
Montana, Missoula, Montana

John T. Truman, M.D., M.P.H.
Professor of Clinical Medicine, College of
Physicians and Surgeons, Columba University,
New York City

Charles T. Wooley, M.D.
Professor of Medicine, Division of Cardiology,
Department of Internal Medicine, The Ohio
State University, Columbus, Ohio

# Preface

The third decade in the life of the American Osler Society ended in 2000. One not unanticipated consequence is the publication of a third decennial volume of papers selected from talks delivered at Society meetings between 1991 and 2000.

It is of great interest that the major threads of Osler's life, clinical topics, medical societies, friendships and the wider philosophical and historical basis of clinical medicine, continue to catalyze the interests of many. In an increasingly scientific and technologic age, with greater focus on biological mechanisms of disease, broad areas of inquiry that amount to the sturdy roots of a comprehensive and thoughtful life for the clinician attract increasing numbers and energize activities across the whole range.

In keeping with the above, one of the charms of the American Osler Society annual meetings, and of the meetings of Osler societies generally, is the remarkable range of subjects discoursed upon. As it did for the first two volumes, this diversity characterizes *Persisting Osler III*. From Benjamin Franklin (Swick) to the launching of the USS *William Osler* (Bryan and Fransiszyn), from America's first medical journal (Kahn) to a trove of Lady Osler's letters (Bliss), and from the founding of the Japan Osler Society (Hinohara) to the Charaka Club (Truman)—the range is eclectic and stimulating.

The selection process has, perhaps, been most difficult for this anthology. The cause has been and increase in both quantity of papers presented— our meetings are becoming longer— and in quality. A number of fine papers simply could not be fitted into the confines of the book.

We continue to hope, in the words of the Preface to the first volume, that "these essays will serve to stimulate thought and further exploration of those timeless issues that captured Sir William's energies, and that remain vital for the modern physician."

Jeremiah A. Barondess, M.D.
Charles G. Roland, M.D.

SECTION I

Personalia

"James Bovell, A Remarkable 19th Century Canadian Physician and the Forgotten Mentor of William Osler"*

 Mark E. Silverman, M.D., M.A.C.P., F.A.C.C.

From age 19 and throughout the rest of his life, William Osler was observed to scribble absent-mindedly the name "James Bovell" again and again. In "The Life of William Osler", Cushing comments about Osler's student book of October, 1869.[1] *"In pencil on the fly-leaf in W.O.'s hand is: 'James Bovell, M.D., M.R.C.P'. . . . ..and through the book the name is scribbled whenever a lapse appears to have occurred in the lecture, or the student's mind wandered—'James Bovell, M.D., M.R.C.P.'; 'James Bovell M.D.' The man must have come to exercise an extraordinary influence over the boy, and to his last days, as will be seen, in moments of absent-mindedness or when trying a pen it was the name of James Bovell that came first to paper, not his own."* Cushing refers to this life-long habit again and again. In like fashion, Marcia C. Noyes, a librarian at Maryland, wrote: *"In my early days at the Library, when Dr. Osler used to sit across from me at my double desk, he would absent-mindedly pick up a pencil and apparently scribble idly on scratch pad, blotter, anything at hand. Finally, it was impressed on my consciousness that it was always the same two words that were written, "James Bovell."*[2] Who was this man who could inspire such an intense devotion in the young Osler? Surprisingly little has been written about James Bovell, one of the three teachers to whom Osler dedicated his "Principles and Practice of Medicine."[3] (Fig. 1A & B)

Revised from a presentation at the American Osler Society, March 26, 1992, San Diego.

Reprinted by permission of the publisher, *Can Med Assoc J,* 1993; 148 (6), pp. 953–957. ©1993 Canadian Medical Association.

Fig. 1A James Bovell, age approximately 17.

Photograph used by permission of the Museum of the History of Medicine, The Academy of Medicine, Toronto.

Early life and schooling

Bovell was born in Barbados, West Indies, in 1817, the eldest son of a wealthy banker.[4–6] At age 17, after early schooling in Barbados, he traveled to England to enter Trinity College, Cambridge but became ill and decided instead to study medicine at Guy's Hospital in London. His teachers were Astley Cooper, Richard Bright, and Thomas Addison, all of whom he revered and would never tire of talking about in later years.[6] At age 18, he married Julia Howard of Barbados. They subsequently had four daughters. From England, he went to Edinburgh to learn morbid anatomy and then to Dublin where he studied under William Stokes and Robert Graves and obtained his M.D. degree in 1838. While in Ireland he contracted typhus. In 1839, he was admitted as an Extra-Licentiate into the Royal College of Physicians, London. Against advice from Stokes, who predicted a great career for him in the British Isles, he

Fig. 1B James Bovell later in life.

Photograph used by permission of the McGill Osler Library of the History of Medicine

returned to practice in the West Indies from 1840 until 1848 when he joined a number of West Indians who decided to migrate to Upper Canada.

Move to Canada and professional recognition

Bovell was now 31 and brought with him a prized microscope, one of the first in Canada, which would eventually figure importantly in his future friendship with Reverend William Arthur Johnson and the young Osler.[4] He settled in Toronto where he quickly became a prominent physician in the town of 30,000 inhabitants.[7] In 1850, Bovell and five other physicians offered their services to Bishop Strachan as medical faculty to Trinity Medical College, a newly formed Church of England University.[7,8] At Trinity, he held the initially unpaid positions of Professor of the Institutes of Medicine and Dean of the

Faculty from 1852 until 1856 when he and other members of the faculty were reprimanded for ignoring instructions of the College Council, incurring unauthorized expenses, inserting unapproved advertisements of medical courses in the press, and negotiating directly with the government.[7,8] This was apparently an effort by the faculty to increase their limited income by enlarging the classes with students who did not belong to the Anglican Church. Although they apologized for their actions, the entire faculty resigned; the Trinity Medical School folded and was not reestablished until 1871.[4,7,8] Bovell, however, remained at Trinity University as Professor of Natural Theology.[8]

During the 1850's, Bovell gained the reputation of being the best trained and educated physician in Canada.[4,9] He helped found and became the editor of "The Upper Canada Journal of Medical, Surgical and Physical Science", was one of the first councilors to the Royal Canadian Institute, a lecturer of Physiology and Pathology at the Toronto School of Medicine, and Professor of Natural Theology at Trinity University. Later he became lecturer in physiology to the Upper Canada Veterinary School.[10] He was regarded as a brilliant lecturer with a keen wit and considerable fluency of expression; however, *"his intuitive grasp of ideas was so rapid that he failed to make allowance for the slower perceptions of less gifted minds."*[6] His kindness, erudition, and enthusiasm for medicine made him a favorite with students.

Medical pioneer and social crusader

About half of his approximately thirty publications were medical.[5] They reflected a scientific zeal and curiosity based on his microscopic interests, and contained a number of important observations enhanced by his scholarly, classical allusions.[4] He pioneered in the use of cow's milk as a transfusion for cholera victims based on an erroneous microscopic impression that the milk globules were transformed into white blood cells.[9,10] Bovell tried this novel approach on seven patients who were near death; two recovered while several others made a dramatic rally. A keen and compassionate reformer, he published in 1862 "A Plea for Inebriate Asylums Commended to the Consideration of the Legislators of the Province of Canada", in which he remonstrated on the consequences of alcohol on society and proposed an institution of rehabilitation, including his own architectural designs, that was never adopted.[11] He was an early crusader for improved hygiene who advocated cleaning up the filthy living conditions and water in the mid-nineteenth century though he did not anticipate the germ theory of disease that would come with the discoveries of Pasteur in the late 1870's and 1880's. In 1863 he was the anesthetist at the time of the first death from chloroform at Toronto General Hospital.[9,12] A jury trial was held and he was exonerated.

Religious beliefs and accomplishments

Bovell was a deeply religious man, devoted to the Anglican Church, and regarded as saintly with a moral nature of unusual delicacy and fineness.[4] He had a frank, kindly disposition which made him loved and deeply respected by his professional colleagues and the community. It was said that *"vice naturally avoided him, virtue was drawn towards him, and the good side of a man instinctively showed itself in his presence."*[6] From 1851 to 1869 he served as Lay Secretary to the Synod of the Diocese of Toronto under the autocratic Bishop Strachan with whom he would have doctrinal disputes leading to his resignation from the medical faculty. He wrote a number of religious treatises and his physiology lectures to the third year arts students at Trinity College were based on his "Outlines of Natural Theology" which attempted to rebut Darwin's revolutionary theories of evolution of 1859 while tracing the divine descent of man.[5,13] His religious beliefs were in the tradition of the ritualists who had brought the Catholic traditions of the Oxford movement to the parishes.[4] For this, he was denounced as "Romish" by the Bishop of Huron in 1860. Despite attempts to prove his loyalty to the church, he was censured.

Bovell becomes friends with the young Osler

In the early 1860's, Reverend William Arthur Johnson founded a private boys school in Weston, near the Humber River, which became known as Trinity College School in 1864. Johnson and Bovell were close friends, based on a shared devotion to the Anglican Church and their enthusiastic interest in natural science as viewed in the microscope.[4] Bovell became the medical director and ex-officio governor of the school spending parts of each weekend with Johnson in the Humber River Valley collecting, staining, and mounting specimens for study. In January 1866, William Osler, the 16 year-old son of Reverend Featherstone Osler, enrolled at the Trinity College School. A classmate recalls the young Osler: *"I can see him now soon after arrival at the rectory—with a red pocket-handkerchief round his neck and a sling in hand taking a survey of any chance birds in the garden."*[14] Osler soon became a companion to the two men on their nature expeditions and was captivated and influenced by them and their microscope. He wrote to his cousin, Jeanette, *". . . I have splendid times with Mr. Johnson out after specimens of all sorts. . . . And if you could only see the Algae, that green stuff that you see on ponds and stagnant water, it is so beautiful, the thousands upon thousands of small animals all alive and kicking that are in it."*[15]

Osler is influenced by Bovell to enter medicine

In 1867, he enrolled in Trinity College in Toronto, apparently planning to study theology and enter the church. His mother wrote Jeanette in 1868, *"While in Toronto I made a point of speaking to Dr. Bovel (Willie's greatest friend) to ask his candid opinion as to the boy's future . . . and which way he would advise me to throw my influence. He said by no means dissuade him from the Church; underneath the surface his feelings were deep and sincere and the boy, having varied talents, was never likely to strikingly excel in any one thing."*[16] During his first year at Trinity, Osler spent considerable time at the Bovell house, collecting and preparing specimens and following Bovell to medical school to hear him lecture. Osler later commented on Bovell's lectures: *"With equal readiness he would discuss the Origin of Species, the theories of Kant, Hamilton, and Comte, or the doctrine of the Real Presence; and what he had to say was well worthy of attention, for his powers of criticism and analysis were good."*[6] Bovell's granddaughter wrote about Osler, *"He was about twenty in those days and literally lived at our house. He adored grandfather and the latter loved him like a son—and they were both crazy about the microscope. Mother says her life was a perfect burden to her with weird parcels arriving which might contain a rattlesnake, a few frogs, toads or dormice. She found quite a large snake meandering around the study one afternoon, and when she protested violently, the two told her she should not have been in there . . . "*[17] The influence of Bovell the physician won out. When Osler returned for a second year, he told Bovell he was determined to go into medicine to which Bovell replied, *"That's splendid, come along with me."*[4] Curiously, as Osler was turning from the church to enter medicine, Bovell was taking the opposite pathway.[9] During the next two years, the two were like father and son as Osler lived in Bovell's house, followed in his footsteps, and became familiar with the extensive collection of classic and scientific books in his library. Years later, Osler looked back at that period, *"Three years of association with Dr. Bovell were most helpful. Books and the Man!—the best the human mind has afforded was on his shelves, and in him all that one could desire in a teacher—a clear head and a loving heart. Infected with the Aesculapian spirit he made me realize the truth of those memorable words in the Hippocratic oath, "I will honour as my father the man who teaches me the Art."*[18]

Bovell's haphazard medical practice

Osler also relates later about Bovell that *"the exacting details of practice were irksome to him, and too often appointments were neglected and patients forgotten in the absorbing pursuit of a microscopic research, or the seductive pages of Hamilton or Spencer."*[6] Bovell put blisters on a patient and forgot about them for three weeks. He misplaced his horse and buggy until they were found in front of a patient's house the next day. On one occasion he advised an ill student to go to bed and remain there until he checked him in the morning. He totally forgot about him until three days later when he took Osler with him to find a patient whose name and address he could not remember. The student, who had recovered, was walking on the street when he spotted Bovell looking distressed and Osler running door to door asking if there was a sick man in the house. Osler tried to bring some order into the haphazard collections from Bovell's consulting practice by collecting and placing fees in the table drawer but as needy patients would come in, Bovell would hand out the money for food and medicine so that none would be left.[19]

Probably on advice from Bovell, Osler decided to switch from Trinity to McGill in 1870 to enhance his clinical opportunities. Before Bovell departed for the West Indies that summer, he provided a letter of recommendation for Osler to Palmer Howard, Professor of Medicine at McGill.

Bovell leaves Canada and forsakes medicine for the church

In 1870, at the age of 53, Bovell decided to visit the West Indies apparently intending to return to Canada.[4] For uncertain reasons, perhaps related to the new medical school at Trinity or to turmoil occurring in the church, he remained in the West Indies except for two brief visits to Toronto. He purchased some property for his family, made arrangements with Osler to take care of his microscopes, and then responded to the call of the Church of England. He was ordained in six months and became rector at St. George's and St. John's parishes in the mountainous island of Nevis, W.I. in 1871 at a time of great poverty. In 1872 he wrote to Osler, *"The Church here is in an awful state, it is being disestablished and disendowed and the negroid life is a very sorry one to work with.* " He considered leaving Nevis for India where *"its teeming population and the immense wealth of its native princes and merchants affords all a professional can desire."* [20]

He decided to remain, however disconsolate, and wrote to James Bovell Johnson, his namesake and the son of Reverend Johnson, *"I am a most miserable recluse and rarely see any but the members of my own family. You see my clothing is Brian O'Lyng's for I have no breeches to wear. . . . .We have had a terrible time of it."* [20] Little is known of his last few years but he maintained his avid interest in the microscope and wrote to James Bovell Johnson, *"I am not idle but have collected a good deal towards a little Class Book on Germs in relation to Disease, but I am kept back for want of a high objective. I had just written to Beck about his 1/20th when your letter comes. Becks is $85 so I felt quite dispirited. Have a talk with Fred, and see if he can squeeze out 65 for Spencers Professional 1/4 which must be a wonderful Glass. I am very poor it is true, but my goodness anything to relieve this cruel monotony."* [20] He suffered a stroke at the age of 63 and died January 16, 1880 in Charlestown, Nevis, West Indies. Bovell is buried in the churchyard of St. Thomas Lowland.

Bovell's lasting influence on William Osler

The parallel medical and religious attainments by Bovell were impressive in themselves; but his lasting tribute became his influence on William Osler. Osler may well have achieved his ultimate success and acclaim without the early guidance of James Bovell, but Osler had the enormous good fortune to find just the right mentor at the formative stage of his career. As one thinks about Bovell—a great physician, humanist, teacher, microscopist, reformer, bibliophile, classicist, and leader—the very traits and interests that Osler cultivated in his own career are easily recognized. Certainly it was Bovell who turned Osler toward a career in medicine.

In an obituary written in 1880, Osler reflects on the beneficent effect that Bovell had upon him and others, *"The influence for good which a life like that of Dr. Bovell exercises in the profession and in society at large is in many ways incalculable. Enthusiasm, high moral principle, and devotion at a shrine other than that of material prosperity, are not the qualities that build a princely fortune, but they tell not only on a man's own generation, but upon the minds and hearts of those who are growing up around him, so that his own high purpose and unselfish life find living echoes when he himself has long passed away."* [6] However, with a twinge of regret at a potential unfulfilled, Osler later remarked, *"Only men of a certain metal rise superior to their surroundings, and while Dr. Bovell had that all-important combination of boundless ambition with energy and industry, he had that fatal quality of diffuseness, in which even genius is strangled. . . . .yet withal his main business in life was as a physician, much sought after for his skill in diagnosis, and much beloved for his loving heart. When in September 1870 he wrote to me that he did not intend to return from the West Indies I felt that I had lost a father and a friend."* [21]

Acknowledgements

The author expresses his deep appreciation to the following for source material: Canon G.P.J. Walker, St. Kitt's, West Indies; W. Bruce Fye, M.D., Marshfield, Wisconsin; Thomas W. Dukes, D.V.M., Ontario, Canada; Wayne LeBel,

Osler Library of the History of Medicine, McGill University, Montreal, Canada; and the Diocese of Toronto Archives, Anglican Church of Canada.

References

1. Cushing H. The Life of Sir William Osler. Vol. 1. Oxford: Clarendon Press;1925:i,57–58.
2. Noyes MC. Medical and chirurgical faculty. Bull. Med. Library Assoc. Vol. 9 NS. July 1919-April 1920. Baltimore, 1920.
3. Osler W. The Principles and Practice of Medicine. New York: D. Appleton and Co.; 1892.
4. Dolman CE. The Reverend James Bovell, M.D., 1817–1880. In: Stanley GFG, ed. Pioneers of Canadian Science. University of Toronto Press; 1966.
5. Dolman CE. Bovell, James. In: LaTerreur M, ed. Dictionary of Canadian Biography. v. X. University of Toronto Press; 1871–1880.
6. Osler W. (Authors name not given). James Bovell, M.D. Can J Med Sci. 1880;114–115.
7. Reed TA, ed. A History of the University of Trinity College 1852–1952. University of Toronto Press; 1952.
8. Spragge GW. The Trinity Medical College. The Ontario Historical Society. 1966;58:63–98.
9. Roland CG. James Bovell (1817–1880): the Toronto years. Can Med J. 1964;91:812–14.
10. Bovell J. On the transfusion of milk, as practised in cholera, at the cholera sheds, Toronto, July 1854. Can Med J. 1855; March: 188.
11. Bovell J. A Plea for Inebriate Asylums Commended to the Consideration of the Legislators of the Province of Canada. Toronto: Lovell and Gibson; 1862.
12. Graham J. First death from chloroform at Toronto General Hospital. Can J Med and Surg. 1911;29:201.
13. Bovell J. Outlines of Natural Theology For the Use of the Canadian Student Selected and Arranged From the Most Authentic Sources. Toronto: Rowsell and Ellis; 1859.
14. Cushing H. The Life of Sir William Osler. Vol. 1. Oxford: Clarendon Press;1925:i,28.
15. Cushing H. The Life of Sir William Osler. Vol. 1. Oxford: Clarendon Press;1925:i,43.
16. Wilkinson A. Lions in the Way: A Discursive History of the Oslers. Ch. 10. Toronto: The MacMillan Company; 1956.
17. Cushing H. The Life of Sir William Osler. Vol. 1. Oxford: Clarendon Press;1925:i,56–57.
18. Cushing H. The Life of Sir William Osler. Vol. 1. Oxford: Clarendon Press;1925:i,63.
19. Cushing H. The Life of Sir William Osler. Vol. 1. Oxford: Clarendon Press;1925:i,54,55,63.
20. Bovell J. Selected letters to William Osler and James Bovell Johnson. Osler Library of the History of Medicine. McGill University.
21. Cushing H. The Life of Sir William Osler. Vol. 1. Oxford: Clarendon Press;1925:i,68–69.

Arnold Meadowcroft Muirhead (1900–1988) and the Story of the Lady Osler Memoir

 Dee J. Canale,M.D.[1] and G. S. T. Cavanagh

Arnold M Muirhead was an Oxford graduate and scholar in the true sense. He became well known, especially as an educator, bibliophile and book seller. Arnold Muirhead was also, in every sense, an Oslerian, but is generally less well remembered for his authorship of the only definitive, albeit brief, biography of Lady Grace Revere Osler. We will focus on the circumstances surrounding his writing of *Grace Revere Osler, A Brief Memoir*[1] (Figure 1).

Arnold Muirhead was born in London on 30 June 1900 and was of Scottish heritage, in which he took great pride[2], his father Horace being a Scot born in Edinburgh. His mother was English, born in the town of Colchester. Arnold and his sister, Elizabeth, were raised in a modest home in a north-west suburb of London[3,4].

Early Years

His early education was at a small local boy's preparatory school, after which he went to University College School, Hampstead. He made a short journey by train each day to this well established independent school, where he excelled in his studies of the classics, Latin and Greek. He was described by his mother as a "rather nervous child", and was said to have remained a fairly highly strung person all his life.

Horace Muirhead suffered a serious setback in his publishing business as a result of the First World War, and the family was never well off financially.

Presented in part at the annual meeting of the American Osler Society April 18, 1991, New Orleans.

Previously published in J Med Biog 1996; *4*: 45–52. Reprinted with permission.

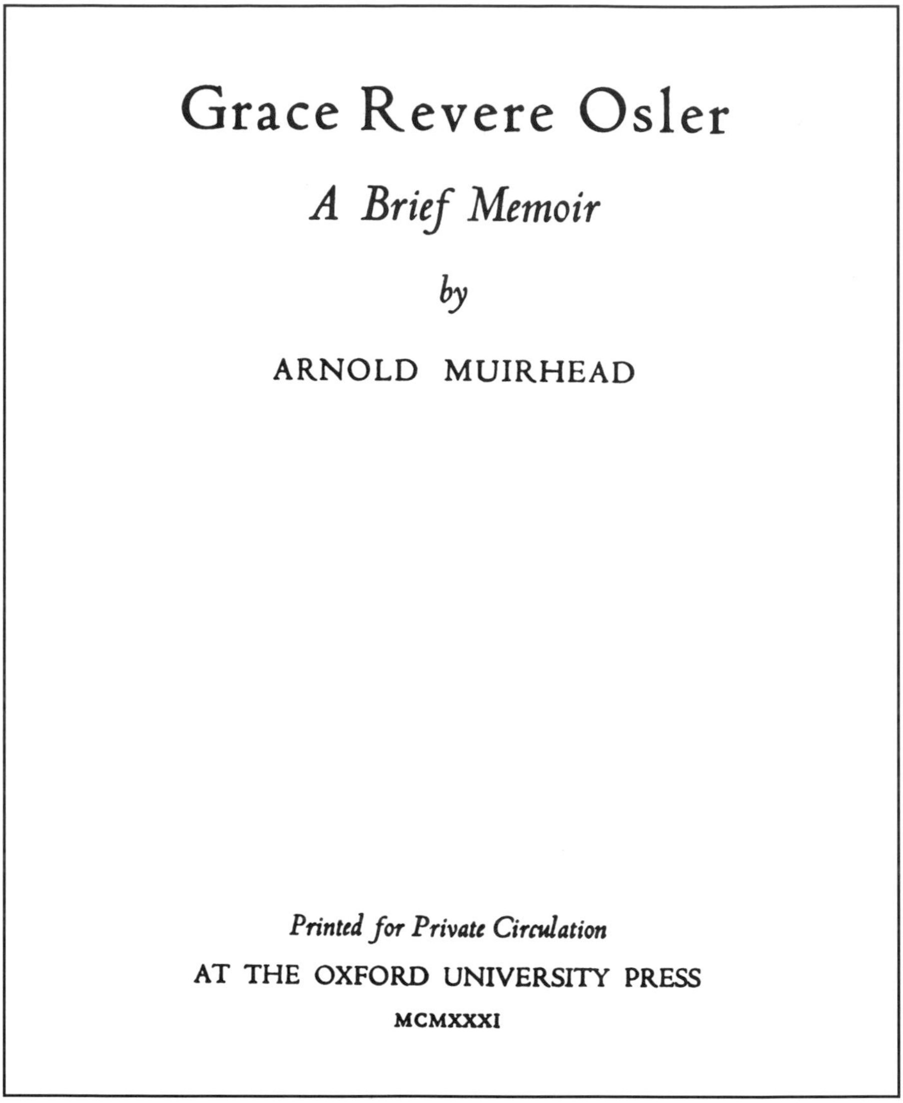

Grace Revere Osler

A Brief Memoir

by

ARNOLD MUIRHEAD

Printed for Private Circulation
AT THE OXFORD UNIVERSITY PRESS
MCMXXXI

Figure 1:   Detail of the title page of *Grace Revere Osler: A Brief Memoir* by Arnold M Muirhead (1931).

It was through the great generosity of a friend of the family that Arnold had the financial resources to enter Brasenose College, Oxford. Muirhead was in his third year at Brasenose when, one July evening in 1921 at his uncle's house in Hampstead, he met by chance a young American girl, who suggested that he look up an American Rhodes scholar attending Magdalen College that October. Muirhead first met this American, John F Fulton, on an autumn afternoon in 1921 in Fulton's room at Magdalen College. This meeting, Muirhead acknowledged, brought him the closest and most enduring friendship of his life. It was through Fulton that Muirhead first met Lady Osler and came under the spell of the "Open Arms", as the home of Sir William and Lady Osler at 13 Norham Gardens was affectionately known.

Becoming a latchkeyer

Fulton had arrived in Oxford with a letter of introduction to Lady Osler. He had been warmly welcomed, invited to stay to meals, to use the library and tennis court, and to bring a friend. It was not long before Fulton and Muirhead advanced to the privileged status of "latchkeyers", which virtually gave them the run of the house and library[5].

Marshall Fulton (no relation to John Fulton) was another latchkeyer, along with Harold Mansell, a young English medical student, and R H Hill. Marshall Fulton, who had entered Oxford as a medical student in the autumn of 1920, perhaps best expressed the privilege of a latchkeyer as being given the opportunity to come to know Lady Osler[6,7].

RH Hill, one of the earliest latchkeyers, was actually given a latchkey by Sir William Osler in 1915. Hill would work evenings in the library performing small tasks, such as paying book bills or cataloguing new books. He returned from military service in 1919, and would later work with W W Francis until the *Bibliotheca Osleriana*[8] was completed. He kept the latchkey until Lady Osler's executors handed the house over to Christ Church College.[9]

Muirhead's friendship with John Fulton grew steadily over the next two years, and they both frequented 13 Norham Gardens (Figure 2). They came to know and enjoy the company of Bill Francis, who was then working on the

Figure 2: Arnold Muirhead and John Fulton at 13 Norham Gardens in 1924. (Used with permission of the Yale University Library.)

Bibliotheca Osleriana at Norham Gardens. Their knowledge of Osler was enhanced by Bill's conversational reminiscences about Sir William. Muirhead especially enjoyed helping Francis with bibliographical details, which he would look up for him at the Bodleian Library, and later, after completing his studies at Oxford, at the British Museum[10,11].

First appointment as a school teacher

Muirhead took his degree in 1923, and accepted his first teaching position at Bexhill-on-Sea, in Sussex[12]. Then began a voluminous correspondence with Fulton, whose first stay in Oxford would conclude with his graduation and PhD in 1925. Muirhead would be the best man in Fulton's wedding in 1923, and he and Fulton would ride to the wedding in an automobile with Lady Osler and her sister, Susan Revere Chapin.

During these years, Muirhead would regularly return to Oxford, staying at Fulton's home if Fulton and his wife Lucia were out of town or at 13 Norham Gardens. If Muirhead was staying at the Fultons' home, Lady Osler would insist that he take his meals with Bill at 13 Norham Gardens, even if she was away. This also afforded Muirhead an opportunity to remain close to Bill Francis[13,14]. It was not long before Lady Osler felt that Muirhead had "become one of the family"[15].

Though not a medical man, Muirhead was of course greatly influenced by the Osler spirit. Lady Osler told Muirhead she was giving him a copy of the Cushing biography of Sir William Osler as a Christmas gift in 1924[16]. It was a most welcome though belated gift, which he would read in the spring of 1925[17]. Muirhead recalled that in April 1925, he was staying with the Fultons at 4 Bradmore Road, just across the way from 13 Norham Gardens, when, one morning at about eight, Lady Osler sent Henry, the gardener, across with gifts of the biography for each of them. He further recalled that they had their "noses in the volumes all that day and for several days afterwards"[18]. He also read and reread Sir William Osler's address, *A Way of Life*[19], and applied it to his own profession[20].

Muirhead was saddened when John Fulton left Oxford to enter Harvard Medical School in the summer of 1925, writing, "The happy incidents of our friendship and my memories . . . are among the very happiest of my life"[21]. Their correspondence continued nevertheless, and even included the swapping of diaries, which both kept on a regular basis. They both seemed to take great delight in locating and sending books to each other, especially as gifts for birthdays and Christmas. It was at this time that Muirhead began in earnest to read and collect books by John Keats and William Cobbett.

Memorable visits with Lady Osler

In June of 1926, Muirhead accepted a new teaching position at the Wanstead High School, which was within 30 minutes of London. There again he taught Latin and Greek. He felt that he had found his vocation as a schoolmaster, telling Fulton that he "would never be happy except in close touch with students and education"[22]. The attraction of Oxford and especially of 13 Norham Gardens would remain ever strong (Figure 3). Of one short visit, he

Figure 3: Lady Osler and Sir Arthur MacNalty on the terrace at 13 Norham Gardens. (A previously unpublished photograph from the primary author's collection.)

wrote, "Those three days spent at 13 Norham Gardens filled me with fresh energy and determination; heavens, what a wonderful house"[23]. On another occasion, he wrote to Fulton:

> "It was a splendid visit. I was the only person staying in the house so I had great talks with Lady O. I had the suite of honour all to myself. Lady O. called our food picnicking, but of course it was like living at the Ritz. The rest of the time I spent among the books – most happily. A great atmosphere always makes me more alert mentally. I seem to go through a process of spiritual purification if you know what I mean"[24].

That Muirhead was regarded as part of Lady Osler's family is perhaps best illustrated by the following account: Muirhead arrived at 13 Norham Gardens a day or two before Christmas 1927, only to find that Lady Osler had suffered a mild stroke. Dr A G Gibson, Sir William's physician, had been called in consultation, and had recommended bedrest. Despite this, she refused to have Muirhead go elsewhere, and he related to Fulton that he and Adelaide Eberts, Lady Osler's goddaughter on holiday from her finishing school in Paris, were the only ones staying in the house. The Francises came for Christmas dinner, but all others were put off[25].

The year 1928 would prove a momentous one for Muirhead, who wrote to John Fulton in January announcing his engagement to Dorothy Murray[26]. In turn, Fulton informed Muirhead that he would be returning to Oxford in

June as a Fellow of Magdalen College, to continue his neurophysiological studies in Sir Charles Sherrington's laboratory[27,28].

Lady Osler died suddenly on 31 August 1928, in her own bed at 13 Norham Gardens, with John Fulton in attendance at the end[29,30]. All who knew her felt a profound loss at her death. Muirhead was especially saddened to think of Oxford without her, as she had been "the centre of any picture at Oxford"[31]. Soon after her death, Muirhead was very occupied with his new appointment, in September 1928, as Latin Master at the Latymer School in north London[32].

Origin of the Lady Osler memoir

The origin of the memoir of Grace Revere Osler was a letter from Muirhead to Fulton on 21 October 1928, in which he wrote, "I wish someone would write a character sketch of her—something in thirty pages or so which would amplify anything that appeared in the biography. If it is to be done, it should be done while our memory of her is vivid"[33]. He suggested that Fulton might manage it.

Fulton suggested, however, that the appreciation of Lady Osler be written by Muirhead, who immediately accepted the responsibility, even though he felt "inadequately prepared for the task". It is not surprising that one of Lady Osler's young men would so want to write her biography. She carried on that tradition of the "Open Arms" and the spirit of Osler in helping and influencing young medical students and their friends visiting 13 Norham Gardens[34]. Muirhead, writing to Sir Arthur MacNalty, after the memoir had been published, said it had been written from a "young man's point of view"[35]. Of the many honours bestowed on Osler, he was said to have been most proud of his unwritten title, "The Young Man's Friend"[36].

Fulton agreed to help Muirhead gather material for the memoir, including his and Lucia Fulton's personal letters from Lady Osler, as well as information from the pre-Oxford period of individuals such as Mrs Chapin, Bill Francis, and others[37]. Fulton would gather many "priceless anecdotes from Bill Francis about the old days in Baltimore before Francis left Oxford to assume his position as the Osler librarian at McGill'"[38].

Fulton played a major role in seeing the memoir through to publication, especially in securing material and editorial suggestions, and in placating Mrs Chapin, who, as it turned out, would have the last word in matters concerning the memoir itself. Early on, both Muirhead and Fulton recognized the need to be "discreet", and this seemed to be an inherent trait of the Reveres. Unhappily, they also learned Lady Osler had requested that all her personal letters be destroyed after her death[39].

With some anxiety, Muirhead made known to Mrs Chapin his intention to write the memoir[40], and was encouraged when she indicated that she was pleased and told him to go "straight ahead"[41]. Muirhead was also anxious that the portion of the memoir during Sir William's life not be a resume of the Cushing biography.

Unfortunately, they were unable to "pump" Aunt Sue, as Mrs Chapin was thereafter referred to. She seemed to be very upset over the problems involved in turning 13 Norham Gardens over to Christ Church College. Fulton concluded that it was not a good time to talk to her about Lady Osler[42], and when she left England in February, Fulton noted her "psychology difficult". No intimate details of Lady Osler's first marriage, to Dr Samuel W Gross, which they eagerly sought, were ever obtained.

Archibald Malloch had his own anecdotes relating to Lady Osler, and sent them to Fulton[43]. John Fulton learned that Harvey Cushing had stacks of Lady Osler's letters[44]. Muirhead wrote to Cushing, thanking him for his approval of the project he and Fulton had conceived, and outlined the nature of the memoir, emphasizing that it would not interfere with any subsequent work on a larger scale. He requested any letters of Lady Osler's that Cushing felt would illustrate in particular the last eight years, following Sir William's death, recognizing "how difficult it is to reproduce in full and without often, considerable editing of any of her letters as she was so outspoken in her correspondence"[45].

Fulton returned to America for a visit in the summer of 1929. This trip included a visit to Montreal in May 1929, to attend the dedication of the Osler library. It was during this trip that Cushing gave Fulton access to all of his files of Osler material, which included some Grace Revere Osler letters of the Baltimore period, which Miss Shipley, Cushing's secretary, originally copied at the time the Osler biography was being written. Cushing generously allowed Fulton to use his own judgement with regard to which letters to use, and additionally expressed "mixed feelings" about using all the letters, hoping one day someone would publish a detailed volume of "letters of a physician's wife"[46]. Moreover, Cushing urged considerable discretion in using the letters, because of uneasiness he experienced over the difficulty he had had in persuading Mrs Chapin to part with some letters in the first instance when he was editing the Osler biography, and he was sure that she was unaware he had had them copied. Muirhead and Fulton faithfully followed Cushing's advice.

As the manuscript was coming together, portions were sent to Fulton at intervals for his review and suggestions, and the first draft of the complete manuscript was sent to Fulton on 4 October 1929. Muirhead met with Mrs Chapin on at least two occasions at Brown's Hotel in London in October, going over the first complete draft of the manuscript, and found that she seemed "quite pleased", but indicated a desire to have Dr Cushing see the manuscript on its completion, before publication. He also noted that she seemed to be much troubled by her inability to remember names and words[47].

It was Mrs Chapin's original intention that the memoir would be published for private distribution only[48]. Muirhead, thinking to minimize the cost of publication, found that Mr Cumberlege, manager of the Oxford University Press in New York, was quite anxious to publish the memoir in New York for American distribution. Mrs Chapin, however, thought it should be printed only by the Oxford University Press in London[49,50]. This insistence on private distribution would later be referred to by Muirhead in letters to Fulton as the "Revere complex"[51].

During this interval, Muirhead was also doing translations for Fulton, including those on works by Galvani, Glisson and Weber[52–54], for Fulton's *Selected Readings on the History of Physiology* (1930)[55].

The meetings with Mrs Chapin had produced promises that she would send other suitable material to be incorporated in the manuscript, including some photographs. Muirhead despaired, however, over the fact that Mrs Chapin had not sent him any additional information or the promised photographs, and wrote to Fulton, "she seems to have been unable to find any of the material she promised me and says her memory is a vacuum"[56]. He was especially annoyed after writing to Lady Summerville and learning that she had sent a number of Lady Osler's letters to Mrs Chapin[57,58].

In July 1930, Harvey Cushing was in London, giving the Lister Memorial Lecture at the Royal College of Surgeons of England[59]. Fulton came down from Oxford to be with Cushing. Upon learning of the difficulties in dealing with Mrs Chapin, Cushing promised Muirhead enthusiastic cooperation in seeing the memoir to completion. He remarked that the old adage, "You cannot do it while the relatives are living", applied to Muirhead as it did to him, and that "the only thing is to ignore any lack of cooperation which you seem to encounter"[60]. While Fulton was in London, he invited Muirhead to a meeting of the Osler Club of London, which had been founded in 1928[61].

The completed draft of the memoir was sent initially to Fulton on 15 September 1930, with a request that he send a copy to Dr Cushing. Muirhead sent separately a copy of the memoir to Mrs Chapin[62]. In addition, Fulton sent copies to Bill Francis, Leonard Mackall, and Archibald Malloch, suggesting that they might "pounce on any errors or add things here and there to enrich the narrative". Ann Revere, who was visiting the Fultons at the time, read the memoir and was enthusiastic over every detail[63]. Helpful suggestions and corrections to the manuscript were received from Fulton and Bill Francis. Moreover, Dr Cushing suggested that it would be better to omit the medical details of Lady Osler's illness[64]. Reginald Hill, who saw so much of Sir William and Lady Osler, reviewed the manuscript and wrote a stirring letter to Muirhead stating, "Those who knew 13 Norham Gardens in our time, will tell you that you have drawn a loving and faithful portrait and they will be very grateful"[65].

Mrs Chapin procrastinated all the while until she had read a copy of Hill's letter. She then gave her approval of the memoir, and stated that she wanted 500 copies published at Oxford University Press for private circulation only[66].

Another three months went by with still no word about the photographs. In January 1931, Fulton went up to Boston to see Mrs Chapin, and after a "long talk," she agreed to send the photographs of Lady Osler that she personally selected to illustrate the memoir. She remained adamant about not having the memoir published for general public circulation. Both Fulton and Muirhead felt that more than 500 copies should be published, and Muirhead even suggested having Mr Cumberlege of the New York Press approach Mrs Chapin personally to see if he could overcome the Revere complex against publication[67,68].

Proofs of the manuscript were reviewed by Fulton, who promptly cabled Muirhead on 15 February 1931[69]. "Most delighted trial proofs. Don't procrastinate". With those magical reminiscent words, "Don't procrastinate", the manuscript was sent without the photographs to John Johnson, Manager of the Oxford University Press[70].

Anxious to help, and presumably at Fulton's suggestion, Dr Cushing visited Mrs Chapin and described finding her in poor health. Writing to Muirhead, Cushing stated:

> "But the main thing is, I found her cogitating about some photographs for your memoir of Lady O and I urged her vigorously to buck up and send them off to you instantly. You know of course how she feels – Grace would be annoyed by all this publicity. It was alright for Willie but not for her."[71]

Again, Dr Cushing encouraged Muirhead to "plow ahead . . . and when the thing is done, she will be as delighted with it as G.O. was with my effort which was looked forward to with dread and apprehension"[71]. Additionally, he sent Muirhead a cheque to help with the expenses, and told him to write to him directly if he needed further assistance.

Dr Cushing was successful in his efforts, for Mrs Chapin cabled Muirhead on 20 February that she was "completely satisfied" and would send the photographs by next mail. The anxiously awaited photographs of Lady Osler as a young child in a hoopskirt standing by a rocking horse in Boston as a young woman on a visit to Oxford in 1894, and in later years on the terrace at 13 Norham Gardens, arrived on 1 March, and were promptly sent off to Mr Johnson at Oxford University Press[72].

Mrs Chapin had wanted the binding of the memoir to be similar to that of the Osler biography, which was done in Oxford blue cloth, but neither Muirhead nor Johnson would agree to this. Moreover, the materials had already been ordered for the parchment spine and grey boards. Fulton fully supported Muirhead regarding the binding[73–75].

Publication of the memoir

The completed bound memoir was delivered by the Press in early June 1931. Almost 100 copies were mailed by the press directly to friends and associates of Sir William and Lady Osler in England, America, and Canada from a list prepared by Muirhead[75]. Review copies were sent to selected journals, including *The Lancet*[77], *The British Medical Journal*[78], *The New England Journal of Medicine*[79], *The Journal of the American Medical Association*[80], *Annals of Medical History*[81], and the *Canadian Medical Association Journal*[82–84]. John Fulton was to receive 20 copies, including one of the four copies done in full morocco binding.

As Dr Cushing had predicted, Mrs Chapin was completely satisfied and greatly pleased over every detail of the book itself, regretting only that she had not been able personally to send a note to accompany many of the mailings[85–87]. Writing to Muirhead, Mrs Chapin acknowledged that she was "utterly satisfied" with the memoir and, moreover, stated that "distance, my inadequate health and irregularities of the mails account for what have been petty annoyances to us both". Mrs Chapin, as promised, paid for the entire cost of the publication of the memoir, which was just short of L95[88].

The reviews were all favourable, and Muirhead received many letters generous in their praise, including those from Osler's personal physician, Dr A G Gibson, William Welch, Arnold C Klebs, Dr Maude Abbott, Sir D'Arcy Power, R Ramsey Wright, Humphry Rolleston, Lady Sherrington, Lady Astor, and others[89,90].

Fulton commented especially on the "most interesting and delightful" letters from Sir Arthur MacNalty and Sir George Newman, and stated, "They would mean almost more than any of the others, since both Newman and MacNalty measure their words carefully and say nothing they do not mean"[91].

Many felt Muirhead had achieved the impossible in so faithfully portraying Lady Osler. John Johnson of the Oxford University Press in a letter to Fulton stated:

> "I am simply delighted with the Muirhead Memoir. I think it is the most delightful intimate memoir that I have ever read. The state biography is a comparatively easy thing to write; the intimate biography such as this is the most difficult thing in the world."[92]

Mrs Chapin soon wrote that she wanted all remaining copies of the memoir held by the Press sent to her. Muirhead arranged for this to be done, which also included the two remaining copies bound in morocco. With his own supply dwindling rapidly, Muirhead again expressed his desire to Fulton to attempt to persuade Mrs Chapin to agree to another printing of the memoir, so it might be more generally available[93,94].

Just when Muirhead seemed resigned to the fact that no additional copies of the memoir could be published, he received a letter from Mrs Chapin in which she stated that she had given Dr A D Blackader, who reviewed that memoir for the *Canadian Medical Association Journal*, permission to print 300 copies of a 15-page abstract of the memoir. Muirhead was furious at Mrs Chapin's decision to allow publication of what he considered to be a small-scale pirated edition without consulting him, the author. To him, this was another in a succession of occurrences in which he had felt slighted. These began with his learning that Mrs Chapin had asked Cushing's opinion as to whether Muirhead's English was "literary enough" for him to write the memoir originally[95,96]. Muirhead promptly wrote a "forceful" letter to Mrs Chapin concerning another printing of the memoir, describing Mr Cumberlege of the New York Press as very anxious to publish it. Fulton was sympathetic to Muirhead's desire for an additional printing; however, neither he nor Dr Cushing could persuade Mrs Chapin to agree to further publication, citing her "very unstable mental condition", and Dr Cushing's advice to "lie low and not worry her further" [97–99].

Mrs Chapin wrote to Fulton and expressed "regret if her decision should make any material difference" to him. That Mrs Chapin might think that a personal profit motivated Muirhead to want more copies printed was a further insult to him. He soon became "fed up with the whole thing", and dropped further efforts to seek an additional printing[100].

Fulton expressed concern that Muirhead was overreacting, and had perhaps misinterpreted Mrs Chapin's use of the phrase "material difference", which he stated was used in America as synonymous with "essential". Moreover, Fulton reminded him that it had been Mrs Chapin's wish from the start that the memoir be private, and that to do otherwise would result in "much unpleasantness all around" from the Reveres, which presumably would include Lady Osler's brother and executor, Mr E H R Revere, as well as Mrs Chapin[101].

Muirhead intended to have Mr Maltby, the well known bookbinder, bind up his manuscript, personal letters from Lady Osler, and the letters received about the memoir. These had originally been promised to the Osler Library[102,103]. The material, bound in three volumes, was eventually given instead to the Osler Club of London[104].

Schoolmaster days

For the remainder of the 1930s, Arnold Muirhead continued to teach at the Latymer School in north London. From one of his former students who attended the school from 1931 to 1938, we have the following description of Muirhead at this time. He was very tall, exceedingly thin, aloof in manner, rather jerky in movement; he had a habit of closing his eyes when speaking and tossing his head in a manner quite intimidating to small children. He gathered round him a small coterie of senior pupils whom he considered worthy of encouragement, mostly girls. After school, the students were invited to the Muirheads' house on The Limes Avenue in Southgate for extra coaching and on weekends for social evenings. They were given access to his well lined book shelves and shown the latest acquisitions. His wife Dorothy would always prepare a delicious meal, which to the students seemed marvellously exotic.

During the 1930s, most of the small sixth form from the Latymer School went on to London University, an occasional boy going up to Cambridge or Oxford[105]. Muirhead would encourage the especially bright girls to try for a university place. Often the girls' fathers were unwilling to allow such feminism; however, it is said that Muirhead tactfully suggested to an unwilling father that his daughter's brains were clearly inherited from her father and must not be wasted on housework. These girls were usually very attractive, with lively personalities, and many later became teachers, doctors, and lawyers in the days when this was rare.[106].

Muirhead and his wife Dorothy made only one trip to the United States, visiting the Fultons from 31 March to 5 May 1939[107]. Muirhead had the honour of representing the Osler Club of London at Harvey Cushing's seventieth birthday party. He sat at the head table and gave a short speech[108].

Fulton next saw the Muirheads a year later, in October 1940, when he flew to England to gather information on behalf of the National Research Council. The Second World War had begun in Europe, and despite the bombing of London, he found Arnold and Dorothy looking extremely well. Both were actively teaching[109].

Book seller and collector

Apparently Muirhead became frustrated with his lot as a teacher, for after the war he gave up teaching and joined the well established London rare-book dealer, Peter Murray Hill Ltd, as a director. Muirhead already had a reputation as an established collector, his library having been reviewed by the *Times Literary Supplement* as an example of what could be achieved by a school master of moderate means. His collection emphasized education, philosophy, and the works of William Cobbett. The Cobbett collection was said to be exceptional[110]. In 1949, while still with Murray Hill, he became the principal organizer of the National Book League's exhibition, "The English at School", gathering together almost 600 items illustrative of English education over five centuries. His own collection of books, many of which were rare and almost all of which were in excellent condition, was sufficient to gain him a distinction, shared with only a dozen or so private owners, of being listed as a location in Wing's short-title catalogue. Muirhead knew Donald Wing[111]. Muirhead was also among those consulted about the design of the Rothschild Library catalogue[112].

Muirhead remained active in the Osler Club of London, and was one of the editors selected by the Club to publish the *Selected Writings of Sir William Osler* in 1951[113]. In the same year Muirhead presented to the Osler Club of London a photograph that Lady Osler had originally given to Mr Maltby of Revere Osler holding a record trout. The photograph was bound with a cover letter from Lady Osler and one from Revere[114].

In 1951 Muirhead left Peter Murray Hill and established himself as a book seller. He issued a series of his own catalogues, calling them the "Lime Tree Miscellanies", for he had lived at 83 The Limes Avenue, Southgate, continuously since he first started teaching at the Latymer School. His very fine Cobbett collection was sold, going to the library at Yale University, and was said to have financed his first steps in book selling[115]. He and Dorothy moved to a delightful Regency house in St Albans, Hertfordshire, in 1954. He continued to be active in the antiquarian book trade for over a quarter of a century. He belonged to a dinner club that he referred to as the "Biblio Boys", and it is said that he knew Geoffrey Keynes, John Hayward, John Carter, Percy Muir and others. Though not thought of as a major book seller, Arnold Muirhead never-theless enjoyed an excellent reputation. His private papers, of which there was a considerable body, went to the Bodleian Library after his death[116].

Visitors to the Muirhead's home in St Albans all have fond memories of the beautiful garden, to which Arnold devoted considerable energy, of Dorothy's outstanding cooking, and of stimulating conversation and fine books[117,118].

Gradually Arnold Muirhead retired. Dorothy was increasingly beset with disabling arthritis; Arnold devotedly cared for her. Despite his own failing health in his last years, he remained alert and retained his considerable charisma to the end. Upon his death on 26 December 1988, the book world lost someone who had made his own distinctive contribution, and Oslerians lost one of the last witnesses to the spirit and legacy of the "Open Arms".

Acknowledgments

The authors will be forever indebted to Ms Janice Braun, Assistant Historical Librarian, at the Yale Medical Library, and to Ms Diane E Kaplan, Archivist (Manuscripts and Archives), Yale University Library, for their invaluable assistance in obtaining the correspondence exchanged between Arnold Muirhead and John F Fulton. Truly, this manuscript could never have been completed to our satisfaction without the help of these two learned ladies.

And thanks to Ms Florence Bruce for her assistance in preparing the manuscript.

References

1. Muirhead A. *Grace Revere Osler: A Brief Memoir.* London: Oxford University Press, 1931
2. Muirhead A to Fulton JF, 8 May 1927
3. Taylor E M. Personal correspondence, 1 November 1990
4. Taylor E M. Personal correspondence, 7 December 1990
5. Muirhead A: John Fulton – book collector, humanist, and friend. *J Hist Med Allied Sci* 1962;**17**:2–14
6. Fulton M: Sir William Osler's better half. In: Barondess JA, McGovern JP, Roland CG, eds. *The Persisting Osler.* Baltimore: University Park Press, 1985:35–8
7. Fulton JF: Grace Revere Osler: her influence on men and medicine. 1949 Bull *Hist Med* 1949;**23**:350
8. *Bibliotheca Osleriana.* Oxford: Clarendon Press, 1929
9. Hill RH. WW Francis. *Tributes from his Friends on the Occasion of the Thirty-Fifth Anniversary of The Osler Society of McGill University.* Montreal: The Osler Society of McGill University, 1956:35–47
10. Muirhead A to Francis WW, 4 November 1926
11. Muirhead A to Francis WW, 7 September 1926
12. Muirhead A to Fulton JF, 17 August 1923
13. Muirhead A to Fulton JF, 9 December 1923
14. Muirhead A to Fulton JF, 1 September 1924
15. Wagner FB. *The Twilight Years of Lady Osler.* Canton: Science History Publications, 1985:69

16. Cushing HW. *The Life of Sir William Osler,* 2 vols. London: Clarendon Press, 1925

17. Fulton JF. *Harvey Cushing, A Biography.* Springfield: Charles C Thomas, 1946:469–70

18. Muirhead A. *Address on the Occasion of Harvey Cushing's Seventieth Birthday, April 8, 1939.* Springfield: Charles C Thomas, 1939:23–4

19. Osler W. *A Way of Life.* Address to Yale students, Sunday evening, 20 April 1913. New York: Paul B Hoeber, 1914

20. Muirhead A to Fulton JF, 12 January 1926

21. Muirhead A to Fulton JF, 26 July 1925

22. Muirhead A to Fulton JF, 28 July 1926

23. Muirhead A to Fulton JF, 12 January 1926

24. Muirhead A to Fulton JF, 7 September 1926

25. Muirhead A to Fulton JF, 28 December 1927

26. Muirhead A to Fulton JF, 15 January 1928

27. Muirhead A to Fulton JF, 19 March 1928

28. Fulton JF. Obituary. *Lancet,* 1960; **i:**1301–2

29. Muirhead A to Fulton JF, 5 September 1928

30. Fulton JF. (*op.cit.* ref 7):341–51

31. Muirhead A to Fulton JF, 10 September 1928

32. Muirhead A to Fulton JF, 21 May 1928

33. Muirhead A to Fulton JF, 21 October 1928

34. Barker LF. Dr Osler as the Young Physician's Friend and Exemplar, *Bulletin No. IX, Sir William Osler Memorial Number.* Montreal: International Association of Medical Museums; J Technical Methods, 1926:251–8

35. Muirhead A to MacNalty AS, 19 July 1931

36. MacNalty AS. Osler at Oxford. *Arch Int Med* 1949;**84:**135–42

37. Muirhead A to Fulton JF, 25 October 1928

38. Fulton JF to Muirhead A, 14 December 1929

39. Wagner FB. *The Twilight Years of Lady Osler.* Canton: Science History Publications, 1985:xi

40. Muirhead A to Fulton JF, 8 October 1928

41. Muirhead A to Fulton JF, 12 November 1928

42. Fulton JF to Muirhead A, 22 December 1928

43. Fulton JF to Muirhead A, 25 March 1929

44. Fulton JF to Muirhead A, 22 December 1929

45. Muirhead A to Fulton JF, 13 January 1929

46. Fulton JF to Muirhead A, 13 August 1929

47. Muirhead A to Fulton JF, 13 October 1929

48. Fulton JF to Muirhead A, 10 September 1929

49. Muirhead A to Fulton JF, 13 October 1929

50. Muirhead A to Fulton JF, 14 October 1929

51. Muirhead A to Fulton JF, 18 September 1930

52. Fulton JF to Muirhead A, 14 October 1929

53. Fulton JF to Muirhead A, 11 November 1929

54. Muirhead A to Fulton JF, 10 November 1929

55. Fulton JF, ed. *Selected Readings on the History of Physiology.* Springfield: Charles C Thomas, 1930:x

56. Muirhead A to Fulton JF, 27 March 1930

57. Muirhead A to Fulton JF, 9 February 1930

58. Muirhead A to Fulton JF, 1 April 1930

59. Cushing H. Neurohypophysial mechanisms from a clinical standpoint. *Lancet* 1930;**ii:**119–27; 175–84

60. Fulton JF to Muirhead A, 16 July 1930
61. Franklin AW. *Proem for The Osler Club of London.* Talk given at joint meeting of The Osler Club of London and The American Osler Club at the Royal College of Physicians honouring the XXIII International Congress of the History of Medicine, London, 5 September 1972
62. Muirhead A to Fulton JF, 18 September 1930
63. Fulton JF to Muirhead A, 25 September 1930
64. Fulton JF to Muirhead A, 3 October 1930
65. Hill RH to Muirhead A, 22 October 1930
66. Fulton JF to Muirhead A, 17 November 1930
67. Fulton JF to Muirhead A, 12 January 1931
68. Muirhead A to Fulton JF, 18 September 1930
69. Fulton JF to Muirhead A, 16 February 1931 (cable)
70. Muirhead A to Fulton JF, 16 February 1931
71. Cushing H to Muirhead A, 17 February 1931
72. Muirhead A to Fulton JF, 1 March 1931
73. Fulton JF to Muirhead A, 17 March 1931
74. Muirhead A to Fulton JF, 23 March 1931
75. Fulton JF to Muirhead A, 6 April 1931 (cable)
76. Muirhead A to Fulton JF, 25 May 1931
77. Lady Osler. *Lancet* 1931;**ii:**25
78. Lady Osler. *BMJ* 1931;**ii:**25
79. Lady Osler. *N Engl J Med* 1931;**205:**548–9
80. Book review – *Grace Revere Osler. A Brief Memoir. JAMA* 1931;**97:** 954
81. Packard FR. Book review – Grave Revere Osler: A Brief Memoir. *Ann Med Hist* 1931;**3:**680–1
82. Blackader AD. Lady Osler – A review. *Can Med Assoc J* 1931;**25:**477–81
83. Muirhead A to Fulton JF, 26 May 1931
84. Fulton JF to Muirhead A, 4 June 1931
85. Fulton JF to Muirhead A, 24 June 1931
86. Muirhead A to Fulton JF, 30 June 1931
87. Muirhead A to Fulton JF, 13 July 1931
88. Muirhead A to Fulton JF, 24 July 1931
89. Muirhead A to Fulton JF, 16 June 1931
90. Muirhead A to Fulton JF, 22 June 1931
91. Fulton JF to Muirhead A, 4 August 1931
92. Fulton JF to Muirhead A, 16 July 1931
93. Muirhead A to Fulton JF, 28 September 1931
94. Muirhead A to Fulton JF, 2 October 1931
95. Muirhead A to Fulton JF, 23 March 1931
96. Muirhead A to Fulton JF, 19 October 1931
97. Muirhead A to Fulton JF, 13 November 1931
98. Fulton JF to Muirhead A, 9 November 1931
99. Fulton JF to Muirhead A, 23 November 1931
100. Muirhead A to Fulton JF, 23 November 1931
101. Fulton JF to Muirhead A, 4 December 1931
102. Muirhead A to Fulton JF, 6 April 1931
103. Muirhead A to Fulton JF, 4 June 1931
104. Osler Club of London. *Oslerian Anniversary.* Oxford: Oxford University Press, 1976:82
105. Cox C. Personal communication, 9 July 1990
106. Kelsall J. Personal communication, 9 July 1990
107. Starling C. Personal communication, 21 November 1990

108. *Speeches, Letters, and Tributes: Harvey Cushing's Seventieth Birthday Party, April 8, 1939.* Springfield: Charles C Thomas, 1939: 23–4

109. Fulton JF. Notes on a recent trip to England. *American Oxonian* 1941; **28**:72–92

110. Cox C. (*op.cit.* ref. 105)

111. Hamlyn MG. News and comment. *Book Collector;* **38**:94–6

112. Cox C. (*op.cit.* ref 105)

113. *Selected Writings of Sir William Osler (July 21, 1849 to December 29, 1919)* (Introduction by GL Keynes MD FRCS). London: Oxford University Press, 1951

114. Osler Club of London (*op.cit.* ref 104):81

115. Cox C. Personal communication, 10 December 1989

116. Hamlyn MG. Personal communication, 10 December 1989

117. Tulloch J. Personal communication, 19 June 1990

118. Fletcher WR. Personal communication, 4 July 1990

An Archeology of Two Oslerian Dreams and a Perspective on Sir William's Historical Significance

 Joseph W. Lella, Ph.D.

Introduction

This paper examines vivid and occasionally bizarre segments of two dreams recorded by Sir William Osler in a journal kept for the most part from 1910 to 1918, approximately one year before his death at the age of seventy. Some scholars have suggested that a psychological and or psychoanalytic approach to understanding Osler's life might prove fruitful.[1] This paper attempts such an approach. The two dreams are explored psychoanalytically, linking them to significant features of Osler's childhood especially relations with parents and educational and professional role models. They are also linked to events and situations around the time of their occurrence. The interpretations are then used to derive a perspective on Osler's significance in the rapidly evolving medicine of his age.

It is clear that, though highly competent, he was not a scientist of the first rank.[2] He was what some might call a superb clinician, clinical teacher, and educational innovator. In all of this and in his inspirational and historical writing, however, he did serve as a guide for many—indeed, he continues to do so.[3] Despite this, as we shall see, one may question his status as a contributor to progressive professional and social change in at least three important areas. First, the historical record gives one room to wonder whether Osler was a leader in elevating the status of women in medicine or whether he strengthened the status-quo.[4] Second, at least one notable Oslerian, Alfred White

Presented at the American Osler Society, May 6, 1999, Montreal.

Franklin, has seen him as conservative in areas of social change linked to preventive medicine.[5] Finally, there are those who see his historical writing as primarily conservative, celebrating the medicine that was and was 'a-borning.'[6] He may well have minimized its negative dimensions. For example, trends established in Osler's time and with his participation have been viewed as promoting reductionist and hyperspecialized medicine, practices which simplify the links among biological, psychological and socio-cultural aspects of human functioning, and focus exclusively and naively upon the individual, or worse, upon organic, or molecular, or cellular and sub-cellular levels.[7] Did Osler offer original insights into the historical record, then, or present an ideologically blinded, or at a best rose-colored view? Was he as teacher, colleague and role model, a person who explored important new directions for physicians, or a man who brilliantly led students and colleagues down established roads?

Space does not allow us to do justice to these questions, nor can definitive justice be done since answers depend at least in part on highly variable value stances toward these particular aspects of Osler's legacy. One critic, however, has reached beyond the particular, stating that his "qualifications for immortality are beyond analysis . . . There must have been something in the spirit of the man which could not be translated clearly through the many tributes which have been written to him throughout the years."[8]

This exercise will try to use what might be called psychoanalysis' humane subtlety and historical grounding to inform the specific 'either-ors' above and to take a small step toward a more informed stance on "the spirit of the man" and his significance or "qualifications for immortality."

A Theoretic and Methodological Note

Dreams have been food for wakeful thought, meditation and serious study from time immemorial. Sigmund Freud loved the biblical story of Joseph and his exegesis of Pharaoh's dreams (Genesis: 37). He became a modern Joseph and the world's most renowned dream interpreter.[9] Since that time scientists, scholars and clinicians have both elaborated upon and severely criticized Freud's work. Some have dismissed its scientific worth completely. Two influential researchers, recently noted "Freud's [theoretic] attempt to relate dream symbolism to . . . infantile sexual/aggressive impulses no longer seem[s] worthy of serious interest by scientific psychology.[10] And yet, the same authors suggest that Freud made "valid observations about the . . . sources of dreams"—that dream images often have multiple and unrelated sources in memory; that images are often condensations which best reflect these sources and, that the dreams themselves weave these sources and images into "reasonably coherent narrative[s] . . . Being in a dream . . . is like acting out a story or experiencing life itself."[11]

Some neurologists see dream weaving as related to the brain's on-going organization of recorded experience. Symbols and both proximate and more remote (and even repressed) memories (top down inputs) meet more primitive (bottom-up) inputs and become sorted into more or less meaningful neural networks.[12] One need not go too far to interpret at least some of this organization, as Arden does, as part of an evolving (and indeed historically grounded) self-referential system which sometimes may, sometimes may not, fit Freudian and or other theoretic categories.

Some cautionary statements. This paper uses Freudian ideas to interpret Osler's reports of two of his own dreams. Since the reports were of necessity written after the fact, it is impossible to say whether they are really what Osler dreamed. No one, including Osler at the time, could say that with any great certainty. Further, in using the Freudian schema, I imply no general scientific significance for it. I mean merely that its concepts can provide a useful way of finding coherence in these two "narratives."

Freud called his interpretive work "archeology." Like an archeologist exploring remains in a modern city, he worked at (or close to) the surface and primarily interpreted what was already visible or made visible through a light dusting off.[13] This dusting off was the work of clients' free associations and Freud's interpretive work with them. The clients were generally Osler's contemporaries. They were Europeans and relatively close to Sir William in culture and social class. Freud's interpretive work would not have been completely foreign to Osler. Indeed, it is known that he did refer at least one patient to him.[14] Osler himself rather obliquely recognized an archeology of the human psyche in a famous lecture to Yale medical students, "A Way of Life." He recommended that the students do as he does—abandon concern with the past to cultivate a life lived in "day-tight compartments." Your "yesterdays," he said, "have no concern for you personally, that is, consciously. *They are there alright, working daily in us, but so are our livers and our stomachs. And the past in its unconscious action on our lives should bother us as little as they do.* [ital. mine] He recommended that we bury (repress?) the past, "deep in the oblivion of each night. . ." to wake again in the morning "a free man with a new life."[15] Perhaps that is good advice for living. As students of the past and of past lives, however, why not study the past's "unconscious action" as carefully as we can, recognizing the tentative nature of our "archeology" even if we cannot do more precise post-mortem dissections like those done on livers and stomachs?

We no longer have Osler with us and have no access to associations he might have made to his dreams nor to interpretations he might have found acceptable. We do have access, however, to his manuscript notes made immediately upon waking that describe some of his dreams. These were handwritten in pencil for the most part from 1910 to 1918. They were edited in 1980 by Charles Roland who "corrected only those spelling errors that seemed likely to cause confusion for a reader." He also added punctuation, "where its use seemed necessary and the author's intent [was] unequivocal."[16] We also have access to Osler's other writings and to historical data about his life. Thus, we can attempt our own associations linking the dreams to what that body of work seems to reveal. I have tried to weave my associations into a fabric of meaning which links Osler's self-reported dream images and narratives to what might have been their sources in his conscious and or unconscious memories and in his symbolic usages. Whether or not my weaving, my interpretations or hypotheses have a grounding in fact (readers may judge for themselves), they have helped me (I hope they will help others) to appreciate better the meaning and significance of Osler's life and work.

A Puzzle: Osler and His 'Fathers'

Accounts of two dreams in Osler's journal struck me as particularly intriguing. They promised to help answer a puzzling question which emerged for me out of the historical record. Why in his writing was Sir William so openly and frequently reverential and affectionate towards the mentors of his youth—his fathers in the art of medicine— while he seemed to neglect or indeed express outright ambivalence toward his own father in the flesh? This was a man whose vocation he had originally sought, and whose ecclesiastical/ministerial work and faith was in some ways a model for his own.

This paper attempts first to document the above discrepancy. It then looks at each of the dreams and interprets them psychoanalytically in order to shed some light on the conundrum. The final section deals with questions concerning Osler's considerable legacy in the light of that interpretation.

Osler's Selective Piety

Among the many facets of Osler's character that struck me when I read Harvey Cushing's biography was piety—in the ancient Latin sense of *pietas*—allegiance to and affection for one's family or, more broadly, one's forebears.[17] Osler cherished all of his 'fathers in the art and science of medicine' but especially, those mentors of his youth, those to whom he dedicated his *Principles and Practice of Medicine*.

'Father' W. A. Johnson, an Anglican Clergyman and amateur scientist, was Osler's teacher from the age of 16 to 18 at Trinity College School. He was the first person intellectually and morally to challenge the young man's mind and heart with a love of scientific investigation. He also introduced Osler to Sir Thomas Browne's *Religio Medici* (A Physician's Religion) reconciling a commitment to science with Christian faith.[18]

In an address dealing with science in the public schools as late as 1902, Osler was effusive in his memories of Father Johnson perhaps especially in his appreciation of how this teacher introduced him to the findings and ways of science.

> Imagine the delight of a boy of an inquisitive nature to meet a man who cared nothing about words, but who knew about things—who knew the stars in their courses and could tell us their names . . . who showed us with the microscope the marvels in a drop of dirty pond water. . .[19]

Osler met *Dr. James Bovell* (a physician/scientist with deep religious faith) while at Trinity College School. Bovell nourished Osler's scientific and humane interests later as his mentor during medical studies at the University of Toronto showing him that both could be harnessed to a life in medicine.

The words 'love' and 'father' recur in descriptions of Osler's relationship with Bovell whose grand-daughter wrote: "He (Osler) adored Grandfather and the latter loved him like a son. . ." Bovell's letters sent his "Love for you dear boy" and were signed, "Yours affectionately."[20]

Later in life, Osler said of Bovell "the best the human mind has afforded was on his shelves and in him all that one could desire in a teacher, a clear head and a loving heart."[21]

Dr. R. Palmer Howard was Osler's teacher at McGill University's Medical Faculty in Montreal. He confirmed the student physician in his love of science and the art of medicine and showed him how to focus his energies on both.

Palmer Howard was a model of concentrated and specialized effort—the "ideal student-teacher." Osler used a phrase from Matthew Arnold's poem "Rugby Chapel" to epitomize this concentrated effort. Howard had chosen a "path to a clear-purposed goal . . . With him the study and the teaching of medicine were an absorbing passion, the ardour of which neither the incessant and ever-increasing demands upon his time nor the growing years could quench."[22]

The poem itself is a lengthy and elaborate Victorian expression of piety and of the Oslerian ideal of what we would now call mentoring. One can understand why Osler was attracted to it. The author (Arnold) addresses his father lying in state in Rugby Chapel.

> Seasons impair'd not the ray
> Of thy buoyant cheerfulness clear . . .
> O faithful shepherd! to come,
> Bringing thy sheep in thy hand.
> And through thee I believe
> In the noble and great who are gone . . .
> Helpers and friends of mankind.[23]

Later in life, Osler said of Palmer Howard: "I have never known [a teacher or a colleague] . . . in whom was more happily combined a stern sense of duty with the freshness of youth."[24]

Willie and "the Guv." Osler's introduction to the *Bibliotheca Osleriana* (from which the above quote was taken) praises the influence of the three mentors on his book collecting. There are many other writings in which these men are affectionately noted. Osler's references to his father, however, are few (it seems there are few letters extant between the two) and when present are brief, some tending to damn him with faint praise or make implicit, negative comparisons to others. To paraphrase him, Father had 1,500 books in his library, *but* they were mostly theological. No novels! Sunday reading under the home regime was a trial! The only enjoyable materials that weren't taboo were father's travel books especially one by a missionary and they couldn't be hurtful even on Sunday. Books written by my *uncle* were a source of the family's literary flavour and a source of family pride.

During his years on the Ontario frontier, in Bond Head, the Reverend Featherstone Lake Osler had worked prodigiously. Arriving there in 1837, when the southern Ontario township of Tecumseth was still being cleared, he was the only Anglican clergyman for miles. His early years saw him away from the family for days at a time.

Despite his hard work, journals, diaries, and correspondence beginning in his young adulthood, portray a man whose clerical vocation, taken up only after a naval career had been blocked, seems a series of duties (albeit energetically pursued), not a loving engagement. Wilkinson sums up her reading of him "He lacked spiritual insight, he lacked humor; the Church had been thrust upon him; he did his always literal best."[25] In contrast, while speaking of "The Master Word in Medicine," Osler states *"that the law of the higher life is only fulfilled by love."*[26]

According to Wilkinson, the Reverend was known for his temper. Understandably, his over-riding concern for the family 'here on earth,' seems to have been for its material existence, and for providing his children with a proper education. The record does provide some evidence of close, affectionate relationships with the children as a group, at least when they were young. A letter from the Reverend to his wife in 1843 states "I long to have the dear boys hanging about me. Tell them Papa is continually thinking about them and hopes they are good." A letter from his wife to him in the same year: " The dear boys were so delighted with [your] nice little notes F[eatherston] was in ecstasies, and B.B.'s quiet joy was not less evident."[27] At this point in the life of the family, the Oslers had two boys, one of them, Featherston, born in 1838, the other, Britton Bath, born in 1839. The third child, Ellen Mary, was born in 1841 and was perhaps too young to understand a letter.

The Reverend's letter to his mother in England, on March 3rd, 1851, however, (when he had eight children) uses language which distanced himself both from his wife and his family and perhaps reflects a certain weariness.

> [The school] will be a great matter for *Ellen's troop of boys* . . . My only anxiety in money matters is that when god may be pleased to take me, *Ellen & her large family* may have some provision . . . I often think, since *Ellen has proved such a breeder* what a mercy it was that we did not remain in England. (ital. mine)[28]

Also, in a letter from this year to his mother, Featherstone noted that "the children were neither very good, nor very bad." As Bliss put it:

> He probably felt the same about his domestic flock a decade later. He had made clear to his boys, particularly the eldest, that he expected them to be industrious and dutiful, and then to make their own way in life; 'I wish to give each of you the best start in my power and then your future prosperity must under God depend upon yourselves.' As he aged, slowing down a bit, perhaps burned out from the early years in Canada, Featherstone tended to fade into the background of family life . . .[29]

Several later references to the Reverend in letters among the Osler children call him rather peremptorily "the Guv," i.e. the boss, and deal with their financial situation.

Willie was born in 1849 when Papa Featherstone was forty four years of age after seven elder children. Perhaps his temper was wearing a little thin over childhood pranks by the time Willie was pulling them. Further, although Wilkinson portrays a household in which the rod was spared, she also refers to a regular, if gentle discipline not calculated to inspire affection toward the father, with whom it was probably identified if only because of his occupation. "Sunday reading was confined to the theological shelves. Morning and evening prayers, regular church-going, and constant, if gentle reminders of their Eternal Home may have contributed to the later lukewarm attitude of the brothers toward the pulpit."[30]

One might even characterize as 'teen-age' rebellion Willie's adoption of Father Johnson as a father figure especially since Johnson was considered by some a 'papist' for his adoption of Roman liturgical uses and his adherence to the 'romanising' Oxford movement.[31] Indeed, the Reverend Featherstone seems to have had little patience for such Romish falderol.[32]

Michael Bliss summarizes his view of the Reverend's relationship with Willie during his formative years in medicine at Toronto and Montreal. He contrasts it with his "father-son" relationship with Bovell. "His real father . . . was a somewhat distant figure in his life in these years, but perhaps wise fathers know when to keep their distance."[33]

Willie and Ellen Free Picton, His Mother. On the other hand, there is much to indicate that Ellen loved and was dearly and unambivalently loved by her son William. He shared her dark complexion.[34] She called him, affectionately, her "Benjamin," her dear youngest son. Many of their letters to one another throughout his life are full of the everyday chat of mother and child, generally keeping one another abreast of how things were going and closing with genuine expressions of affection. These observations and what we have seen of Osler's feelings toward his father provide a background for understanding the dream symbolism that follows.

The Dreams

Analysis of the first dream argues for Osler's ambivalent identification with his father, with masculinity, and with his professional identity as a physician. Analysis of the second, reinforces the argument concerning his ambivalent identification with his father, and by extension his ambivalent identification with masculinity and his profession.

1. *A Fearful Snake—Osler Has Breasts and is Pregnant with A Girl!* The first dream account was dated July 23, 1911 some eleven days after Osler's sixty second birthday. It is a long account, but pared to certain elements which seem key to its plot, the dream tells the following story. Willie is abed with his wife. A snake is coiled under his armpit, and he can't move lest he be bitten. He is "simply terrified" in a "sort of convulsion" and "trembling violently." Later, with this and other snakes now gone, a physician examines him and asks:

> 'Have you always had these large breasts, Osler?' 'No,' I said. 'My God,' he said, 'there's milk in them . . . He put his hand on my abdomen, which for the first time I noticed to be very big, and said 'We are ruined. You are in the family way . . . Now I understand why you have been bothered with the snakes—they smelt the milk in your breasts and will do anything for a drink.'[35]

It was close to Osler's sixty-second birthday (July 12). Getting older, one can imagine him at least sub-consciously wondering about the meaning of his life, with dreams rising up to express and disguise night-time anxieties at this late-life review. (In a famous, or infamous speech upon leaving Hopkins for Oxford, Osler had jocularly recommended that people over sixty be chloro-formed since they were now beyond creativity. He paid dearly for the remark with the press uproar that greeted it.)

What experiential elements of memory and of symbol might have been associated (or 'condensed') in Osler's mind with a fearful snake? The most obvious, because of his deep interest in the history of medicine, would seem the ancient Greek cult of the god Asclepius[36] and by customary extension, the profession of medicine itself (both symbolized by a snake). But whence the threat? Could medicine have been felt by Osler as a threat? Perhaps only in conjunction with the snake's threat to him as female. Did Osler, then, have a latent identification with his affectionate Mother, a desire to be creative in a female way, to be nurturing in a feminine way? Could he have felt that his iden-tification with masculinity, and with medicine had deprived him throughout his life of this sort of creativity?

With what other memory or memories might the snake be associated to help explain this? A penis comes readily to mind. Could medicine have been associated in Osler's mind with his masculinity, and as such with his own fear-ful penis, or his father's? Perhaps so if Osler had an affectionate identification with—desire for—his mother, and an ambivalence toward or fear of his father. The dream seems to indicate and at the same time explain this. (The next dream will reinforce this interpretation.)

His adult life, too, had missed another sort of femininity, that which a daughter might have provided. He and his wife Grace had only one child to survive to adulthood, a son named Revere. The final elements of the dream see Osler told by his wife, that he is pregnant with a girl. He records, "I protested that I was rather old to have a baby—but it did not seem strange on account of my sex . . . I'll have a Caesarian done," I said,"[37] suffering perhaps, one might add, the punishment of this invasive surgical procedure (perhaps even symbolic of castration), in order to enjoy his forbidden desire to identify with (or possess) Mother. These last sentences have a calm, and a resignation, which the earlier elements of the dream lack. It is almost as though the dreamer is happy both to have finally accomplished this hidden desire and, within the dream, to have banished the fearful snake and his own fearful penis, the source of all this anxiety.

And so, as a sixty-two year old, Osler's mind perhaps wove a story expressing his subconscious fears of dying, of leaving life deprived (because of a masculine medical identity) of a feminine (maternal) sort of creativity which he subconsciously desired in childhood and perhaps continued to desire—soft, protective, and nurturing. The dream has a happy ending—he is a woman and pregnant with a girl.

2. *An Italian Boy Murders a Bishop in Rome And Is Hanged for It. Two Women Watch and Grieve.* This dream was dated August 10, 1918, approximately one month after his sixty-ninth birthday and twenty days before the first anniversary of Revere's death on the battlefields of France. The death of his son has been described by all who knew Osler as particularly traumatic for him possibly shortening his life because of his deep grieving. Osler described the dream as follows:

> Most distressing dream about the execution by hanging of a boy of 9 in London, at the instigation of the Italian Govt. for the murder of a Bishop in Rome the year before. The boy had been smuggled out of Italy and abandoned in London and picked up by a woman who kept a shop in the East End—not anything like a London shop as it had a clapboarded front and a small window. The woman had a remarkable face, with an expression of concentrated grief such as I had never seen before. She lay in a wooden bunk at the back of the shop and an Italian sister was trying to comfort her. The side of the shop opened directly into a big church from which noises of a service could be heard. The woman rolled from side to side, moaning "They tied his hands behind him, they put a rope about his small neck, and they did not bandage his eyes." The sister explained that the boy had been executed that morning in front of the high altar. All day the face of the woman recurred.[38]

A conjuncture of symbols make one wonder whether the boy is Willie himself; the murdered bishop, his father; the shop-woman and Italian sister, both of them, perhaps, his mother. Bear with me.

Willie's father (the bishop, a senior ecclesiastic, like his father) has been murdered. Willie (the young boy, dark complexioned, "Italian") is the murderer. Willie has the exclusive attention of this woman, his mother with her "Italian sister" in attendance. Perhaps the woman herself was dark-complexioned "Italian" too. The woman rolls from side to side, in bed—moaning for Willie. The moans are, perhaps, of some sexual significance. Willie is hanged in church for the murder; thus suffering the most extreme punishment possible for what may have been his latent wish. His hands are tied behind him, and his eyes are not covered.

One wonders if Willie's dream expresses a 'fearful' sight, experienced or imagined as a child—that which Freud called the "primal scene" —his mother and father in the act of making love. Here we see the woman, his mother, moaning. The boy, Willie himself, perhaps not understanding his mother's sounds, thinks, as children often do, that she is being hurt. He is furious at his father, perhaps from hostility, jealousy, and worry over his mother, but "his hands are tied." In the dream, time is collapsed, his eyes are not covered and he is punished for what he (is seeing) has seen and for the murder which he has desired.

The woman "kept a shop" in the East End (a poor district of London). The shop was a rather rudimentary structure, with a wooden cot in the back, one small window in the front, and clapboarded, perhaps symbolizing the Osler family's early residence in Bond Head, a pioneer and undeveloped rural area in Ontario.

"All day long," and perhaps all his life, "the face of that woman recurred."

But why did Osler dream that the murderous boy was nine years of age? At eight years old, Willie moved with his family from the rural Bond Head to the town of Dundas near Hamilton, Ontario. After nineteen years, his father had asked for a transfer so that his children could have a more adequate education. Ellen agreed to move but was not enthusiastic. One can imagine that the young Willie, from all accounts a frisky child[39], was not at all thrilled to leave his friends all because of schooling. The Oslers first stayed with family in Toronto waiting for the Rev. Featherstone to return from a funeral in Tecumseth before moving to Dundas. A train, on which some have said they were scheduled to leave, suffered a horrendous accident. A trestle collapsed and a large number of passengers were killed, among them several clergy of the church of England.[40] Perhaps the young boy feeling that the family and he had narrowly missed death, and learning that a number of clergy had been killed, sub-consciously blamed his father (who wanted the move in the first place) and wished his father dead, or at least fantasized that he had been killed in the wreck (he was at a funeral) and then felt guilty about the parricidal wish, and or fantasy.

Why was the boy aged nine in the dream? He had murdered the bishop in Rome a year before his execution, i.e. he was eight years old when the murder took place—Osler's age at which the move and accident and perhaps the murderous fantasies occurred.

Osler's dream records that he was executed because of the "Italian Govt." Osler's father was often referred to as "the Guv" the boss, the authority, by his children. Why were the governmental authority and the Bishop Italian? Perhaps, to signify ever present collusion among the parents. The mother, Ellen, as the woman in the dream was attended by the "Italian" sister.

But Osler was dreaming all of this at age sixty-nine, in the month of August, 1918 shortly before the first anniversary of his son's death at the hands of the German army. The death of his son had devastated him. Was he not also subconsciously wishing that he had been killed in his son's place (as another dream seems to indicate),[41] and perhaps more justly since he had psychologically murdered his own father?

If these interpretations and those of the "snake dream" are correct, the former would strengthen the latter. The execution dream more clearly indicates Willie's repressed hostility toward his father. The snake dream expresses an identification with 'feminine' feelings. It expresses ambivalence toward the profession of medicine and his masculinity and but only indirectly toward his father. Taken together I submit, the interpretations present a stronger argument for the over-all analysis

To take this analysis one step further—Osler's ambivalence toward masculinity and his profession in conjunction with the very affection and love which he showed toward his mentors, would have us argue that he overcame his ambivalent feelings toward his father by "identifying with the aggressor," i.e. with fatherly, masculine and professional images and roles close to that toward which he was ambivalent and anxious, but with which he could identify independently of his father in ways which were for him satisfying, and which became, for his era in society and for his profession, extremely fruitful.

Our discussion above, has shown that Osler began his journey toward a masculine/occupational identity first by 'staying close to home.' His first ambition was to enter the ministry, like his father. While still identified with this, he chose a role model different from but somewhat like the first—Father Johnson, a 'romanising' minister/amateur scientist. He then moved one step further and identified with a professional physician/scientist, Bovell, who had theological interests and became a minister. He identified with the former aspect of this mentor choosing medicine as a vocation. Finally, he met and identified with an unambiguously medical mentor, R. Palmer Howard, a man who had chosen a "path to a clear-purposed goal" a model of focused effort—a person with a passion for medical teaching, one through whom Osler could believe in 'the noble and great who are gone—the helpers and friends of mankind.' Osler distanced himself from *his* father, but identified with *other* fathers, and through them with *fathers*—helpers and friends of mankind, like his own father, the minister, but different too. He became a sort of medical minister.

A Reflection on Osler's Accomplishments

But why bother with all this? Do these interpretations of Osler's dreams help us to do justice to his achievements while crediting justifiable criticism? Let us look more closely at the criticisms noted in our introduction and then try to answer this question.

Women in Medicine. Before he was at Hopkins, and later, during his tenure there, Osler commented clearly and powerfully upon the place of women within medicine. He recommended against the establishment of women's medical schools in Canada (there was a movement for at least one or two of them)—on the eminently practical grounds that there was as yet no market for their products, women doctors. In addition, the cost of new medical schools would be prohibitive (especially given no such market).[42] He was by no means enthusiastic about admitting women to Hopkins on equal footing with men. He did, however, examine successful French experiences with women in medical schools and recommended their admission so that Hopkins might receive a desperately needed grant to open the medical school.[43]

Osler, however, who often spoke from the bully pulpit of his celebrity, could have done more than this—to help create a market for women in medicine and to help establish them on a more equal or secure footing with men. However encouraging he could be to a number of women who by dint of their own striving ultimately leapt the severe barriers to enter his profession, he only grudgingly and in a very local way helped to bring those barriers down. It seems clear that he believed that "a woman's place is in the home" and that only exceptional women (not always desirable exceptions) would be capable of medical careers, and these would remain male dominated for 'natural' reasons.[44] To illustrate his traditional views on sex-roles, one need only quote his dictum, "So truly as a young man married is a young man marred, is a woman unmarried, in a certain sense, a woman undone."[45] It is only within the past thirty to forty years that medical school enrollments have gradually approached a proportion of 50% women in the United States and Canada. The profession is still predominantly male in numbers but especially in its power structure.

Preventive Medicine and Social Class. Toward the end of his distinguished career, A.W. Franklin, a British pediatrician, co-founder and long-time organizational mainstay of the Osler Club of London, made the following mildly critical comments about the man he and his club called their "Patron Saint." Osler, he noted, "had a kindly regard for the less privileged person but, [as] a man of his time. . . had no general sympathy for the poor. They are always with us, and do not necessarily inspire social action. . . His privileged position in a secure society allowed him to surround himself with books, concentrating on those important in the history of science and medicine. . ."[46] It would seem that for Franklin, Osler should have been more concerned with bettering the social condition of the poor. He then would have been a more complete patron Saint.

When he stated the above, Franklin was at the height of a successful career as a London pediatrician, a pioneering neonatologist and influential member and president of a range of professional societies including the International Society for the Prevention of Child Abuse and Neglect. He was deeply involved in a range of clinical and preventive matters having to do with children and was thus keenly aware of the impact of social conditions on their health and well-being.[47] One of his biographers noted: that "Alfred recognized that it was necessary for pediatricians to become knowledgeable and active in their diagnosis of children suffering from abuse and neglect and to seek ways of preventing it."[48]

Franklin was surely well aware of Sir William's long and committed fight in Baltimore for public sanitation and for clean water, his concern to vaccinate British soldiers against typhoid and typhus in the Boer War and other similar campaigns. But he also had probably read Osler's 'Lay Sermon' on "Man's Redemption of Man"[49] in which redemption is described as entailing "physical salvation" i.e. physical health which derives from "modern science." And further, "The new socialism of Science cares not a rap for the theories of Karl Marx, of Ferdinand Lasalle, or of Henry George."[50] Perhaps A.W. Franklin was thinking of this when he stated that Osler "was not inspired to "social action" that is, action to eliminate or change those social factors which condition the occupational and family lives of the poor and which thus are the breeding grounds of so much disease.[51] Direct action on humanity's social condition, of the sort which Marx, and others espoused was generally far from Osler's mind. He fought for biological science, for the individual patient, and against pathogenic microbes and their more proximate breeding grounds. He thought little about the economic exploitation of man by men, which helps 'soften up' the human macro-organism for those micro-organisms. Perhaps, if he had lent the weight of his prestige and the eloquence of his voice to the fight against these conditions, the strides which some modern societies have made since his death would have been made earlier— strides, for example, towards more equitable living conditions, toward occupational health and greater accessibility to health care.

Osler's View of Medicine's Historical Record and the Fragmentation of Patients. After analyzing the character of Osler's literary styles, Faith Wallis concludes that Osler was committed to "health as a new gospel, and doctors as a modern priesthood." She notes, "This vision leaps out of the pages of his non-technical writings to any eye alert to Biblical allusion, but is even more profoundly implanted in the . . . voice of his textbook. . . [It is] . . . at once the oracle of a prophet and the preaching of a new apostle, and that was what the medical profession of Osler's day was at last ready to hear."[52] Tom Middlebro has seen Osler conferring the "notes of the Church" on medicine. It is "one" in "fraternal solidarity;" "holy", in its "singular beneficence;" "Catholic" in its universally accepted methods; and, "apostolic" in its noble ancestry.[53]

Philip Teigen sees Osler's reading of the historical record as focused primarily on the profession as a "point of reference." Osler's medical history is written to bring [physicians] together [in] "sympathy and pride," to inspire their mutual efforts, to keep that heritage alive.[54] As Osler himself said, "The profession in truth is a sort of guild or brotherhood, any member of which can take up his calling in any part of the world and find brethren whose language and methods and whose aims and ways are identical with his own." Osler's historical plot line stresses medicine's apotheosis in the 19th—the greatest of centuries.[55] He looks forward to much greater triumphs. "There seems to be no limit to the possibilities of scientific medicine, and . . . philosophers see, as in some far-off vision, a science from which may come in the prophetic words of the Son of Sirach, 'Peace all over the earth.' "[56]

But has modern medicine really been so unqualifiedly glorious, and climactically happy? Not too long after Osler's death in 1919, the great Mahatma Gandhi wrote that western medicine "ignores the soul altogether and strains at nothing in seeking to repair [that] fragile instrument . . . the body." Thus, he said "The profession puts men at its mercy and contributes to the diminution of human dignity and self-control."[57]

If anything this and related critiques of modern medicine have become louder and more stringent, even among those of our own tradition. Some have blamed these developments upon the modern physician's tendency to become highly specialized, with work and authority based wholly upon laboratory-based knowledge of ever smaller sub-divisions of the human organism, or narrower slices of the life course, or upon technical procedures; with behavior rule-governed by groups and sub-groups, departments and sub-departments.[58] Some analysts have attributed the frequency and high price of malpractice suits to patients' perceptions of physician 'callousness' or 'unresponsiveness' or 'discourtesy' resulting from specialism embedded in bureaucracy.[59] Various movements for patients' rights, self-help, etc. have surfaced especially among women in order to make up for this depersonalization.[60] Alternative health care practitioners who base their work on non-scientific health practices have thrived.[61] Some of them are within medicine itself.

In sum, we might ask, did Osler's glowing account of Asclepius' triumph[62] mask or underplay associated developments which were less progressive? Perhaps, if Osler had not repressed his rebellious instincts and so fully "identified with the aggressors" i.e. his substitute fathers, and the developing tradition out of which they came, he could have seen more clearly and called attention to these problems—largely unrecognized but nonetheless latent in the scientific medicine of his day. He may have used his professorships, his "bully pulpits," more insistently to call his colleagues' attention to them. Perhaps we would not have drifted so far so soon.

Questions and Conclusions: A Life Which Was A Gem

One is tempted to wonder, only half jokingly, if Osler had been analyzed by his contemporary Sigmund Freud could he have acknowledged his suppressed conflicts, and learned to tap in a more positive way into his 'underside?' Would his life have been even more fruitful for others and more satisfactory for himself if he had identified more fully with his rebellious feelings, with his disruptive and disorderly, zany alter-ego, what some have called his "McConnachie?"[63] Would his life have been more productive if he had identified more explicitly with his 'feminine side?' Would his legacy and immortality be more assured if he had more consciously and judiciously rejected more of what those medical "fathers" close to him represented, at least enough to nudge medicine further along the road toward professional developments which have come later and with difficulty? Perhaps.

But perhaps not. Perhaps such efforts would have diluted the very brilliant facets of a life, which, as it was, was a gem. Perhaps, because of the psychosocial dynamics we have seen, Osler chose the ideal of "unswerving devotion" to a "clear purposed goal" and a medical life in the profession largely as it was handed to him by his professional fathers. He pursued and enhanced it as best he could; and he did it brilliantly as a man of his time and not too far ahead of it.

Building on what his mentors taught him, Osler saw that the twin pillars of a physician-teacher's work are "a clear head [open to and/or pursuing science] and a loving heart"[64] [open to the humanity and needs of his patients and students]. And perhaps because of this, he did glimpse his profession's problems. Though posing no serious challenges to institutional sexism, he was mentor to individual women in medicine. He expressed discomfort with hyper-specialism at the bedside and in teaching.[65] Perhaps, he should have resisted these more vigorously, but because of who he was, and when, whence, and from whom he came—that was not to be. He took as a maxim, "Your business is 'not to *see* what lies dimly at a distance, but to *do* what lies clearly at hand.' "[66] It was to be the work of others.

As model of a physician with a "clear head and loving heart" his achievements were far more than one has a right to expect from any man. He identified with his professional fathers, and with paternity itself—with fathers as progenitors of a great, living tradition and with sons (even if some few were daughters) as bearers of its future. He taught lovingly and enthusiastically and through him, I suspect, many have learned that physicians must be responsible to their collective past and future and that their collective responsibilities must be exercised with a deep respect and concern for science and scientific progress, yes, but always and necessarily with a concern for practice and patients and for teaching and students.

Perhaps it is because Osler was spread so thin that his greatness is not obvious to all. Perhaps he was overly identified with transmitting the paternal past to the filial future and could not fully grasp that potential daughters, and the poor and oppressed were being slighted, and that his history of medicine was somewhat gilded. Perhaps, and yet who could fault him? As it was and as a man of his time he lived a life that was a gem and in it he accomplished more than enough. Indeed he accomplished far more than most of us who like our fellow human beings harbor I fear the seething psychic cauldron that Freud and other keen observers of the human condition have portrayed so well.

References

*Earlier versions of this paper have been presented at meetings of the American Osler Society (Montreal, 1999), King's College Faculty Seminar Series, University of Western Ontario and the London Medical History Association (March, 1999). The author is grateful to colleagues who have made helpful suggestions. Any faults in this paper are, of course, his own.

1. C.G. Roland, "On the Need for a New Biography of Sir William Osler," in J.A. Barondess and C.G. Roland eds., *The Persisting Osler—II: Selected Transactions of the American Osler Society 1981–1990* (Malabar, Florida: Krieger, 1994), 73–84, p. 78. See also: W. B. Bean, "The Egerton Yorrick Davis Alias," in J. P. McGovern and C.R. Burns, eds., *Humanism in Medicine* (Springfield, Ill.: Charles C. Thomas, Publisher, 1973), 49–59, p. 51; and, Joseph W. Lella, *Willie: A Dream: A Dramatic Monologue Portraying Sir William Osler (With Commentary and References)*, Osler Library Studies in the History of Medicine, vol. 6 (Montreal: Osler Library, McGill University, 2000).

2. Michael Bliss, *William Osler: A Life in Medicine* (Toronto: University of Toronto Press, 1999), p. x. See also, Charles Roland, "The Palpable

Osler: A Study in Survival," in J.A. Barondess, J.P. McGovern, and C.G. Roland, eds., *The Persisting Osler* (Baltimore: University Park Press, 1985), 3–18, pp. 12–13; and, Charles G. Roland, "Reputation Unrevised: Celebrating the Osler Sesquicentennial," *Can. Med. Assoc. J.*, 1999, 161, 827–8.

3. Ibid.

4. Bliss, (n. 2) *Osler: A Life*, pp. 147–48, 205–6, 230–31.

5. A.W. Franklin, "Osler Transmitted: A Study in Humanism," *Med. Hist.*, 1972, 16, 99–112, pp. 103–4.

6. Faith Wallis, "The Literary Styles of Sir William Osler," *The Osler Library Newsletter*, 1986, 51 (Feb), 1–3; Tom Middlebro, "Dr. William Osler: Some Reflections," *Studies in Canadian Literature*, 1980, 260–70; Philip Teigen, "William Osler's Historiography: A Rhetorical Analysis," *Can. Bull. Med. Hist.* 1986, 3, 31–49.

7. See a range of apposite, summary articles in M. Lock and D. Gordon, eds., *Biomedicine Examined* (Dordrecht, Netherlands: Kluwer, 1988); also, Bliss, (n. 2) *Osler: A Life*, pp. 283, 450–51, and Michael Bliss, "William Osler at 150," *Can. Med. Assoc. J.*, 1999, 161, 832–833.

8. P.K. Bondy, "What's So Special About Osler?" *Yale J. Biol. Med.*, 1980, 53, 213–217, quoted favorably by Roland, (n. 2) "Reputation Unrevised," p. 828.

9. Marianne Krull, *Freud and His Father* (New York: WW Norton and Co., 1986), p. 161.

10. Corrado Cavallero and David Foulkes, eds. *Dreaming as Cognition* (New York: Harvester Wheatsheaf, 1993), p. 135.

11. Ibid., pp. 3–5.

12. John Boghosian Arden, *Consciousness, Dreams, and Self: A Transdisciplinary Approach* (Madison, Connecticut: Psychosocial Press, 1996). See also: Gerald M. Edelman, *Neural Darwinism: The Theory Of Neuronal Group Selection* (New York: Basic Books, 1987).

13. H. Ferguson, *The Lure of Dreams: Sigmund Freud and the Construction of Modernity* (London: Routledge, 1996), p. 34.

14. Bliss, (n.2) *Osler: A Life*, p. 392.

15. William Osler, "A Way of Life," [originally published in 1913] in J.P. McGovern and C.G. Roland, eds., 3 vols. *The Collected Essays of Sir William Osler*, I, *The Philosophical Essays* (Birmingham, Alabama: The Classics of Medicine Library, 1985).433–45, pp.437–38.

16. C.G. Roland, "Sir William Osler's Dreams and Nightmares," *Bull. Hist. Med.*, 1980, 54, 418–46, p. 420.

17. Harvey Cushing, *The Life of Sir William Osler*, 2 vols. (Oxford: At the Clarendon Press, 1926), I, *passim*. In what follows, most non-referenced assertions of fact about Osler's life are derived from Cushing's biography, documented by him and well-accepted by Oslerian scholars. Specific quotations and controversial assertions are given supporting documentation and or references.

18. Thomas Browne, *Religio Medici and Other Writings*. [Originally published in 1635] London: Dent-Everyman's Library, 1965.

19. Cushing, (n. 17) *Osler*, I, 34–35.

20. Ibid., p. 67.

21. William Osler, "The Collecting of a Library," Introduction to *Bibliotheca Osleriana: A Catalogue of Books Illustrating The History of Medicine and Science Collected, Arranged and Annotated by Sir William Osler, Bt. and Bequeathed to McGill University*, ed. W.W. Francis, R.H. Hill and A. Malloch [originally published in 1929] (Montréal and London: McGill-Queen's University

Press, 1969), xxi–xxxvii.

22. William Osler, "The Student Life," [originally published in 1905] in J.P. McGovern and C.G. Roland, eds., (n.15) *The Collected Essays*, II, *The Educational Essays*, 255–85, pp. 282–83.

23. John Bryson, ed. *Matthew Arnold: Poetry and Prose* (London: Rupert Hart-Davis, 1954), pp. 197–201.

24. Osler, (n. 22), p. 283.

25. Anne Wilkinson, Lions in the Way (Toronto: Macmillan, 1956), p.62.

26. William Osler, "The Master Word in Medicine," [originally published in 1903] in J.P. McGovern and C.G. Roland, eds.,. (no. 15) *The Collected Essays*, I, 183–206, p. 204.

27. Wilkinson, (n. 25), pp. 83–84.

28. Ibid., pp. 89–90.

29. Bliss, (n. 2) *Osler: A Life*, pp. 30–31.

30. Wilkinson, (n. 36) *Lions*, p. 96.

31. Ibid., pp. 122–23.

32. Ibid., pp. 75–76, 86.

33. Bliss, (n. 2) *Osler: A Life*, p. 59.

34. Cushing, (n. 17) *Osler*, I, 15.

35. Roland, (n. 16), pp. 423–33.

36. Asclepius, Greek god of healing, was honored in a number of sacred places. Perhaps the most famous was his temple at Epidauros where sick pilgrims came to consult the Oracle, to sleep, and to be cured. The serpent was a symbol of the Asclepian cult and has become a symbol of medicine. See: *Bulfinch's Mythology* (New York: The Modern Library), pp. 105–106; also, "Asclepius," *The New Columbia Encyclopedia*. 1975 ed. p. 163.

37. Roland, (n. 16), p. 434.

38. Ibid., p. 444.

39. Bliss, (n. 2) *Osler: A Life*, pp. 27–28.

40. Ibid., pp. 25, 29, 30. On page 29, Bliss states that the "story that Willie had the croup, thereby saving the family from being on the fatal train is not true. When the wreck occurred, Ellen was in Toronto with the little ones waiting for Featherstone to come from a funeral in Tecumseth." He cites letters from B.B. Osler to brother Featherston (Fen) and EO to Fen Osler on 13 Mar. 1856. The move to Dundas is said to have taken place in 1857. Further investigation is needed to establish whether the letter citation is a typographical error and whether the move was or might have been postponed because of "Willie's croup."

41. Roland, (n. 16), p. 419.

42. William Osler, "The Growth of a Profession," [originally published in 1895] in J.P. McGovern and C.G. Roland eds., (n. 15) *The Collected Essays*, II, 9–32, pp. 29–30.

43. Bliss, (no. 2) *Osler: A Life*, pp. 205–6.

44. See: Ibid., pp. 147–48, 205–6, 230–31; as well as, J.B. Shrager, "Three Women at Johns Hopkins: Private Perspectives on Medical Coeducation in the 1890's," *Ann. Intern. Med..* 1991, 115, 564–69 and Faith Wallis, "Piety and Prejudice," *Can. Med. Assoc. J.* 1997, 156, 1549–51.

45. William Osler, "Nurse and Patient," [originally published in 1897] in J.P. McGovern and C.G. Roland eds., (n. 15) *The Collected Essays*, I, 86–98. p. 94.

46. A.W. Franklin, "Osler Transmitted: A Study in Humanism," *Med. Hist.* 1972, 16, 99–112, pp. 103–4.

47. See the following: A.W. Franklin, *Family Matters: Perspectives on the Family and Social Policy: Proceedings of the Symposium on Priority for the Family* (Oxford:

Pergamon Press, 1983); A.W. Franklin, ed., *Child Abuse: Prediction, Prevention and Follow Up* (New York: Churchill Livingstone, 1978); and, A.W. Franklin, *Widening Horizons of Child Health* (Lancaster: M.T.P. Press, 1976).

48. GW/VL, "Franklin, Alfred White," in Richard Robertson Trail, ed., *Munks Roll: Lives of the Fellows of the Royal College of Physicians of London* (London: Royal College of Physicians of London, 1984), 166–7.

49. William Osler, "Man's Redemption of Man," [originally published in 1910] in J.P. McGovern and C.G. Roland eds., (n. 15) *The Collected Essays,* I, 371–431.

50. Ibid., p. 427.

51. Bliss, (n. 2) *Osler: A Life,* pp. 283, 450–51.

52. Wallis, (n. 6), p. 3.

53. Middlebro, (n. 6), pp. 262–63. See also William Osler, "Chauvinism in Medicine," [originally published in 1902] in J.P. McGovern and C.G. Roland eds., (n. 15) *The Collected Essays,* I. 152–80.

54. Teigen, (n. 6).

55. Ibid. See also: William Osler, "The Evolution of Internal Medicine," in William Osler, ed., *Modern Medicine: It's Theory and Practice* (Philadelphia: Lea Brothers, 1907), vx–xxxiv.

56. Osler, (n. 53), p. 157.

57. Mohandas K. Gandhi, "Young India," *Unknown,* no. June 11. 1925.

58. For descriptions of this evolution see: Rosemary Stevens, *Medical Practice in Modern England: The Impact of Specialization and State Medicine* (New Haven: Yale University Press, 1966); and, her *American Medicine and the Public Interest* (New Haven: Yale University Press, 1971); also, Paul Starr, *The Social Transformation of American Medicine* (New York: Basic Books, 1982. Critiques of this evolution abound. Among them are the following introductory examples: George Engel's classic statement, "The Need for a New Medical Model: A Challenge for Biomedicine," *Science,* 1977, 129–36; Aaron Antonovsky, *Health, Stress, and Coping* (San Francisco: Jossey-Bass, 1977); Lock and Gordon, eds. (n. 7).

59. David Mechanic, *The Growth of Bureaucratic Medicine: An Inquiry into the Dynamics of Patient Behavior and the Organization of Medical Care* (New York: Wiley, 1976), pp. 272–73.

60. Arthur Frank, *The Wounded Healer: Body, Illness and Ethics* (Chicago: University of Chicago Press, 1995), p. 12.

61. Again, the literature is voluminous. For introductions see: Michael S. Goldstein, *Alternative Health Care: Medicine, Miracle, or Mirage?* (Philadelphia: Temple University Press, 1999); and, P.B. Fontanarosa and G.D. Lundberg, eds., "Alternative Medicine," J. Am. Med. Assoc, 1998, 280 (Theme Issue), 1549–1640.

62. Teigen, (n. 6).

63. Cushing, (n. 17) *Osler,* I, 240.

64. Osler, (n. 21), p. xxiii.

65. William Osler, "Remarks on Specialism," [originally published in 1892] in J.P. McGovern and C.G. Roland eds. (n. 15), *The Collected Essays,* I, 97–107.

66. William Osler, "The Army Surgeon," [originally published in 1892] in J.P. McGovern and C.G. Roland eds., (n. 15), *The Collected Essays,* I, 67–84, p. 74.

New News from Norham Gardens: The Osler Letters to Kate Cushing

 Michael Bliss, M.D.

Every historian or biographer lives in terror of new documents being discovered just after his work has gone to press. So we scour archives and attics making sure we capture every last scrap of relevant paper. Most of the time we know that complete success will elude us, for new sources are almost certainly out there just waiting to be found.

In producing *William Osler: A Life in Medicine* I tried very hard to see all the relevant Osler material that had been accumulated over many years, satisfied myself that I had, and was delighted to be able to incorporate some major new last minute finds. But Osler and his circle were such voluminous correspondents that I knew much Osler material could survive out there, hidden away. No one knows quite how much there is, where it might be, when it will appear. What I did not anticipate was that almost immediately after the biography was published, I myself would stumble on a major new run of Osler letters.

In examining most archival collections, I made a point of looking in every box and every file and at every piece of paper, and this way turned up quite a bit of material that previous biographers had not used. One particularly rich source was the Harvey Cushing papers at the Osler Library. These were the files Cushing generated in doing the first Osler biography, and had donated to McGill. I also spent a large amount of time in the much, much larger collection of Cushing papers at Yale, which are the records of Cushing's own life. I found that there was a great deal of material in the Yale papers relating to Cushing's Osler biography, to Cushing's relationship with Osler, and to the Hopkins circle and related projects.

It would have been next to impossible and seemed unnecessary to go

May 17, 2000. Revised for publication, August 2000.

Presented at the American Osler Society, May 7, 2000, Bethesda, Maryland.

through all the papers relating to Cushing's life for a life of Osler. Using the good finding aid to the Cushing Papers, and examining about a quarter of the whole collection, I though I had found every relevant file and had located all the Osler references of any value. I had found many more Osler letters than Cushing referred to in the biography, for example, and was able to make particularly extensive use of files of Grace Revere Osler's letters that Cushing had semi-surreptitiously had copied for posterity but had felt he dared not use for fear of her objections. Grace's letters are remarkably rich in fleshing out the narrative of the Oslers' lives, especially in their Oxford period.

After finishing the Osler biography, I decided to write more about Cushing. On literally the day after the American edition of *William Osler: A Life in Medicine* was published in November 1999, I received a further shipment of microfilm of Cushing papers and dove into files that the Finding Aid had identified as his wife's, Kate Crowell Cushing's, family correspondence. To my great surprise, these files in fact contain, among other letters Kate Cushing chose to keep, eighty-seven notes and letters she received from Grace and William Osler. Although other Osler letters to Kate exist, some of which Harvey Cushing quotes in the biography, this is the master series of Osler letters to Cushing's wife. Neither Cushing nor anyone else had ever referred to them. Here is the substance of these letters:

The first letter is from Grace to Kate on August 15, 1903, on hearing of the birth of the Cushings' first child. Harvey had been a next-door neighbour of the Oslers in Baltimore since 1901 and was well on his way to becoming a protegé and surrogate son when he married Kate in June 1902 and brought her into the community. The Oslers, on vacation in England are "dancing & singing for joy" about the Cushing news, Grace writes. She goes on to say, "Take the advice of a strong woman and stay *flat* on your back as long as you can. You will never regret it and rarely have such a good excuse. Men— *husbands & doctors* are always in such a hurry to get one up and it does make a difference later—And don't forget about the bandage if you want no stomach. Miss Collins [Kate's attendant] has sense about frivolities like flat stomachs."

Grace passes on news of their summer in England which has been delightful except for her "asthmatic cough . . . . I have been rather a wreck all summer but am improving now. Dr. Osler insists on my splending two weeks at Harrogate to drink the Sulphur waters—I hate the idea but have promised to go." She urges Kate to be "old-fashioned" in caring for her baby.

The correspondence resumes the next summer as Grace is visiting relatives and then summering on the St. Lawrence while Osler and Harvey Cushing are in England. Grace's desire for privacy, well-documented in the biography, is given a new twist in a comment she makes on August 1, 1904, "Murray Bay is filling up. I have great difficulty in avoiding people—Fortunately nearly all the invitations are for Bridge and as I do not play it is a splendid excuse. The women here play day and night and already look worn out." Grace is pleased to hear of the splendid ovations Osler received during the BMA's meeting at Oxford, but says nothing to Kate of the deliberations about the Regius Chair until the men have arrived home.* Then on August 17 she

---

*Kate, however, would have known that Osler was considering the position from a July letter her husband sent her on July 24 after he first learned of the offer; a close study of Cushing's diary of his 1904 England trip, another source missed for the biography, reveals that Osler then kept Cushing in the dark about his final decision until Cushing accidently learned the truth on their voyage home. In his diary Cushing noted of: 107/1047. HC Diary of Oxford Trip, 1904. "The passage Homeward bound. One thing alone stands out above all others – a depressing thing it is. On the second day out I found a 'Daily Note' book of Dr Os which had slid off from a pile of books by his bunk onto the floor. Two or three loose sheets I replaced and at the top of one of them – I read to my grief the following – 'The story of my acceptance of the chair at Oxford may be briefly told' – that was all".

writes how thankful she is to have her dear man back, "because these have been very trying weeks—Such a serious matter settled and now I am in possession of an Oxford Professor. My heart is heavy & light in turn. And I hardly know what to do or say. I have had very worrying weeks over it. I am trying only to look on the bright side and think of the many advantages of comparative ease for Dr. Osler and a charming chance for Revere. Please forgive us—and remember how easy it is to cross the sea. . . . ."

On September 1 Grace thanked Kate for a comforting letter and expanded on the problem of planning their departure from America the next spring: "I wish I could simply vanish—I dread the breaking up more than anything but the leaving you all is the worst. Dr. Osler is very bright and cheerful over it And satisfied absolutely now that it is settled. Of course he was awfully worried while away and I can imagine how the boys must have suspected. . . . Mother is bearing up pluckily and feeling very proud of her son-in-law."

Two days later Osler himself wrote Kate, offering some fascinating lines of self-analysis: "The really hard part is to leave all my good friends. For a naturally soft hearted man I must have a hard strain somewhere to be able to do it. I must have a mixture, of Puritan blood which is bad for a Celt—bad in some ways but I dare say good in others, tempering & giving stability to character." Grace dreaded having to go home to Baltimore that fall to face the music. "We are inundated with letters from both continents", she wrote Kate on September 11, "Dr. Osler was delghted with your remark—'No one will ever know what you really think'. I think *he* thinks he has done the right thing."

We pick up Grace's inner feelings eight months later, as the family has left Baltimore and is en route for England. She thanks Kate profusely for her support through the winter, and adds, "There have been days when I have felt I must cry halt and not go on with the plans for the new life—but they were selfish moments & I have tried to conquer them." Now they were having a wonderful voyage, having found their cabin "baracaded with flowers—fruits & Champagne boxes—to say nothing of telegrams & letters".

On June 2, 1905 William wrote Kate from 7 Norham Gardens, (the first Oxford house they stayed in) to add his views on their life after 6 days "in the new old land. . . . You know the poem Home-sick in Heaven—well that was our condition on Sunday & Monday—heavenly days & celestial surroundings but— we were really sad at heart away from all the dear ones who have come so close into our lives. We have cheered up now and, I think, shall be very happy. . . . I have been introduced to many young colleagues & have begun to find my way about. My first official duty is this afternoon—a meeting of the Curators of the Bodleian. . . . The English girls have colour but there is a great difference."

A month later (July 13) Osler writes Kate that he is loafing and getting rested and that Sargeant [*sic*] has begun the group painting of himself, Welch, Halsted, and Kelly. "He is a wonderfully rapid artist—starts at once, without a sketch on the canvass. He put W's face in with about three touches so that it was recognizable. He says it will be magnificent. He has our robes draped {?} He would not look at my scarlet gown—impossible—awful! Grace is in good form— getting accustomed to the ways & doings." Grace herself wrote Kate with news of their comings and goings that is familiar to us from other sources, but added her harshest comments on British women. "They are growing so hideous and so untidy, it is very distressing. The really smart ones are so bedizened there is no pleasure in them—Even young girls have their cheeks & lips done up."

On October 26, 1905 Grace described to Kate in delicious detail what life in Oxford was like that autumn:

> We have had the best luck in weather ever since we came and are now
> rejoicing in a real American Autumn—The Oxonians not having anything

else to grumble at now fuss because it is cold and the flowers have been killed. They are chronic grumblers. The climate suits me admirably and I have cheeks like beets. . . .

I am nearly worn out with guests—that does not seem very hospitable but we have been alone two weeks since we arrived and I never get a moment to myself. Dr. Osler looks perfectly splendid & about 30—We had a jolly week in Paris—it was reeking with Americans—all fussing about clothes. I cant find a dress maker here & I shall soon be in rags . . .

Oxford is agog again. Term is in and the place is alive with undergraduates. They re all busy playing foot ball & rowing & the Heads giving dinner parties—We have seven invitations for one night—Our dining room is only large enough to seat ten formally so I fear we must have many detachments [sic] to return civilities. No chance of a house yet. Dr. Osler is over come with joy today over the beautiful gift from the Hopkins Graduates. 12 vols of reprints of all the graduates. He says no teacher ever had such a gift. It is really stunning. . . . Dr. Osler had his first clinic yesterday 15 men present. He was most amusing over it. The Rhodes men [Rhodes Scholars] are some of them every nice—others awful."

On March 24, 1906, Grace wrote that both she and her husband had periods of homesickness, and mentioned that she had just been to see the Sargent painting of the Four Doctors: "It is perfectly wonderful. Really I could not believe so beautiful a picture could be done of men." The only person who did not like the portrait, Grace wrote, was Bill Francis (Osler's second cousin and surrogate son), who thought Sargent had made Osler look too old.

There is one letter in the series from Marjorie Howard, yet another of the Oslers' surrogate children, reporting from Norham Gardens on June 12, 1906 that she "found all the dear things in this household simply flourishing! Reggie is more wicked than ever, Aunt Grace more angelic, Tommy [Revere] too dear & English for words". By that summer Grace was complaining (July 19, 1906) that Osler was "terribly involved" mostly with visitors. "Oxford is packed with Americans—and half of them know the Oslers—Ewelme [the nearby village where Osler was the Master of the alms house] means peace in a graveyard and I hope no one discovers it."

She comments constantly in these letters on her husband's appearance. She worries about his health and, in one undated note remarks to Kate, "I am so afraid Dr. Osler gets ill away from me."

In December 1906, the Oslers were back in America for a visit and Grace wrote Kate from Toronto, on the 15th, "sometimes I am almost sorry we came—it makes me long so to be back with you all—but like Dr. Osler I feel that it is a good thing for old people to move on and when one finds the vacancies filled so perfectly one can but be thankful. . . ." This was the one hundredth birthday of Osler's mother. "Dr. Osler only arrived this morning—but came extra happy as his Mabel [almost certainly Mabel Brewster, a former patient and good friend] gave him a rare Shelley. Ha—Ha!! Who wouldn't be the wife of a popular MD or Surgeon?"

None of Kate Cushing's letters to the Oslers have been located, so we get very little Cushing news in this correspondence. Of course Grace is happy to pass on nice comments, such as young doctor Campbell Howard's remark in 1906 that 'Harvey Cushing is the best known Hopkins man in German [sic] and the most talked of." (Sept. 19). And as Cushing, a rising superstar, began to consider offers to move from Johns Hopkins, the Oslers felt free to advise: "Do hold off all appointments or offers and wait for *Harvard*", Grace wrote in March 1907. "I am sure there will be a call for the Brigham and it will be so delightful to see the Cushings meandering back to New England." The distinguished Oxford physiologist C.S. Sherrington, and his wife were asking about Harvey, Grace also reported (July 15, 1907). "They are such satisfactory people," she said of the Sherringtons.

Thanks to a Grace Osler letter in August, 1908 we now know that the Oslers' first automobile was a 14 horsepower Renault landau, which ran along smoothly at 20 miles per hour. On their Scottish trip, she reported "Dr. Osler is bowling and playing the games of the country." Grace constantly inquired about the Cushing children and said she wanted to stand to them as a surrogate grandmother. Most of her later letters to Kate are signed "Tanta Grace". "Sometimes I just cry when I think how wonderful my life has been in connection with all you young people and how good you have all been to me, never treating me as though I was so much older—Oh—dear—I want to cry now!" (Sept. 2, 1910). Grace's letters are full of brief comments about her son, Revere, which suggest that Grace saw in the boy from an early age a quick wit and precociousness. He "has an extraordinary insight for 14 years", she wrote in 1910, "Even if he can't do Greek verbs."

The notes tend to be brief and routine until the outbreak of the European war in 1914, and then they are characterized by Grace's intense hatred of the conflict—"now the world is upside down and no one can be happy" (Dec. 10, 1914)—along her concern for her two men. We have on May 15, 1917 a new view of 21-year old Revere's arrival for what proved to be his last leave from his artillery unit in France:

> I didn't know him when he literally fell on me out of the train. He is so
> enormous & with a very smart moustache & his cheeks brown & pink. . . .
> He has stood the 7 months wonderfully. Seems to be undamaged by nerves
> and sees amusement in many things with which he is surrounded. . . . Of
> course he is like his father—seeing only Good in everyone. Kate isn't it
> simply horrible, cruel & beyond words—a sorrow—that WO should have
> this to bear? It is pathetic to see him with the boy—who is half a head taller
> than his father and stands with his arm around his neck. I can hardly bear
> to look at them—Thank God your boy is so young? . . . .

On August 19 Grace passes on the latest news of Revere at the front and asks Kate, "Will it ever end? The suspense grows worse—poor Reggie is almost a skeleton and worries me to death. He keeps busy every moment but sometimes cannot sleep & it makes one very anxious. I dread the winter for him—to say nothing of Revere—if it is to be as bad as last year."

For Revere it ended ten days later, with Cushing present at the boy's death, and in the biography I have quoted Grace's agonized lament to Kate Cushing, which is in a different file in the Cushing collection. In these files we have a new letter from Grace's sister, Susan Chapin, writing about the Oslers on September 19th:

> It is not necessary for me to tell you that they are magnificent in their
> courage—you would know it—but Oh! it is heart breaking to see them—
> WO seems to be shrinking away & dear Grace's face is sad beyond words.
> The strained look has gone—It has seemed in all these anxious months that
> sometime something would snap—she has been so over-strained—& with it
> all the continual pressure of people—people—people—& every one else's
> interests & demands to be attended to.

And we have a letter of Grace's, written on December 6, 1917, movingly describing their situation:

> Docci O looks a wreck and is terribly thin. He is so pathetic it breaks my
> heart to look at him—He says he has nothing to live for and all joy has

gone—which is quite true—But he works harder than ever and is called on to do a thousand things at once. . . . Kate the customs of war time are awful. You can't stop to be alone with your sorrow as you would like—you have to be up and doing all the time—calling on officers wives to come to the hospital—have strange people in all the time—and smile as though your heart wasn't bursting with grief and disappointment. I can hear Revere say 'Dont mind Muz, I'm all right—go on' And that's the reason we must— And help other sufferers as best we can— . . . there are always people walking in & out and the everlasting jabbering going on. . . .

"If only Grace might run away some where & just scream—I think it would do her good", Susan Chapin had written the day before: "but always there is some one there & when there isn't poor Willy looks as if he could not stand it. It is so awful for each to see the other's suffering & to have me looking on was too much—that was the reason I felt I must get 'a job' " [and leave Oxford].

There is more of the same sense of grief in the letters, but otherwise no new information on the Oslers' last years, his final illness, or Grace's widowhood.

* * * * * * * * *

On balance these letters would not cause me to change any of the judgments or factual statements in *William Osler: A Life in Medicine,* but they are so rich in detail, and so specially infused by Grace Osler's delightful personality that I deeply regret not having had them at hand to quote in the biography. I have no doubt that further significant Osler material will come to the surface over time, thus further enriching our understanding of this remarkable family.

Sources: All of the letters cited are contained in the Harvey Williams Cushing Papers at the Yale University Library, Series IV, Box 198, Folders 55–60 (microfilm reel 157), Cushing, Katherine Crowell, Correspondence. 1897–1940.

William Osler and The *New York Times,* 1897–1931

 Charles F. Wooley, M.D.

The Oslerian corpus, which had nineteenth-century origins, continued to grow after the death of William Osler (1849–1919), expanding throughout the twentieth century. The institutions and organizations in Canada, the USA and England that honour him as their own also contributed to the phenomenon with regular renewals of their claims to Oslerian heritage. The man (Figure 1), his works, and the legend are well documented in the specialized literature dealing with the history and literature of medicine, medical biography and bibliography, and the medical humanities. However, the popular press in the USA approached Osler in a quite different manner. A prime example may be found in the *New York Times* from 1897 to 1931. Over those years, opinions expressed about Osler changed remarkably as he moved across the pages first as a source of recurring controversy during his lifetime, then emerging posthumously as a newly discovered legend.

We turn to a different time, when the daily press was the sole source of daily news, the newspapers forming, refining, or destroying reputations while informing the reading public. In fact we return to a very different world, with Cunard's Liners, the railroad, and the Marconi wireless, the world before, during, and shortly after World War I. Barbara Tuchman speaks of attempting to cross that gulf: "The Great War of 1914–18 lies like a band of scorched earth dividing that time from ours . . . a physical as well as psychological gulf between two epochs."[1]

Presented at the American Osler Society, May 5, 1998, Toronto.

Previously published in J Med Biog 1999, 7:130–139. Reprinted with permission.

Copyright © by the *New York Times* Co. Reprinted by permission.

Sir William Osler
1849 - 1919

Physician, Teacher, Historian, Biographer, Bibliophile

1872   McGill University, Montreal
        Two years study in Europe

1874   McGill Institute of Medicine
        Lecturer/Professor

1884   University of Pennsylvania
        Chair of Clinical Medicine

1889   Johns Hopkins University
        Professor/Chief, Medical Department

1905   Oxford University
        Regius Professor of Medicine

Figure 1.   Osler's professional life. (Top picture couresy of the Osler Library of the History of Medicine, McGill University, Montreal; bottom picture courtesy of the Illustrated News Picture Library, London.)

Dr. William Osler speaks

William Osler was a Professor of Medicine at Johns Hopkins in Baltimore in 1897 when the *New York Times* reported his address to the British Medical Association in Montreal, the first overseas meeting of the British Medical Association in its 42 years of existence. Over 1000 physicians and surgeons were in attendance at the meetings, including nearly 300 Americans. "Montreal is en fete," said the *New York Times*. Lord Lister, champion of asepsis in surgery, President of the Royal Society and President of the British Association for the Advancement of Science, was the outstanding figure at the meetings. The *New York Times* noted "When Lord Lister was presented the cheering was deafening, the greatest enthusiasm prevailing"[2].

The principal paper was read by Dr William Osler, FRCP, Professor of Medicine in Johns Hopkins University, Baltimore. Osler's address, "British medicine in Greater Britain," traced the development of medicine in North America to the worldwide influence of British medicine at a time when the revival of medicine in England paralleled the growth of the colonial settlements. The English physicians in the New England colonies came primarily from Great Britain until the first US medical schools were established in 1765 to 1782. Osler's presentation dealt with great moments and great names, and was later published in the collected essays that accompanied Aequanimitas, Osler's classic valedictory address to Philadelphia students given on 1 May 1904.[3]

The *New York Times* in 1897 presented Osler as a respected figure in US medicine and an important participant in international medical circles. This was before the storm. It all started innocently enough with a two-paragraph note in August 1904:

OXFORD POST FOR DR. OSLER
Johns Hopkins Professor to Succeed
Sir John Burdon-Sanderson

London, August 16—King Edward has approved the appointment of Prof. William Osler of the Johns Hopkins Medical School, Baltimore, as Regius Professor of Medicine at Oxford University, in succession to Sir John Burdon-Sanderson.

Prof. Osler, who has been Professor of Medicine and physician to the hospital of the Johns Hopkins Medical School since 1889, is a Canadian by birth and is fifty-five years old. After being graduated from McGill University, at Montreal, he studied in Europe. From 1874 to 1884 he was a professor at McGill University, and then for five years was Professor of Clinical Medicine at the University of Pennsylvania.[4]

Osler's impending departure returned to the news in early 1905. The Johns Hopkins University 1905 birthday celebrations incorporated an outpouring of tributes to the soon departing Osler. President Remsen of the University requested that Osler present an address for the occasion. On 22 February Osler read his valedictory, entitled "The fixed period", at the event, an address that seemed innocuous enough to the packed audience, which included a large gathering of alumni. Osler was then presented to President Remsen as the single candidate for an honorary degree, and the university LLD was conferred.

But the content of the address was misinterpreted. The unintended legacy was instantaneous controversy. The storm broke on 24 February 1905. Under headlines reading "Fixed Limit of Man's Usefulness at Forty", "Dr Osler Asserts Belief That Value to the World Ends Then", "Suggests Death at Sixty", "Retiring Johns Hopkins Professor Quotes Anthony Trollope's Idea of Chloroform for Superannuated", the *New New York* Times began by stating that Dr. William Osler "has aroused interest by his remarks on the relative usefulness of man before and after a certain age limit."[5] It went on:

After expressing the opinion that professors ought to live like peripatetic philosophers and not permit themselves to grow stiff and stale by too long a stay in one place, Dr Osler spoke of the feasibility and advisability of fixing the period of a teacher's time of service and age. This question, he said was delicate, but must be approached because it was of infinite importance to university life. He mentioned the time limit of twenty years of service set by some London hospitals, and said that, to his knowledge, no educational institutions had followed this example.

THE LIMITS OF USEFULNESS

"I have two fixed ideas," he then said, "With these I have sometimes bored my friends, but I have heretofore never uttered them in public. The first is the comparative uselessness of men above forty years of age. This may seem shocking, and yet, read aright, the world's history bears out the statement. Take the sum of human achievement in action, in science, in art, in literature—subtract the work of the men above forty, and while we should miss great treasures, even priceless treasures, we would practically be where we are today. It is difficult to name a great and far reaching conquest of the mind which has not been given to the world by a man on whose back the sun was still shining. The effective, moving, vitalizing work of the world is done between the ages of twenty-five and forty—those fifteen golden years of plenty, the anabolic or constructive period, in which there is always a balance in the mental bank and the credit is still good.

"In the science and art of medicine there has not been an advance of the first rank which has not been initiated by young, or comparatively young men. Vesalius, Harvey, Hunter, Bichat, Laennec, Virchow, Lister, Koch—the green years were yet upon their heads when their epoch-making studies were made. To modify an old saying, 'a man is sane morally at thirty, rich mentally at forty, wise spiritually at fifty-or-never.'

"The young men should be encouraged and afforded every possible chance to show what is in them. If there is one thing more than another upon which the professors of this university are to be congratulated it is this very sympathy and fellowship with their junior associates, upon whom really in many departments—in mine certainly—has fallen the brunt of the work.

"My second fixed idea is the uselessness of men above sixty years of age and the incalculable benefit it would be in commercial, in political, and in professional life if, as a matter of course, men stopped work at this age. Donne tells us in 'Biathanatos' that by the laws of certain wise states sexagenarii were precipitated from a bridge, and in Rome men of that age were not admitted to the suffrage, and they were called depontani because the way to the Senate was per pontem and they from age were not permitted to come thither."

Dr. Osler himself is fifty years old. . . Among those who held seats on the stage of McCoy Hall and listened to his remarks were the following well-known men, all of whom are above forty: . . .

Among those who held seats on the stage of McCoy Hall listening to Osler, the paper listed the President of the Johns Hopkins University, the President of the Carnegie Institution, trustees of the Johns Hopkins University, a bishop, a US Supreme Court judge, an editor, and so on. The article ended with a review of Osler's own record, noting that a great deal of his fame had been acquired since he passed his fortieth year.

Osler's complete address occupies 18 pages of the *Aequanimitas* collection of essays.[6] "The fixed period" that Osler referred to in his farewell speech was the title of a little read satire by Anthony Trollope. Set 100 years in the future, the Parliament of the small imaginary Pacific island of Britannula has passed a bill that would lead to national happiness and prosperity, ending the miseries of old age and the financial problems attendant on the care of the non-productive elderly by setting a fixed period of life, following which men and women would be admitted to a college for a year for preparation for euthanasia by chloroform. Trollope's futuristic satire dealt with the eventual collapse of social programs because of the factor of human nature, namely, the reaction of the planners when their own time comes.

OSLER WRITING ESSAY ON MAN'S CRISIS AT 40
Only a Joke About Chloroform at Sixty, He Says

HE ANSWERS HIS CRITICS

Baltimore, Feb. 24.-Dr. William Osler, surprised and apparently somewhat annoyed over the widespread adverse criticism made on his statement that a man's usefulness in the world begins to decline when he is forty, this evening reiterated his statement and continued:

"I mean just what I said, but it's disgraceful, this fuss that the newspapers are making about it.

"I know there are exceptions, but they only serve to illustrate the rule. I have spent some time writing an essay entitled 'La Crise De Quarante Ans', (The Crisis of Forty Years), which will prove what I say. I have not yet finished the essay, and I have been years in accumulating the facts it contains.

"As to chloroforming men at sixty that was only a pleasantry," and the doctor laughed heartily.

"I was alluding to Anthony Trollope's story, which hinges upon the chloroforming of an old fellow at sixty.

"After forty man can lead a useful life as a citizen and he can make money, but making money is not the great work that tells. The creative mind seems not to care to make money.

"The work that counts is the essential, fermentative, vitalizing creations of the mind, and history shows that men under forty have done the best and the largest part. In fact, nearly all of that."[7]

Chicago, Feb.24.-President James B. Angell of the University of Michigan does not subscribe to Dr. Osler's statement that men lose their usefulness when they reach the age of sixty years. In an address at the annual banquet of the Chicago Alumni Association of the University of Michigan he said:

"I would like to extend the time of a man's life instead of shortening it. The experiment of killing off old men has been tried in Africa for centuries, and I would suggest to the distinguished physician that civilization has not advanced very rapidly there."[8]

There was more two days later:

DR. OSLER STICKS TO VIEWS
Has Been Misquoted, but Believes
Men Under 40 Do World's Work

Baltimore, Feb.26- Dr. William Osler, in reply to criticisms and misstatements made in connection with his recent remarks on the limit of man's utility, to-night gave out the following statement:

"I have been so misquoted in the papers that I should like to make the following statement:

"First-I did not say that men at sixty should be chloroformed: that was the point in the novel to which I referred, and on which the plot hinged.

"Secondly-Nothing in the criticisms have shaken my conviction that the telling work of the world has been done and is done by men under forty years of age. The exceptions which have been given only illustrate the rule.

"Thirdly- It would be for the general good if men at sixty were relieved from active work. We should miss the energies of some young-old men, but on the whole it would be of the greatest service to the sexagenarii."[9]

Osler also sent a letter to the Editor:

DR. OSLER MISREPRESENTED
Did Not Urge That Men Over Forty
Should Be Chloroformed

To the Editor of the New York Times

I wish you would contradict in your paper the statement that has been so foolishly circulated and so widely in the press that I urged that men over sixty should be chloroformed. W. Osler.

Baltimore, Md., Feb. 27, 1905.[10]

By March first, the New York Times returned to Osler's impending departure:

FAREWELL DINNER TO OSLER
Charaka Club Members Laud Him in
Poems and Speeches

Dr. William Osler of Baltimore attended a farewell dinner given in his honor at the University Club, Fifth Avenue and Fifty-fourth Street, by the Charaka Club. Dr. Osler leaves for Oxford next June.

The Charaka Club had no more than 15 members, who were men of New York and other cities interested in literature, art, and medicine. (The Club was formed in New York City by an elite group in 1902. Some major personalities, including Osler, Harvey Cushing, Weir Mitchell and Charles Dana, gave papers to the group. In time these presentations were issued in printed volumes.)

After a discussion of the speakers and honours bestowed on Osler, for those who might have missed the tempest the *New York Times* fanned the flames—referring to Osler as "the man who has been discussed so widely within the last few weeks because of his views upon the age limit of usefulness," noting that Osler in his response to the honours "made no reference whatever to his recently expressed theories."[11]

Two brief articles dealt with Osler's successor at Johns Hopkins. The first, from 22 March 1905, mentioned Dr William T Councilman of Harvard as the man likely to succeed Osler based upon a visit to Boston by Dr William Welch, Professor of Pathology at Hopkins, allegedly with overtures to Dr Councilman. The second, dated 4 April 1905, reported the election by the trustees of Johns Hopkins University of Dr Franklin Barker, head of the Department of Anatomy in the University of Chicago and Rush Medical College, to the Professorship of Medicine made vacant by the resignation of Dr William Osler.

Osler's farewell address to the Medical and Chirurgical Faculty of Maryland urging fusion of the medical colleges in Baltimore and in other cities in the country, and bringing the homeopathic brethren into the fold, was reported 28 April 1905. His next stop was New York City. On 3 May 1905 the *New York Times* ran an article under "500 Physicians Say Bon Voyage to Osler", "He Talks of His Ideals", "Honored at Dinner as He is About to Become the Regius Professor at Oxford". There is a change in the tone of this laudatory article. More than 500 physicians representing every part of the country and Canada, with foreign guests from places as distant as Cairo, Egypt, gathered in the large banquet hall of the Waldorf-Astoria "to do honor and bid farewell". The *Times* listed the guests including "names familiar not only in this country but all over the world". The speakers and the toasts to which they responded were mentioned, reminiscences of their companionship with Osler in Montreal, Philadelphia, and Baltimore were presented, along with "frequent and cordial tributes to his professional skill and learning as well as to his personal charms". Osler's family, "including his mother-in-law, his wife, and his young son, occupied the center box in the first gallery. Their appearance there when the dinner proper was about half through, was a signal for the entire assembly on the main floor to rise and applaud. Both tiers of boxes were filled with women in gay dresses, who had gone there to listen to the speeches."[12]

The detailed description of the formal medical and social event, the menu, the participants, and the proceedings provides a tableau from another era, with echoes of European royal pageantry and class distinctions. It was certainly a major happening in the lives of many of the participants who recalled the event decades later.

And so Osler went to Oxford. The acute phase of the storm had subsided. The pause lasted until December 1905, when Osler returned home with Mrs Osler and their son, ER Osler to spend the holidays.

DR. OSLER IS BACK AGAIN

Anti-Chloroform Argument Greets Him

on Pier, but Doesn't Please Him

Dr. William Osler, who disbelieves in old age, came home from Oxford University on the Cunard liner Caronia yesterday to spend the holidays here. With him were Mrs. Osler and their son, E.R. Osler.

The doctor's arrival had been heralded in advance, and a group of reporters was at the pier to meet him. Dr. Osler made it quite clear that he no longer liked reporters. He denied himself to a timorous one in the group, who began with the inquiry:

"Is this Dr. Osler?"

"No," snapped the physician, without further comment.

Alittle later, however, the timorous one, having proved his suspicions to be correct, went up to Dr. Osler again with the passenger list in his hand.

"Dr. Osler," he began, "will you tell us something about your plans? We think the public would be interested to know them."

Somewhat mollified, Dr. Osler then explained that he had come home to spend the holidays, that he was going directly to Boston, then a little later to Canada, and that he would eventually go to Johns Hopkins University at Baltimore, where he formerly had a Chair in the Faculty.

By the time Dr. Osler had gotten as far as the pier to look after his baggage his presence had become known to several Government officials connected with the Custom House. One of them, Deputy Inspector Bishop, having noticed Pier Captain Watson about, saw the possibility of a practical illustration to Dr. Osler that his theories about old age has exceptions. Capt. Watson served in the civil war, followed the sea for many years, and has now been Pier Captain for many years. He is about 70 years old.

Grabbing Capt. Watson, Mr. Bishop took him up to Dr. Osler and said:

"I wish to introduce you to Capt. Watson. He doesn't believe in your chloroform theory."

The vigorous Capt. Watson gave the hand of the physician a shake that made him squirm. Dr. Osler didn't appear to like the incident.[13]

President Angell of the University of Michigan and Pier Captain Watson of New York were soon joined by Dr. Felix Adler.

OSLER ONLY HALF RIGHT, SAYS DR. FELIX ADLER
Inner Life of Old Age Overlooked
by Physicians

CITES THE CASE OF DANTE
Also, Milton, Kant, and Others Who
Did Immortal Work Late in Life –
Thinks Belief in Future Life Waning

Dr. William Osler's remarks on old age were the text of the address given by Dr. Felix Adler in Carnegie Hall before the Ethical Culture Society yesterday morning.

"When the physician speaks the whole world listens," said Dr. Adler. "He is the custodian of health, the savior of life, and life and health have never been rated more highly than in this age when the confidence in another life is abating. He is the alleviator of pain and a kind of father confessor and priest. He is reticent, and the seal on his lips makes him a professional expert in keeping his own counsel.

"No wonder, then, that the whole world listens when the physician speaks, as Dr. Osler has done in his 'Counsels and Ideals,' a somewhat scrappy collection of his writings. The author seeks to impress splendidly idealistic views of life. The student, he urges, should not consider his life as a business, but as a consecrated service, and the practice of his profession not as art, but as a science. He enjoins travel, friction with other minds, and what he quaintly terms 'quiquennial brain-dusting,' that is, he should go back to school, as it were, every five years.

"He advises, too, the threefold classification of cases into the clear cases, the doubtful, and the mistakes."[14]

There was more in March 1906.

JOHNS HOPKINS ALUMNI
HEAR OF OSLER'S WOES
His Name Now a Verb, He Travels
Incog., Dr. Remsen Says

FAMOUS SPEECH DISTORTED

Dr. Osler was the theme at the annual dinner of the Johns Hopkins Alumni in New York, held last night at the University Club.

It was declared that he had suffered from faulty reports of his famous address in which he had made himself the champion of young men's ambitions and was reported to have suggested the killing off of their elders.

"We suffered a great loss when Dr. Osler resigned and went to a place he should have never gone to. His name suggests the notoriety of a year ago. If those who quote Osler quoted him rightly they would have not quoted him as they did. It is a common error of the world to attribute to him nonsensical remarks he never said, I would explain, except that I might be a second to have my name changed into a verb. He has had to travel incognito since the misquotation of his remarks.

"He went to Atlantic City incognito after that speech, and he did the same when he went to England. He is a very sensitive man, and if you ever meet him again; don't ask him about his alleged theory."[15]

Osler returned again in December 1906.

DR. OSLER ARRIVES
He and Mrs. Osler Come from England,
En Route to Toronto

Dr. William Osler, who once said that all men more than 60 years old had outlived their usefulness, and who is now a lecturer at Oxford, arrived from England yesterday on the White Star liner Celtic. He was accompanied by Mrs. Osler. They are going to Toronto.

"I am glad to see you," he said as reporters approached him, but when they questioned him he backed away. "I have nothing to say," he said.[16]

On 10 December 1906, the paper had a different story on Onsler.

OSLER ON OUR COLLEGES
Says Few Rhodes Scholars from This
Country Will Get Degrees

Baltimore, Dec. 9.- Dr. William Osler of Johns Hopkins University and now Regius Professor of Oxford, in a talk to the Medical Journal Club last night spoke rather disparagingly of the work of American colleges. In referring to the Rhodes scholars from this country at Oxford he said many of them would not attain their degrees because they had not been properly taught.

He suggested that in this country teaching was followed by men for other reasons than to promote the welfare of those whom they taught, by saying that in England school teaching was taken up as a life profession, and was a calling that was looked upon as an honored one. In this country in many of the Western colleges Greek was looked upon as a study of barbarianism, and consequently when a young man who graduated from one of these institutions obtained a Rhodes scholarship and went to Oxford he was greatly surprised because he was so far down the scale in the classics.[17]

Four days later the *New York Times* carried an article from Toronto, Ontario, about Mrs Featherstone Osler celebrating her one hundredth birthday. Children and grandchildren, kindred and friends gathered to rejoice with her. Never in the history of Canada, the paper asserted, had any woman been the mother of four such distinguished men as Judge Osler of the Ontario Court of Appeals; EB Osler, MP; Dr William Osler of Oxford, and the late B B

Osler, one of the most distinguished lawyers who ever pleaded in a Canadian court.

In April 1909 the *New York Times* carried a brief editorial about Osler dealing with American Rhodes scholars and a sailing notice about Osler leaving Southampton for New York.

In May Osler was in Washington urging war on tuberculosis: "Osler Urges War on Tuberculosis. . . Declares the People Must Solve the Problem of Furnishing Money to Fight"[18]. This was a wake up call to the public about the devastating effects of the disease and the need to actively combat the scourge. Osler addressed the meeting of the National Association for the Study and Prevention of Tuberculosis, which took place in Washington. "Cannon, at 73, Defies Him. . . Speaker Shakes His Fist Under Doctor's Nose and Boasts His Age". Lest the public forget, the *New York Times* also included the opening remarks of Joseph G Cannon, Speaker of the House of Representatives, who aroused the audience to laughter when, turning to Dr Osler he said, "Dr Osler, I have reached the age of 73 and I shake my fist in your face"[18]. It went on to say that Dr Osler laughed heartily at this defiance of his old-age theory. One can almost hear Osler's laughter at this distance.

Osler felt the sting of the *New York Times* versions of his speech for the next decade as his wry humour was transformed into a call for euthanasia, and Osler's name became a verb-as in to "Oslerize" the elderly.

In November 1910, an editorial addressed Osler and vaccination as follows:

DR. OSLER ON VACATION

At last Dr. William Osler has broken his "curious silence" about vaccination. The anti-vaccionists had remarked upon it, had made the most of it. In the American Magazine for December the Regius Professor of Medicine in Oxford issues this defiance:

"I would like to issue a Mount Carmel-like challenge to any ten unvaccinated priests of Baal. I will go into the next severe epidemic with ten selected vaccinated persons and ten selected unvaccinated persons. I should prefer to choose the latter-three members of Parliament, three anti-vaccination doctors, if they could be found, and four anti-vaccination propagandists."

And he makes this promise:

"Neither to jeer nor to jibe when they catch the disease, but to look after them as brothers, and for the four or five who are certain to die I will try to arrange the funerals with all the pomp and ceremony of an anti-vaccination demonstration."

Rather a grisly joke. But there would be grislier reality everywhere if the anti-vaccinationists had their way.[19]

In June 1911, the coronation honour list carried the notification that William Osler was named as a baronet. William Osler became Sir William Osler. One week later Osler's reputation was discussed in the *New York Times'* Letters to the Editor section[20] (in between articles about the superiority of metric weights and measures and the matter of night garbage collections):

SIR WILLIAM OSLER
His Elevation to a Baronetcy and the
Perverted "Chloroform" Address

New York, June 25, 1911

"To the Editor of The New York Times:

Apropos of Dr. William Osler's elevation to a Baronetcy, I have noticed several references in newspapers to his supposed remarks in his now famous address in Baltimore some years ago. There have been many other references in the papers from time to time as well as from pulpit and stage and platform. This is one instance in which the press has done a grave injustice to one of the noblest and sweetest-natured men it has been my fortune to know or know about.

Dr. Osler, in his farewell address to the members of the faculties of the Johns Hopkins University and the Johns Hopkins Medical School, made some jests at the expense of his colleagues, and they were given a serious import which was never intended or deserved, and the point of his serious remarks was perverted until a great part of the public has actually come to believe that he thinks men pass the age of usefulness at 60, and that he advocates chloroforming them.

He was nearing 60 himself at the time of delivering the address and his own mother died a year or two later at the age of 100 years. I have personal knowledge that he has the tenderest regard for age, and it is doubtful if but few men living have done so much for the relief and prevention of the physical sufferings of people of all ages.

JAMES KENDALL BURGESS.

Osler's last visit to America

The year is 1913 and events in Europe are hurtling towards a war unlike any other in history; however, the mood in the United States does not yet reflect a world on the abyss. Osler returned to North America for what became his last visit to his home and to the medical centres involved in the Oslerian medical and cultural network that connected Canada and the USA with Oxford University.

His schedule was full and tight. Invited lectures, dedication proceedings, family visits, meetings and dinners with old friends filled the calendar. He had been engrossed with the preparation of the invited Silliman Lecture series to be delivered at Yale University while keeping a busy schedule at Oxford from January through to April. Other scheduled events included lectures or talks at the opening of the Phipps Clinic at Johns Hopkins University and a lecture at Harvard preceding the opening of the Brigham Hospital in Boston. The following two pieces appeared in early and mid-April.

Sir William Osler Coming Here
By Marconi Transatlantic Wireless Telegraph to
The New York Times

London. Sir William Osler is leaving on the Cunard Line steamship Campania to attend the opening of the new Johns Hopkins clinic for mental diseases. Accompanying him are Dr. F. W. Martin of London and Dr. J. Mackenzie, an Oxford alienist. Sir William said that he would lecture several times and visit the Rush Medical School in Chicago, remaining in America six weeks.[21]

OSLER HERE ON VISIT

Among the passengers arriving yesterday from Liverpool on the Cunard liner Campania was Sir William Osler, better known in the United States as Dr. Osler, the physician who was credited with the statement several years ago that the world had no room for a man after he was 60 years old. He was accompanied by Dr. W. McDougall, a teacher of mental philosophy at Oxford University, where Sir William is now Regius professor of medicine, and Dr. F.W. Mott, the London brain specialist. They have come to attend the opening of the Phipps Psychiatric Clinic at the Johns Hopkins Hospital, Baltimore.

Sir William appeared to be in the best of health, but declined to be interviewed, and to avoid publicity had his name kept off the passenger list.

The party will spend six weeks in America and visit Philadelphia, Chicago, Boston, and Washington after leaving Baltimore.[22]

After his arrival on Sunday, 13 April, Osler spent the next day in Philadelphia visiting Weir Mitchell and attending a dinner with old friends. The next four days were in Baltimore, where he stayed with friends and participated in the programmes surrounding the opening of the Phipps Clinic.

He left to go to New Haven on Saturday when he put the finishing touches to his address for the undergraduates at Yale. Osler gave this address on Sunday evening, the day before the first of the three Silliman Lectures at Yale University. Entitled "A way of life", this was a sermon based upon his own philosophy of life.

LIVE TODAY, SAYS OSLER
Forget Past and Future, Savant's
Advice to Yale Students

New Haven, April 20. Speaking before a gathering of Yale men to-night Sir William Osler, formerly of Johns Hopkins University at Baltimore, but now a member of the Faculty of Oxford University, said:

"My method in life is the freshest, oldest, simplest and usefulest. Forget the past, forget the future. Touch a button that will shut off the past and another that will shut off the future, and you will have a vaccine that will insure you against all morbid thoughts. When the load of tomorrow is added to the load of yesterday many men fall on the way.

"As things stand to-day many of you would rather sing over and over again psalms for the sins of the past than follow Christ into the slums. The day of man's salvation is to-day. Live earnestly. Make the limit of your life the twenty-four hours of a day.

"The first two hours of a day determines the day. If you have been romping with the younger Aphrodite the night before you will be as bleary-eyed as a fish when you get up, and the day will be lost. Quit tobacco and liquor. Bright eyes are the thing, and bright eyes never came from the free indulgence of wine, women, and song.

"The control of the mind as a working machine is the end of all education. This can be accomplished with deliberation."[23]

CLERGYMAN DEFENDS OSLER
Replies to Cardinal That Physician
Did Not Attack Catholics

Baltimore, April 20. Regarding to Cardinal Gibbons' criticisms of Sir William Osler's remarks at the opening of the Phipps Clinic here concerning the saints, the Rev. William Crawford Frost, in St. Mary's Protestant Episcopal church in Emmerton said in his sermon today:

"Cardinal Gibbons and Sir William Osler are two of the few first-class intellects, as well as two of the most efficient and useful men in the world today."

Rev. Crawford further went on to say, "Sir William stated one of the most important truths. As a race, we are just emerging from the state of comparative childhood when we trusted to miracles or acts of supernatural origin to cure our troubles, and we are just beginning to see that this is the wrong kind of trust in God or in the saints. The Christian Scientist represents the extreme form of this delusion. He expects God to do for him what he ought to do for himself.

"God apparently considers it better for our development that we should apply ourselves to the study of hygiene and sanitation to avoid disease and of medicine and surgery to relieve or cure it."[24]

In August 1913, Osler attended a congress held at the Albert Hall, London. Cushing described it in his biography of Osler:

The XVIIth international congress, likely to be the last of those unwieldy periodical gatherings of medical men from all over the world, was held in London from Wednesday, August 6th to Tuesday the 12th, under the presidency of Sir Thomas Barlow. Thirty-two years before, in 1881, another of these great congresses had been held in London, which Palmer Howard of McGill and his protégé William Osler had attended.[25]

The scale of the congress and the accompanying pageantry, dinners, receptions and entertainments would not be repeated in the wake of the two World Wars that marked the first half of the twentieth century.

MEDICAL CONGRESS
HONORS AMERICANS
Delegate from This Country
Heads Those Presented to
Prince Arthur of Connaught

SUFFRAGISTS TRY TO ENTER
Papers by Drs. Murphy and Harvey
Cushing Eagerly Awaited -
Sir William Osler Gives a Dinner

By Marconi Transatlantic Wireless
Telegraph to The New York Times

London, Aug. 6. Prince Arthur of Connaught on behalf of King George opened the great International Congress of Medicine in the Albert Hall to-day, when 7,400 doctors from all quarters of the world met to make and hear reports of past conquests and to gather new strength and new knowledge for their struggle with disease. Specialists in all the ills that beset humanity filled the great hall.

Sir William Osler gave a big dinner to delegates to the congress tonight at the Automobile Club, and many of his old friends at Johns Hopkins University were present.[26]

In June 1914, the French honoured Sir William Osler and elected him as the Foreign Associate of the Academy of Medicine.

World War I

The war brought extraordinary changes to every walk of life in England. The medical community was mobilized along with the rest of the nation and Osler's position as Regius Professor of Medicine at Oxford evolved into a series of military and civilian supervisory activities. With the onset of World War I, the tone of the *New York Times* articles changed as Osler assumed consultative positions of authority in England, becoming a wartime witness with US ties.

FEWER WOUNDS KILL THAN EVER BEFORE
Sir William Osler Believes War
Will Set Low Record for
Such Deaths

Typhoid Can Be Guarded Against,
But, Pneumonia Cannot, and Danger
of it Will Be Great

London, Oct 20. Sir William Osler, Regius Professor of Medicine at Oxford, and since the beginning of the war, in close supervisory touch with hospital work in England, said to *The New York Times* correspondent today:

"I think this war will set a new record for low mortality among the wounded. Formerly, with the best first aid and hospital work, a mortality record of five or six percent of those who reached the base hospitals was considered creditable. Up to date there has been but one fatality our of more than 700 wounded who have reached the base hospital at Oxford. This death was caused by tetanus.

"All fighting forces should take advantage of the knowledge that the human body can be protected from typhoid fever by vaccination. The success of this measure in the armies of the United States and France is proof enough."[27]

"ALLIES FIGHTING FOR US," SAYS OSLER

"I think that the enlightened public opinion of the United States appreciates what this position would be, and feels closer to England and closer to Canada than ever before since 1776."[28]

Oslers Thank Americans for Belgian Professors. . .
By Cable to the Editor of the New York Times

Oxford, Dec. 23. May we, through you, send thanks and Christmas greetings from twenty-one Belgian Professors and their families, comfortably settled largely through the great generosity of the Rockefeller Foundation and of our friends in New York, Philadelphia, Boston and Baltimore?

WILLIAM OSLER
GRACE REVERE OSLER

Sir William Osler, who signs the message above, is Regius Professor of Medicine at Oxford, and was formerly at Johns Hopkins University. Lady Osler is the daughter of the late John Revere of Boston.[29]

AMERICANS TO RUN BIG WAR HOSPITAL
Three Universities to Send 32 Surgeons
and 75 Nurses
At Britain's Request

EMINENT MEN TO BE CHOSEN
Party to be Selected by the Medical
Schools of Columbia, Harvard, and
Johns Hopkins

England has called on American surgeons to man her newest and largest field hospital. The medical schools of Columbia, Johns Hopkins, and Harvard Universities, as the three foremost centres of medical learning in this country, offered to supply the men and nurses, and a cablegram has been received from the Director General of the English Army Medical Corps accepting the offer.

Sir William Osler, formerly of Johns Hopkins University, but now Professor of Medicine in Oxford University, conceived the idea of having the new field hospital manned by American surgeons picked by men with whom he was professionally associated in this country. The idea met the approval of Lord Kitchener. Sir William cabled to the three universities that England thought very highly of the work done by volunteer American surgeons, but that he was anxious to add to the laurels won by medical men from the United States by having a unit in charge of men sponsored by the three American medical schools most highly thought of in Europe.[30]

CALLS PNEUMONIA
BEST "WAR KILLER"
But Dr. Osler Says Soldiers Develop
Greater Resistance Than
Civilians to Tuberculosis
Because Earlier in the War Medical

Examinations Were Lax and
Infected Recruits Enlisted.

Discussing tuberculosis in the British Army in France, The New York
Medical Journal quotes Sir William Osler, Regius Professor of Medicine at
Oxford and formerly of Johns Hopkins.[31]

Illness and death of Osler

Osler's last two years of life were shadowed by the death of his only son,
Revere, in France in 1917. His seventieth birthday, in July 1919, was celebrated
at the Royal Society of Medicine and featured a presentation by Sir Clifford
Allbutt, his brother Regius Professor of Medicine at Cambridge and long term
friend. During the autumn Osler developed a respiratory infection with pro-
gression to pneumonia with pulmonary complications including empyema
which caused his death at the year's end.

Sir William Osler Worse
Special to The New York Times

Baltimore, Md. Dec 10. A cablegram from England received today by Dr.
Thomas B. Futcher announced that the condition of Sir William Osler, who
has been ill for several weeks with pneumonia, has taken a decided turn for
the worse, and that physicians now regard his condition as serious. The
message was from Lady Osler, who has been in almost constant attendance
at her husband's bedside during his illness.

A short time ago the announcement was made that the famous
scientist had passed the crisis of malady. The message therefore indicates
that he has suffered a serious relapse.[32]

HEAR OF OSLER'S HEALTH
"Empyema Operation, Making Good Fight,"
He Cables.

Baltimore, Dec. 25. Following recent disconcerting reports regarding the
health of Sir William Osler, the Superintendent of the Johns Hopkins
Hospital received the following cablegram dated Oxford, England, from the
eminent physician today:

"Empyema operation. Making good fight. Christmas greetings all old
friends."

William Osler[33]

SIR WILLIAM OSLER
DEAD AT OXFORD
Noted Physician Stirred World
With Theory That Man's Greatest
Work is Done Under 40

"CHLOROFORM AT 60" A JEST
Regius Professor of Medicine at
Oxford Was Chief Physician at
Johns Hopkins for 15 Years

Oxford, England. Dec. 29. Sir William Osler, the noted physician, who had
been ill for several weeks past, died here this evening. Sir William was
stricken with pneumonia in November, and about the middle of that month
was reported convalescent. A fortnight ago, however, reports reached
America that he had taken a turn for the worse. Cabled advices shortly

afterward announced that his condition was somewhat improved, while on Christmas Day a message was sent to the Johns Hopkins Hospital in Baltimore in which the famous physician extended Christmas greetings to all his old friends and announced that he was "making a good fight" after an empyema operation.

Sir William Osler, though his fame rests on his work as a diagnostician, investigator, and teacher, is familiarly known because of the association of his name with the theory that the greatest work of man is done before he is 40 and that it would benefit society in general if chloroform was administered to all on their reaching the age of 60 years.

He reached the age of 70 himself, and his last ten years formed a period of great activity and of his greatest influence. During the last five years he devoted himself with great vigor to the great problems thrust upon his profession by the war—the treatment of shell shock and other nervous diseases, trench diseases and the development of better methods of treating wounds.

He was himself one of the outstanding examples of a man doing great work and benefiting the world to the end of a long life. As a matter of fact, he was 53 years old when he delivered his famous address at the Washington's Birthday exercises of the Johns Hopkins University at Baltimore, which was reduced to the crude formula that a man was "through" at 40 and ought to be chloroformed at 60. He was addressing an audience in which many of the most eminent men had crossed the "deadline" of 60 and his great friends in the medical profession were hovering around that mark.

Dr. Osler was shocked at the great hue and cry caused by the part of his speech, which was intended to produce merriment. It was necessary for him to deny the constrictions placed on his address and to explain himself again and again. The verb "to Oslerize" came into being and he was widely regarded as an advocate of the most cold-blooded and inhuman theories, in spite of his efforts to prevent his jests being taken literally. This episode caused him great chagrin for some years, not because of the bloodthirsty character which he had become in popular estimation, but of account of his belief that the widespread discussion of the subject had had a depressing and discouraging effect on men who had passed 40 and 60.

Dr. Osler was Physician in Chief at Johns Hopkins Hospital from 1889 until he accepted the appointment of Regius Professor of Medicine at Oxford in 1905, his address on usefulness at different ages being in the nature of a farewell address. At Johns Hopkins his powers of diagnosis were considered little less than miraculous. He was credited with the power of looking over a room full of patients whom he had never seen before, men and women afflicted with various ailments which had previously defied diagnosis, and telling at a glance what was the trouble with each one and how it should be treated.

Dr. Osler was born at Tecumseh, Ontario, July 9, 1849. After being graduated from McGill University in 1872, he studied in London, Berlin, and Vienna. He taught medicine at McGill from 1874 to 1884 and was Professor of Clinical Medicine at the University of Pennsylvania from 1884 to 1889, after which he went to Johns Hopkins. He was the author of a large number of books on medicine. He was created a Baronet in 1911.[34]

BALTIMORE PAYS TRIBUTE
Johns Hopkins Associates Say Prof.
Osler's Death Will Leave a Great Void.
Special to The New York Times

Baltimore, Dec. 29. The announcement of the death of Sir William Osler, Regius Professor of Medicine at Oxford University and for fifteen years, from 1889 to 1904, Professor of Medicine at Johns Hopkins University, was a great shock to Drs. William S. Halsted, Henry M. Hurd, Thomas B. Futcher, William S. Thayer, William H. Welch, and others on the medical staff who were his associates.

Cardinal Gibbons said tonight when told of Dr. Osler's death:

We were warm friends for many years and the news of his passing is a great shock to me.[34]

Taking a new view of Sir William Osler

In May 1920, a review in the *New York Times* book review section[35] signalled a sea change in the reporting about Osler. Brander Matthews reviewed two books with origins in the last year of Osler's life.

The Old Humanities and the New Science was Osler's 1919 presidential address to the Classical Association of Great Britain, delivered before a scholarly audience at Oxford, a crowning achievement in his career as scientist and humanist. Osler, dissecting his thoughts about the balance between the humanities and science, addressed a major source of concern and controversy for centuries at Oxford at a time when traditional certainties, already disrupted by nineteenth century scientific developments were further shaken by the devastation accompanying World War I.

Contributions to Medical and Biological Research was a two volume collection of articles dedicated to Sir William Osler on his seventieth birthday. Written by his former pupils and co-workers in Canada, the USA and Great Britain, the collection contains a wide spectrum of contributions to medical and biological science. It fell to Sir Clifford Allbutt, Regius Professor of Medicine at Cambridge University, another man of science and letters, to provide the dedication.

Sir William emerges posthumously as the learned physician, a man of science and a man of letters.

Harvey Cushing's biography, *The Life of Sir William Osler,* was reviewed by Van Buren Thorne in the *New York Times* in May 1925. A picture of the mature Osler was central to the article. The tone of the review sets a new standard for viewing the man and his life. Thorne extracted the essence of Osler's career from Cushing's "month-to-month record of a great life", a 1413 page, two-volume epic that subsequently brought a Pulitzer Prize to Cushing, simultaneously elevating Osler to legendary status.

Cushing presents the scope and the sweep of Osler's career in a fast forward mode; Thorne, commenting on this whirlwind existence in Osler's life, concludes, "All of which impelled this reviewer to write that the reader of this biography lives a breathless seventy years with Osler for his energy never flagged and the spirit of youth remained with him to the end."[36]

Sixty years later Sir John Walton MD FRCP, Professor of Neurology, Newcastle University School of Medicine, then President of the British Medical Association, while addressing the topic "The medical book I would most like to have written", considered the medical books that influenced his life. He recalled with that intensity of pleasure, almost akin to revelation, his first exposure to the writings of Sir William Osler in *Aequanimitas* and *An Alabama Student,* "from which I derived an inspiration and a love of clinical science and medical history which have had a pervasive influence on my career". He then spoke of the superb *Life of Osler* by Harvey Cushing: "we have a pen picture of the master, perhaps a trifle dated in its prose, perhaps a little protective of its subject's peccadilloes, but nevertheless one of the greatest biographies ever published."[37]

The John Singer Sargent portrait of Sir William Osler graces the review of a short life of Osler by Edith Gittings Reid, *The Great Physician*. The reviewer, RL Duffus begins, "If ever a story was worth telling twice, the life of William Osler deserves that distinction," and at the end questions, "How in the perspective of twelve years, can Dr. Osler be measured?" In between we learn that Mrs Reid knew the Oslers well, and brings a distinctly feminine point of view to her tasks. The positive review ends with partial answers to the question, with thoughts of Osler not as one of the remote and austere heroes of mankind, but as a friend of the suffering, "the patient felt only that a strong hand stretched out to help him, and curiously, he felt the room empty of all except his physician and himself and power."[38]

Osler and the *New York Times*—perspective

And so it is that William Osler moves across the pages of the *New York Times*, in pursuit, as he described it, of his "vagrant career", from Toronto, Montreal, Philadelphia, Baltimore, to Oxford. Along the way the paper documents certain of his activities, from the emergence of the young Canadian physician and professor to his position in the USA as clinician and medical educator, moving on to his status as a scholarly leader in British medicine.

Much, too much, was made of his farewell talk at Johns Hopkins University, the US press refusing to drop the eye-catching press captions—"Chloroform at sixty," Osler's name as a verb to Oslerize. Osler's statements were, at the least, ill considered, and as many a politician has learned, self-destruction by ill advised comments about the aged is a repetitive theme in the USA.

However, at some point in the journey through the pages of the *New York Times*, William Osler, physician, scholar, and educator, became Sir William Osler, a man for the ages. Although his contemporaries canonized him during life, it is not until his posthumous resurrection in the book review section of the *New York Times*, from 1925 to 1931, that we hear the press speak triumphantly of Osler's eminence, Osler as the learned physician, the man of letters, the prince of physicians, and medicine's great modern exemplar.

How do we create our legends? And how do reputations grow or persevere, enriched in the retelling? For much of history the development of legends depended upon a band of disciples retelling the stories of the master, with a group of scribes to write them down. Within the creation of the Oslerian legend, we have seen how the modern press can create or invent a version of a life at odds with the recollections of the disciples and the scribes.

By the 1930s there were several published versions of the Oslerian journey—Harvey Cushing's remarkable biography encompassing the scope and sweep of Osler's career, the events the press deemed newsworthy during his life, and turn around expressed in the posthumous contributions and reflections in the *New York Times*.

Osler's reputation evolved over time, germinating in the nineteenth century, and reaching legendary status during the twentieth century. With the new Osler biography by Michael Bliss[39] of Toronto, renewed interest in the Oslerian tradition and the Oslerian heritage seems assured well into the twenty-first century. Perhaps the *New York Times* will speak again of Sir William, his life and his work.

References

1. Tuchman BW. *The Proud Tower.* New York; Macmillan,1966:xiii
2. *New York Times.* 2 September 1897; 4–3
3. Osler W. British medicine in Greater Britain. In *Aequanimitas With Other Addresses* (3rd edn). Philadelphia: Blakiston,1932:163–88
4. *New York Times,* 17 August 1904:6–6
5. *New York Times,* 24 February 1905:6–7
6. Osler W. The fixed period. In *Aequanimitas With Other Addresses* (3rd edn). Philadelphia: Blakiston, 1932:373–93
7. *New York Times,* 25 February 1905:5–1
8. Ibid.
9. *New York Times,* 27 February 1905:1–6
10. *New York Times,* 1 March 1905:8–5
11. *New York Times,* 14 March 1905:9–1
12. *New York Times,* 3 May 1905:1–1
13. *New York Times,* 25 December 1905:1–2
14. *New York Times,* 8 January 1906:6–3
15. *New York Times,* 3 March 1906:5–1
16. *New York Times,* 8 December 1906:7–5
17. *New York Times,* 10 December 1906:11
18. *New York Times,* 15 May 1909:5–1
19. *New York Times,* 24 November 1910:10–2
20. *New York Times,* 27 June 1911:8–5
21. *New York Times,* 15 April 1913:3–1
22. *New York Times,* 14 April 1913:11–2
23. *New York Times,* 21 April 1913:2–2
24. *New York Times,* 21 April 1913:5–3
25. Cushing H. *The Life of Sir William Osler, Vol.II.* Oxford: Oxford University Press, 1925:368–9
26. *New York Times,* 7 August 1913:4–2
27. *New York Times,* 21 October 1914:2–6
28. *New York Times,* 8 November 1914:6–5
29. *New York Times,* 24 December 1914:1–2
30. *New York Times,* 21 May 1915:1–4
31. *New York Times,* 8 October 1916:12–7
32. *New York Times,* 11 December 1919:13–2
33. *New York Times,* 26 December 1919:2–7
34. *New York Times,* 30 December 1919:13–1
35. *New York Times,* 23 May 1920:263–2
36. *New York Times,* 31 May 1925:6–1
37. Walton J. The medical book I would most like to have written: *"Life of Osler."* *BMJ* 1982;**285:**59
38. *New York Times,* 23 August 1931:1
39. Bliss M. William Osler: A Life in Medicine. Oxford. 1999. Oxford University Press

William Osler's Bibliomania

 W. Bruce Fye, M.D., M.A.

A century ago, William Osler (1849–1919) was the English-speaking world's most prominent physician and medical educator.[1] He was also a bibliomaniac.[2] Osler's family and friends knew of his irrepressible passion for books; he made no attempt to hide his addiction. Indeed, his legacy is due in large part to his collecting habit. Osler's bibliomania led him to create one of the finest libraries of medical books ever assembled and to write more than one-hundred historical and biographical papers.[3] His influence on medical book collectors, institutional libraries, and on the emerging field of medical history was substantial, and it persists to this day. For Osler, book collecting, historical research, and writing were complementary pursuits. He collected works written by authors in whom he had a special interest and sought books that were viewed as important historically—those that illustrated the history of medicine. Osler's library, in turn, stimulated him to study and write about the lives and contributions of influential figures in the history of medicine and science.[4]

It is of some interest to trace the origins of Osler's bibliomania. He grew up in a family that enjoyed reading and in a home filled with books. His father, a country parson, owned about 1500 volumes, mainly on theology. When Osler was seventeen, his oldest brother, Featherston, encouraged his interest in rare books by giving him for Christmas a copy of J. Hain Friswell's *Varia: Readings from Rare Books*.[5] Shortly thereafter, young Osler bought his first books: the popular Globe edition of Shakespeare's works and the 1862 Ticknor and Fields edition of Thomas Browne's "Religio Medici." The Shakespeare book was later stolen, but half a century later Osler characterized this Browne volume as the most precious book in his library.[6]

Osler was first exposed to scientific books when, at sixteen, he entered Trinity College School in Weston, Ontario. The school's founder and warden, Reverend William A. "Father" Johnson, owned a library that included books by Charles Lyell, Charles Dana, William Carpenter, and several other 19th century scientific authors. Osler enjoyed exploring Father Johnson's books and later remarked that "browsing in a large and varied library is the best introduction to

Presented at the American Osler Society, May 6, 1999, Montreal.

a general education."[7] When he moved in with Dr. James Bovell of Toronto in 1869, Osler discovered a vast new world of books—medical books with extraordinary engravings and spellbinding real life stories of diseases, doctors, and death. He spent his evenings roaming and reading in Bovell's extensive library of medical and scientific classics. This adolescent experience fueled Osler's passion for books—his bibliomania. He wrote in 1914, "I date my mental downfall from that winter, upon which, however, I look back with unmixed delight."[8]

As a student at McGill Medical College between 1870 and 1872, Osler came under the influence of Dr. Palmer Howard, who also owned a large medical library. He spent the next two years studying abroad, where he was exposed to several large institutional libraries and to many antiquarian booksellers. Osler's very limited budget allowed him to purchase very few books in Europe, mainly textbooks necessary for his studies. Soon, however, Osler came to view books as a necessity, and they would compete successfully for his time and his income. Reflecting on his rich and varied life in 1901, he told an audience at the opening of the new building of the Boston Medical Library, "Books have been my delight these thirty years, and from them I have received incalculable benefits."[9]

When Osler moved to Philadelphia in 1884, his bookish and historical interests were stimulated by new friends and colleagues such as S. Weir Mitchell and Howard A. Kelly and by the resources and ambiance of the College of Physicians of Philadelphia and its library. Considering Philadelphia's important role in the early history of medicine in the United States, it is not surprising that Osler began to collect medical Americana while living there. He acquired some "special treasures," as he called them, including John Morgan's very rare book *A Discourse upon the Institution of Medical Schools in America*, published in 1765.[10]

Osler evolved gradually from an ambitious young pathologist and aspiring doctor who wanted to have a useful working library into the world's best known physician who assembled a spectacular book collection illustrating the history of medicine. The published catalogue of his library, Bibliotheca Osleriana, reveals much about Osler's passion for books. In his introduction he explained, "A library represents the mind of its collector, his fancies and foibles, his strength and weakness, his prejudices and preferences."[11] As his career unfolded, Osler gravitated toward men and institutions that shared his passion for books and history.

If Osler's interest in medical history and biography took root in Philadelphia, it blossomed in Baltimore. A few months after the Johns Hopkins Hospital opened in 1889, Osler, Howard Kelly and William Welch launched the Johns Hopkins Historical Club. With John Shaw Billings of the Surgeon General's Library, a frequent visitor to Johns Hopkins, they shared a common interest in the history of medicine and rare medical books.[12] Osler began to collect more aggressively as his income grew dramatically as a result of his successful consultative practice and the royalties from his medical textbook, first published in 1892. Indeed, in 1904 his income was $47,280 (including his $5,000 salary from Johns Hopkins, $5,200 in royalties from his popular textbook, $2,000 from investments, and $35,000 from private practice).[13]

This huge income fueled Osler's bibliomania. He explained later that he began to buy, "first, the early books and pamphlets relating to the profession in America; secondly, the original editions of the great writers in science and in medicine; and thirdly, the works of such general authors as Sir Thos. Browne, Milton, Shelley, Keats, and others."[14] But Osler did not buy old books just to have them. He used his growing library in his research and writing, both clinical and historical. Osler also used his books when teaching. He hoped to stimulate others to read the older literature, to appreciate the classics of medicine, and to collect books and offprints.

Osler purchased most of his books from three traditional sources: bookshops, catalogs, and auctions. But a powerful force that animates bibliomaniacs—the fun of the hunt—also led him to rummage through bookstalls and seek out little known dealers.[15] During his Baltimore years Osler spent most summers abroad, and his letters reveal his passion for bookhunting. When he visited Holland in 1901, Osler tried to be a tourist—until bibliomania overpowered him. His wife Grace informed Harvey Cushing, "Dr. Osler has been really sightseeing on this trip and is very amusing. He looks at one picture in the collection and then flies to a book shop."[16] In another letter she told Cushing, "We really had a delightful trip, though Drs. Dock and Osler became utterly disgusted at every place where old books were not forthcoming and promptly wanted to leave."[17] Bibliomaniacs, like other passionate collectors, recognize this behavior. They often find traditional cultural attractions uninteresting because they represent a distraction and consume valuable bookhunting time. While abroad Osler's itinerary was often defined by visits to bookshops. Other activities, beyond formal appearances at medical meetings and other professional duties, were secondary.

George Dock described Osler's visit to an Amsterdam shop that had a large selection of old medical books:

> W. O. would begin early in the morning and continue all day. In a large and light room they had put out the Index Catalog [of the Library of the Surgeon General's Office] on a table, and on other tables, books that people had gathered for him between visits. . . . There was a pitcher of drinking water. He would take off his coat, roll up his sleeves, and work systematically, putting the books he wanted on a pile, to be shipped later. In smaller shops he worked less intensely, but probably not missing much of value.[18]

Osler spent the summer of 1903 in Europe. Writing to Cushing from Paris, he boasted, "I have bagged two 1543 Fabricas! 'Tis not a work which should be left on the shelves of a bookseller."[19] A week later, he wrote again, "Besides the two copies of the '43 edition of the De Humani corporis fabrica I have just ordered a third. We cannot have too many copies in America & no Medical Library is complete without one."[20] But Osler's hunting trips were not always so successful. Like all bibliomaniacs he got frustrated whenever reality fell short of expectation. On one such occasion he complained to Cushing,

> I had a fall in blood pressure of 125 mm. yesterday afternoon. In an antiquariat's here I was pulling over some old books . . . and on a chair near at hand were two fine quartos, very finely bound, one the History of the Strawberry Hill & the other, Walpole's Noble Authors, the two £1.15.0! I jumped on them . . . but alas the Delilah in charge knocked me over by saying that she had just sold them—not an hour before, to Sir Tristram??— Shandy I suppose-damn him!! I was disgusted.[21]

Cushing understood. He, too, was a bibliomaniac.[22]

Speaking of Osler's final years at Hopkins, Cushing explained, "[his] infection with the bibliomania was becoming chronic."[23] Excerpts from an unpublished manuscript "Burrowings of a Bookworm" that Osler wrote in 1902 (under his pseudonym Egerton Yorrick Davis, Jr.,) support Cushing's conclusion. Referring to bibliomania—and writing from personal experience—Osler's alter ego confessed,

> In the final stage of the malady, sung of so sweetly by John Ferriar, and described so minutely by Dibdin, the bibliomaniac haunts the auction rooms and notes with envious eyes the precious volumes as they are handed about for inspection, or chortles with joy as he hears the bids rise higher and higher for some precious treasure already in his possession. Of this final enthraldom the chief symptom, not mentioned indeed by Dibdin, is the daily perusal of the catalogues of auction sales. . . . Like the secret drinker with a full bottle by his side and the kettle on the trivet the victim in this last stage indulges his passion alone and is never so happy as with a Sotheby catalogue . . . . Into this final stage, I confess to have lapsed, gradually and insensibly, and without the loss of my self-respect.[24]

At about this time, Osler spoke at the Boston Medical Library, a focal point of medical history activities and collecting in the city. He described three classes of physicians: teachers, practitioners, and

> . . . a third class of men in the profession to whom books are dearer than to teachers or practitioners—a small, a silent band, but in reality the leaven of the whole lump. The profane call them bibliomaniacs, and in truth they are at times irresponsible. . . . Loving books partly for their contents, partly for the sake of the authors, they not alone keep alive the sentiment of historical continuity in the profession, but they are the men who make possible such gatherings as the one we are enjoying this evening. We need more men of their class, particularly in this country. . . .[they] keep alive in us an interest in the great men of the past and not alone in their works, which they cherish, but in their lives, which they emulate.[25]

Exhausted by the demands of his practice and concerned about his health, Osler left Johns Hopkins in 1905 to become Regius Professor of Medicine at Oxford, a position of great prestige but with few responsibilities.[26] He knew that serious medical book collectors found most of their treasures in European bookshops and auction houses.[27] After moving to Oxford Osler was in a position to visit British and continental booksellers more frequently and to participate in book auctions more actively. During his Oxford years, Osler spent many Mondays in London attending Sotheby's book auctions.

Osler worked hard to build his collection. Speaking of his early Oxford period, Cushing recalled that wherever the Regius professor went, "whether by train, tram, or car, he usually carried with him a bundle of . . . book catalogues or auction lists, and the number of these things that he could go through in a short time with the unerring scent of the true collector was amazing. He had a rare nose for books, and could track to its lair anything that lurked in them."[28] Increasingly, however, it seemed there were never enough books to satisfy Osler's cravings. An addict, he was struggling to feed his habit. When William Keen and Osler were both in Italy in 1907, the Philadelphia surgeon beat the Oxford professor to most of the bookshops. Keen purchased more than two dozen incunabula and other rarities for the library of the College of Physicians of Philadelphia. Although Osler was a longtime benefactor of that institution, he was annoyed that Keen won the race for books. He sent a postcard to Keen that began with just two words, "You Pig," written boldly on the first line.[29] But Osler had a double standard. He would buy several copies each of the first edition of Vesalius, the editio princeps of Celsus, and other medical classics, thereby depriving some other bibliophile of the thrill of possessing those treasures.

Osler's detailed knowledge of the history of medicine and of medical authors worked to his advantage when he bought books from general booksellers. Emile Holman, an American student at Oxford during the First World

War, recalled Osler telling a group of students how, while searching the "dusty shelves of a little bookshop in Rome," he had discovered a small octavo incunable, priced at just one lira. Holman continued, "Unbelieving, shaking with excitement, he quickly paid the lira, and hurried out lest the proprietor recognize the book for what it was and revoke the sale."[30] But Osler also bought big and expensive books in Italy. Describing a 1909 visit to Rome when Osler bought two more copies of the first edition of Vesalius, Cushing exclaimed, ". . . he evidently had an orgy in the book shops."[31]

Osler's bibliomania sometimes resulted in behaviors that do not quite fit Max Brödel's image of him as "The Saint." That well-known drawing depicts Osler as an angel hovering above the Johns Hopkins Hospital. Osler acquired his copy of the first edition of Copernicus's *De revolutionibus orbium coelestium* (1543) from Heffer in Cambridge for 18 pounds sterling. He explained, "It was formerly in Marichal College, and there is no duplicate mark; but I have resisted the prickings of conscience which suggest asking how it got out of the library!"[32] Now, contrast Osler's admission that he did not confirm how this copy of Copernicus's extremely rare book reached the market with his feelings about the potential loss or theft of one of his own special books. He wrote on the fly-leaf of his interleaved copy of the first edition of his *Principles and Practice of Medicine:* "Private copy. May all the curses of the good Bishop Ernulphus light on the borrower-and-not-returner or upon the stealer of this book."[33]

Despite his substantial income at the peak of his career (nearly $^3/_4$ million dollars per year in current dollars) Osler often expressed concern that he could not afford his book habit! In 1911 Osler at once bragged and whined to Cushing, "I have had some luck lately—several beauties! but next year I must go slow. I have spent too much this year on books."[34] Compulsive collectors like Osler—all addicts for that matter—suffer from a certain lack of self-discipline. Osler even went so far as to tell his colleagues that he was "sanctifying" his consultation fees by purchasing rare books—some for libraries but most for his own collection.[35] What a marvelous example of what might be called double rationalization—high fees and bibliomania, each seemed to justify the other.

By 1908, Osler's books—thousands of them—were displayed in the new oak-paneled library that was the centerpiece of his large home on Norham Gardens Road in Oxford. It was important to Osler that his books were readily accessible, so he could use them or show selected volumes to his bookish friends or to first-time visitors who expressed the slightest interest in medical history or his collection. Before long, Osler's books spilled out of his library into other rooms in the house. Yale historian and bibliophile Edward Streeter recalled, "The library, grown too great for the lower floors, had mounted the groaning stairs and bid fair to have the run of the rooms above. Books everywhere, invading all the premises."[36]

Osler's friends and family knew he was a bibliomaniac, obsessed with building his collection. So did the world's leading booksellers. In 1911, he confessed publicly at a meeting of members of the International Association of Antiquarian Booksellers,

> . . . you see here before you a mental, moral, almost, I may say, a physical wreck—and all of your own making. Until I became mixed up with you I was really a respectable, God-fearing, industrious, earnest, ardent, enthusiastic, energetic student. Now what am I? A mental wreck, devoted to nothing but your literature. Instead of attending to my duties and attending to my work, in comes every day by the post, and by every post, all this seductive literature with which you have, as you know perfectly well,

gradually undermined the mental virility of many and many a better man than I.[37]

Even physical illness could not cool Osler's passion for books. Confined to bed with influenza in 1916, he thanked his friend and former student Charles Camac for giving him a very rare work by Thomas Browne, the seventeenth century physician and philosopher. Having collected Browne's works for half a century, Osler exclaimed, "There was an acute paroxysm of bibliomania a few minutes ago when your parcel came. I jumped on it at once. What a beautiful present. . . . it is a great addition to the Browne collection which now lacks but one important item."[38]

By this time Osler's library was both very large and very valuable. He was now in his sixties and, like every bibliomaniac, he had to decide what would become of his collection—the fruit of decades of passionate but focused collecting. By 1912 he had decided to bequeath his library to McGill University, his medical alma mater.[39] And Osler would give McGill much more than several thousand rare and important books and offprints in the history of medicine and science. He would give them a detailed road map of his collection: an annotated catalogue in which the books would be arranged in a unique and most compelling way. A year before his death in 1919, Osler told Leonard Mackall, "My library continues to grow and I am trying to get a proper Catalogue . . . . my scheme will be on interesting lines. I have divided the library into seven groups—Prima, Secunda, Historica, Biographica, Bibliographica, Incunabula, and Manuscripts."[40]

Osler's library and its catalogue contains seven sections. Prima, the centerpiece of his collection, includes 1,702 entries, most representing very important and rare books. Arranged in chronological order, the entries provide a bio-bibliographical account of the evolution of medicine and science up to the discovery of x-rays. Osler chose to include in Prima separate sections devoted to works by and about sixty-seven individuals from Hippocrates to Roentgen. Several other authors' works were included under subsections of Prima.

Osler was especially interested in two major developments: Harvey's discovery of the circulation and the invention of inhalation anesthesia. Anesthesia was the only entry that represented a subject rather than an individual, and Osler was especially proud of this special collection. His persistent effort to build a comprehensive anesthesia collection reveals his recognition of the importance of acquiring periodical contributions in addition to printed books. After decades of collecting Osler wrote to Boston surgeon J. Collins Warren in 1916, "My Anaesthesia collection grows . . . . [but] I lack—and want badly—the Bost. Med. & Surg. Journal for 1846."[41] He appealed to Warren to see if the Massachusetts General Hospital library had a duplicate copy of this volume that contained the original description of the first use of ether anesthesia. When he finally got a copy of this journal during his last month of life, Osler had it inscribed: "All things come to him who waits—but it was a pretty close shave this time!"[42]

Prima also reveals that Osler was not always successful in getting specific books to complete his special author or subject collections. For example, the Osler library copy of the rare 1653 first English translation of Harvey's book on the discovery of the circulation appears in the addenda section of the catalogue because John F. Fulton donated it to the collection after Osler's death.[43] Osler was proud, however, that he possessed what he considered to be the "rarest" Harvey item, the first edition of *Exercitatio anatomica de circulatione sanguinis*, published in Cambridge in 1649. This classic volume includes the first description of the coronary circulation and the results of new experiments Harvey performed to support his theory of the circulation.[44]

Secunda, consisting of 2,596 entries, includes the works of individuals who had made notable contributions to medicine and the life sciences or whose works especially interested Osler. Although the authors and their publications were less significant that those included in Prima, some very important individuals appear in this section such as Leopold Auenbrugger, Giorgio Baglivi, Charles Bell, Hieronymus Fracastorius, Jean Baptiste van Helmont, Giovanni Maria Lancisi, and Thomas Willis. Osler's own publications, including seven bound volumes of his offprints, appear in Secunda. Litteraria, consisting of 1,311 entries, greatly interested Osler. In 1918 he told George Dock, "The literary section will be the most interesting—poets, novels, plays, works, by Doctors, or in which the profession is portrayed."[45] This genre had long intrigued Osler.[46]

Historia, consisting of 956 entries, represents Osler's reference collection of secondary sources. These books and offprints on medical history were an indispensable part of his working library. He used them to learn more about the history of medicine and the individuals and institutions that were a part of that history. Biographia, consisting of 297 entries, was another area of special interest to Osler. His Baltimore associate William Sidney Thayer recalled, "Throughout all his life Osler was a student of the lives of those who had gone before. Biography was to him of compelling interest. . . .he stimulated in his students a reverence for the great names of medicine."[47] Osler published dozens of biographical studies, several of which were reprinted in his popular 1908 book *An Alabama Student and Other Biographical Essays*.[48] He explained in its preface that he not only enjoyed reading biographies, but he held a strong conviction that they were useful as an educational tool.

Bibliographica, consisting of 538 entries, includes items that helped Osler place his books and their authors in context. They also helped him identify rare and obscure publications that he might have otherwise overlooked. By the turn of the century bibliography had become increasingly sophisticated. Osler explained in 1902, ". . . medical bibliography is worthy of a closer study than it has received heretofore in this country. The subject presents three aspects, the book itself, the book as a literary record, i.e., its contents, and the book in relation to the author."[49]

Incunabula, consisting of 105 entries, includes the so-called cradle books of medicine, items printed before 1501. Thirty additional incunabula are catalogued in the prima section of Bibliotheca Osleriana. This remarkably large number of 15th century publications reflects Osler's special interest in early printed books and, more importantly, that many incunabula were still on the market a century ago. Today, almost all medical incunabula are in institutional libraries. Osler's collection was an important stimulus for his pioneering bibliographical study of 214 medical books printed between 1467 and 1480.[50]

Manuscripts, consisting of 163 entries, included unique items spanning several centuries. Somewhat surprisingly, Osler did not actively collect autographs or letters. He did, however, add a few selected letters to his collection if they were by individuals in whom he had a special interest. Osler's description of his acquisition of a remarkable collection of letters to and from British physician and botanist William Withering reveals the workings of this bibliomaniac's mind. He informed his former pupil and longtime friend Joseph Pratt in 1918:

> My library grows, and I am working at a catalogue. Did you know that I made a great haul of Withering's letters &c? A man came in one day with a bag & said—are you interested in W? I said 'rather' & he pulled out a big bundle of letters & papers & his Edin. diploma. I offered him £20, at which he nearly expired, as he had hoped for not more than £5. I should have gone to double at auction. I have them all in chron. order & beautifully bound.[51]

Osler's books remained at Norham Gardens almost nine years after his death while the catalogue was being completed.[52] Shortly after Lady Osler died in 1928 almost 8,000 books were shipped from Oxford to Montreal where they were installed in a special room in the McGill library.[53] Osler instructed his alma mater that his library was "for the use of students of the history of science and of medicine, without any other qualifications."[54] His legacy of old and rare medical books and reference works would be an accessible working library, not a stagnant museum collection.

Osler loved libraries and greatly enjoyed the company of knowledgeable librarians, whom he viewed as kindred spirits. Baltimore physician and historian John Ruhräh stated it well when he wrote in 1920, the year after Osler died, "Wherever he happened to be his interest in the medical library was paramount."[55] Osler's special affection for libraries was related in part to his love of books, but it also reflected his beliefs that libraries hatched scholars and that physicians knowledgeable about the history of their profession were better practitioners. Osler believed that physicians had a duty to familiarize themselves with the rich history of their profession. He thought that the best way to learn about the history of medicine was to read books and articles written by and about the leading physicians and medical scientists of earlier generations. Libraries and private book collections were the focal point of this important intellectual endeavor.

Osler gave thousands of books, journals, and offprints to libraries as he moved from one location to another or as he ran out of space. He was equally generous when it came to individuals. His practice of giving books to friends and acquaintances as a token of his affection or as an incentive to study and collect the history of medicine grew dramatically through the years. In 1916 he informed Charles Sayle of the University of Cambridge library, "I send books at Xmas to about 100 of my old students, and this year I have selected your 'Ages' & the just-issued edition (trans.) of Galen's 'Natural Faculties'."[56] Boston physician and historian Henry Viets recalled Osler's "annual shed" of duplicates during his final years: "I have seen delighted students carry away a small library in their arms and many a nucleus for a private medical library has been started in this way."[57]

Of all the books and collections Osler gave to libraries over the years, the gift that surely had the greatest emotional impact was his bequest to the Johns Hopkins University of his only child's small but significant collection of English literature of the Tudor and Stuart periods. Osler had characterized his son Revere, just twenty years old when he was killed in France during World War I, as a "chip off the old block in his devotion to books."[58] He supplemented Revere's collection with his own "general literature" books, including works by Milton and Shelley. These books formed the nucleus of a library that would be the focal point of the new "Tudor and Stuart" literary club at Hopkins.[59]

Osler had a profound impact on the emerging field of medical history a century ago.[60] Bibliomania fueled his interest in the history of medicine, which, in turn, led him to acquire more books. For Osler, book collecting and historical research and writing were inseparable interests and activities. Although several American physicians such as John Shaw Billings, Samuel D. Gross, and Joseph M. Toner had researched and written about the history of medicine before Osler got interested in the subject, he, more than any other person, catalyzed widespread interest in medical history as a pleasant pastime and as a subject of scholarly endeavor.[61] Osler encouraged his colleagues to contribute biographical sketches and articles on historical subjects that interested them.

Moreover, he set an example by publishing more than one hundred biographical and historical papers.

Speaking of Osler's impact on the history of medicine, Owsei Temkin declared fifty years ago, "To Osler, more perhaps than to anybody else in this country, does medical history owe inspiration and academic representation at a time when it lacked departments or full-time appointments. Through papers, books, and personal contacts, Osler impressed the historical spirit upon American medical research and literature."[62] In a more recent study of Osler's historiography Philip Teigen concludes that ". . . whether one views Osler's historical writing favourably—and many do not—it was a major event in 19th-century medicine."[63] By any measure, Osler's influence on medical history in the English-speaking world has been profound.

Notes

1. Osler infected several prominent American medical book collectors such as Harvey Cushing, John Fulton, and Lawrence Reynolds with bibliomania.[64] Many more recent medical bibliomaniacs, including this writer, can trace their addiction to Osler, at least indirectly. And while serious present-day medical collectors may be grateful for Osler's inspiration and his example, they are no doubt grateful that he is not here to compete with them for the few old and rare medical books that come on the market.[65] Cushing, *The Life of Sir William Osler* (London: Oxford University Press, 1925). A valuable new study based on extensive archival research is Michael Bliss, *William Osler: A Life in Medicine* (Toronto: University of Toronto Press, 1999).

2. See Leonard L. Mackall, "Sir William Osler as a bibliophile," in *Sir William Osler Memorial Number,* ed. Maude E. Abbott (Toronto: International Association of Medical Museums, 1926), 9: 97–103 and Leonard Payne, "Osler as a Bibliophile," in *Oslerian Anniversary* (London: The Osler Club of London, 1976), pp. 38–47. A recent survey of bibliomania is Nicholas A. Basbanes, *A Gentle Madness: Bibliophiles, Bibliomanes, and the Eternal Passion for the Book* (New York: Henry Holt, 1995). See also Charles G. Roland, "Bibliomania," *J. A. M. A.* 1970, 212: 133–135.

3. Osler's book collection, donated to McGill University upon his death in 1919, is described in detail in William W. Francis, Reginald A. Hill, and Archibald Malloch, eds. *Bibliotheca Osleriana: A Catalogue of Books Illustrating the History of Medicine and Science Collected, Arranged, and Annotated by Sir William Osler* (Oxford: Oxford University Press, 1929). Hereafter, Bibliotheca Osleriana. For Osler's publications, see Richard L. Golden and Charles G. Roland, eds., *Sir William Osler: An Annotated Bibliography with Illustrations* (San Francisco: Norman Publishing, 1988). See also Ellen B. Wells, "Books for the Bibliotheca: A study of Sir William Osler's book bills," in Golden and Roland, *Sir William Osler,* pp. 163–167.

4. William Osler, "Remarks on the medical library in postgraduate work," *Br. Med. J.,* 1909, 2: 925–928.

5. J. Hain Friswell, *Varia: Readings from Rare Books* (London: Sampson Low, Son, and Marston, 1866).

6. Osler, "Sir Thomas Browne," in *An Alabama Student and Other Addresses* (New York: Oxford University Press, 1908), pp. 248–277.

7. Osler, "The collecting of a library," in *Bibliotheca Osleriana,* pp. xxi–xxxii, quote from p. xvi.

8. Osler, "Letter to Jefferson Medical College students," *The Jeffersonian*, September 1914, 15: 1–2.

9. Osler, "Books and Men," *Bost. Med. Surg. J.* 1901, 144: 60–61, quote from p. 60.

10. Interest in "Medical Americana" peaked during the first half of the twentieth century. In recent decades, medical collectors in the United States have tended to focus more on the literature of the medical and surgical specialties. This reflects both the dramatic growth of specialty medicine during the twentieth century and the disappearance of eighteenth and nineteenth century medical imprints from the market. See Leonard L. Mackall, *Catalogue of an Exhibition of Early and Later Americana* (New York: New York Academy of Medicine, 1926) and W. Bruce Fye, "Collecting medical books: Challenges and opportunities in the 80s," *Bull. N.Y. Acad. Med.*, 1985, 61: 250–265.

11. Osler, "The collecting of a library," p. xxi.

12. See John Shaw Billings, "Rare medical books," *Johns Hopkins Hosp. Bull.*, 1890, 1: 29–31.

13. For a detailed study of Osler's practice and his various sources of income based on his diaries and daybooks, see Edward H. Bensley and Donald G. Bates, "Sir William Osler's autobiographical notes," *Bull. Hist. Med.*, 1976, 50: 596–618 and George T. Harrell, "Osler's practice," *Bull. Hist. Med.*, 1973, 47: 545–568.

14. Osler, "The collecting of a library," p xxii.

15. See Edward C. Streeter, "Osler as a bibliophile," *Boston Med. Surg. J.*, 1920, 182: 335–338.

16. Grace Osler to [Harvey Cushing], July 1901, quoted in Cushing, *Sir William Osler*, 1: 558.

17. Grace Osler to [Harvey Cushing], July 1901 [another letter], quoted in Cushing, *Sir William Osler*, 1: 558–559.

18. George Dock to Willard Goodwin, nd, published in, Willard Goodwin, "William Osler and Howard Kelly; Physicians, Medical Historians, Friends, as revealed by 19 letters from Osler to Kelly," *Bull. Hist. Med.*, 1946, 20: 611–652, quotation from p. 630.

19. Osler to [Harvey Cushing], 17 July 1903, quoted in Cushing, *Sir William Osler*, 1: 612–613.

20. Osler to [Harvey Cushing], 25 July 1903, quoted in Cushing, *Sir William Osler*, 1: 613.

21. Osler to [Harvey Cushing], 29 August 1903, quoted in Cushing, *Sir William Osler*, 1: 614–615.

22. Cushing shared Osler's passion for medical history and book collecting. See Emile Holman, "Sir William Osler and Harvey Cushing: two great personalities and medical bibliophiles," *Stanford Med. Bull.*, 1961, 19: 173–185, and Elizabeth H. Thomson, "Early manifestations of bibliomania in three collectors: Harvey Cushing, Arnold Klebs, and John Fulton," *J. Albert Einstein Med. Center*, 1962, 10: 98–107.

23. Cushing, *Sir William Osler*, 1: 579.

24. E. Y. Davis. Jr. [William Osler], "Burrowings of a Bookworm," c1902, quoted in Cushing, *Sir William Osler*, 1: 579–580. Additional material from this unpublished essay and supplementary notes were published recently, see Richard L. Golden, *The Works of Egerton Yorrick Davis, M.D.: Sir William Osler's Alter Ego* (Montreal: McGill University, 1999).

25. Osler, "Books and Men," quote from p. 35.

26. See W. Bruce Fye, "William Osler's departure from North America: The price of success," *N. Engl. J. Med.*, 1989, 320: 1425–1431.

27. See Fielding H. Garrison and F. Neumann, "How to collect old medical books in Europe: Where to go and what to look for," *J. A. M. A.* 1911, 57: 895–898.

28. Cushing, *Sir William Osler,* 2: 84.

29. W. W. Keen, "A tribute to Sir William Osler," in *Sir William Osler Memorial Number,* ed. Maude E. Abbott (Toronto: International Association of Medical Museums, 1926), 9: 246–248.

30. Holman, "William Osler and Harvey Cushing," p. 176.

31. Cushing, *Sir William Osler,* 2: 166.

32. *Bibliotheca Osleriana,* entry 566, p. 57.

33. *Bibliotheca Osleriana,* entry 3544, p. 315. See also Francis A. Neelon, "Osler and Ernulf's curse," *Lancet,* 1997, 350: 1245–1246.

34. Osler to [Harvey Cushing], 9 July 1911, published in Cushing, *Sir William Osler,* 2: 279.

35. See Cushing, *Sir William Osler,* 2: 166–167.

36. Streeter, "Osler as a bibliophile."

37. Osler, "Address before the International Association of Antiquarian Booksellers at the Criterion Restaurant, Piccadilly, Jan. 26, 1911," *Bookseller,* 3 February 1911, p 144.

38. Osler to Charles Camac, 19 December 1916, published in Earl F. Nation and John P. McGovern, *Student and Chief: The Osler-Camac Correspondence,* (Pasadena, CA, The Castle Press, 1980), p. 104.

39. Cushing, *Sir William Osler,* 2: 318.

40. Osler to Leonard L. Mackall, 6 August 1918, quoted in *Sir William Osler Memorial Number,* ed. Maude E. Abbott (Montreal: International Association of Medical Museums, 1926) 9: 99–100.

41. Osler to J. Collins Warren, 4 December 1916, quoted in Cushing, *Sir William Osler,* 2: 546.

42. Bibliotheca Osleriana, entry 1357, p. 136.

43. See William W. Francis, Reginald H. Hill, and Archibald Malloch. "Editors' preface," in *Bibliotheca Osleriana,* pp. ix–xiv.

44. See D. Evan Bedford, "Harvey's third circulation: de circulo sanguinis in corde," *Br. Med. J.,* 1968, 4: 273–277.

45. Osler to George Dock, 5 May 1918, quoted in Cushing, *Sir William Osler,* 2: 601–602.

46. Osler, "Physic and physicians as depicted in Plato," *Boston Med. Surg. J.,* 1893, 128: 129–133, 153–156, quote from p. 129.

47. William S. Thayer, "Osler," in *Sir William Osler Memorial Number,* ed. Maude E. Abbott, (Montreal: International Association of Medical Museums, 1926) 9: 286–293.

48. Osler. *An Alabama Student and Other Biographical Essays* (London: Oxford University Press, 1908).

49. Osler, "Some aspects of American medical bibliography," [1902], in *Aequanimitas: With other Addresses to Medical Students, Nurses and Practitioners of Medicine* (Philadelphia: P. Blakiston's Son & Co., 1904), pp. 307–326, quote from p. 311.

50. Osler, *Incunabula Medica: A Study of the Earliest Printed Medical Books, 1467–1480* (Oxford: Oxford University Press, 1923).

51. Osler to Joseph H. Pratt, 24 August 1918, quoted in Cushing, *Sir William Osler,* 2: 616.

52. John F. Fulton, "The story of the Osler catalogue, 1922–1929, by a somewhat prejudiced observer," in *W. W. Francis: Tributes from his Friends* (Montreal: Osler Society, 1956), pp. 28–34.

53. *The Osler Library* (Montreal: Osler Library, McGill University, 1979).

54. Osler, "The collecting of a library," quote from p. xxvi.

55. John Ruhrah, "Osler's Influence on Medical Libraries in the United States," *Ann. Med. Hist.*, 1919, 2: 170–183, quote from p. 170. See also Thomas E. Keys, "Sir William Osler and the medical library, *Bull. Med. Lib. Assoc.*, 1961, 49: 24–41, 127–148.

56. Osler to Charles Sayle, November 1916, published in Cushing, *Sir William Osler,* 2: 545–546.

57. Henry R. Viets, "Glimpses of Osler during the War," in *Sir William Osler Memorial Number,* ed. Maude E. Abbott (Montreal: International Association of Medical Museums, 1926) 9: 402–406, quote from p. 405.

58. Osler to Mabel Brewster, December 1914, quoted in Cushing, *Sir William Osler,* 2: 453.

59. Osler to Archibald Malloch, Spring 1918, published in Cushing, *Sir William Osler,* 2: 600. See also *The Book of the Tudor and Stuart Club of the Johns Hopkins University* ([Baltimore: Johns Hopkins University], 1927).

60. John F. Fulton, "William Osler as a medical historian," *Univ. Manitoba Med. J.,* 1949, 20: 113–119.

61. See Genevieve Miller, "In praise of amateurs: Medical history in America before Garrison," *Bull. Hist. Med.,* 1973, 47: 586–615.

62. Owsei Temkin, "Introduction [to the William Osler memorial number]," *Bull. Hist. Med.,* 1949, 23: 319–320, quote from p. 319.

63. Philip M. Teigen, "William Osler's historiography: a rhetorical analysis," *Can. Bull. Hist. Med.,* 1986, 3: 31–49, quote from p. 45.

64. See Thomas E. Keys, "Libraries of some twentieth-century American bibliophilic physicians," *Library Quart.,* 1954, 24: 21–34.

65. See W. Bruce Fye, "Medical book collecting: A retrospect and a forecast," *J. Med. Soc. New Jersey,* 1992, 89: 835–841.

Reginald H. Fitz, Appendicitis, and the Osler Connection—A Discursive Review.

 Richard L. Golden, M.D.

On June 18, 1886 in Washington, D.C., a stocky, balding, mustachioed, 43-year-old man mounted the podium at the inaugural meeting of the Association of American Physicians and delivered a monumental address on "Perforating Inflammation of the Vermiform Appendix, with Special Reference to its Early Diagnosis and Treatment."[1] With this report on 257 cases, Reginald Heber Fitz (1843–1913), Shattuck Professor in Pathological Anatomy at Harvard University, initiated the modern concept of appendicitis and launched a revolutionary change in medicine and surgery (Fig. 1). In recognizing the true nature of appendicitis, he thus consigned to obsolescence and oblivion the old ideas of typhlitis, perityphlitis and paratyphlitis. These terms, unfortunately inconstant in definition, referred respectively to inflammation of the cecum; inflammation of the peritoneum covering the cecum; and inflammation of the connective tissue behind the cecum. Fitz described the pathologic condition and clinical features of the disease and stressed the importance of early diagnosis and surgical intervention. No doubt the prestigious inaugural meeting of the Association of American Physicians and the presence of approving luminaries such as William Osler provided Fitz with a forum that greatly enhanced the impact of his presentation. This, together with the progressive scientific climate of the late nineteenth century, were undoubtedly major contributory factors to Fitz's success.

William Osler (1849–1919), renowned clinician, teacher, bibliophile, and humanist, was a founder of the organization and a participant in this first meeting. He wrote: "The coming-of-age party of clinical medicine in America was held in June, 1886, in Washington, with the inauguration of the Associa-

Published also in *Surgery*, 1995, *118:* 504–509. Reprinted with permission.

Presented at the American Osler Society, May 9, 1994, London.

Figure 1. Reginald H. Fitz, Professor of Pathological Anatomy, Harvard University (1879–1892). Source: Reference 20 (journal now defunct)

tion of American Physicians. . . . The meeting was made memorable by two papers of the first rank, that of Reginald Fitz on 'Inflammation of the Vermiform Appendix,' a landmark in our knowledge, and the study of F. W. Draper on 'Pancreatic Hemorrhage'."[2] Fitz, too, was to make a major contribution to the understanding of pancreatic disease several years later—the second of the twin pillars of his fame. In 1889 he delivered the Middleton-Goldsmith Lecture in which he classified acute pancreatic diseases and described their pathologic condition and symptomatology, achieving for pancreatitis the recognition and acceptance that he had brought to appendicitis.[3] Osler[4] later attested to this when he said, "The history of our knowledge of pancreatic disease might be divided into three periods—that time when the pancreas was believed to be of little if any importance, the time when the work of Fitz appeared, and the later times of the discoveries of the influence of pancreatic ferments and the relationship of the pancreas to the production of diabetes."

Osler and Fitz had missed each other by about three years in the course of their respective, postgraduate, Vienna and Berlin stays in the early 1870's, both returning as earnest devotees of Virchow and the methods of German medical science. Osler's association with Fitz began in 1877, when as Professor of the Institutes of Medicine of McGill University, he visited Harvard to familiarize himself with the method of instruction then current in the medical school. Among the sessions he attended was the course in pathology given by J. B. S. Jackson and his assistant Reginald H. Fitz.[5] The following year Osler's first observations on the cecum and appendix were published. He reported on the autopsy of a 19-year-old man with a perforation of the cecal wall and noted that, "Perforation of the caecum is rather an unusual accident, much more so than perforation of its appendix." He also commented on three cases in which postmortem examination of the appendix demonstrated, ". . .firm concretions of faecal matter, oval in form, and about the size of date stones."[6] In another (post-typhoid) autopsy revealing a normal cecum, perforation of the appendix, and peritonitis, Osler remarked: "The typhoid fever may be regarded as the primary affection. Another source of infection, however, was present, viz: the inflammation of the appendix vermiformis, which formed the starting-point of the disease in three or four of the recorded cases; but I see no reason in this instance to regard the ulceration and perforation of the appendix as anything more than an accidental occurrence, arising from obliteration of the orifice—probably the result of typhoid fever—and retention of secretion."[7]

In 1881, a case of "perityphlitis" was presented at the Medico-Chirurgical Society of Montreal, in which Osler demonstrated an abscess at the head of the cecum in the course of the postmortem examination.[8] In the discussion, Dr. Robert Palmer Howard, Professor of Medicine, observed: "Confusion exists in the books: inflammation of the caecum is one thing, of the appendix quite another." In his commentary, "Dr. Osler referred to the fact that no part of the body varied so much as the appendix vermiformis. It coils in various directions, and owing to its changed situation may get inflamed." Apparently Osler and the McGill group were close to an understanding of appendicitis at this time.

The Canadian Medical Association met at Chatham, Ontario, on September 2, 1885, and William Osler delivered the presidental address, "On the Growth of a Profession".[9] He was also on the program for a paper, "The Clinical and Pathological Relations of the Caecum" which was apparently read but uncharacteristically not quickly published, perhaps obscured by his presidential address.[10] What probably encompassed the essence of his remarks was ultimately published in 1888 with descriptions of 7 cases of anomalous position of the appendix and cecum, 11 cases of ulceration of the appendix, 4 cases of obliteration of the lumen, 6 cases of perforation with perityphlitic abscess, and 2 cases of perityphlitis from cecal disease. He wrote, "I have never met with a foreign body of the appendix. . . . Moulds of faeces are not uncommon . . . Sometimes these form concretions and may cause ulceration." Osler also noted two occasions in which foreign bodies found in the appendix were brought to his attention and he states: "It is rather surprising considering the situation of the appendix, that we do not more often find foreign bodies in it."[11] Cushing, with tenuous hindsight, calls attention to the fact that had this report been promptly published it would have "antedated Fitz's classical paper on the subject by two years."[12]

When Osler accepted the chair of Professor of Clinical Medicine at the University of Pennsylvania in 1884 (Fig. 2), Fitz, in an insightful testimonial letter to Dr. James Tyson (Professor of Pathology) observed: "It is my impression that he would prefer the scientific professorship providing a sufficient salary were paid—and give up all his time to the teaching rather than teach clinically at a small salary and give most of his time to practice."[13]

Figure 2. William Osler, as Professor of Clinical Medicine, at the University of Pennsylvania (1884–1889).
Personal collection of the author

On December 29, 1885 Osler and Fitz attended a founders meeting of the Association of American Physicians in the New York office of Dr. Francis Delafield, Professor of the Practise of Medicine at Columbia University. Delafield was elected the first president of the new Association at its inaugural meeting in 1886. In a memorable address he said: "We want an association in which there will be no medical politics and no medical ethics; an association in which no one will ask who are the officers, and who are not; in which we will not ask from which part of the country a man comes, but whether he has done good work, and will do more, whether he has something to say worth hearing, and can say it. We want an association composed of members, each of whom is able to contribute something real to the common stock of knowledge, and where he who reads such a contribution feels sure of a discriminating audience. . . . we also want a society in which we can *learn* something." It was to further these goals that Osler and Fitz served as founders and in this spirit that Reginald H. Fitz presented his seminal paper.[14]

In a lengthy editorial in 1886 on "Perforating Appendicitis", Osler reports favorably on Fitz's "exhaustive study" and concludes: "The carefully collected facts in Fitz's article will materially assist in the diagnosis of this grave disease, and will embolden surgeons to practise an early operation which can alone, in many instances, give the patient a chance of recovery."[15] In 1887 he reported a case of hernia of the cecum and appendix with perforative appendicitis, perityphlitis and peritonitis.[16] At a meeting of the Philadelphia County Medical Society on December 11, 1887, a symposium was conducted on "Pericaecal Inflammation" with addresses by John H. Musser, William Pepper and Thomas G. Morton. In the discussion that followed, William Osler remarked on the large number of cases of "appendix disease" that recover without surgical intervention and he also commented on cases of cecal disease resulting from fecal impaction.[17] His final major communication on the subject was given one year later at the Toronto Medical Society on December 26, 1888, in which he again distinguished between cases of typhlitis and those of appendicitis, stating: "The opinion has been expressed, and is I believe widely held, that such cases as I have here described (typhlitis] are also in reality due to appendix disease; that typhlitis and peri-typhlitis mean in all cases tubal [appendix] affection. I confess that there is often great doubt as to the true nature of a case, but, clinically, I believe we can recognize a stercoral typhlitis." In his discussion of appendicitis he advises: ". . .it is better in these days of safe laparotomy to give the patient the benefit of any diagnostic doubt, even without the existence of local tumor, and to explore thoroughly the peri-caecal region."[18]

Osler answered the call to Johns Hopkins University in 1889 where he assumed the chair of Professor of Medicine, and Physician-in-Chief of the newly opened Johns Hopkins Hospital. It was a major departure in American medical education with the hospital divided into separate units, clinics and laboratories, each with its own chief as in the German tradition. With the later advent of the medical school, students with baccalaureate degrees were carefully chosen for admission and later served as clinical clerks and dressers in the English and Scottish fashion. Research was stressed, bedside instruction was the rule, postgraduate residencies followed, and a true university spirit prevailed.[19] It was only a few months after the opening of the hospital, in the autumn of 1889, that Reginald H. Fitz came from Boston to see this new institution that had inspired so much interest. In reporting on his experience, he "likened the life to that of a monastery, with the unusual feature that the monks did not appear to bother their minds about the future."[19]

In the recognition of appendicitis, as in every major scientific advance, there is a long list of unsung contributors, culminating in Fitz's paper in 1886.[20] Fitz was neither the discoverer nor the first to describe appendicitis. His contribution was to name the disease and define its pathologic condition, symptoms and treatment, thereby dispelling the myths of earlier generations, and to focus the attention of the profession on this life-threatening condition.[21] It is not within the scope or purpose of this paper to review the history of appendicitis. Neither should there be construed any intention of suggesting Osler's precedence, his address of 1885 notwithstanding, but rather the objective is to depict the contributions of Osler and the evolution of his understanding of appendicitis, as well as his relationship to Fitz.

There are interesting parallels between William Osler and Reginald H. Fitz. They were both well grounded in pathology as a result of their postgraduate studies in Europe and their long hours at the autopsy table. Fitz, an early pupil of Rudolph Virchow, was deeply imbued with his concepts of cellular pathology. Although Fitz had an active clinical practice and was later a visiting physician at the Massachusetts General Hospital and Hersey Professor of the Theory and Practice of Physic at Harvard, he remained primarily a pathologist.[22] Osler, on the other hand, also possessed a vast experience in pathology having performed at least 949 recorded autopsies, but was primarily a clinician whose abilities were based on a solid foundation of morbid anatomy.[23] His skills at the bedside and in the dissecting room allowed him to recognize at an early date, the role of the appendix in inflammatory disease of the right lower quadrant.[6,7,10,11,15,16]

The impact of the Paris clinical school, which flourished in the first half of the nineteenth century, in laying the foundation for the observations of Osler and Fitz was of paramount importance. The fusion of pathologic anatomy, and clinical diagnosis in this school, together with statistical analysis, gave rise to a methodology permitting the correlation of findings at the bedside with those of the autopsy table.[24,25] Were there other factors that together with these advances in science and medicine now permitted Fitz and Osler to properly conceptualize the disease, to "see" appendicitis where they had previously "seen" typhlitis? The findings at autopsy had not changed, only the interpretation. The solution may be found, at least to some degree, in the evolution of the ways in which physicians have viewed the body and its disease states. This type of philosophic-psychologic analysis is offered in the works of M. Foucault, who reasoned: "At the beginning of the nineteenth century, doctors described what for centuries had remained below the threshold of the visible and the expressible, but this did not mean that after over-indulging in speculation, they had begun to perceive once again, or that they listened to reason rather than to imagination; it meant that the relation between the visible and the invisible—which is necessary to all concrete knowledge—changed its structure, revealing through gaze and language what had been previously been below and beyond their domain. A new alliance was forged between words and things, enabling one *to see* and *to say*."[26]

Osler was quite familiar with the association of luminal obstruction, fecaliths, ulceration, and perforation in his reported cases. Perhaps after Fitz's paper he put aside any thoughts of future major publications in this regard. Osler, however, was not totally convinced that appendicitis was all encompassing and initially clung to the notion of "stercoral typhlitis" (or "stercoral caecitis"), as did Fitz, in the differential diagnosis. In the first edition of the **The Principles and Practice of Medicine** in 1892, he wrote: "At present inflammation of any sort, accompanied by pain in the right iliac fossa, is generally thought to be due to disease of the appendix; and, so far as postmortem statistics indicate, a vast majority are due to this cause. Clinically, however, authors still recognize typhlitis (inflammation of the caecum) associated with lodgement of faeces (*typhlitis stercoralis*)."[27] In the second edition (1895) he appears as a total convert, affirming: "Formerly the 'iliac phlegmon' was thought to be due to disease of the caecum—*typhlitis* and of the peritonaeum covering it—*perityphlitis;* but we know now that with rare exceptions the caecum itself is not affected, and even the condition formerly described as stercoral typhlitis is in reality appendicitis." Dr. Osler paid tribute to American physicians in recognizing the importance of appendicitis, and especially to Fitz, "whose exhaustive article in 1886 served to put the whole question on a rational basis."[28]

The two men maintained numerous scientific and social contacts over the years, They shared a warm personal and professional relationship, of which Osler said, "Fitz was one of my best friends & one of the few men who always addressed me affectionately as 'William'. I met him with Henry Bowditch [Professor of Physiology, Harvard] on the occasion of one of my early visits to

Boston, 1876 or '77, and we became greatly attached to each other. He was a clear-headed sensible fellow, the very best type of clinician, & we owe to him splendid work on appendicitis and diseases of the pancreas."[29]

In 1890, Fitz and Osler, together with Abraham Jacobi, William Welch, William Pepper and James Stewart, were members of the American Committee of the Xth International Medical Congress in Berlin. It was here that Robert Koch made his sensational, and unfortunately erroneous, announcement of tuberculin as a cure for tuberculosis.[30] When Osler's magnum opus, **The Principles and Practice of Medicine,** appeared in 1892, Fitz wrote to Osler offering his congratulations and commenting, "An excellent (I won't say shrewd) feature is the constant reference (I say it with pleased modesty) to American work."[31] Fitz in 1894 served as President of the Association of American Physicians and was succeeded by Osler in 1895. In Osler's presidental address he appraised the Association's first decade and paid tribute to Fitz's paper on appendicitis at the first meeting.[32] During Osler's vacation in the summer of 1896 he visited with his Boston friends and with Fitz at Beverly, Mass.[33] Their paths crossed in 1897 in Montreal at the first overseas meeting of the British Medical Association[34] and again in 1903 at the VIth triennial Congress of American Physicians and Surgeons in Washington,[35] where Fitz spoke on pancreatitis and Osler delivered an address on "British Medicine in Greater Britain",[36] later to grace the pages of "Aequanimitas".[37]

In May 1907 William Osler, now Regius Professor of Medicine at Oxford, attended the Congress of American Physicians and Surgeons in Washington. He participated in a symposium on "the historical development and relative value of laboratory and clinical methods of diagnosis" possibly suggested by Reginald Fitz, who served as the President of the Congress.[38] At Christmas 1910, Fitz, on his "18 Arlington Street [Boston]" stationery, wrote to "Dear William" discussing the vaccination controversy in which Osler was embroiled, and Fitz's studies of the early American tracts of the colonial pamphleteers in the debate on inoculation. "Nearly two hundred years and doubting Thomas still is loose." The note ends with a description extolling his trip to California for the Lane Lectures and the natural wonders of the West. ". . .make up your mind to take them all in—for life is short and you can do it in two months."[39] The letter clearly demonstrates the close relationship between the two men and their shared interest in books and the history of medicine. Fitz's research apparently culminated in a scholarly paper on Dr. Zabdiel Boylston, and his role in inoculation in Colonial Boston.[40]

After Fitz's death in 1913 and with the advent of World War I, Reginald Fitz (Fitz's son), Harvey Cushing, and other American medical officers of the Harvard Unit, visited the Oslers in Oxford on May 26, 1917, just a few days before proceeding to France to establish Base Hospital Number 5 with the British Expeditionary Force at Camiers.[41] Fitz had previously met Osler in Oxford (1912), when he began his residency at the Peter Bent Brigham Hospital with a remarkable tour of the great clinics of Europe, led by his chief, Henry A. Christian, and accompanied by other staff members including Francis W. Peabody (later Professor of Medicine, Harvard University).[42] In 1918, while still agonizing over the death in Flanders of their son, Revere, Sir William and Lady Osler presided over the marriage of Captain Reginald Fitz, to Pheobe Wright, a Canadian V.A.D. (Voluntary Aid Detachment) on June 19, 1918. Pheobe's father, Dr. Henry [Harry] Pulteney Wright, was an old friend with whom Osler had shared rooms during their student days at McGill. When Wright died at an early age Osler became a quasi-uncle to the seven Wright children. (Pheobe's sister, Ottilie, married Campbell Palmer Howard, [later Professor of Medicine at McGill and Iowa] Osler's godson and the son of his mentor, Robert Palmer

Howard.) Thus, it was quite natural that when Pheobe came to England she spent a good deal of her spare time with the Oslers in Oxford. In a rather formal letter, Lady Osler wrote to Mrs. Reginald H. Fitz assuring her that Pheobe would make an attractive addition to the Boston scene. The wedding, held at Christ Church, Oxford, in the Latin Chapel of the Cathedral, was followed by a large reception on the lawn at the Osler residence at 13 Norham Gardens, known affectionately as the "Open Arms" to the myriad of friends and visitors who found welcome there. (R. H. Fitz, personal communication, July 1993)[43,44]

Fitz and Osler were both well served by their excellent training and broad experience in pathology and clinical medicine. There is no question that Osler had an early, perspicacious awareness of the pathogenesis and diagnosis of appendicitis and was a significant contributor to the understanding of this disease. However, his near miss of 1885 notwithstanding, the major breakthrough in the recognition of appendicitis came with Fitz's seminal paper which was the final step in the evolution of medical and surgical knowledge of this disorder. Osler's role as a founder of the Association of American Physicians and his presence at the inaugural meeting may have been a significant factor in providing Fitz with a proper forum to successfully disseminate his views. In their relationship, William Osler and Reginald H. Fitz enjoyed a long friendship and a deep mutual professional esteem. Several years after Fitz's death, an even more intimate family relationship began with the Oxford marriage of his son, and the wedding reception at the "Open Arms". The knowledge of the Osler-Fitz relationship provides greater insight into the history of appendicitis and the lives and achievements of these two illustrious physicians.

Acknowledgments

I gratefully acknowledge the help of Dr. Reginald H. Fitz; Joyce Bahr, Librarian of the Suffolk Academy of Medicine, Hauppauge, New York; Ruth Glick and Angela Governale, medical librarians of the Huntington Hospital, Huntington, New York; and Wayne LeBel, assistant history of medicine librarian, the Osler Library of the History of Medicine, McGill University, Montreal.

References

1. Fitz, RH. Perforating inflammation of the vermiform appendix; with special reference to its early diagnosis and treatment. Tr Assoc Am Phys. 1886; 1:107–43.

2. Osler W. The coming of age of internal medicine. *Internat* Clin. 1915; ser 25, 4:1–5.

3. Fitz RH. Acute pancreatitis; a consideration of pancreatic hemorrhage, hemorrhagic suppurative, and gangrenous pancreatitis, and of disseminated fat necrosis. Boston Med Surg J 1889; 120, 181–7, 205–7, 229–35.

4. Osler W. The diagnosis of acute pancreatitis. (Remarks in Discussion, British Medical Association, Exeter, July 27 to Aug. 2, 1907) BMJ 1907; ii: 1132–5.

5. Cushing H. The life of Sir William Osler. Oxford: Clarendon Press, 1925; 1: 152–4.

6. Osler W. Round ulcer of caecum—perforation; concretions in appendix;

perforation of appendix. Montreal Gen Hosp Path Rep, No. I. Montreal: Dawson Bros, 1878: 49–50.

7. Osler W. Suppuration of portal vein following typhoid, perforation of appendix, abscesses in mesentery, empyema. Montreal Gen Hosp Path Rep, No. I. Montreal: Dawson Bros, 1878: 65–71.

8. Armstrong G. Perityphlitis. Autopsy and Discussion by Dr. Osler, Canada Med & Surg J 1881–82; 10: 18–20.

9. Osler W. On the growth of a profession. Canada Med & Surg J. 1885–86; 14: 129–55.

10. Osler W. The clinical and pathological relations of the caecum and the appendix. (by title). Canada J Med Sci. 1885;10: 283.

11. Osler W. Cases of diseases of the appendix and caecum. *Med & Surg Reporter*. Philadelphia, 1888; 59: 419–22.

12. Osler W. The life of Sir William Osler. Oxford: Clarendon Press; 1925; 1: 258fn.

13. R. H. Fitz, Boston, to J. Tyson, Philadelphia, 30 June 1884. "Testimonials Submitted by Prof. Wm. Osler . . . in Application for the Chair of Clinical Medicine, in the University of Pennsylvania", accession no. 8312, Osler Library, McGill University, Montreal.

14. Means JH. The Association of American Physicians: its first seventy-five years. New York: Blakiston Div, McGraw-Hill Book Co., Inc, 1961:5,8,10.

15. Osler W. Perforating appendicitis. Med News. Philadelphia, 1886; 49; 461–2.

16. Osler W. Hernia of the caecum and appendix; perforation of latter; old perityphlitic abscess; recent larger one; general peritonitis. Tr. Path. Soc. Phila. (1885–1887), 1887; 13: 64–6.

17. Osler W. Pericaecal inflammation. Discussion by Dr. Osler. Med & Surg Reporter, Philadelphia, 1888; 58: 14–8.

18. Osler W. Typhlitis and appendicitis. Canada Lancet. 1888–89; 21: 193–6.

19. Cushing H. The life of Sir William Osler. Oxford: Clarendon Press, 1925; 1: 321.

20. Smith DC. A historical overview of the recognition of appendicitis. New York State J Med 1986; 86: 571–83, 639–47.

21. Major RH. Classic descriptions of disease. Springfield and Baltimore: Charles C Thomas, 1932: 620–22.

22. Means JH. The Association of American Physicians: its first seventy-five years. New York: Blakiston Div, McGraw Hill Book Co, Inc, 1961: 4, 7.

23. Rodin AE. Oslerian Pathology: an assessment and annotated atlas of museum specimens. Lawrence, Kansas: Coronado Press; 1981: 11–6.

24. Rosen G. Medical thought and the rise of specialism. In: Ciba Symposia. Summit, New Jersey: Ciba Pharmaceutical Products Inc, 1949; 11: 1126–1134.

25. Ludmerer K. Learning to heal: the development of American medical education. New York: Basic Books, Inc, 1985: 20–4.

26. Foucault M. The birth of the clinic: an archaeology of medical perception. New York: Pantheon Books, 1973: xii.

27. Osler W. The principles and practice of medicine. 1st ed. New York: Appleton, 1892: 405–13.

28. Osler W. The principles and practice of medicine. 2nd ed. New York: Appleton, 1895: 429–43.

29. Osler W. Bibliotheca Osleriana. Oxford: Clarendon Press,1929: #6655.

30. Cushing H. The life of Sir William Osler. Oxford: Clarendon Press, 1925; 1: 333.

31. R.H. Fitz, Boston, to William Osler, Baltimore, 13 April 1892. "Scrapbook of review and letter on textbook," accession no. 9432, Osler Library, McGill University, Montreal.

32. Means JH. The Association of American Physicians: its first seventy-five years. New York: Blakiston Div, McGraw-Hill Book Co., Inc, 1961: 54–9.

33. Cushing H. The life of Sir William Osler. Oxford: Clarendon Press, 1925:I: 439.

34. Cushing H. The life of Sir William Osler. Oxford: Clarendon Press, 1925: I: 457.

35. Cushing H. The life of Sir William Osler. Oxford: Clarendon Press, 1925: I: 607.

36. Osler W. British medicine in Greater Britain. Br Med J 1897; 2: 576–81.

37. Osler W. Aequanimitas with other addresses to medical students, nurses and practitioners of medicine. Philadelphia: P Blakison's Son & Co, 1904: 1156–61.

38. Cushing H. The life of Sir William Osler. Oxford: Clarendon Press, 1925; 2: 89.

39. RH. Fitz, Boston, Christmas 1910, to W. Osler, Oxford. Inserted in: "Reginald Heber Fitz: memorial addresses delivered at the Harvard Medical School, Nov. 17, 1913," accession no. 6655, Osler Library, McGill University, Montreal.

40. Fitz RH. Zabdiel Boylston, inoculator, and the epidemic of smallpox in Boston in 1721. Bulletin Johns Hopkins Hospital, 1911; 22: 315–27.

41. Cushing H. From a surgeon's journal. Boston: Little, Brown, and Co, 1936; 108.

42. Paul 0. The caring physician: the life of Dr. Francis W. Peabody. Boston: Francis A Countway Library of Medicine, 1991; 36–8.

43. Cushing, H. The life of Sir William Osler. Oxford: Clarendon Press, 1925; 1:72; 2: 598, 607.

44. Howard, RP. The chief: Dr. William Osler. Canton, Massachusetts: Science History Publications, 1983; 88: 131, 175–7.

Serving Two Masters: The Relationship between Sir Charles Tupper and Sir William Osler

 T. Jock Murray, M.D.
Janet K. Murray, M.D.

Even though William Osler had a busy daily schedule by any standard, he was not adverse to criticizing such behavior in his patients. He was particularly critical of physicians, businessmen and politicians, and generalized about their unhealthy lifestyle, which he felt would hasten them towards an early grave. He expressed this view in his relationship with a more senior colleague, Sir Charles Tupper, who was both a physician and a politician. Tupper was referred to Osler by his mentor, Dr. Palmer Howard, who expressed concern about some ominous signs of renal disease.[1]

In The New York Medical Journal, 23 November 1901, under the title "*On the Advantages of a Trace of Albumin and a Few Tube Casts in The Urine of Certain Men Above Fifty Years of Age*", Osler wrote, "Year by year I see an increasing number of cases which justify the somewhat paradoxical heading of this brief paper".[2] He then described the effects of hectic schedules on business and professional men, and the wear and tear this unhealthy life style has on their bodies. One sign of this wear and tear was the presence of albumin and casts in the urine. Although many physicians of the day believed such urine changes were ominous, signalling the possibility of serious and even fatal Bright's Disease, Osler argued that they may only be nature's danger signal to slow down, like the red lights on the railroad. He developed the railroad analogy further, and we add it in some length, as an example of Osler's frequent use of railroad, automobile and steamship analogies for bodily function in his

Presented at the American Osler Society, May 11, 1994, London.

writing and speeches. Sadly, an editor today would red pencil such colorful and illustrative prose.

> "The successful business or professional man, who lives intensely and strives hard to get wealth or reputation, or both, and who takes plenty of good food three times a day, with two or three glasses of spirits, and smokes six or ten cigars, works in blissful ignorance that his bodily mechanism is constructed on much the same principles as a steam engine. In the one, as in the other, fuel, combustion, transformation of energy, and the accumulation of waste materials tell the story of the day's work. The engineer as a rule understands his machine better, and accommodates the amount of coal burnt to the size of the engine and to the amount of work required. He does not 'stoke' No. 15, a small yard engine employed to shunt empty cars, as he would No. 580, the superb machine drawing a limited express. Another important difference is the automatic action of the human engine in getting rid of its ashes and clinkers. The waste-pipes bear the strain of the extra work when the amount of fuel consumed in energy liberated is out of all proportion to the work demanded. No 15 'stoked, as if it were No 580, drawing the lightening limited, would go to pieces very rapidly'. So it is with our business friend . . . Careless stoking with high pressure for 25 years and bad treatment of his machine mean early degenerations, and his waste-pipes—kidneys—are often the first to show signs of ill usage."[2]

Osler warned that this busy, successful, professional man will receive a rude shock when he is told that there is a slight trace of albumin and a few tube casts in his urine, as this is thought to signal potentially fatal renal disease.

Osler described in more detail the case of "a very distinguished man in public life in Canada" who was found to have albumin and tube casts in his urine when applying for additional life insurance. The man was nearly 60, leading a very active life in politics, but he had been careless in his habits of eating and drinking. This prominent politician was very anxious and distressed when told by his physician, Dr. R. Palmer Howard, that this finding indicated that his career would be cut short. Dr. Howard was concerned enough about the prognosis to refer the prominent politician to Osler in Montreal.

Osler said "in the summer of 1881 I went to England on the same steamer with him[1] and in London I discussed his condition with Sir Andrew Clarke, who took a very sombre view of the case." Indeed, Sir Andrew took a sombre view of any busy politician, or anyone else, whose fast living life style ignored "the Laws of Health".

Sir Charles Tupper

Fourteen years after the publication of Tupper's case and 34 years after the original consultation Osler revealed that the prominent Canadian politician in this article was Sir Charles Tupper. He revealed this when he wrote Tupper's obituary in the British Medical Journal, The Lancet and the Canadian Medical Journal.[3]

When Sir Charles consulted Osler, it was a meeting of a nationally prominent physician and politician at age 58, and a younger colleague, age 31. Tupper was known throughout Canada as a powerful and visionary Father of

---

[1] I have not been able to find out how they came to travel together, whether by coincidence, or related to their patient-doctor relationship.

Photograph by Bradley & Rulofson, San Francisco

SIR CHARLES TUPPER, BART. (1881)

Figure 1 Sir Charles Tupper at age 60, the year Osler brought him to be examined by Sir Andrew Clark in London. Despite the ominous view taken by Palmer Howard and Clarke about his urinary findings, Tupper looks hale and hearty, younger than his age, as his did for the next three decades. Source: reference 11

Confederation, a tough physician with a surgical mentality, who was a key person in the formation of the confederation of Canada, and the "enforcer" for the first Prime Minister, Sir John A. Macdonald.[4-14] In the early 1860's Tupper had a vision for the future of Maritime Canada, expanded later to a larger confederation of Canada, but recognized that his tough, straight-forward style did not suit the complex political sensitivities of the times and he saw that Macdonald had great diplomatic skills. Macdonald, on the other hand, had the political skill to recognize the ability of Tupper to strong-arm change. When someone was blocking an issue, the call went out, "Send Tupper".[4]

As an experienced country doctor and physician, Tupper did not hesitate when he saw what needed to be done. He approached politics like a surgeon, and when he saw what should be done he marshalled all skills and procedures, whatever the difficulty and the pain, in order to produce a positive outcome. No niceties of the lawyer's subtle political dancing for Tupper. If you know what you need to do, you do it, and use whatever sharp lancet or

Figure 2. William Osler was asked by his mentor Palmer Howad to see Sir Charles Tupper because he was concerned about albumin and casts in his urine, found on a routine insurance examination. Source: Cushing, reference 1, vol 1

blunt instrument necessary. And he was skilled in using the sharp and blunt instruments of politics—the sharp argument based on facts rather than rhetoric, and the blunt instrument of patronage.

Charles Tupper was born in Amherst, Nova Scotia, on July 2, 1821, the elder son of a Baptist Minister. Both of his parents were the descendants of New England Planters or settlers, who had been given land in the British colony of Nova Scotia after the French Acadian settlers had been expelled by the English governor.[15, 16] Charles was well educated, first at home, then in small private schools, and apprenticed in medicine under Dr. Benjamin Page and Dr. Ebenezer Harding. He studied medicine at Edinburgh under Simpson, Syme, Miller, Christenson and other great Edinburgh professors, graduating in 1843, with a thesis on parturition under his mentor Simpson. He returned to Nova Scotia, where he had a very successful country practice in medicine, surgery and obstetrics for 13 years.[4]

In 1855, he was encouraged to run for election, and defeated the great senior Nova Scotia hero of a free press and responsible government, the Honorable Joseph Howe. While sitting in the House, Tupper also assumed the role of the City Medical Officer in Halifax, the capital, where he also engaged in a busy medical practice and was editor of a weekly newspaper called the British Colonist. In 1864, at the age of 43, he became Premier of Nova Scotia.[8] One of his first acts was to introduce free education for all children in the colony, an act that met with considerable opposition at the time, including from his own party and most of the taxpayers.

Also in 1864, he called for and organized a meeting of the four Atlantic coast British colonies to discuss Maritime union, and invited representatives of Upper and Lower Canada—Ontario and Quebec—to attend. In 1867, representatives of Ontario and Quebec, together with delegates from the colonies of Nova Scotia, including Tupper, and New Brunswick, presided over the confederation of the four colonies into the Dominion of Canada.[14]

Tupper played major roles in the Dominion government. He wrote the National Policy on Tariffs and Trade; was Minister of Transportation during the building of the great Canadian Pacific Railway from coast to coast; and represented Canada in the Fisheries talks with the United States. He was also the founding President of the Canadian Medical Association, and the only president ot serve more than one term, serving three.[17] For a very brief period he was Prime Minister of Canada, and later Canadian High Commissioner in London.

When we began the research for a biography of Tupper some years ago[4], many we interviewed repeated an oft told story that Osler didn't like Tupper because he tried to serve two masters. In fact that is a misunderstanding of the statement Osler made of Tupper in his obituary:

> *"His life is an illustration of the brilliant success of the doctor in politics. . . . . But, he never really served two masters; from 1855 he was a politician first, and practitioner when stranded by the exigencies of party."*[3]

Some felt Osler was criticizing Tupper for trying to serve both medicine and politics, but Osler clearly meant the oposite, and this is evident in reading the obituary and a note in the biography of Osler by Harvey Cushing.[1, 3] Although Bliss notes that Osler avoided politics himself,[18] he felt it was important for physicians to involve themselves in politics, in order to change things in a larger society. Virchow, admired by Osler, was all his career an influential and visionary pathologist while also a politician, said that politics was just medicine on a grand scale, and this sentiment must have been known to Osler when he visited Virchow.

Sir Andrew Clarke

Sir Andrew Clarke shared Palmer Howard's dim view of Tupper's urinalysis. His conclusions carried considerable weight as he was one of the most prominent English consultants and was six times president of the Royal College of Physicians.[2] Sir Andrew had a tireless work schedule and in his dramatic and even histrionic manner of speaking, lectured his patients and public audiences on the importance of lifestyle to health.[19] Like Osler, he was critical of those with excessive schedules which were often much less than his own.[20]

---

[2]Sir Andrew Clarke, born in Aberdeen in 1826, overlapped at Edinburgh in his medical studies with Charles Tupper in 1842–1843 and it is likely they had known each other in medical school. Clarke became one of the most eminent consultants in England, with a clientele of the prominent and famous. His portrait hangs in the Royal College of Physicians of London, painted by Watts, who was also his patient.[4]

Figure 3.   Sir Andrew Clark, prominent medical consultant, six times President of the Royal College of Physicians, had described a syndrome of "urinary inadequacy" with no demonstrable renal pathology, and shared Palmer Howard's ominous view of Tupper's finding. He also shared Osler's view that politicians led lives that led to ill health. Source: reference 4

Although he felt business and professional people suffer from offences from their excessive diet, alcohol and hectic schedules, it is worth noting that many people at the time of his fatal stroke expressed the belief that his overwork was probably the cause.

Sir Andrew also assumed that a prominent, busy politician like Tupper would have health problems related to excesses of diet, alcohol and schedule. He said, "Health is that state of the body in which all the functions of it go on without notice or observation, and in which existence is felt to be a pleasure, in which it is a kind of joy to see, to hear, to touch, to live. *That* is health." But he could not resist adding that this state cannot be benefited by alcohol in any degree.[3][21]

---

[3]In his lecture on alcohol, *"An Enemy of the Race"*[20] on alcohol and temperance, Sir Andrew indicated that he saw ten thousand people a year (which we calculate as 40 consultations per day, an amazing number considering the nature of London medical consultations of that day) and inquired into each patient's lifestyle habits.

Like Osler, he did not think it inappropriate for a physician like Tupper to be a politician, but such a life would require special caution about diet and rest. A person should avoid "Hurry, worry, scurry, strain and lifting". If in business or politics, a person should have a "quiet, regular, occupied, tranquil life", and retire to bed early (even if Clarke didn't follow these directions himself).[4]

When he was being assessed and lectured by Clarke, Tupper was recovering from an attack of bronchitis, and what he described as "a tightness around the head, which rendered him unequal to any work." Sir Andrew thought his urinary findings were ominous, similar to the disorder he had published as "renal inadequacy", a form of renal disease with urinary findings but no pathology in the kidney (which later authors said was a non-existent disease[22]). But his conclusion was that Tupper had "suppressed gout" as the root of his trouble, and recommended a healthy regimen, coupled with a stern warning to steer away from alcohol in any form. He then gave him a prescription for syrup of hypophosphates.

Tupper was puzzled. He wrote in his journal, "I could hardly believe it, as I had been a very abstemious man, and my father had been still more so."[5] He had some trouble having the prescription filled, but he did begin to follow the strict regimen advocated by Sir Andrew, and he steadily improved. One reason he may have improved was that he was feeling depressed about the possibility that his medical problem would stop his career, and because his father had recently died, giving Tupper a sense of his own mortality. With Clarke's healthy regime and Osler's reassurance, Sir Charles resumed a busy public life and good health. Osler was able to say twenty years later that following a year of rest, the politician got over his fright, resumed work, accomplishing as much as he had in the previous twenty years. Osler concluded proudly, "he is still alive—an octogenarian of exceptional vigor".[6] To further explain Tupper's good health in later years, Osler wrote, "A few months ago he, in reply to a question as to what he attributed his kindly old age, said: "a good constitution, a good digestion, and a capacity to sleep".

Osler, referring to the writings of Oliver Wendell Holmes, another physician who had a busy and varied career, concluded, "Very few of us are made as was the Deacon's masterpiece, the wonderful *One Hoss Shay*, and lurking somewhere there is a weakest spot, very often in our modern mode of life, the kidneys, which to use the language of the Autocrat's fine poem, may begin to show "a general flavour of mild decay" in the fourth or fifth decade."[2]

Osler says that a few hyaline casts and a trace of albumin are simply the expression of this mild decay in the kidneys and concludes that adopting a more healthy lifestyle would reverse this process. He quotes Aphorism 13 of George Cheyne's, *"Essay on Regimen"*. "Every wise man, after 50, ought to

---

[4]Although Clarke avoided the dreariness of daily politics, he did believe in speaking out on political issues that were socially relevant, particularly if they related to education, temperance, religion and morals, social and sanitary reform, or the need to support hospitals. He did not shy away from medical politics and was a frequent and eloquent speaker at medical meetings.

[5]His Father, the Reverend Charles Tupper, founded the first temperance organization in Eastern Canada, and his son Sir Charles Tupper, rarely used alcohol, was physically fit and strong, always looking younger than his age.

[6]In that paper he also described another politician with much the same benign outcome. He alludes to a third case, a man he had seen years before who approached him while visiting the Cathedral at Antwerp. Osler felt a tap on his shoulder and a voice said, "Not dead yet!" On turning he saw a gentleman that he had seen ten years before when the man was 53. He had also been rejected for insurance because of the suspicion of Bright's disease, and the opinion that he would not be long for this world, but Osler had correctly concluded that the condition was benign.

begin to lessen at least the quantity of this aliment; and if he would continue free of great and dangerous distempers, and preserve his senses and faculties clear to the last, he ought every seven years to go on abating gradually and sensibly, and at last descend out of life as he ascended into it, even into the child's diet."[2]

Although he emphasizes the benign nature of the urinary changes, he returned to his engine/transportation metaphor to warn that a trace of albumin and a few tube casts were danger signals, red lights which may mean an open draw bridge or a wrecked road ahead, or simply warnings to "go slow."[2]

Osler said of Tupper, "His life is an illustration of the brilliant success of the doctor in politics. We have to go to France or to the South American Republic to parallel his career. He never really served two masters; from 1855 he was a politician first, and a practitioner only when stranded by the exigencies of party."[3]

Osler makes clear his attitude towards physician-patients and physician-politicians, and specifically to Tupper:

Photograph by Pictorial Agen
SIR CHARLES TUPPER, BART., G.C.M.G., C.B.
(JANUARY, 1914)

Figure 4.   Sir Charles Tupper at Bexley Heath, London, age 93, alert and interested in the politics of the day, but in failing health. Osler visited him many times as a colleague and friend but also as a consultant to Tupper's physicians. Source: reference 8

"A doctor who comes to me with broken nerves is always asked two questions—it is unnecessary to ask about drink, as to the practised eye that diagnosis is easy—about Wall Street, and politics. It is astonishing how many doctors have an itch to serve the state in parliament, but for a majority of them it is a poor business which brings no peace to their souls. There is only one way for a doctor in political life—to belong to the remnant, the saving remnant of which Isaiah speaks, that votes for men not for parties, and that see equal virtues (and evils) in 'Grits' and Conservatives. I have had one political principle (and practice), I always change with the government. It keeps the mind plastic and free from prejudice. You cannot serve two masters, and political doctors are rarely successful in either career. There are great exceptions, for example, Sir Charles Tupper, a first-class surgeon in his day and a politician of exceptional merit. Nor do I forget that the great Clemenceau is a graduate in medicine of Paris, and that we have three members of the profession in the Imperial Cabinet, one a professor of anatomy at McGill. All the same, let the average man who has a family to support and a practice to keep up, shun politics as he would drink and speculation. As a right-living, clear-thinking citizen and with all the interests of the community at heart the doctor exercises the best possible sort of social and political influence."[2]

When Tupper finally withdrew from active public life in 1900 at the age of 80, he and his wife divided their time between England and Canada, and in 1909, they retired to England, where he lived at the Mount, a beautiful old mansion in Bexley Heath, near his only daughter, Emma, and her family.[19] The Mount was on the edge of a golf course, and at the age of 89, he played golf, went to London to dine or to visit friends, and wrote letters to his family and friends, letters to many editors, and his Recollections. In 1913, his wife of 66 years died, and he accompanied her body to Canada where she was buired in Halifax. He then went across the country to British Columbia and Manitoba, where he visited his sons, and then he returned to England. His son, Stewart came to visit him, and suffered what appears to have been a stroke. He was in a nursing home in Oxford, where Osler visited him and relayed reports to Tupper. Stewart died in 1914. During this period Tupper was often depressed. He was very disturbed by the war. His granddaughter's husband had been killed, his grandson Captain Victor Gordon ("Gordie") was killed at Vimy Ridge at age 21 and buried in France, and his grandson, Reggie, seriously injured at the front.

In his last year, Tupper was repeatedly examined by Osler, who was then the Regius Professor of Medicine at Oxford, when consulted by Tupper's two physicians, the young local physician Dr. Thomas W. Hinds, and the prominent Sir Richard Powell, but he would also visit on his own as social calls. In Tupper's notebooks we counted 15 visits to Tupper by Osler during the last year of his life.[4] When Tupper was in Oxford, or when Osler was in London, these visits were often daily, and Lady Osler also frequently visited Tupper on her own.

In April Tupper went to Oxford where he was examined by Osler, who told his daughter Emma the gradual deterioration of his health was due to his age. Emma reported that Osler found his arteries wonderful for a man of his years, with a good pulse and still generally strong.

But Tupper was failing, dreaming each night of his "His Darling Frances". On July 12 in 1915, he went to London to consult Sir Douglas Powell because he was feeling ill. He was suffering from what he called bronchial irritation. On September 22, Tupper had a heart attack. The doctor was called, and prescribed rest, and although he initially seemed to be recovering, on October 26, Dr. Hinds was sent for again. He came, bringing Osler with him. Tupper had been laid up in his room for three weeks, was depressed and talking repeatedly about his concerns for his grandson, Reggie, who was severely injured in battle, and was being shipped back home across the Atlantic. His daughter Emma said he continually thought of Reggie, and "he is glad to think he is such a good man as well as a brave one." The old man died a few days later, October 30, 1915, at age 94.[7] His body was shipped to Quebec on the warship *Metagama,* and then by train to Nova Scotia where a state funeral was held on a clear sunny day of November 16." The funeral cortege walked from St. Paul's to St. John's Cemetery, where, with full state honours, he was laid to rest beside Frances.

Recognizing the friendship, medical journals asked Osler to write the obituary and this account of his life was printed by The Lancet, the British Medical Journal and the Canadian Medical Journal. Some of that final account will give the view of Osler about his senior friend and patient:

> "Few men have lived more vigorously, first in the rough and tumble of a
> large general practice in Nova Scotia and then in a more turbulent area of
> politics, yet he retained good health of mind and body nearly to the end."

Osler mentioned that Tupper never tired of talking of his happy days at Edinburgh and only months before his death Osler had encouraged him to write his experiences as a medical student. Osler talked about his successful practice in Nova Scotia before politics, saying, "He was fond of surgery, and was one of the few men remaining who could talk of personal experiences in pre-anaesthetic days. He told the writer of an amputation at the hip joint for sarcoma performed on a farmer's wife on the kitchen table, with a sailor as assistant".

Osler talked of Tupper's successful medical practices in Halifax, Ottawa and Toronto, and his role in founding the Canadian Medical Association. "Canada owes a deep debt to Sir Charles Tupper, and his political opponent, Sir Wilfred Laurier, very truly said that next to Sir John A. Macdonald, the man who did most to bring about the federation of the Canadian provinces was Sir Charles Tupper. With a strong and daring personality, he had all the qualities for success in the public life—calmness and clear judgement in victory, resolution and hopefulness in defeat. Nothing in his history was more remarkable than to have "stumped the country" successfully for his party when in his 80th year." Osler added that his life was an illustration of the brilliant success of the doctor in politics.

Osler commented that Tupper was alert and clear to the last few months, and his arteries were healthy and " scarcely palpable when the blood stream was pressed out." He concluded with the exclamation, " Yet here was a man who in 1880–1881 was ready to throw out the sponge, as he was believed to have Brights disease!". Osler said that his observation that these findings constitute a benign disease, coupled with the sensible advice of Sir Andrew Clarke enabled Tupper to lead a healthy and productive professional life for another 34 years.

Sir William Osler was a physician and friend to Sir Charles Tupper, and over 35 years these two prominent men, despite their differences in years and directions in life, developed a lasting friendship that was based on understanding and respect.

Osler felt he had made an important observation with Tupper, separating a benign warning from fatal Bright's disease, and said in his publication of Tupper's case:

---

[7]Reggie eventually got home and lived. His younger brother, Captain Victor Gordon Tupper, known as Gordie, was not so fortunate. He was killed in action at Vimy Ridge, 9 April, 1912, and is buried in France. He was 21.

"I do not wish to minimize the importance of the information to be obtained by an examination of the urine, but we must ever bear in mind the adage—true to-day as well as in the times of the old "Pisse-Prophets"; *urina est meretrix, vel mendax*—the urine is a harlot or a liar."[2]

Bibliography

1. Cushing, Harvey; The Life of Sir William Osler. Oxford, Clarendon Press; Vol 2, pp 618–619, 1925.

2. Osler, WO. On the advantage of a trace of albumin and a few tube casts in the urine of certain men above fifty years of age. New York Med J 23 November 1901.

3. Osler, Sir William, The Obituary of Sir Charles Tupper, Bart. British Medical Journal, Nov. 6, 2: 2862; 694–695, 1915; (Also in The Lancet, Nov. 6, 2:4810; 1049–1050, 1915, and the Canadian Medical Journal, Nov 1915).

4. Murray TJ, Murray JK. Sir Charles Tupper: Fighting Doctor to Father of Confederation. Markham, Ont, Fitzhenry and Whiteside, 1999, Chapter 8. P. 95–106.

5. Longley, J.W., The Makers of Canada Series: Charles Tupper. Makers of Canada (Morang) Ltd.; Toronto; 1916; (Parkman Edition).

6. MacIntosh, Alan Wallace, The Career of Sir Charles Tupper in Canada, 1864–1900. Phd thesis (unpublished); University of Toronto, 1960. (Killam Library, Halifax copy, F1033T86M25).

7. Saunders, E.M.,D.D. Three Premiers of Nova Scotia. Toronto, William Briggs, 1909.

8. Saunders, E.M.,D.D., Editor. The Life and Letters of Rt. Hon. Sir Charles Tupper, Bart., K.C.M.G. Volume I and II. Cassell and Company Ltd. London. 1916.

9. Simpson, J.H.L., The Life of Sir Charles Tupper. Canadian Medical Association Journal, June 1939. Also read before the Halifax Medical Society, Halifax NS, February 22, 1939.

10. Thibault, Charles, Biography of Sir Charles Tupper. Montreal. L'Etendard Print. 1883.

11. Tupper, Rt. Hon. Sir Charles, Bart., G.C.M.B., C.B. Recollections of Sixty Years.London, Cassell and Company. 1914.

12. Tupper, Sir Charles Hibbert. Supplement to the Life and Letters of the Right Hon. Sir Charles Tupper Bart., K.C.M.G. Toronto, The Ryerson Press; 1926.

13. Tupper Papers. Inventory of manuscripts in the Public Archives of Nova Scotia. Halifax 1976.

14. Waite, Peter B., The Charlottetown Conference. Toronto: The Canadian Historical Association, 1970.

15. Tupper, E., Tupper Genealogy: In The Interest of the Tupper Family Association of America. Beverley Mass; The Reporter Press; Paul K. Blanchard Inc. North Conway N.H. 03860.

16. Steele, Rev. D.A., and Rogers, G.M., One Hundred Years With the Baptists of Amherst, N.S., Amherst, 1911.

17. MacDermot, H.E., History of the Canadian Medical Association 1867–1921. Toronto, Murray Printing Company, Limited; 1935.

18. Bliss, M. William Osler: A Life in Medicine. Toronto, University of Toronto Press, 1999.

19. Pitcairn E.H., Personal Reminesces of Sir Andrew Clark. Strand Magazine, 1894;7(9):65–76.

20. Clark, A. An Enemy of the Race: a lecture on Alcohol and Temperance. London, National Temperance Publishing Depot, 1881. (Pamphlet of 15 pages, price one penny).

21. Clark, A. The Physician's Testimony for Christ. Preface by Sir Dyce Duckworth. London . Natioanl Temperance Publishing Depot, 1894.

22. Johnson, George. Sir Andrew Clark's Theory and Treatment of "Renal Inadequacy". Brit Med J 1894,(ii) July 28, 169–170.

23. Foxley, G L; A History of the Bexleyheath Golf Club—1907–1977. Dartford, England, S.B.Printing Co. 1980.

SECTION II

 Writings

Mr. Gates's Summer Vacation: A Centennial Remembrance

 Charles S. Bryan, M.D.

A novelty item sold in recent years consists of a brass plaque inscribed "At this site in 1897 nothing happened." Such gentle whimsy would be inappropriate at a certain site on Lake Liberty, New York, although in 1897 a passerby would have found nothing remarkable about a man reading a book. The man was Frederick Taylor Gates (Figure 1) and the book was the second edition of William Osler's *Principles and Practice of Medicine*.[1] Gates became a principal champion of medicine and launched a series of initiatives that, arguably more than any other, fostered scientific medicine and research-oriented clinical departments in the United States.[2–7]

Born in Broome County, New York, Frederick Gates was the son of a small-town clergyman. Osler was also the son of a clergyman but the similarities end there. Although Featherstone Osler could send his eighth child to a boarding school where natural science and Sir Thomas Browne's *Religio Medici* shaped the boy's interests, Granville Gates needed his son's help to keep the family from living in poverty. Young Frederick Gates acquired business acumen through such activities as selling harrows to farmers and buying their calf hides for a tannery 20 miles from home. He worked his way through college and seminary, led the Fifth Avenue Baptist Church of Minneapolis through a successful fundraising campaign, and came to the attention of such prominent Midwest Baptists as George A. Pillsbury, the flour magnate. In 1888, Gates left the pulpit to help form the American Baptist Education Society, and he became its executive secretary. He stated, "This Society, under my administration, founded the University of Chicago, for which I raised the first million dollars, and in this way became acquainted with Mr. John D. Rockefeller."[8]

Presented at the annual meeting of the American Osler Society, April 3, 1997, Williamsburgh.

Reprinted with permission from *Annals of Internal Medicine, 127:* 148–153, 1997.

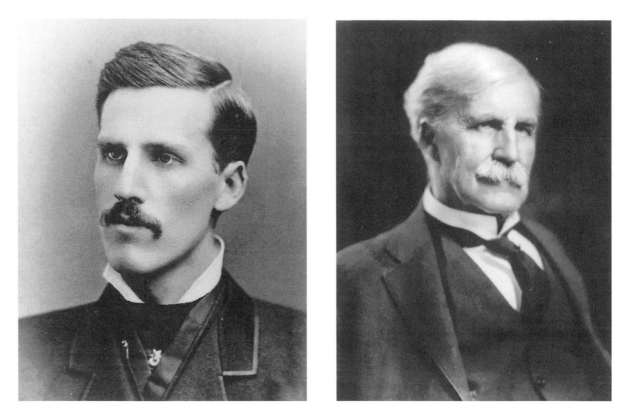

Figure 1. Frederick Taylor Gates (1853 to 1929) as a young man and in later life. Rockefeller Archives Center

Rockefeller was impressed with the "extraordinary ability" of Gates "to get at facts, to analyze them, and to draw sound conclusions from them."[9] In 1891, Gates moved to the eastern United States to help Rockefeller with his philanthropic endeavors. Although a study in contrasts—the taciturn, fastidious Rockefeller was a model of self-restraint and Gates, by his own admission in 1891, was "eager, impetuous, insisting, and withal exacting and irritable"[10]—they got along famously. Rockefeller was beset by thousands of requests for contributions each year. As Gates phrased it, Rockefeller was "constantly hunted, stalked, and hounded almost like a wild animal."[11] Gates established a policy of refusing all individual requests for funds and concentrated on agencies that could be held accountable. Rockefeller also sought the help of Gates with investments and thereby learned that he had often been swindled by others. In 1893, Rockefeller brought Gates to his private New York offices at 26 Broadway as a full-time advisor.

In effect, Rockefeller became Gates's congregation of one. Gates counseled him in private and defended him in public, calling him a man whose "ruling passion was by no means a love of money" but rather "a taste for excellence," and whose genius was "for taking pains, doing everything possible just as well as it can be done by steady observation, reflection, and rigid self discipline day by day."[12] Gates gave practical advice laced with spiritual prognosis: "Your fortune is rolling up, rolling up like an avalanche! You must distribute it faster than it grows! If you do not, it will crush you, and your children, and your children's children."[13] The textbook by Osler convinced Gates that an excellent investment for the Rockefeller fortune would be scientific medicine.

The Reading of *The Principles and Practice of Medicine*

Gates embellished the story with time, especially in response to a request in 1920 from Harvey Cushing for biographical information about Osler. Cushing wrote:[14]

> Nothing can possibly interest me more . . . than the note pasted on the flyleaf of your Principles and Practice. . . . If you could bring yourself to write the narrative of your first encounter with Osler's "Practice", with the subsequent reaction of Mr. Rockefeller, all of which led up to the gift to the Johns Hopkins after the fire, to the Rockefeller Institute, and much else beside, it would certainly be one of the most interesting stories I shall have to tell. I would greatly like to have it in your own words.

When Gates prepared his autobiography in 1928, he used the same version that he had given to Cushing:[15,16]

> I read the whole book without skipping any of it. I speak of this not to commemorate my industry but to illustrate Osler's charm. Osler's *Principles and Practice of Medicine* is one of the few scientific books possessed of literary attraction. There was a fascination about the style itself that led me on and, having once started, I found a hook in my nose that pulled me from page to page, and chapter to chapter, until the whole of about a thousand closely printed pages brought me to the end.

Although almost a quarter of a century elapsed between Gates's reading of the book and Cushing's request for a good story, several aspects are beyond dispute.

First, Gates did not pick up the textbook by chance. A great-grandfather and several other relatives had been physicians, and his father had read about medicine on his own for 3 years before choosing to enter the clergy. Gates "had been for years convinced that medicine as generally taught and practiced in the United States was practically futile."[17] He had witnessed his older brother and only sibling, Frank, bled from the temporal artery for brain fever and later watched helplessly as Frank died of rheumatic heart disease. He had seen his first wife, Lucia Fowler Perkins Gates, "the gentlest spirit that ever drew breath," die of undiagnosed illness the year after they were married. He himself had survived a life-threatening illness that was never diagnosed. He had heard physicians in his Minneapolis congregation confide that much of what they did was humbug. By 1897, Gates "determined at length that I would find out what really lay in the minds of doctors in active practice. I would read the text books they studied."[18] For reading advice, he turned to Elon O. Huntington, a former parishioner from Minneapolis who, being alone in New York City as a medical student, sometimes spent weekends with the Gates family in Montclair, New Jersey. Huntington prescribed Osler. Gates purchased the textbook from a bookstore in New York City and packed it for vacation.

Second, the vacation was designed to benefit the Gates children, not medicine. Believing that the best learning occurs in large families and that well-educated people have a special duty to procreate, Gates was in both respects his own best example. The 1897 summer entourage of Gates and his wife, Emma Lucille Cahoon Gates, included four sons and three daughters ranging in age from 7 months to 10 years. Like earlier vacations on the New Jersey coast, the trip to the Catskills was "arranged by us on the modern theories of education, to give our children fresh interests and experiences in the greatest possible number and variety."[19] Lake Liberty afforded "endless play in the water," a carpenter's shop, and a dam that provided "a small water-power for which the boys made a suitable wheel, to which they attached a small churn, and actually made butter from the cream saved from the morning cereal." Moreover, "many happy hours spent in frogging supplied our family table with frogs' legs." Gates completed the reading of an entire textbook of medicine because, like Osler, he had learned to manage his time, balance sociability and solitude, and focus his energy.

Finally, the episode was unquestionably pivotal to the Rockefeller philanthropic endeavors. The considerable evidence for this includes a 1902 letter in which Gates introduced himself to Osler for the first time:[20]

> Some years ago, in carrying out a determination to become more intelligent as a layman on the subject of the current and common diseases, I purchased a copy of your "Principles and Practices of Medicine," on the advice of a bright young medical friend. Happening to receive it just as I was about to start on a vacation[,] I took the book with me and read it from beginning to end, with absorbing interest, and with a medical dictionary at my side.
>
> In reading it, I was impressed specially with the vast number of diseases that are certainly or probably originated by bacteria and with the success that has attended the efforts to isolate the germs of disease in so many instances, and equally with the fact that as yet only one specific seems certainly to have been found, in the antitoxin of diphtheria; and the vast possibilities for good lying in this field of research opened up before my imagination and fired my enthusiasm. I acquainted myself in a general way with what is being done in Paris and Berlin, and with the fact that with the exception of the work of Johns Hopkins, comparatively little seems to have been accomplished in the United States.

Gates later elaborated that Osler's

> . . . chapter on any particular disease would begin with the definition of the disease and its extension throughout the world, the history of discovery about it, the revelations of innumerable post mortems, the symptoms, cause, and probable results of the disease, and the permanent complications and consequences likely to follow; but when he came to the vital point, namely the *treatment* of the aforesaid disease, our author, who had up to this time been treading on solid ground with the confidence and delight of sure knowledge, would almost invariably lapse into a mental attitude of doubt, scepticism, and hesitation.[21]

Gates decided that the United States needed a medical research institute similar to the Koch Institute in Berlin and the Pasteur Institute in Paris where scientists could work unfettered by outside demands.

On 24 July 1897, Gates returned to New York City, brought Osler's book to the Rockefeller headquarters, and dictated his vision for John D. Rockefeller, Sr. Gates never saw the memorandum again. However, the following October, he gained a valuable ally when John D. Rockefeller, Jr., a recent graduate of Brown University, chose to work with him rather than with the Standard Oil Company. Thereafter the younger Rockefeller approached his father at opportune moments with well-reasoned proposals from Gates. In this setting, Gates thrived as the ultimate corporate liberal. He eventually came to view health as an index of social progress, medicine as a way to reduce tensions in society, and science as a supplement to religion.[22,23] Science, education, and health would thereafter dominate the Rockefeller philanthropic endeavors.[24]

The first endowment was the Rockefeller Institute for Medical Research (now Rockefeller University) which opened in 1901. Through his association with this research facility, Gates met William H. Welch, a pathologist who was

Osler's colleague at Johns Hopkins University and who became president of the scientific directors at the Rockefeller Institute.[25] After the institute became established, the General Education Board was chartered in 1903, the Rockefeller Foundation was incorporated in 1913, and the Laura Spelman Rockefeller Memorial was founded in 1918. An initiative begun as the Rockefeller Sanitary Commission for the Eradication of Hookworm Disease evolved into the Rockefeller Foundation's hugely successful International Health Board. Gates also became preoccupied with the structure and function of clinical departments at medical schools in the United States, which led to a controversy between Gates and Osler.

The Full-Time Controversy

The decision to keep the Rockefeller Institute for Medical Research separate from existing medical schools was made in part because Gates had unhappy memories of a failed 1894 attempt to merge Rush Medical College with the University of Chicago. However, a movement to combine medical education and research within the university framework had begun in the 1870s and had gained momentum when The Johns Hopkins University School of Medicine opened with its own hospital, close ties to its university, and an emphasis on research. As is well known, a report by Abraham Flexner in 1910 on the poor condition of most medical schools in the United States featured Johns Hopkins as a paradigm for comparison.[26,27] During the heady early days of Johns Hopkins University, however, a serious rift between basic science and clinical faculty developed over the issue of whether faculty members should be in private practice. Osler, whose own practice became quite lucrative,[28] held that third- and fourth-year students should be taught by clinicians who were responsible for patients and the treatment of disease. Franklin Paine Mall, an anatomist who had returned from his training in Germany, was convinced that clinical professors should eschew practice-derived income to focus on teaching and research. When Osler left Baltimore in 1905 to become Regius Professor of Medicine at Oxford University, he saw the tide running in Mall's favor. At the end of his final faculty meeting at Johns Hopkins University, he turned to Mall and said: "Now I go, and you have your way."[29]

In 1911, Gates invited Flexner to lunch and asked him what he would do if given $1 million with which to start reorganizing medical education. Flexner answered that he would give the money to Welch.[30] Gates consulted Welch, who replied that "unless you inform me to the contrary I shall include the hospital side, as well as the laboratories in my statement of our needs."[31] The idea that medical school departments should be organized and funded on the same basis as other departments within the university system appealed to Gates; indeed, he had previously reached the same conclusion. Gates therefore reinforced Welch's support of the so-called full-time plan for clinical faculty, an idea that Flexner did not originate but of which he became the avowed champion.[32–36] Rockefeller patronage of medical research would extend to the clinical departments of medical schools, where professors would no longer benefit financially from practice. When the younger Rockefeller proposed the idea to his father in August 1911, he included a memorandum by Gates indicating that Johns Hopkins would be "as free from commercialism as the Rockefeller Institute."[37] Osler, who by 1911 had been Regius Professor of Medicine at Oxford for almost 6 years, was among those who received a copy of the proposal.

Osler did not like it. He circulated a "family letter" addressed to Ira Remsen, president of the Johns Hopkins University, in which he pleaded that the money not be accepted on Rockefeller terms. Remsen, the letter continued, should "divert the ardent souls who wish to be whole-time clinical professors from the medical school in which they are not at home to the Research Institutes to which they properly belong, and in which they can do their best work."[38] Osler's protest failed. In 1913, shortly after Flexner became secretary of the General Education Board, Johns Hopkins University accepted a $1.5 million endowment to establish its departments of medicine, surgery, and pediatrics on a full-time basis. Osler later complained that the full-time plan "had been forced on the profession by men who know nothing of clinical medicine, and there has been a 'mess of pottage' side to the business in the shape of big Rockefeller cheques at which my gorge rises."[39] By 1928, the General Education Board had spent $60 million to support medical education, most of which went to implement the full-time plan.[40] Although clinical faculty would eventually be allowed to secure some private practice (the so-called geographic full-time plan, or the Harvard plan) and Osler would modify his own views toward the end of his life, he had correctly seen the passing of an era.

In retrospect, Osler missed an opportunity to influence the eventual outcome by failing to cultivate a close personal relationship with Gates. When Osler thanked Gates in 1904 for a $500 000 Rockefeller gift to Johns Hopkins University, Gates wrote back:[41]

> Medical science has made comparatively small progress until lately, because chemistry and physics have until very lately never furnished medical science with suitable instruments of research. . . . It has seemed to me that if now medical science, with its new workshop, could be given the same financial encouragement that other sciences have received, we might expect in the next generation or two to reduce medicine, if not to an exact science, certainly to something approximating an exact science, and we might reasonably expect results as revolutionary, as far-reaching, as beneficent on human well-being as any which have been derived from the practical applications of physical and chemical sciences. . . . Am I not right in this train of reflections? Right or wrong, I have made lists for Mr. Rockefeller and his son of achievements already accomplished, and other and yet longer lists of problems needing to be solved.

Gates admired Osler as "the greatest modern physician," and Osler had sent Gates most of his publications.[42] Osler may have missed the opportunity to influence Gates well before the direct involvement of Abraham Flexner with the General Education Board. In fairness to Osler, he was a very busy man on the verge of burnout.[43] In fairness to Gates, clinical science as we know it might not have evolved had part-time professorships remained the norm. Gates eventually acknowledged that the Rockefellers' intentions with the first full-time gift to Johns Hopkins were "not yet fully disclosed. We aimed at nothing less than a wide reform in the teaching and ultimately in the practice of medicine, and Hopkins was only the place of beginning."[44] A century has passed since Gates read Osler, and the extent to which clinical professors should engage in private practice remains an issue.[45]

Epilogue

Gates, Osler, Welch, and Flexner deserve major credit for sponsoring scientific medicine and academic departments of medicine in the United States, but their perspectives sometimes differed in ways that still reverberate today. Gates, whose main cause was research, eventually believed that academic medicine in the United States should rely heavily on seven great privately-endowed schools: Harvard University, Johns Hopkins University, Yale University, the University of Rochester, Vanderbilt University, the University of Chicago, and Washington University at St. Louis. Flexner, whose main cause was education reform, believed that all medical schools should aspire to the standards set at Johns Hopkins University. In 1922, Gates and Flexner clashed over whether the General Education Board should aid a state-supported medical school, the test case being the University of Iowa. Flexner prevailed.[46] Gates's influence over medical education declined but his interest did not, nor was he reluctant to express his views.

In 1925, Gates again opposed Rockefeller aid to state medical schools in a paper that listed 10 "basal facts" about medicine (Table). He maintained that clinical medicine should be subordinate to basic research and disease prevention:[47]

> What is the practical object of the science of medicine? It is not to multiply physicians and Medical schools, nor is it primarily to cure disease. . . . The place of the cure is secondary. The high aim and ideal of the science of medicine is no less than to prevent sickness altogether, to usher humanity into a new world, by banishing sickness from human life and bringing about universal health, an object of course never to be fully obtained. . . . This practical aim, of health, dominates the science itself, and prescribes the logical order of its research. . . . The order is to study the diseases severally, to trace each to its cause; when the cause is found to find out how the disease may be prevented, and to publish the findings immediately, far and wide; then as a final, terminal incident, to seek the cure for those cases that can not be humanly prevented. . . . Physicians, as curative agents, pure and simple, have a necessary place, but it is a subordinate and declining place. For, as health increases we shall need ever fewer physicians and Medical schools, and health *is* increasing.

In conclusion, Gates quipped: "I wonder who can tell me where, after finishing this paper, I borrowed something like the following: 'Medicine must always be a science, or else an empirical method of getting a living out of the

Table. Gates's 10 Basal Facts about Medicine*

---

1. Good medical schools require substantial capital investment.
2. "There has been for fifty years or more, is now, and always will be, an enormous surplus of medical colleges, medical students, and practicing physicians in the United States."
3. Technology enhances efficiency to the extent that "two physicians can now, in 1925, easily cover the ground and do the work of five, in 1900, and do it much better."
4. Sanitary science and preventive medicine reduced the amount of sickness in the United States between 1900 and 1925 "by fifty per cent, thus reducing the practise of physicians by half."
5. Preventing an illness cuts off the potential for secondary illnesses, "several times as many perhaps as the one prevented. Thus, health too becomes contagious, like disease."
6. Big business can, should, and must reinforce preventive medicine because health is profitable. Preventive medicine should further reduce the need for doctors.
7. Much of what physicians do consists of a "fictitious" practice of taking care of imaginary or functional illnesses with methods that lack a scientific basis.
8. The location of medical schools "has no relation whatever to the distribution of physicians."
9. The science of medicine "can be taught only in medical schools that have adopted the academic basis."
10. Research laboratories, graduate medical institutions, and schools of public health are "powerful reinforcements to the science of medicine, without increase in medical schools, and constantly adding to the efficiency of medicine."

---

*adapted from reference 47

ignorance of the human race.'" Today, many articulate spokespersons within medicine would criticize this viewpoint as narrowly preoccupied with the science of medicine—the biomedical model of disease—to the detriment of the "art" of medicine.[48,49] Yet how does the public really value medicine in social, political, and economic terms? We should not forget that informed, concerned, and energetic laypersons, such as Gates, will probably have the final word.

Life was kinder to Gates than it was to Osler, who died broken-hearted after his son and only surviving child, Revere, was killed in World War I. Gates lived to see all seven of his children begin successful careers, marriages, or both. All four of his sons finished college and were elected to Phi Beta Kappa; two survived the war as combat aviators, and one was a medical graduate of Johns Hopkins University and became a researcher at the Rockefeller Institute. Gates retired comfortably and devoted his time to hobbies, such as golf and farming, and to his 17 grandchildren. Unlike Osler, Gates derived enormous personal benefit from medical research. In 1923, Gates and his wife, who both had diabetes, were among the first persons to receive insulin. The dramatic results prompted Gates to secure $150 000 to make insulin available at 15 hospitals within the United States and Canada.[50,51] Gates died of acute appendicitis, a condition on which Osler—his era's foremost reconciler of the old art with the emerging new science—had been a pioneering authority.[52]

Acknowledgments

The author thanks Thomas E. Rosenbaum of the Rockefeller Archive Center, North Tarrytown, New York, and June Schachter of the Osler Library of the History of Medicine, McGill University, Montreal for their assistance, and their respective institutions for permissions to excerpt from unpublished materials.

References

1. Golden RL. Osler's legacy: the centennial of *The Principles and Practice of Medicine*. Ann Intern Med 1992; 116: 255–60.
2. Fosdick RB. The Story of the Rockefeller Foundation. New York: Harper & Brothers; 1952: 8.
3. Bordley J III, Harvey AM. Two Centuries of American Medicine. Philadelphia: W. B. Saunders; 1976: 165–8.
4. Ludmerer KM. Learning to Heal: The Development of American Medical Education. New York: Basic Books; 1985: 201–2.
5. Berliner HS. A System of Scientific Medicine: Philanthropic Foundations in the Flexner Era. New York and London: Tavistock; 1985: 53–9.
6. Wheatley SC. The Politics of Philanthropy: Abraham Flexner and Medical Education. Madison: The University of Wisconsin Press; 1988: 27–8.
7. Flexner S, Flexner JT. William Henry Welch and the Heroic Age of American Medicine. Baltimore: The Johns Hopkins University Press; 1993: 269–72.
8. FT Gates to AS Ochs, 18 January 1912. Rockefeller Foundation archives. Frederick T. Gates collection, box 1, folder 51. Rockefeller Archive Center.
9. Rockefeller JD Jr. Address to honor the memory of Frederick Taylor

Gates, 15 May 1929. Rockefeller Foundation archives. Frederick T. Gates collection, box 3, folder 36. Rockefeller Archive Center.

10. Fosdick RB. The Story of the Rockefeller Foundation. New York: Harper and Brothers; 1952: 1.

11. Gates FT. Chapters in My Life. New York: The Free Press; 1977: 161.

12. Gates FT. Gates on Rockefeller. Rockefeller Foundation archives. Frederick T. Gates collection, box 3, folder 57. Rockefeller Archive Center.

13. Nevins A. Study in Power: John D. Rockefeller, Industrialist and Philanthropist. New York: Charles Scribner's Sons; 1953: ii, 217.

14. H Cushing to FT Gates, 4 May 1920. Rockefeller Foundation archives. Frederick T. Gates collection, box 1, folder 19. Rockefeller Archive Center.

15. Cushing H. The Life of Sir William Osler. London: Oxford University Press; 1925: I, 454–6.

16. Gates FT. Chapters in My Life. New York: The Free Press; 1977: 180–2.

17. Gates FT. Chapters in My Life. New York: The Free Press; 1977: 180.

18. Gates FT. Chapters in My Life. New York: The Free Press; 1977: 180–1.

19. Gates FT. Chapters in My Life. New York: The Free Press; 1977: 136–8.

20. FT Gates to W. Osler, 4 March 1902. Osler Library of the History of Medicine, McGill University, Montreal.

21. Gates FT. Chapters in My Life. New York: The Free Press; 1977: 181.

22. Berliner HS. A System of Scientific Medicine: Philanthropic Foundations in the Flexner Era. New York and London: Tavistock; 1985: 77–8.

23. Gates FT. Corporations (undated). Rockefeller Foundation archives. Frederick T. Gates collection, box 1, folder 17. Rockefeller Archive Center.

24. Gates FT. Philanthropy and civilization (1923). Rockefeller Foundation archives. Frederick T. Gates collection, box 4, folder 79. Rockefeller Archive Center.

25. Corner GW. A History of the Rockefeller Institute, 1901–1953: Origins and Growth. New York: The Rockefeller Institute Press; 1964: 1–29.

26. Flexner A. Medical Education in the United States and Canada. A report to the Carnegie Foundation for the Advancement of Teaching. Bulletin No. 4. Boston; Updyke; 1910.

27. Hudson RP. Abraham Flexner in perspective: American medical education, 1865–1910. Bull Hist Med 1972; 46: 545–61.

28. Harrell GT. Osler's practice. Bull Hist Med 1973; 47: 545–68.

29. Fleming D. William H. Welch and the Rise of Modern Medicine. Boston: Little, Brown and Company; 1954: 171.

30. Flexner A. I Remember. New York: Simon and Schuster; 1940: 176–84.

31. WH Welch to FT Gates, 8 January 1911. Rockefeller Foundation archives. Frederick T. Gates collection, box 3, folder 74. Rockefeller Archive Center.

32. Harvey AM. Science at the Bedside: Clinical Research in American Medicine, 1905–1945. Baltimore: The Johns Hopkins University Press; 1981: 133–87.

33. Lepore MJ. Death of the Clinician: Requiem or Reveille? Springfield, Illinois: Charles C. Thomas; 1982: 20–77.

34. Berliner HS. A System of Scientific Medicine: Philanthropic Foundations in the Flexner Era. New York and London: Tavistock; 1985: 139–61.

35. Ludmerer KM. Learning to Heal: The Development of American Medical Education. New York: Basic Books; 1985: 207–13.

36. Flexner S, Flexner TJ. William Henry Welch and the Heroic Age of Modern Medicine. Baltimore: The Johns Hopkins Press; 1993: 297–328.

37. JD Rockefeller Jr to JD Rockefeller Sr, 2 August 1911, with undated mem-

orandum prepared by FT Gates. Rockefeller Foundation archives. Frederick T. Gates collection, box 3, folder 74. Rockefeller Archive Center.

38. Chesney AM. The Johns Hopkins Hospital and the Johns Hopkins University School of Medicine. A Chronicle. Volume III, 1905–1914. Baltimore: The Johns Hopkins Press; 1963: 176–83.

39. Osler W. The coming of age of internal medicine in America. International Clinics 1915; 4: 1–5.

40. Berliner HS. A System of Scientific Medicine: Philanthropic Foundations in the Flexner Era. New York and London: Tavistock; 1985: 168.

41. FT Gates to W Osler, 13 April 1904. Osler Library of the History of Medicine, McGill University, Montreal.

42. Gates FT. Notes on homeopathy, no. 1 (undated). Rockefeller Foundation archives. Frederick T. Gates collection, box 2, folder 39. Rockefeller Archive Center.

43. Fye WB. William Osler's departure from North America. The price of success. N Engl J Med 1989; 320: 1425–31.

44. Gates FT. Chapters in My Life. New York: The Free Press; 1977: 232.

45. Abrahamson S. Time to return medical schools to their primary purpose: education. Acad Med 1996; 71: 343–7.

46. Wheatley SC. The Politics of Philanthropy: Abraham Flexner and Medical Education. Madison: University of Wisconsin Press; 1988: 102–6.

47. Gates FT. Untitled essay (1925). Rockefeller Foundation archives. Frederick T. Gates collection, box 2, folder 28. Rockefeller Archive Center.

48. Engel GL. How much longer must medicine's science be bound by a seventeenth century world view? In White KL. The Task of Medicine: Dialogue at Wickenburg. Menlo Park, California: Henry J. Kaiser Family Foundation; 1988: 113–36.

49. Elks ML. Rituals and roles in medical practice. Persp Biol Med 1996; 39: 601–9.

50. FT Gates to JD Rockefeller, 28 April 1923. Rockefeller Foundation archives. Frederick T. Gates collection, box 2, folder 36. Rockefeller Archive Center.

51. Gates FT. Appropriations and pledges (Insulin Fund). Rockefeller Foundation archives. Frederick T. Gates collection, box 2, folder 44. Rockefeller Archive Center.

52. Golden RL. Reginald H. Fitz, appendicitis, and the Osler connection—a discursive review. Surgery 1995; 118: 504–9.

William Osler on Jean-Martin Charcot Lessons from *On Chorea and Choreiform Affections*

 Christopher G. Goetz, M.D.

Introduction

The late nineteenth century was marked by major scientific advances in numerous areas of neurobiology.[1] In association with these laboratory- and hospital-based discoveries, the literary, artistic and musical world incorporated a new interest in the function of the brain and anatomical basis of behavior.[2] Whereas this movement was an international one, the medical focal point was France and was embodied in Jean-Martin Charcot and his neurological service at the Salpêtrière hospital in Paris[3] (Figure 1). As the first chaired professor of Clinical Diseases of the Nervous System at the University of Paris, Charcot had established his primacy by delineating multiple sclerosis from Parkinson's disease, defining fundamental clinical-anatomic correlates of several spinal and cortical diseases, and defining amyotrophic lateral sclerosis[3]. Charcot drew to his classroom international medical and scientific luminaries as well as social, political and artistic leaders of his time. In addition, his classroom was populated with younger visitors from France, the rest of Europe, South America, Russia and North America. These young physicians came to study with Charcot and thereby gained experience and the necessary credentials to return home as the next generation of neurologists. From the United States, such figures as J.J. Putnam, M.A. Starr, S.W. Mitchell, and B. Sachs came as visitors.[4]

Based in part on a talk given to the American Osler Society, May 5th, 1999, Montreal. This manuscript was published in a briefer format in the *Annals of Neurology*, *Annals of Neurology* 2000;47: 404–407. Reprinted with permission.

Figure 1: Portraits of William Osler (left) and Jean-Martin Charcot (right). Source: College of Physicians of Philadelphia and Bibliotheque Charcot, Paris

Among the most successful contributors to the field of neurology from this next generation, William Osler (Figure 1) considered himself an internist and never a neurologist *per se*. No more dangerous members of our profession exist than those born into it, so to speak, as specialists"[5] (p. 457). Despite this view, Osler contributed to many areas of the field including studies on cerebral localization, subdural hematomas, brain tumors, cerebrovascular syndromes, peripheral neuropathies and movement disorders[6]. Within this last category, and perhaps the most noteworthy of his neurological contributions was his monograph called *On Chorea and Choreiform Affections*[7] (Figure 2).

Charcot's authority fostered great fidelity and also hostility during his life and after death.[3] As such, contemporary accounts are often webbed with a mixture of idolatry and open anger or cloaked resentment. Because Osler was neurologically adept, but not specifically a neurologist, not trained in Europe, and not a protegé of Charcot, he offers a particularly useful vantage for the modern neurologist to examine Charcot's contributions with a maximal freedom from bias. This study examines Osler's view of Charcot and his role in medicine and science with a primary focus on references from *On Chorea*. The text delineates areas of strong agreement and fundamental disagreement, thereby helping the modern neurologist to place these two men and their different generations into the historical context of the late nineteenth century.

Source documents for this study include the first edition of *On Chorea*, dated 1894 and several materials from Charcot: his formal neurological lectures given in the 1870's–90, compiled by Bourneville as the *Complete Works* or *Oeuvres Complètes*[8]; his impromptu patient demonstration sessions, known as his Tuesday lectures or *Leçons du mardi*[9,10], and additional archival documents drawn from the Bibliothèque Charcot and Académie de Médecine, both in Paris.

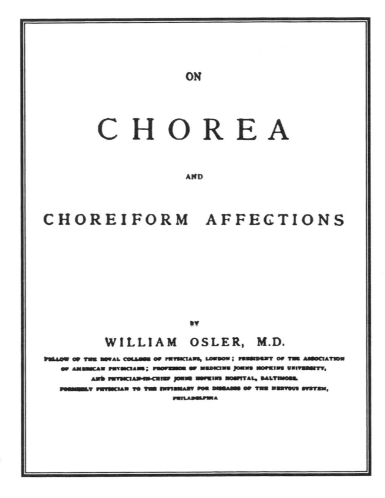

ON

CHOREA

AND

CHOREIFORM AFFECTIONS

BY

WILLIAM OSLER, M.D.

FELLOW OF THE ROYAL COLLEGE OF PHYSICIANS, LONDON; PRESIDENT OF THE ASSOCIATION
OF AMERICAN PHYSICIANS; PROFESSOR OF MEDICINE JOHNS HOPKINS UNIVERSITY,
AND PHYSICIAN-IN-CHIEF JOHNS HOPKINS HOSPITAL, BALTIMORE.
FORMERLY PHYSICIAN TO THE INFIRMARY FOR DISEASES OF THE NERVOUS SYSTEM,
PHILADELPHIA

Figure 2: Frontpiece from Osler's *On Chorea and Choreiform Affections* (1894).

On Chorea

For neurologists, *On Chorea* stands as a unique and important contribution in the English language on a topic that had a long medical history filled with much folklore and misinformation. As Osler himself colorfully described in the opening of the book:

> In the whole range of medical terminology, there is no such *olla podrida* as chorea, which for a century has served as a sort of nosological pot into which authors have cast indiscriminatively[7] (p. I).

In this short monograph, Osler summarized the current knowledge of choreic disorders and supplemented the text with extensive information from his own clinical practice and experience. Although the book was written after he moved to Johns Hopkins Medical School, Osler relied most heavily on his work with S.W. Mitchell at the Philadelphia Orthopedic Hospital and Infirmary for Nervous Disorders. This hospital was the first American civilian neurological specialty hospital and was modeled closely on the Philadelphia military neurological hospital called Turner's Lane that opened and closed in close juxtaposition with the American Civil War.[11] Largely due to Osler's insightful analysis and large patient series on which he published not only clinical but also pathological information, the entity of chorea gained its own phenomenological category in the nosology of neurology, and the specific forms of chorea, Sydenham's and Huntington's as prototypes, became distinctly delineated.

In traditional format, Osler's discussion of chorea was divided into four primary topic areas: Clinical description, Etiology, Treatment and Differential diagnosis. For each area, Osler drew heavily on Charcot and French predecessors, but added his own important contributions to define himself clearly as a new contributor to the field. Osler considered two primary divisions of chorea, childhood and adult, or by eponyms, Sydenham's and Huntington's, chorea. For the first category, the distinguishing clinical hallmarks were its sporadic nature, its association with rheumatic heart disease, and its general self-limitation. In contrast, the adult form of chorea, was familial, associated with dementia, not heart disease, and was a relentlessly progressive disability.

Osler did not deal with two other major categories of choreic disorders. The first, known as chorea major, was a form of hysteria and included the dancing mania and numerous highly rhythmic and bizarre repetitive movements, such as incessant arm waving or body rocking[8]. This topic, one in fact that was extensively studied by Charcot and the French, was dismissed in the introduction. Charcot likewise considered the denomination "chorea" for such conditions improper and placed these conditions nosographically outside the topic of chorea[8]. The second topic, allied to the traditional denomination of chorea but set outside the scope of Osler's text, included the numerous forms of involuntary movements due to degenerative or irritative lesions of the motor cortex. These included cases of what was called posthemiplegic chorea, better named by WA Hammond as athetosis and a wide variety of motor phenomena associated with epilepsy[12].

References to Charcot and the French School

As part of his introduction to the discussion of chorea, Osler reviewed contributions on chorea by various predecessors, writing specifically on Charcot:

> In France the brilliant lectures of Trousseau, but especially the monograph of Sée in 1850 and the extensive article of Roger were among the most important contributions. Charcot and his pupils have contributed enormously to the proper appreciation of the varieties of chorea and to our knowledge of the choreiform affections[7] (p. 5).

Specifically in regard to childhood chorea, Osler credited the French writers, with offering in his words "A the strongest support to the rheumatic theory of the origin of chorea."[7] (p. 14). Charcot himself commented in his impromptu patient interviews, known as the *Leçons du mardi* about the relationship of rheumatism and chorea:

> Rheumatism is part of the past history of this case. We should think of arthritis as a tree whose main branches are gout, rheumatism, certain migraines, skin rashes, etc. On the other hand, the neurological tree has for its branches, neurasthenia, hysteria, epilepsy, all types of mental conditions, progressive paralysis, gait ataxia etc. The two trees live side by side; they communicate through their roots and they interrelate so closely sometimes that one may wonder if the two are not the same tree. If you understand this concept, you will appreciate what occurs in most neurological conditions; without this understanding you will be lost. Whenever you find yourself before a subject with neurological disease, you must consider the

neurological manifestations as only one aspect or phase of a larger illness[9] (lesson of Dec. 6, 1887), [10] (p. 74).

Whereas the studies presented by Sée, Roger, and Charcot clearly showed the association of chorea and rheumatism through individual cases, Osler added his own detailed statistics. Writing on his experience with 554 cases seen in Philadelphia, Osler found 15.5% had a history of rheumatism in the family, 15.8% had a personal history of acute or subacute joint swelling, and 6 % experienced rheumatic pains. Turning to his experience at Johns Hopkins, of 175 cases seen, 18% had a history of arthritis.

In describing the neurological elements of clinical presentation, Osler focused primarily on chorea, weakness, and mental changes. In his description of the chorea, he deferred immediately to the French writers, especially Trousseau who also was lauded by Charcot for his exquisitely rendered clinical descriptions. With regard to the hallmark of weakness in Sydenham's chorea, known as "flaccid chorea", "lump chorea" or "chorée molle" by the French, Osler drew on many sources, emphasizing that patients become feeble, but not paralyzed. The anatomical distribution of weakness, often a monoparesis with flabby and lax muscles that only occasionally had atrophy, had been studied by Charcot's former intern, Fulgence Raymond, and Osler referenced this French source in his presentation[13]. In discussing the wide gamut of mental changes, from apathy to severe restlessness and memory loss, he leaned most prominently on French sources:

> Marcé, whose essay on the subject remains the most important and
> Axenfeld and Huchard laid great stress on hallucinations by day and in the
> intervals between sleeping and waking[7] (p. 35).

Differentiating Sydenham's from Huntington's Chorea

In regard to adult chorea, however, a marked contrast can be seen in Osler's deference to the French, and here Osler looked to American sources, those of Huntington[14], Waters[15] and others as well as the Germanic school[16]. In fact, because of the issues of controversy on the etiology of adult progressive chorea, this section of the monograph represents one of the major areas of neurological disagreement between Osler and Charcot.

Charcot considered primary neurological diseases to be essentially and categorically hereditary in nature[1]. In his concept, predating the wide acceptance of Mendelian genetics, Charcot considered that families with neurological disorders were distinct in that they passed on to each generation a propensity to neurological disorders. This propensity could present itself clinically in the form of any number of diseases that would be seen throughout the family tree as varied manifestations of the same neurological deficit. As such, in discussing Sydenham's chorea, Charcot presented family trees where chorea occurred in the patient being studied, but other family members had such varied manifestations as general paresis, locomotor ataxia, epilepsy or aphasia[9,10]. The propensity for neurological disease in offspring was especially pronounced when the trait could be identified in both sides of the family tree. Importantly, the actual manifestations of neurological disease changed from generation to generation, largely due to hypothesized environmental influences. In Charcot's words, "Each generation may modify the expression of the familial illness"[9] (lesson of Dec 6, 1887),[10] (p. 75).

If this concept appears primitive by modern genetic standards, it was the pivotal anchor of neurological pathogenesis in the nineteenth century. As such, tabes dorsalis, known to be associated with syphilic infections, was not considered to be due to infection per se. Rather the propensity to disease, the neurological trait, was hereditary and the syphilis simply weakened the patient[9,10]. The concept of the constitutional predilection to neurological disease did not end with Charcot, and continued well into the mid-twentieth century as evidenced in the early editions of such texts as Greenfield's *Neuropathology*.[17]

Taking this premise to its logical next step, when Charcot presented cases of adult, progressive chorea, he recognized the work of Huntington, but emphasized the unity, not the distinction, of these adult cases with those of childhood chorea:

> Gentlemen, all that I have said leads me to declare that, in my opinion, Huntington's chorea does not represent a distinct, well-delineated or specific pathological entity to be definitively set apart from a condition like ordinary chorea. It is only an aspect or a single form in the larger sphere of chorea. In other words, it is ordinary chorea with an exceptional presentation of late onset and chronicity in selected families. The predominant or in some cases the exclusive influence of similar hereditary transmission is indeed a remarkable feature, but it does not sufficiently justify our creating a nosographic category[9] (lesson July 17, 1888)[10] (p.85).

Osler fundamentally disagreed. He found that the very gradual and progressive onset of this disorder was totally different than the subacute Sydenham's disease. He felt that gait dysfunction was seen particularly in adult disease, rather than the predominance of rapid movements. Furthermore, there was no characteristic linkage between motor and behavioral manifestations, and Osler found that motor impairment typically far antedated behavioral changes. Today, this feature would be debated, and more selective neuropsychological indices suggest in fact just the opposite[18]. Nonetheless, Osler in his focus on motoric features, even found the involuntary movements to be different in Huntington's and Sydenham's choreas. Acknowledging that indeed the adult patients had involuntary, unpredictable and arrhythmic movements of chorea, he was impressed with the slowness of the movements in contrast to the very rapid jerks of Sydenham's chorea. Neurologists today recognize the bradykinesia that underlies hyperkinesia as one of the hallmarks of Huntington's disease.[19] Secondly, he emphasized that at rest, Huntington's disease patients had few spontaneous movements, unlike the Sydenham's chorea subjects, but in fact developed most of their choreic problems as they moved. Because there was no weakness as in the children, the clinical picture was one of marked adventitial jerking and poor coordination associated with volitional movement. As such, Osler stood up to the preeminent world neurologist of the time and concluded:

> With the exception of Charcot and his pupil Huet, all the writers on chronic progressive chorea regard the disease as totally different from chorea minor, a view which seems to me just when we take into consideration the clinical features particularly the character of the movements, the progressive course, the heredity, and the anatomical lesions[7] (p. 112).

In regard to this last point, the distinction on anatomy is ambiguous, unless Osler meant cardiac lesions, because in both Sydenham's chorea and Huntington's disease, he concluded that there was no specific anatomical lesion that characterized either disorder. He actually published a paper on the pathology in Huntington's disease, but failed to notice caudate atrophy.[20]

Treatment of Chorea

Osler and Charcot concurred that the predominant treatment for the childhood chorea was rest or seclusion therapy. Charcot was a strong advocate of rest therapy and this involved isolating the patient from his home environment, giving a nourishing but modest diet, eliminating all possible stimuli, and encouraging the patient with a supportive staff.[21] The origin of this intervention in neurological therapy has been variously attributed to Charcot himself and to SW Mitchell.[4] The removal from home was considered paramount to Osler who commented:

> The remarkable influence of this procedure in allaying the severity of movements is often seen in hospital practice, and a case which in the outpatient department has seemed of extreme severity has at the end of 2 or 3 days been, without any medication, changed to one of comparative lightness[7] (p. 69).

Charcot emphasized the importance of seclusion from the family, whereas Mitchell emphasized rest. Osler seems to have leaned with his French colleague in writing about the importance of hospitalization and removal of the patient from home:

> In private practice it is a measure usually resented by mothers, and may be very difficult to carry out. I have often insisted, where the family could afford it, upon the presence of a special nurse[7] (p. 69).

In terms of medication, Osler and Charcot agreed that the often recommended treatment with arsenic had little benefit. Osler mentioned the use by others of a wide variety of agents. It is of interest historically that he mentioned that physostigmine was "warmly recommended"[7] (p. 70) by others as beneficial. This observation precedes the recognition of cholinergic/dopaminergic balance at the level of the striatum and the marked, though short-lived, efficacy of parenteral physostigmine in chorea.[21]

Charcot added to the list an extra caveat, and that concerned the avoidance of harmful interventions. A long tradition dating even from the time of Sydenham himself was blood letting in chorea. Charcot noted the danger of this treatment and the weakening of patients:

> Let us throw a veil over Sydenham's therapeutic discussions on bleeding, bleeding and more bleeding. It makes your hair stand on end. How did those little English children survive all that?[9] (lesson of July 17, 1888),[10] (p.90).

Personal Interactions

The usual credentials for a North American physician making an international neurological mark included a visit or study period in the Charcot classroom, and Osler indicated in *On Chorea* that he had visited the Salpêtrière. The exact timing of that visit and the events surrounding it are not documented in materials at the McGill University Library or in the Osler collection of archives at Johns Hopkins University. His first documented trip to Europe was in 1881 when he traveled to London to attend the International Medical Congress.[1] This meeting drew the medical elite of the world and the young stars of the next generation. Charcot was one of the honored guests of this congress, lecturing on syphilic joints and receiving great accolade, including a fireworks display of his portrait[3]. Among the Charcot letters and personal notes in the Bibliothèque Charcot in Paris, there is no correspondence or personal communication from Osler, and likewise no correspondence between Charcot and Osler is documented in the Osler papers at McGill or Johns Hopkins Universities. In terms of the exchange of scientific materials, Charcot had none of Osler's books in his extensive private library and his reprint collection includes only Osler article on Jacksonian epilepsy, marked at the top in Osler's script: "With respects the author." In contrast, however, in the Bibliotheca Osleriana[22] that documents Osler's extensive book collection, Charcot's nine volume Complete Works, his short monograph on faith healing and therapeutic suggestibility, *La foi qui guérit*, and Charcot's essay on syphilic arthropathies are cited.

Charcot's Obituary by Osler

When Charcot died unexpectedly in 1893, Osler authored of an obituary notice written for the Johns Hopkins Medical Bulletin[23] (Figure 3). It is a revealing document that on a cursory reading seems to be a traditional laudatory eulogy. It cites Charcot's influence, his major works, his establishment of a French neurological school, and his noted teaching. In this way, it reads like so many other eulogies printed internationally in the wake of Charcot's death.

But, on closer reading, the essay is draped in words of caution and relativism, with a reevaluation of Charcot as a fine clinician but not a revolutionary medical scientist. This document serves as an important source of Osler's reflections on Charcot's reputation during life and his ultimate role after death. He sets up the context, writing:

> Now and again, there is given to medicine a man whose life and work make an enduring impression, and who, escaping the thralls of nationalism, becomes a cosmopolitan teacher and leader. The latter half of this century has had only three or four such men: Lister in Great Britain, Virchow and Koch in Germany, Pasteur in France—men who have revolutionized medicine by brilliant discoveries[23] (p. 87).

Because this essay is a eulogy, the reader naturally awaits Osler's offering Charcot to be added to this list, but, in fact, his words are different:

> In this select circle, by virtue of extraordinary labors, the suffrages of our Guild, the world over, had placed Jean-Martin Charcot whose sudden death on August the 16th has been so universally deplored[23] (p. 87).

Two points are worthy of emphasis: the subject of the sentence is not Osler but the suffrages, the population of world-wide doctors. Secondly, "had placed" is used rather than "placed", suggesting that even if a majority vote was acknowledged, the placement into this select circle had somehow already ended.

Facts and compliments are showered on Charcot as the essay resumes a traditional character. But the ending returns to this question of where Charcot should sit in the Pantheon of science. Given the introduction, the names of Lister, Pasteur, Virchow, and Koch are clearly on the altar, and Osler's final sentence is:

> The memory of Charcot is secure. It will rest safely cherished beside that of Laennec and Trousseau[23] (p. 88).

SEPTEMBER, 1893.]   JOHNS HOPKINS HOSPITAL BULLETIN.   87

their parents. (4) Each part must have its first principle. Passing over the first, Aristotle answers to the second that healthy children often come from maimed parents. To the third, that while many children resemble their parents, in some the resemblance extends to such things as the voice; and again, that many children resemble ancestors, from whom they can have gotten nothing. Finally, perhaps, in answer to the first argument he adds, "the female has no sperm," and says that this is a convincing proof that sperm does not come from the whole body.

He is an ardent supporter of the doctrine of epigenesis, which maintains that "the actual arises from the potential," as opposed to those who hold the theory of evolution, which conceives of the whole animal as existing in miniature and being gradually unfolded.

His ideas, although imperfect, express in a general way correctly the mode in which the foetus receives nourishment from the mother. He is right in saying that the upper half of the body is developed first, and is nearly correct when he describes the blood as being filtered upon the tissues. As he supposed that the hard shell of an egg was due to the effects of heat, and the soft shell to the effects of cold, so he attributed changes in further development to heat and cold, and thinks that by being dried up by internal heat the tissues become muscles and tendons. Again, deformity, he says, is often caused by an excess of heat. He compares the development of the body to the growth of a picture under the artist's hands, the rough sketch being gradually filled in with the finer details.

The third book is more like a note-book than a piece of set writing. The discussion as to the soul is necessarily unsatisfactory, but he says definitely that there is a sensitive soul and a vital principle (this being perhaps the best translation of the word ψυχή, the meaning of which must, however, be always obscure). He then takes up the question as to the influences which determine the sex of the infant. Empedocles held that sex depended upon the warmth or coldness of the womb; Anaxagoras, that the sperm from the right testicle procreated a male, and that from the left a female child. Democritus thought that everything depended upon the preponderance of the male over the female. Aristotle argues that twins of different sexes are found in the same uterus, thus refuting Democritus, and that men with one testicle have been the fathers of both male and female children.

He criticizes severely the habit of "prophesying from opinion what will be the fact, and anticipating in lieu of observing what the fact is." Unfortunately he then proceeds to set forth opinions which we can only hope are not original; among them that "males are conceived during the prevalence of a north wind, because it is more drying and the secretion is less and therefore the sperm can be better cooked." He is not alone in supposing that hard or soft drinking water had an influence upon sterility.

We are to-night discussing Aristotle as a teacher in medicine and not as a philosopher. Where philosophy could be brought to bear on a subject there Aristotle excels, and we have pointed out how at other times he became entangled by his philosophical bias.

Though he failed to fully carry out his precepts of putting everything to the test of experience, though he accepted too hastily the statements of others, and finally, although if we judge him by his anatomy and physiology we may be tempted to think that the loss of his work on medicine has not been an irreparable one for our science, we cannot but assume, at the risk of incurring the imputation of being *laudatores temporis acti*, that we could better have spared some of the works of those who wrote in a time in which they enjoyed better opportunities and a far greater amount of light.

JEAN-MARTIN CHARCOT.[1]

Now and again there is given to medicine a man whose life and work make an enduring impression, and who, escaping the thralls of nationalism, becomes a cosmopolitan teacher and leader. The latter half of this century has had only three or four such men: Lister in Great Britain, Virchow and Koch in Germany, Pasteur in France—men who have revolutionized medicine by brilliant discoveries and by the introduction of new methods, and who have moulded anew our works and ways, and have widened the horizon of our thoughts. In this select circle, by virtue of extraordinary labors, the suffrages of our Guild, the world over, had placed Jean-Martin Charcot, whose sudden death on August 16th has been so universally deplored.

The facts of his life are briefly these: Born in 1825, the son of a carriage-builder, he received the Paris doctorate in 1853. A year of his *internat* was passed at the Salpêtrière, where he gleaned the material for his graduation thesis on asthenic gout and chronic rheumatism, and doubtless became impressed with its resources as a field for clinical research. In 1853 he was made *chef de clinique*, and in 1856 a hospital physician. In 1860 he was made *professeur agrégé*, and in 1862 physician to the Salpêtrière. In 1872 he was elected Professor of Pathological Anatomy, and in 1882 a special clinical chair of Diseases of the Nervous System was created for him by the Paris faculty. By far the most important event in this list was his election in 1862 as physician to the Salpêtrière, a large asylum for women with chronic maladies of the nervous system; to which, after 1870, were also sent the non-insane epileptics and hysterical patients. Here, in a rich, unexplored mine, he found the work of his life.

Broadly drawn lines divide his labors into three groups: 1, studies in the general pathology and symptomatology of diseases of the abdominal and thoracic organs, particularly in old age; 2, researches on diseases of the brain and spinal cord; and 3, studies on hysteria and hypnotism. So much had the latter subjects absorbed his energies during the past decade, that those not familiar with his life regarded Charcot as a specialist in nervous diseases; but his works on chronic pneumonia, on rheumatism and gout, on endocarditis, on tuberculosis,—in which he remained a consistent unicist—on diseases of the liver and diseases of the kidneys, all characterized by close observation and clear reasoning, remain most important contributions, and are among the most valuable volumes in his collected publications.

In diseases of the spinal cord and brain the following may be mentioned as among the most original of his researches: Localization of the lesions in the spinal cord in the progressive muscular

[1] Memorial notice by Professor Osler.

Figure 3: Obituary notice on Charcot, written by Osler in 1893.

Indeed, Laennec and Trousseau are clinical luminaries, whom Osler respected, and, in fact, Laennec is represented in Osler's Bibliotheca Prima in the Bibliotheca Osleriana. But, in finding a place for Charcot beside these men, Osler strikes him from the spot formerly held on the altar of medical science. In the context of his time, Osler's evaluation was singular in its balance and sobriety. Its content also proved ultimately true, and today, Charcot, and Osler as well, sit most aptly on the tier of great clinicians of medical history.

Osler-Charcot Disease

There is one instance where Osler and Charcot's names are linked in an eponym, and though not related to neurology, it shows the very strong general medical consciousness that both men maintained throughout their careers. Originally known as Hamman-Rich syndrome and its variants, progressive pulmonary fibrosis or fibrosing alveolitis was more recently suggested by Sharma to be more correctly dubbed Osler-Charcot syndrome. More than 50 years before Hamman and Rich, Osler wrote in his textbook of medicine an apparently clear description of the same condition with reference to Charcot:

> In one of Charcot's cases. . . . death occurred about three months and a half after the onset of the acute disease and the lung was two thirds of the normal size, grayish in color, and hard as cartilage. In the only case of the kind which has come under my observation, the patient died about a month from the onset of the chill. The lung was uniformly solid and grayish in color. Microscopically, these areas showed advanced fibroid changes and great thickening of the alveolar cells. . . . [24] (p. 533).

Generations Juxtaposed

Osler's *On Chorea* was published in the United States in 1894, one year after Charcot's death. Simultaneously, other physicians and scientists worldwide were reevaluating Charcot and his contributions. In France, largely due to Charcot's domineering power and unopposed authority during life, a backlash movement occurred, and most of Charcot's students fared poorly in academic medicine in the next generation.[3] Joseph Babinski never received a professorship position in France, and Pierre Marie waited almost his entire career to ascend to the Charcot chair as an aging and bitter man.[25] Much of the neurological writing from the turn of the century and the scientific axes of research in Europe reflected this reaction against Charcot, and several generations passed before his works were reviewed without emotion.[26] This legacy confounds an unbiased analysis of Charcot's long-lasting influences and especially limits a clear understanding of the status of his scientific importance at the turn of the century. Osler's independence from Charcot, his geographical separation from Europe, and his medical, rather than neurological, self-designation provided the necessary distance to provide a solid and scientifically credible critique of Charcot. *On Chorea* exemplifies the transition and passing of the scientific "baton" between two generations on a single neurological topic without political or emotional confounding. With clarity and respect, Osler fully delineated Charcot's contributions on chorea and the clinical and anatomical insights that were embodied in the advances of the nineteenth century. Yet, moving beyond these traditions, Osler represented the next generation of younger and independent physicians, now vested with a clearer understanding of genetics and bacteriology.

References

1. Finger S, *Origins of Neuroscience.* New York, Oxford University Press, 1994.
2. Perrot M. *A History of Private Life.* Cambridge, Harvard University Press

3. Goetz CG, Bonduelle M, Gelfand T. *Jean-Martin Charcot: Constructing Neurology*. New York, Oxford University Press, 1995.

4. Goetz CG. Jean-Martin Charcot and Silas Weir Mitchell. Neurology 1997; 48:1128–1132.

5. Osler W. Remarks on specialism. Boston Med and Surg Journal 1892;126: 457–459.

6 Ebers GC. Osler and Neurology. Canad J Neurol Sci 1985;12:236–242.

7. Osler W. *On Chorea and Choreiform Affections*. Philadelphia, P. Blakiston, Son and Company, 1894

8. Charcot J-M. *Oeuvres Complètes*. Paris, Bureaux du Progrès Médical. (Nine volumes) 1870–1889. In English: J-M Charcot. *Lessons on Diseases of the Nervous System*. Transl Sigurson G, Savill T. London. New Sydenham's Press (1874–1894).

9. Charcot J-M. *Les Leçons du Mardi: 1987–1888, 1888–1889*. Paris, Bureaux du Progrès Médical, 1888, 1889

10. Goetz CG. *Charcot, the Clinician: The Tuesday Lessons*. 1987, New York, Raven Press, 1987.

11. Pappert EJ. Philadelphia Infirmary for Nervous Disease: America's original model of institutional neurology. Neurology 1998;50:1847–1853.

12. Hammond WA. *Treatise on Diseases of the Nervous System*. New York, Appleton, 1871.

13. Raymond F. Danse de St. Guy. *Encyclopédie des Sciences Médicales* Ed. Dechambre (no initials). Paris (no publisher), 1879;(Série I):234–256.

14. Huntingon G. On chorea. Medical and Surgical Reporter 1872;26: 320–321.

15. Waters CO. Description of chorea. In: Dunglison R. *Practice of Medicine*, Philadelphia, Lea and Blanchard, 1842;312–313.

16. Huber A. Chorea hereditaria der Erwachsenen (Huntington'sche chorea). Arch Pathol Anat Physiolog (gathered by R Virchow) 1887;108: 267–285.

17. Greenfield JW. Neuropathology. 1958, E. Arnold, London.

18. Di Maio L, Squitieri F, Napolitano G, Campanella G. Onset symptoms in 510 patients with Huntington's disease. J Med Genet 1993;30:289–292.

19. Thompson PD, Berardelli A, Rothwell JC, Day BL. The coexistence of bradykinesia and chorea in Huntington's disease its implications for theories of basal ganglia control of movement. Brain 1988;111:223–244.

20. Osler W. Remarks on the varieties of chronic chorea, and a report upon two families of the hereditary form with one autopsy. J Nerv Ment Dis 1893;18:97–112.

21. Klawans HL, Rubovits R. Central cholinergic and anticholinergic antagonism in Huntington's chorea. Neurology 1972;22:107–116.

22. Osler W. Bibliotheca Osleriana. Oxford, Clarenden Press, 1929.

23. Olser W. Jean-Martin Charcot. Johns Hopkins Hospital Bulletin 1893;2:87–88.

24. Osler W. Practice of medicine. New York, Appleton 1892.

25. Goetz CG. The Salpêtrière in the wake of Charcot's death. Archives of Neurology 1988;45:444–447.

26. Castaigne P. Introduction au centenaire de la clinique des maladies du système nerveux de la Salpêtrière. Revue Neurolique 1982;57:879–886.

William Osler and *The Cerebral Palsies of Children*

 Lawrence D. Longo, M.D.
Stephen Ashwal, M.D.

"I that am curtailed of this fair proportion,
Cheated of feature by dissembling Nature,
Deform'd, unfinish'd, sent before my time
Into this breathing world, scarce half made up,
And that so lamely and unfashionable,
That dogs bark at me as I halt by them."
(Shakespeare, Richard III, Act 1, Scene I)

Cerebral palsy remains a common and serious neurological disorder in children, characterized by aberrant control of movement or posture appearing early in life (Nelson & Ellenberg, 1978; Volpe, 1987). During the latter portion of the nineteenth century, when both neurology (McHenry, 1969) and pediatrics (Ruhräh, 1925) developed as clinical specialties, cerebral palsy received special attention by two notable physicians, William Osler (1849–1919) and Sigmund Freud (1856–1939), both of whom are known better for their contributions to other areas of medicine. This essay examines the writings of Osler to gain an understanding of his ideas regarding the etiology and pathogenesis of this condition. (We have dealt with both Osler and Freud and the evolution of ideas elsewhere; Longo & Ashwal, 1993). Specific questions which we will address include: What were the late nineteenth century antecedents of Osler's work? What was the basis for Osler's interest in this problem? What were his contributions to classification of this syndrome? What were his contributions to an understanding of the etiology and pathogenesis of this condition? And, what problems did Osler overlook or misunderstand?

Presented at the American Osler Society May 12, 1993, Louisville.

Cerebral Palsy in the Nineteenth Century

The history of cerebral palsy in the early to mid nineteenth century bears comment. Although both Johann Christian Reil (1759–1813) in 1815–1816, and Jean Baptiste Cazauvieilh (?–?) in 1827 reported cerebral atrophy in an individual with congenital paralysis, and Charles Michel Billard (1800–1832) in 1828 described pathological changes in the infant brain, it was Jean Cruveilhier (1791–1874) in 1829, Claude François von Lallemand in 1834, and Carl Rokitansky (1804–1878) in 1835, who first reported isolated cases of cerebral atrophy in children. Later, Eduard Heinrich Henoch (1820–1910) in his 1842 dissertation "De Atrophia Cerebri", described cerebral changes associated with infantile hemiplegia.

A particularly seminal contribution was that of William John Little (1810–1894), a London orthopedist, who in 1843–1844 published his lectures on *Deformities of the Human Frame* (Little, 1843/44; See also Schifrin & Longo, 2000). In the eighth and ninth lectures, Little detailed "a peculiar distortion which affects new-born children which has never been elsewhere described, . . . the spasmodic tetanus-like rigidity and distortion of the limbs of new-born infants, which . . . [he had] traced to asphyxia neonatorum, and mechanical injury to the foetus immediately before or during parturition" (Anonymous, 1854, p 21). In Lecture VIII, Little observed "in many instances the spasmodic affection is produced at the moment of birth or within a few hours or days of that event. . . . The subjects were born at the seventh month, or prior to the end of the eighth month of utero-gestation. In two cases the birth occurred at the full period of gestation, but owing to the difficulty and slowness of parturition the individuals were born in a state of asphyxia, resuscitation having been obtained, at the expiration of two and four hours, through the persevering efforts of the acoucheurs" (Little, 1843–1844, p 319). In lecture IX, Little briefly described spastic diplegia and greater involvement of the lower extremities, among the several types of paralysis (Little, 1843/4, pp 346–349).

The 1853 monograph of Little's lectures, *On the Nature and Treatment of the Deformities of the Human Frame,* contained numerous additions, deletions, and rearrangements of the 1843–44 text, as well as a number of illustrations and several detailed case histories. In addition, Little tabulated data of twenty-four patients with generalized spasticity, noting associations with varying degrees of prematurity (12 cases), difficult protracted labor requiring forceps delivery (7 cases), and severe asphyxia with convulsions (7 cases) (Little, 1853, p 117).

In 1861 Little presented his ideas to the Obstetrical Society of London. In this "learned bombshell" (Neale, 1958, p 23), based on about 200 cases in twenty years practice, Little argued that asphyxia at birth could cause permanent central nervous system damage (Little, 1861/2). He evidenced surprise, that with few exceptions, previous medical authors "seem quite unaware that abnormal parturition, besides ending in death or recovery, not unfrequently has . . . a third termination in other diseases" (p 295). Little's "third termination" included an entire spectrum of long-term deformities and disabilities, which he postulated were secondary to " . . . interruption of the proper placental relation of the foetus to the mother, and non-substitution of pulmonary respiration, [rather] than from direct mechanical injury" (p 298), acting on the brains of "too early and unripe-born foetuses" (p 314). In an appendix, Little tabulated 47 cases of spastic rigidity of the newborn, and 11 related cases.

In the discussion following Little's presentation, one listener recounted a case of a child born with spastic hemiplegia who was shown to have intracerebral bleeding following a "lingering labor" (p 343). However, many of the audience probably agreed with a discussant who stated "the difficulty . . . in discussing this excellent paper, arose, no doubt, from the entire novelty and originality of the subject" (p 342). In closing his report, Little recited the quotation introductory to the present essay, stating that the physique of King Richard III was that of an individual afflicted with such a deformity from birth, and that this was probably a hemiplegia or other palsy secondary to birth asphyxia. Little suggested that in these few lines Shakespeare had outlined the clinical and pathological dimensions of cerebral diplegia. He also referred to Sir Thomas Moore's statement that Richard was born "the feet forward" (p 344). Richard III was also said to have been born prematurely, experiencing a difficult delivery, and requiring resuscitation (Collier, 1924; Accardo, 1980).

About the same time, Jakob von Heine (1799–1879) reported in the second edition of his *Spinale Kinderlähmung*, that symmetrical paralyses of the lower extremities resulted from cerebral rather than spinal disease (Heine, 1860). In 1868, Jean Louis Cotard, under the guidance of Jean Martin Charcot (1825–1893), in his dissertation, *Étude sur l'atrophie cérébrale*, described several conditions causing cerebral paralysis and partial atrophy of the brain. Richard Heschl (1824–1881) introduced the term "porencephaly" for brain lesions characterized by focal cerebral atrophy. (Heschl, 1859). Fairly large series of cases of cerebral paralysis were reported by others (Kundrat, 1882; Audry, 1888; Gaudard, 1884; Wallenberg, 1886), and cerebral sclerosis in children received attention by several French neurologists (Bourneville, 1881; Cotard, 1868; Richardière, 1885; Jendrassik, 1885). Some suggested that congenital hemiplegias might result from localized encephalomalacia secondary to venous congestion, stasis, and thrombosis with hemorrhage (Parrot, 1873; Huxinel, 1877), and that most, if not all, cases of spastic paraplegia in infancy were due to ". . . a porencephalous defect of the cortical motor centres" (Ross, 1882, p 491). In 1885, Ernst Adolf Strümpell (1853–1925) provided a fresh impetus to the study of these disorders by claiming that they were a form of central nervous system infection, which he termed "polioencephalitis" (Strümpell, 1885). That same year, William Richard Gowers (1845–1915), of London, mentioned eight cases of seizures occurring soon after birth ". . . the labor in several of these cases having been difficult, and in some the forceps applied" (Gowers, 1885, p 18). Several years later he reported that the majority of patients with birth palsies were first-born children (Gowers, 1888).

Thus, until the 1880s, there remained much uncertainty about a confusing array of severe neurological conditions seen in young children. There was no systematic classification of these disorders, nor any determinable correlation between clinical presentation and neuropathology. The importance of pre- and perinatal factors was unclear, as was the distinction between congenital and acquired forms of these disorders. Although there was reluctant acceptance that these diseases were "cerebral", rather than "spinal" in origin, the role of hemorrhage of the brain or spinal cord was questioned. In addition, at this time few appreciated or understood the contributions of Little in defining diplegia and hemiplegia.

Osler's Interest in Cerebral Palsy

William Osler, the great clinician, educator, and historian, had a considerable interest in both neurology and pediatrics. Following his graduation from

McGill University School of Medicine in 1872, Osler had worked in London with John Scott Burdon-Sanderson (1828–1905), and in Berlin under Rudolph Ludwig Karl Virchow (1821–1902), and others. From 1874 to 1884, he taught physiology and pathology at McGill and pursued research in pathology. Osler's experience under Virchow and others helped to develop his conviction of the need to correlate pathological findings with clinical symptoms. This approach became the essence of his method, and undoubtedly played a key role in his success as a diagnostician. Of his 1200 papers and books, 100 concern pediatric topics (Robbins & Christie, 1963).

From 1884 to 1889, Osler was Professor of Medicine at the University of Pennsylvania. During this time in Philadelphia, he described at length three basic categories of muscular atrophy: pseudohypertrophic muscular dystrophy, Erb's disease, and Duchenne's disease (Osler, 1885), concluding that they were similar. He also wrote on Friedreich's ataxia (Osler, 1888b), Thomsen's disease (Osler, 1886), and rare forms of idiopathic atrophy involving the face and scapulohumeral muscles (Osler, 1889c). In addition, Osler wrote on idiocy and feeblemindedness (Osler, 1889b), and later produced his well-regarded monograph on chorea (Osler, 1894).

As part of his responsibilities, Osler cared for patients at the Infirmary for Nervous Diseases in Philadelphia. In 1888, he delivered a series of five lectures at the Infirmary on *The Cerebral Palsies of Children*, which he published in the *Medical News* of Philadelphia (Osler, 1888a). This was the first use of the term "the cerebral palsies", and applied collectively to a group of disorders. [A short report of "cerebral birth palsy" appeared in Britain the same year Osler's lectures were published (Burgess, 1888; see Wolf, 1969)]

Osler's lectures were published as a monograph the following year (Osler, 1889a). In this work Osler followed a pattern of his other writings. He classified the cases, presented brief clinical descriptions of the natural course of the disorder from his own experience, described the pathological findings, and reviewed the pertinent literature. The 1889 monograph contains only minor changes from the lectures published the previous year. For instance, he added case No. 20 to the bilateral spastic hemiplegia series (p 69), and added a few topical headings throughout the text. In the original publication, Osler credited one of his residents Charles Walts Burr (1861–1944) for "much valuable assistance in the preparation of these lectures" (Osler, 1888a, p 29). This acknowledgment did not appear in the 1889 volume.

In *The Cerebral Palsies* Osler reviewed 151 cases, both his own and those from the literature (120 of infantile hemiplegia, 20 of bilateral spastic hemiplegia, and 11 of spastic paraplegia). These he classified by distribution/location, correlating them with the neuroanatomical pathology. Many of the patients described were from the Pennsylvania Institution for Feeble-Minded Children at Elwyn, which may explain why a large number showed severe mental retardation. Osler credited Strümpell's 1884 paper with arousing his interest in the problem. He also referenced other reports (Gaudard, 1884; Wallenberg, 1886) as stimulating his thinking in this regard (Osler, 1889a, pp 40–43).

Infantile Hemiplegia

Osler devoted Chapters I and II to infantile hemiplegia (55 pp), categorizing the cases by age of onset. Regarding etiology, among the "congenital cases", 10

of 15 had a history of birth injury, although only a limited number were associated with intrauterine disease or an accident during parturition. In regard to
abnormal pregnancy in the pathogenesis of the condition, he noted "it is very
doubtful how far such influences can be connected with affection of the child"
(p 6). Osler associated paralysis and mental defects with difficult or abnormal
labor, noting that his colleague Wharton Sinkler (1847–1910) (1875, 1885,
1887) had called attention to this subject. Six of nine infants delivered by forceps in this series, were injured during delivery. Osler also reviewed 50 cases
which occurred after the first year of life (p 4), including following a childhood
infectious disease (p 14) or head injury (pp 12–13). He also associated several
cases which began with teething or with convulsions. (p 26).

With respect to physical signs of infantile hemiplegia, Osler noted that
the face was not always affected, ". . . the residual paralysis is most marked in
the *arm* . . . The *leg*, as a rule, recovers more rapidly and more completely than
the arm, and the palsy may completely disappear . . . . *Rigidity* . . . [is] so marked
. . . [a] feature of spasm that the disease has been termed spastic infantile hemiplegia. . . . The rigidity disappears during sleep [and is] . . . increased by emotion . . . " (pp 34–35). "*Sensation* is not often disturbed . . ." (p 36). Osler
observed that speech was affected in 13 cases, five of which were under three
years of age, and epilepsy was "One of the most common and distressing symptoms" (p 40). Osler reviewed the early diagnostic features of hemiplegia,
including: frequent onset with convulsions, absence of rapid muscle wasting,
and a response to electrical stimulation. Later signs included: muscle rigidity,
hyperactive reflexes, characteristic gait, distribution of residual palsy, impaired
intellect, and relatively frequent seizures. He noted that some cases, particularly those of monoplegia, presented diagnostic difficulties (p 53). In regard to
prognosis, Osler observed that the younger the subject, the greater the liability
to serious and permanent damage. He recorded, "Not only are the attacks dangerous in themselves, but they undoubtedly tend to aggravate existing mental
defects" (p 55).

Concerning the morbid anatomy of infantile hemiplegia, Osler observed, "although the clinical features . . . are well characterized . . . our
knowledge of the pathological conditions on which the former depends is, in
comparison, still very defective" (p 43). He continued, "The great majority of
the post-mortems have been made after the hemiplegia has lasted for months
or years, when all trace of the primitive lesion has disappeared" (p 43). Osler
analyzed the records of 90 autopsies in cases of hemiplegia which developed
in infancy or childhood, extending the list of 48 autopsies reported earlier
(Wallenberg, 1886). He grouped the lesions according to: embolism, thrombosis, and hemorrhage (16 cases), atrophy and sclerosis (50 cases), and
porencephaly (24 cases). He reviewed the reports on porencephaly by previous workers, listing 6 cases as congenital, 11 cases in early life following
seizures, with most cases showing changes in the distribution of the middle
cerebral artery (pp 45–50).

Osler recognized Strümpell's theory of polioencephalitis, a cerebral counterpart of the spinal variety, was plausible and supported by the occurrence of
this disorder following infectious diseases (see also Osler 1886). Nonetheless, he
cautioned that the pathological changes seen were, in most instances, necrotic
rather than inflammatory. After mentioning the evidence for cerebrovascular
embolism and thrombosis, he observed that the proof of pathogenesis was lack-
ing; the demonstration of it had yet to be made. In an effort to get at the causes
of paralysis and rigidity in these cases, Osler also noted the need to study the
pyramidal tracts in the spinal cord and spinal centers.

Bilateral Spastic Hemiplegia

In Chapter III, Osler described 20 cases of what others referred to as "spastic rigidity of the newborn", "spastic diplegia", or "Little's disease". Many of these were associated with difficult deliveries, some instrumental, one with kernicterus. He noted that the great majority of these cases occurred within the first three years of life, and that in contrast to infantile hemiplegia, a large proportion arose at birth from injury at time of delivery. Osler credited Little for establishing their relation to abnormal parturition, and Heine (1860) for recognizing their cerebral origin. He noted that in bilateral spastic hemiplegia the extremities were spastic, the legs were involved more than the arms, sensation was preserved, reflexes were hyperactive, and intelligence was often low.

In summarizing his findings of the speech of children with spastic diplegia, two spoke plainly, six with difficulty, 13 not at all (p 70). Osler collated reports of 16 autopsies of this condition, recording that "destruction of the motor centres of the cortex" was "the essential lesion" (p 74). He also noted the common features of diffuse cerebral atrophy with sclerosis, and in some cases diffuse sclerosis, and/or porencephaly.

Spastic Paraplegia

In Chapter IV, Osler defined this condition as spastic paralysis of the lower extremities dating from birth or within the first years of life. Clinically, the patients had varying degrees of talipes equinus or equino-varus deformities, adductor spasm, a stiff gait, and toe walking. Although the intellect was impaired, it was not as severe as in bilateral hemiplegia. Osler presented 11 case reports, stating that 24 of Little's patients were in this category (p 82). In figures he presented footprints of the scissoring gait of two such patients. Case 9 in Figure 5 walked on the toes and balls of her feet, while Case 11, Figure 6, planted the entire sole of the foot on the ground. Regarding the morbid anatomy, Osler reviewed autopsy findings from a single case in the literature, which showed a "moderate grade of general cortical sclerosis, with slight dilatation of the ventricles" (p 86).

Pathology

In Chapter V, Osler considered pathology, reviewing the autopsy findings of Elwyn inmates by Alfred W. Wilmarth (1855–1896). Osler recorded

> . . . we are impressed, on the one hand, with the extent to which sclerotic and other changes may exist without symptoms if the motor areas are spared, and, on the other hand, with the degree of permanent disability which may exist with even slight affection of this region. Our knowledge is so limited to the appearances and states years after the onset of the symptoms, the final results of processes long past, that we are scarcely in a position to discuss accurately, in all its aspects, the pathology of this interesting group of cases. It is something, however, to get an outline for our ignorance and to ascertain in which direction facts are needed to sustain, or, it may be, to upset our theories" (p 88).

Concerning the role of intracranial hemorrhage in the pathogenesis of these disorders, Osler concluded that for palsies associated with birth, ". . . the evidence points strongly to meningeal haemorrhage as one of the chief causes of this disorder", while it accounted for only a small percentage of cases of hemiplegia in older children (p 89). He noted the association at birth of difficult deliveries, asphyxia requiring prolonged resuscitation, and seizures. His review of cases from the literature noted arachnoid and subarachnoid bleeding, but made no mention of intraventricular bleeding. In a cautionary note, Osler admitted "unfortunately we are . . . entirely without information upon the state of the brains of children dying during or shortly after the attack; and the question resolves itself into an explanation of the conditions most commonly met with years after the onset, *viz.* sclerosis and porencephalus" (p 92).

Osler briefly mentioned treatment, advocating supportive therapy, warmth, massage, and electricity to maintain the nutrition of the paralyzed limbs. He played down the potential for surgical relief of cortical epilepsy, observing "the nature of the lesion is such that not much can be anticipated" (p 102). He concluded that the lesson to be learned from these cases was ". . . with patient training and kind care many of these poor victims may be rescued from a condition of hopeless imbecility and reach a fair measure of intelligence and self-reliance" (p 103).

Osler's Further Contributions

In 1889 Osler moved to the Johns Hopkins University School of Medicine where, as professor of medicine, he helped to develop this as the first truly academic medical institution in the United States and, in the process, to transform medical education throughout the country. In *The Principles and Practice of Medicine* of 1892, which became the most influential textbook of medicine in its time, Osler devoted several pages to cerebral palsy. He admitted problems with classification of this group of disorders, and a lack of understanding of the primary pathological changes. Of hemiplegia, he summarized the findings from his 1888 series, adding 15 or so cases from his Baltimore experience. Osler used the term "spastic diplegia" for what previously he called "bilateral spastic hemiplegia". He noted, "the cases usually date from birth, and a majority are born in first labors or are forceps cases" (p 909). Again, Osler ascribed the condition to meningeal hemorrhage, with sclerosis developing secondary to brain compression by blood clots (Osler, 1892a, pp 906–911).

Osler's thinking regarding the cerebral palsies was undoubtedly influenced by his Philadelphia colleagues Sinkler and Silas Weir Mitchell (1829–1914), and by Sarah J. McNutt (1839–1930) of New York. Osler had dedicated his monograph to S. Weir Mitchell "in grateful acknowledgement of innumerable acts of friendly service". He also credited Mitchell and Sinkler for the use of some of their cases. Sinkler, in 1875, had published *On the Palsies of Children* (Sinkler, 1875). In this report of 140 cases of paralysis in young children, many of whom were from the Infirmary for Nervous Diseases, he included two "congenital" cases, as well as three cases of "cerebral hemiplegia" which were "apparently the result of forceps in delivery" (p 360). In an 1885 paper to the Obstetrical Society of Philadelphia, Sinkler had considered briefly the cerebral palsies which "may result from some injury at the time of birth, either from forceps or from pressure of a prolonged labor" (Sinkler, 1885, p 523). Subsequently, he reiterated this theme in the discussion of a paper on "Injuries of the Foetus during Labor", observing "a very large proportion of the cases of paralysis . . . in infants, have followed instrumental or prolonged and difficult labors" (Sinkler, 1887, p 579).

Probably the most convincing evidence in this regard came from McNutt, who in 1885 published two papers which subsequently were quoted by Osler and others. In "Apoplexia Neonatorum", which she delivered to the American Neurological Association, McNutt reviewed ten cases of spastic hemiplegia associated with prolonged or difficult delivery of term or near-term infants. Three of the cases were breech deliveries. Most of the infants lived less than a week, and each was shown to have sustained intracerebral hemorrhage, either at the base of the brain or over the cerebral hemispheres. One child had intraventricular hemorrhage (McNutt, 1885a). McNutt presented a two and a half year old child who had suffered a traumatic delivery and clinically showed severe bilateral spastic cerebral palsy and marked developmental retardation. The autopsy showed marked severe generalized atrophy of the brain. She correlated this autopsy with another patient, that of an infant who died on the 28th day of life. The infant had been born by an easy delivery, had convulsions on the fourth day and on the twelfth day developed a left-sided hemiplegia. At autopsy, a large hemorrhage had destroyed much of the right hemisphere. McNutt concluded that had this child survived she would have been severely compromised and shared the severe neuropathological abnormalities seen in the first patient. Moreover, she concluded that meningeal hemorrhage was a common cause of spastic and diplegic forms of cerebral palsy (McNutt, 1885a.).

Subsequently, McNutt reported an additional case which developed seizures and paralysis following a difficult breech delivery, and subsequently lived two and one-half years. The brain showed severe cerebral atrophy in the region of the rolandic fissure. She tabulated 34 other reports from the literature with autopsy findings, categorizing them as to whether the condition occurred antepartum, intrapartum, or postpartum. Among this latter group, she acknowledged the reports of Little (1862) and Ross (1882) in suggesting hemorrhage from injury during the birth process (McNutt, 1885b). Gowers in his lecture "Birth Palsies" acknowledged McNutt's contribution as ". . . by far the most valuable contribution to medical science that the profession has yet received from its members of her sex." (Gowers, 1888, p 710).

Years later, Hector Charles Cameron (1878–1958) recounted that in 1913 Sir William Osler, Regius Professor of Medicine at Oxford, "recommended me to make a special study of children with cerebral palsies . . . ", as "he knew of no group of sufferers who responded more quickly to care and training". Osler also urged Cameron to read Little's original paper on the subject (Cameron, 1958).

Freud's Interest in Cerebral Palsy

Sigmund Freud also had a long-standing interest in neuroanatomy, neurology, and neuropathology, prior to his many contributions to psychiatry (Amacher, 1965; Bernfield, 1973; Jelliffe, 1937), which we have considered elsewhere (Longo & Ashwal, 1993). Briefly, during his medical studies at the University of Vienna from 1873 to 1881, Freud spent an extra three years working in the laboratory of Ernst Wilhelm von Brücke (1819–1892) on problems of neuroanatomy. Upon completion of his doctorate in 1881, he worked at the Vienna General Hospital, and in 1883 was appointed Junior Sekundärarzt in

Theodor Hermann Meynert's (1833–1892) department where he continued to conduct original neuroanatomical studies. Using an idea from Paul Emil Flechsig (1847–1929), he developed a new histological staining technique using gold chloride, devoting the next two years to studies of brain stem nerve tracts. Freud, realizing that in the fetal brain only a few myelinated tracts were initially present in the medulla, used this model to study the process of myelination, as well as to understand better the complex organization of these pathways (Freud, 1885a). In a related paper, Freud traced the pathways of the inferior cerebellar peduncle, showing for the first time its complex connections with the posterior columns and cerebellum (Darkschewitsch & Freud, 1886). In a third paper, Freud demonstrated that the four sensory cranial nerves (trigeminal, acoustic, glossopharyngeal, and vagal) were homologous with the dorsal root ganglia of the spinal cord (Freud, 1886b). Overall, these studies helped to pave the way for the neuron theory (Bernfield, 1973). For about a year Freud also studied clinical neurology and neuropathology, and acquired a reputation as a superb and accurate clinician.

In the winter of 1885–1886, Freud studied in Paris at the Salpêtrière, attending the "Lessons" of Jean Martin Charcot (1825–1893), who was at the height of his fame and capabilities. Upon learning that Charcot was interested in someone translating the third volume of these lectures into German, Freud quickly volunteered. In his letter to Charcot supporting his abilities, Freud admitted "Concerning my capacity for this undertaking it must be said that I . . . have motor aphasia in French, but not sensory aphasia" (Jones, 1953, p 209). Charcot agreed, and shortly thereafter Freud completed "Neue Vorlesungen über die Krankheiten des Nervensystems, insbesondere über Hysterie" (New Lectures on the Diseases of the Nervous System). Freud took pride in the fact that his translation appeared several months before the French edition (Charcot, 1886, 1872–87).

Freud also spent several weeks in Berlin at the pediatric clinic of Adolf Baginsky (1843–1919). On his return to Vienna, he accepted a position as head of a new neurological department in the first public Institute for Children's Diseases. In 1888, while at the Institute, Freud described for the first time the association of hemianopsia and cerebral palsy in two children (Freud, 1888). He discussed localization of the lesion, and also grouped the cases with those of the unilateral cerebral paralyses of children, which he was now beginning to study in more detail. Between 1891 and 1897 Freud published three monographs and several papers on cerebral palsy. The first was written in collaboration with Oscar Rie, a pediatrician at the Children's Institute (Freud & Rie, 1891a). Thirty-five cases seen by Freud formed the basis of this study, which included an exhaustive review of the literature, and an analysis of the clinical presentation, neuropathology, differential diagnosis, and treatment. The report focused on the hemiplegic form of cerebral ; and they described a new form of cerebral palsy "choreatiform paresis", in which the patients showed evidence of hemichorea, rather than paralysis which had been present earlier. In this work, the authors also stated that many children who were diagnosed as epileptic, actually had this movement disorder and were being misdiagnosed, and rejected Strümpell's view that polioencephalitis could cause cerebral hemiplegia.

Two years later, Freud published a 168 page monograph concentrating primarily on the cerebral diplegias of children (Freud, 1893a), detailing 53 cases which he had observed. Freud divided cerebral palsy into four groups: 1) general cerebral spasticity ("Little's disease"), 2) paraplegic spasticity, due to bilateral cerebral lesions, a condition that previously had been called "spastic tabes", and erroneously regarded as due to spinal cord disease, 3) bilateral spastic hemiplegia, and 4) generalized congenital "chorea" and bilateral athetosis. Freud showed that there was no specific etiology or neuropathological correlate for any of these clinical presentations.

In 1897, Freud published a lengthy review "Infantile Cerebral Paralysis" for Wilhelm Hermann Nothnagel's 24 volume *Handbuch der Allgemeinen Specielle Pathologie und Therapie.* (Freud, 1897a). The work was also published as a separate monograph, and is essentially the last original work that Freud published in neurology (Freud, 1897b). *Die infantile Cerebrallähmung* was a monumental work, 327 pages in length and divided into ten chapters (Freud, 1897b). Most importantly, he emphasized the need to classify these disorders based on a careful unifying clinicopathological framework.

Freud examined in detail possible mechanisms between the initial precipitating events and the final pathological picture, doing this for all known forms of cerebral palsy and most of the previously described pathologies. He summarized the major pathologic entities and attempted to outline a classification based on etiologies, dividing the cases into three broad groups, congenital, those related to some difficulty that occurred at birth and those that were subsequently acquired. He reviewed the various infectious etiologies of the acquired forms of cerebral palsy, including syphilis, and further explored the concept and importance of Little's disease. He also considered the distribution of pathological changes and clinical symptoms, recognizing that there was limited correlation.

Several major themes recur throughout this work. Freud showed that there was no definitive relation between etiological factors and the type of deficit. He demonstrated transitional forms of cerebral palsy that others had considered distinct entities either clinically or pathologically. He correlated the degree of mental impairment with the degree of motor deficit. He described how an infant's clinical symptoms could change over time as a function of development. He credited Little with drawing attention to the importance of prematurity and birth asphyxia as causes of cerebral palsy, but also proved that in many cases no etiology could be determined. He emphasized the relation of cerebral diplegia to prematurity, and of spastic quadriplegia to a combination of prematurity and birth injury.

Freud's monograph was a superb achievement and alone would suffice to assure his name a permanent place in clinical neurology (Jones, 1953, p 219). By this time however, his interests had already shifted toward psychiatry, and it was with some effort that he completed the task. For instance, in a letter to Wilhelm Fliess (1858–1928) he complained "I am fully occupied with the children's paralysis, in which I am not the least interested" (Bonaparte, 1954, p 134). "The completely uninteresting work on children's paralysis has taken all my time" (Bonaparte, 1954, p 169). In a subsequent letter he recorded that he felt like "Pegasus yoked to the plough!" (Bonaparte, 1954, p 170).

Osler's Classification of Cerebral Palsy

It was not happenstance that Osler (and also Freud) made major contributions concerning the cerebral palsies of children. In view of the confusion about these disorders which existed in the late nineteenth century, perhaps Osler's most significant contribution was his attempt to categorize the various clinical forms of cerebral palsy which had been described. This was not a simple task. Not only were clinical neurology and pediatrics just developing as fields of medicine, but neuropathology was just emerging as a distinct discipline with many of the standard histological techniques still being developed and applied. Also, for all practical purposes, interest in the diseases of the new-born were viewed rather fatalistically, attracted limited interest, and rarely were post-mortem neuropathological studies performed. Considering these circumstances, it was an important achievement that, at the same time that Charcot was bringing order to adult neurology by his insistence on neurological taxonomy, Osler and Freud were applying these methods to the most common and devastating neurological disorder affecting children.

Osler's five articles in 1888, reprinted in monograph form in 1889, on three categories of cerebral palsy (hemiplegia, bilateral spastic hemiplegia, spastic paraplegia) was the first well-defined description of these entities in the medical literature. Osler was well aware that Gowers was writing on the same topic for the *Lancet,* and one suspects a degree of competitiveness in the organization and writing up of this material on Osler's part (Cushing, 1925). In a systematic fashion, Osler discussed the pathology and clinical correlates of each of three major forms of cerebral palsy. He was cognizant of movement disorders as part of this general condition, but chose to include them under the category of "post-hemiplegic movements" rather than as a distinct category (Osler, 1889a, p 30). Included here were children with post-hemiplegic tremor, chorea, and mobile spasm and athetosis. Also of importance, Osler stressed the clinical and pathological differences between spastic paraplegia and bilateral spastic hemiplegia in reference to etiologies and prognosis and associated neurological deficits. In short, Osler's compilation was the first lucid and critical analysis that initiated the beginnings of a system of classification of these disorders.

Generalized or paraplegic rigidity or "Little's disease" or what we now would refer to as "spastic diplegia" could be distinguished from bilateral or double hemiplegia by the greater involvement of the lower extremities. In addition the patients with bilateral hemiplegia were more likely to have more severe neurological impairment with marked spasticity, corticobulbar involvement, mental retardation, and epilepsy. These classifications remain more or less in use today although they have over the past ninety years undergone modification (American Academy of Cerebral Palsy, 1956).

Osler's Recognition of the Role of Vascular Pathology

Osler in his studies on cerebral palsy had examined 90 brains and found vascular lesions in 16 of them, with seven being due to hemorrhage and nine to embolism. However he also realized that a large number of the cystic conditions may be due to hemorrhage or embolism, and that many cases quoted as typical atrophy or porencephalus may also belong to the same category (Osler, 1889a; See also Sachs 1895, p 542). Osler was also cognizant of the important observations made by Gowers that thrombosis of the superficial cerebral veins was another vascular etiology of cerebral palsy. Also worthy of mention in reference to fetal cerebrovascular compromise is another case described by Osler of a pregnant woman who died of typhoid fever during the sixth month of pregnancy. Within the left cerebral hemisphere of the fetus was a "cavity with ragged, irregular walls containing a large recent clot which had broken through the ganglia into the lateral ventricle of the same side . . . no special changes were noted in the arteries" (Sachs & Hausman, 1926, p 224). The implication of this case was that maternal infection could have a profound effect on the fetus and that one complication was that of fetal cerebral hemorrhage.

Osler also examined the issue as to whether traumatic delivery was associated with cerebral palsy. He had obtained a history of forceps delivery in nine out of 15 patients with hemiplegic cerebral palsy. However in only three of these patients did he believe that brain injury was due to trauma (Ingram, 1964, p 24).

Related Phenomenon

Osler had collected a series of patients in whom cerebral palsy was associated with abnormal movements. At the time, the terminology used by others was that of "double athetosis" or "chorea spastica". Osler referred to these patients as having spastic diplegias plus post-hemiplegic disorders of movement. He noted that "the history is the same as in ordinary cases; the trouble has persisted from birth or shortly after and there is a condition of feeble-mindedness or idiocy, though in some instances the intelligence is fair. Very often there has been difficult labor (Osler, 1889a; Ingram, 1964, p 290). He then presented five typical cases and also commented on the presence of abnormal teeth in these cases, a subject that has recently attracted renewed epidemiological interest. It is interesting to note that in his case 18, there is the first mention of jaundice in infancy as a possible etiological factor. However, as noted by Ingram, it is likely that Osler may not have realized its significance as he cryptically glossed over this point: " . . . had jaundice when eleven days old, after which the paralysis occurred" (Osler, 1889a, p 67; Ingram, 1964, p 290).

Both Osler and Freud believed that children with cerebral palsy suffered a much higher incidence of convulsions and that this was one of its most serious complications. There was, however, a point of disagreement between Osler and Freud. Osler (as well as Sachs) firmly believed that convulsions in themselves could cause cerebral palsy. Freud, in his 1891 monograph, disagreed believing that although there might be a temporal relation this did not provide sufficient proof of causation (Freud, 1968, p 124; Sachs & Hausman, 1926, p 226).

Controversies About Cerebral Palsy

In both the United States and in England, the work of Sarah McNutt had gained wide acceptance. Freud strongly disagreed. In his 1897 monograph, Freud showed that McNutt's patients suffering from subdural hemorrhages did not have either generalized rigidity or bilateral hemiplegia and that the patient who did have generalized rigidity did not have such bleeding. In searching the world's literature, Freud was also unable to find cases to support McNutt's contention of meningeal or subdural hemorrhage as a cause of spastic diplegia and did not believe this to be a major factor (Collier, 1924, p 7).

What Aspects of Cerebral Palsy Did Osler Overlook or Misunderstand?

Although Little had drawn attention to prematurity and birth asphyxia as important factors causing cerebral palsy, neither Osler nor Freud considered the significance of maternal disease during pregnancy as an important etiological factor. Osler mentions in passing "abnormal conditions" of the mother, "accidents", "sudden fright", or "unusual mental distress" (Osler, 1889a, p 5), but then states that "... it is very doubtful how far such influences can be connected with the affection of the child". One case in which both parents had a "marked history of alcoholism" and another case in which the mother may have had syphilis were reported. Considering that many of Osler's patients with congenital cerebral palsy had no specific etiology determined, it is surprising that he neither alluded to nor studied these "maternal influences" in greater detail. However, in general it was not until the early 1900s that this area of obstetrics received more attention and investigation (Ballantyne, 1902–04).

Hemorrhage, thrombosis, and embolism were the vascular pathologies recorded by both Osler and Freud, and much was made of the work of Sarah McNutt and meningeal hemorrhage. What is striking from our current perspective is the almost complete absence either in the literature of the time or in either Osler's or Freud's cases, of the mention of intraventricular or subependymal hemorrhage as possible etiologies. Osler and Freud both recognized that intraparenchymal hemorrhages were recognizable lesions but neither reported evidence of intraventricular blood.

Both Osler and Freud were remarkable in their ability to analyze large amounts of personal clinical material and compare this to literature on cerebral palsy. One striking omission, however, is the lack of mention of either spinal cord or brachial plexus injuries, either as additional injuries to the young child's nervous system, or in reference to the differential diagnosis of palsy or paralysis. Although giving credence to the importance of cranial trauma, there is no mention of cord or plexus injuries, problems which were discussed in detail by Gowers in his *Lancet* papers on "Birth Palsies" (1888), with which Osler and Freud were familiar. Perhaps these omissions were intentional, as their monographs were focused on the "cerebral" aspect of these palsies. The later works of Ehrenfest on *Birth Injuries of the Child* (1922) and Ford, Crothers, and Putnam (1927) drew attention to the importance of both of these phenomena.

Cerebral Palsy's Heritage From Osler

Osler's legacy to generations interested in the cerebral palsies of children is considerable. His prominence and authority helped, once and for all, to designate the "cerebral" rather than "spinal" causes for these disorders. He initiated a system of clinical classification which, with modifications, is still in use today. He provided careful clinical descriptions, added new terminology, and correlated the motor deficits with other neurological symptoms. Of equal, if not more, importance was the contribution to the clinicopathological study of these disorders. He impartially dissected theories, weighed the historical and contemporary evidence of others, and incorporated their own personal observations to formulate reasonable and balanced theories as to the etiologies of the congenital and acquired forms. This consolidation of the literature and development of a conceptual framework were responsible, in part, for the explosion of interest in these disorders as manifested by the fact that during the early years of the twentieth century, several thousand books and articles on cerebral palsy were published (Wolf, 1969, p 7). Osler's interest, analysis, and publications in this area had a not inconsiderable influence on determining the future scope and direction of clinical and pathological research in this field over the past century.

References

Accardo, P.M. Deformity and character. Dr. Little's diagnosis of Richard III. *JAMA* 244:2746–2747, 1980.

Amacher, P. Freud's neurological education and its influence on psychoanalytic theory. *Psychological Issues* 4:9–87, 1965.

American Academy of Cerebral Palsy, 1956.

Anonymous. Biographical sketch of W.J. Little, M.D. *Lancet* 1:16–22, 1854.

Audry, J. Les porencephalies. *Rev. Méd.* 8:462–488, 1888.

Ballantyne, J.W. *Manual of Antenatal Pathology and Hygiene.* Vol. I, *The Foetus,* Vol. II, *The Embryo,* Edinburgh, Wm. Green & Sons, 1902–1904.

Bernfield, S. Freud's scientific beginnings. In: *Freud As We Knew Him,* Ruitenbeek, H.M. (Ed), Detroit, Wayne State University Press, 1973, pp 222–248.

Billard, C.M. *Traité des maladies des enfans nouveau-nés et à la mamelle,* Paris, J.B. Baillière, 1828.

Bonaparte, M. , A. Freud, and E. Kris. *The Origins of Psycho-analysis. Letters to Wilhelm Fliess, Drafts and Notes: 1887–1902 by Sigmund Freud.* London, Imago Publishing Co. Ltd., 1954.

Bourneville, D.M. and E. Brissaud. Contribution a l'étude de l'idiotie. *Arch. Neurol.* 1:69–91, 1881.

Burgess, D. A case of cerebral birth palsy. *Med. Chron. Manchester* 9:471, 1888–89.

Cameron, H.C. Spasticity and the intellect. Dr. Little versus the obstetricians. *Cerebral Palsy Bull* 1:1–5, 1958.

Cazauvieilh, J.B. Recherches sur l'agénésie cérébrale et la paralysie congénitale. *Arch. Gén. Méd.* 14:5–33, 347–366, 1827.

Charcot, J.M. Ataxie locomotrice progressive; arthropathie de l'épaule gauche resutats nécroseopiques. *Arch. Physiol. Norm. Path.* 2:121, 1869.

Charcot, J.M. Leçons sur les maladies su système nerveux faites à La Salpêtriere. 3 Vols, Paris, A. Delahaye, 1872–1887.

Collier, J. The pathogenesis of cerebral diplegia. *Brain* 47:1–21, 1924.

Cotard, J.L. Étude sur l'atrophie cérébrale. Thèse de Paris, 1868.

Crawford, J.R. *The Yale Shakespeare. The Tragedy of Richard the Third,* New Haven, CT, Yale Univ. Press, 1957.

Cruveilhier, J. *Anatomie pathologique du corps humaine* . . . . Paris, J.B. Baillière, 1829–1842.

Cushing, H. *The Life of Sir William Osler.* Oxford, Clarendon Press, 1925.

Darkschewitsch, L. and S. Freud. Ueber die Beziehung des Strickkörpers zum Hinterstrang und Hinterstrangskern, nebst Bemerkungen über zwei Felder der Oblongata. *Neurol. Centralbl.* 5:121–129, 1886.

Ehrenfest, H. *Birth Injuries of the Child.* New York, D. Appleton, 1922.

Ford, F.R., B. Crothers, and M.C. Putnam. *Birth Injuries of the Nervous System. Part I. Cerebral Birth Injuries. Part II. Cord Birth Injuries.* Baltimore, The Williams and Wilkins Co., 1927.

Freud, S. Beitrag zur Kenntniss der Olivenzwischenschicht. *Neu. Centralbl.* 4:268–270, 1885a.

Freud, S. Ueber den Ursprung des N. Acusticus. *Monats. F. Ohrenheilkunde* 20:245–251, 277–282, 1886b.

Freud, S. Ueber Hemianopsie im frühesten Kindesalter. *Wien med. Wsch.r* 32:1081–1086, 1116–1121, 1888.

Freud, S. *Zur Kenntniss der cerebralen Diplegien des Kindesalters (im Anschlusse an die Little'sche Krankheit).* Wien, 1893a.

Freud, S. Zur Kenntnis der cerebralen Diplegien des Kindesalters. (Im Anschluss an die Little'sche Krankheit). *Kassowitz Beiträe*, N.S., 3, Leipzig, F. Deuticke, 1893b.

Freud, S. *Die infantile Cerebrallähmung. Nothnagel's Specielle Pathologie und Therapie.* Wien, 1897a.

Freud, S. *Die infantile Cerebrallähmung.* Vol. 9, part 2, section 2, Wien, A. Hölder, 1897b.

Freud, S. *Infantile Cerebral Paralysis.* Trans. by L.A. Russin. Coral Gables, FL, Univ. Miami Press, 1968.

Freud, S. and O. Rie. *Klinische Studie über die halbseitige Cerebrallähmung der Kinder.* Wien, Verlag von Moritz Perles, 1891a.

Freud, S. and O. Rie. *Klinische Studie ueber die halbseitige Zerebrallähmungen des Kindes. Kassowitz Beiträge,* old series, 3, 1891b.

Gaudard, E. *Contribution à l'étude de l'hémiplégie cérébrale infantile.* Genève, Thesis, 1884.

Gowers, W.R. *Epilepsy and Other Chronic Convulsive Diseases: Their Causes, Symptoms and Treatment.* New York, William Wood & Co, 1885.

Gowers, W.R. Birth palsies. *Lancet* 1:709–711, 759–760, 1888.

Heine, J. *Spinale Kinderlähmung,* 2nd ed. Stuttgart, J.G. Cotta'scher, 1860.

Henoch, E. *De atrophia cerebri.* Dissertation. Kiel, 1842. (Summarized in *Lectures on Children's Diseases,* translated by J. Thomson, 1889, London).

Heschl, R. Gihirndefect und Hydrocephalus. *Vjisch.r prakt. Heilk.* 61:59, 1859.

Huxinel, V.H. Contribution à l'etude des troubles de la circulation veineuse chez l'enfant ct en particulier chez le nouveau-né. Paris, 1877.

Ingram, T.T.S. A historical review of the definition and classification of the cerebral palsies. In: *Clinics in Developmental Medicine No. 87. The Epidemiology of the Cerebral Palsies,* F. Stanley and E. Alberman (Eds.), Oxford, Blackwell Scientific Publications Ltd., 1984, pp 1–11.

Ingram, T.T.S. *Paediatric Aspects of Cerebral Palsy.* Edinburgh, E & S Livingstone, Ltd., 1964.

Jendrassik, E. and P. Marie. Contribution a l'étude de l'hemiatrophie cérébrale par sclérose lobaire. *Arch. Physiol. Path.* 5:51, 1885.

Jelliffe, S.E. Sigmund Freud as a neurologist. *J. Nerv. Ment Dis.* 85:696–711, 1937.

Jones, E. *The Life and Work of Sigmund Freud.* New York, Basic Books, 1953.

Kundrat, H. *Die Porencephalie. Eine anatomische Studie.* Graz, Verlag von Leuschner & Lubensky, 1882.

Lallemand, C.F. von. *Recherches anatamo-pathologiques sur l'encéphale et ses dépendances.* Paris, 1830–34.

Little, W.J. Course of Lectures on the Deformities of the Human Frame. *Lancet* 1:5–7, 38–44, 70–74, 209–12, 230–33, 257–60, 290–93, 318–20, 346–49, 350–54, 1843–44.

Little, W.J. *On the Nature and Treatment of the Deformities of the Human Frame. Being a course of lectures delivered at the Royal Orthopaedic Hospital in 1843 . . .* London, Longman, Brown, Green, and Longmans, 1853.

Little, W.J. On the influence of abnormal parturition, difficult labours, premature birth, and asphyxia neonatorum, on the mental and physical condition of the child, especially in relation to deformities. *Trans. Obstet. Soc. Lond.* 3:293–344, 1861–1862.

Longo, L.D. and S. Ashwal. William Osler, Sigmund Freud and the evolution of ideas concerning cerebral palsy. *J. Hist. Neurosci.* 2:255–282, 1993.

McHenry, L.C., Jr *Garrison's History of Neurology. Revised and Enlarged with a Bibliography of Classical, Original, and Standard Works in Neurology.* Springfield, IL, C.C. Thomas, 1969.

McNutt, S.J. Apoplexia neonatorum. *Am. J. Obstet. Dis. Women Child.* 1:73–81, 1885a.

McNutt, S.J. Double infantile spastic hemiplegia, with the report of a case. *Am. J. Med. Sci.* 89:58–79, 1885b.

Neale, A.V. Was Little right? *Cereb. Palsy Bull.* 1:23–25, 1958.

Nelson, K.B. and J.H. Ellenberg. Epidemiology of cerebral palsy. *Ad.v Neurol.* 19:421–435, 1978.

Osler, W. The primary muscular atrophies. *Med. News* (Phila.) 47:681–682, 1885.

Osler, W. Infantile paralysis of cerebral origin. *Med. News* (Phila.) 48:75–76, 1886.

Osler, W. The cerebral palsies of children. Lectures I-V. *Med. News* (Phila.) 53:29–35, 57–66, 85–90, 113–116, 141–145, 1888a.

Osler, W. Note on a case of Friedreich's ataxia, with exhibition of patient. *Tran.s Coll. Physicians Phila.*, 3rd Ser., 10:277–278, 1888b.

Osler, W. *The Cerebral Palsies of Children. A clinical study from the Infirmary for Nervous Diseases,* Philadelphia, P. Blakiston, 1889a.

Osler, W. Idiocy and feeble-mindedness in relation to infantile hemiplegia; a report of twenty-two cases at the Pennsylvania Institution for feeble-minded children. *Alienist & Neurol.* (St. Louis) 10:16–23, 1889b.

Osler, W. On a case of simple idiopathic muscular atrophy, involving the face and the scapulo-humeral muscles. *Am. J. Med. Sci.* (Phila.) N.S., 98:261–265, 1889c.

Osler, W. *The Principles and Practice of Medicine,* New York, D. Appleton & Co, 1892, pp 906–911.

Osler, W. *On Chorea and Choreiform Affections.* Philadelphia, P. Blakiston, Son & Co., 1894.

Parrot, J. Etude sur le ramollissement de l'encephale chez le nouveau-né. *Arch. de Physiol.* 1873.

Reil, J.C. *Entwurf einer allgemeinen Pathologie.* Halle, Curt, 1815–16.

Richardière, H. *Études sur les scléroses encephaliques primitive de l'enfance.* Paris, 1885.

Robbins, B.H. and A. Christie Sir William Osler the pediatrician. *Am. J. Dis. Child.* 106:124–129, 1963.

Rokitansky, C. von. *Handbuch der pathologischen Anatomie.* 3 Vols., Wien, Braumüller u. Seidel, 1842–44-46.

Ross, J. On the spasmodic paralyses of infancy. *Brain* 5:344–363, 473–491, 1882.

Ruhräh, J. *Pediatrics of the Past. An Anthology . . . .* New York, PB Hoeber, 1925.

Sachs, B. *A Treatise on the Nervous Diseases of Children.* New York, Wood, 1895.

Sachs, B. and L. Hausman. *Nervous and Mental Disorders from Birth Through Adolescence,* New York, Hoeber, 1926.

Schifrin, B. and L.D. Longo. William John Little and cerebral palsy: A reappraisal. *Eur. J. Obstet. Gynaecol. Reprod. Med.* 90:139–144, 2000.

Sinkler, W. On the palsies of children. *Am. J. Med. Sci.* 69: 348–365, 1875.

Sinkler, W. The different forms of paralysis met with in young children. *Med. News* (Phila.) 47: 521–523, 1885.

Sinkler, W. Discussion. In T. Parvin, Injuries of the foetus during labor. *Med. News* (Phila.) 51:561–580, 1887.

Strümpell, A. Ueber die akute Encephalitis der Kinder (Polioencephalitis acuta, cerebrale Kinderlähmung). *Jb. Kinderheilk.* 22:173–178, 1885.

Volpe, J.J. *Neurology of the Newborn.* Philadelphia, W.B. Saunders Co., 1987.

Wallenberg, A. Ein Beitrag zur Lehre von den cerebralen Kinderlähmungen. *Jb. Kinderheilk.* 24, 384–439, 1886.

Wolf, J.M. Historical perspective of cerebral palsy. In: *The Results of Treatment in Cerebral Palsy,* JM Wolf (Ed.), Springfield, IL: Charles C. Thomas, 1969, pp 5–44.

Penis Captivus, William Osler's Captivating Penchant

 Charles G. Roland, M.D.

One of Osler's most provocative publications was the pseudonymous letter of 1884 on penis captivus, or vaginismus. Most Oslerians, at least those of this overinformed and sometimes jaded dying decade of the millennium, know about the E.Y. Davis letter in the *Medical News* of Philadelphia.[1]

Interestingly, Cushing managed to avoid identifying the subject matter of the letter in his *Life* of Osler,[2] even though this biography was published in the sometimes naughty 1920s. Similarly, Osler's ultra-protective second cousin, W.W. Francis, wrote about some of the E.Y. Davis flights of *joie de vivre* without mentioning penis captivus.[3] Even in the sexually liberated 1970s, Bill Bean — scarcely one to blanch at naming a shovel — wrote a long paper on Egerton Yorrick Davis and never alluded to vaginismus or penis captivus.[4]

My purpose is threefold: first, to review the infamous letter and some commentaries written upon it by individuals less reticent that Cushing and Bean; secondly, to survey briefly the historical observations on this topic; and thirdly, to suggest a possible source for Osler's awareness of the subject and, perhaps, his interest in it.

First, however, some definitions are called for. "Vaginismus" was defined by J. Marion Sims, who invented the term. He said, ". . . by the term Vaginismus I propose to designate an invol untary spasmodic closure of the mouth of the vagina, attended with such excessive supersensitiveness as to form a complete barrier to coition."[5] "Penis captivus" has been identified as that condition " . . . in which the penis is caught inside the vagina, is held there by the muscular spasm, and cannot be withdrawn."[6]

Some writers use the term vaginismus to encompass penis captivus, while others differentiate between them. Osler, or Davis, was of the first group.

Presented at the American Osler Society, April 3, 1997, Williamsburgh.

The Davis Letter of 1884

The Davis letter is introduced in the *Medical News* as having been received through the courtesy of the editor of *The Canada Medical and Surgical Journal*. In 1884 the editors were George Ross and Thomas G. Roddick.[7] The letter was stimulated by an anonymous editorial entitled "An uncommon form of vaginismus."[8] Unlike Davis, Osler was on the editorial staff of the *Medical News* and knew that Theophilus Parvin had written this item.[9] Parvin wrote, in the course of his editorial, that Hildebrandt, a contemporary German gynecologist, had stated ". . . that cramp of the levator ani may cause contraction of the upper part of the vagina, so that a speculum, or a swollen glans penis, as in coition, may be forcibly retained."[10]

"Davis" was reminded by Parvin's editorial of a case he had seen when he was in practice in Pentonville, England. He was sent for late one evening by a gentleman described as being ". . . in a state of great perturbation. . . . " The letter then details the case:

> At bedtime, when going to the back kitchen to see if the house was shut up, a noise in the coachman's room attracted his attention, and, going in, he discovered to his horror that the man was in bed with one of the maids. She screamed, he struggled, and they rolled out of bed together and made frantic efforts to get apart, but without success.

As an aside, I would suggest here, as a precipitating factor, the officious intrusion by the employer of the coachman and the maid. Her understandable shock and terror at suddenly seeing her master appear — so unwelcomely — in the midst of ecstasy surely must have induced the extreme constriction of the circum-vaginal muscles that thus led to the situation "Davis" described. But let me resume the quotation:

> He was a big, burly man, over six feet, and she was a small woman, weighing not more than ninety pounds. She was moaning and screaming, and seemed in great agony, so that, after several fruitless attempts to get them apart, he sent for me. When I arrived I found the man standing up and supporting the woman in his arms, and it was quite evident that his penis was tightly locked in her vagina, and any attempt to dislodge it was accompanied by much pain on the part of both. It was, indeed, a case "De cohesione in coitu." I applied water, and then ice, but ineffectually, and at last sent for chloroform, a few whiffs of which sent the woman to sleep, relaxed the spasm, and relieved the captive penis, which was swollen, livid, and in a state of semi-erection, which did not go down for several hours, and for days the organ was extremely sore. The woman recovered rapidly, and seemed none the worse.
>
> I am sorry that I did not examine if the sphincter ani was contracted, but I did not think of it. In this case there must have been also spasm of the muscle at the orifice, as well as higher up, for the penis seemed nipped low down, and this contraction, I think, kept the blood retained and the organ erect. As an instance of Jago's [*sic*, Iago's] "beast with two backs," the picture was perfect. I have often wondered how it was, considering with what agility the man can, under certain circumstances, jump up, that Phineas, the son of Eleazar, was able to thrust his javelin through the man and the Midianitish woman (*vide* Exodus); but the occurrence of such cases as the above may offer a possible explanation.

It was typical of Osler to close with a Biblical reference. It was also typical that in writing this section, Osler obviously did not trouble to check his references, since there are several minor errors in the text.[11]

There is a nice satirical touch in placing Davis's site of practice in Pentonville. This is a district of London containing a major British prison. "What better location," Tigertt asks, "for an example of penile incarceration?"[12]

The Commentaries

There have been numerous commentaries either specifically about the Davis letter, or that included some mention of it. Others have referred to the concept of penis captivus in general. Several of these will be mentioned in the course of the discussion. But I should perhaps quote from one of the general group of commentaries. This is less concerned with the physical entity than with its subconscious motivation. Kroger states: "Vaginismus is often the muscular expression of an unconscious sadistic desire to castrate the man by using the vagina to suck in the penis, to cut it off, and possibly retain it as an organ for themselves."[13] Being neither a Freudian nor a woman, I have no comment.

Historical Descriptions of Penis Captivus

There exist, first, several apparently hearsay reports about anonymous victims. These seem highly questionable. The captivity usually took place in or near a holy place; the victims are freed only after confessing sins or otherwise placating the diety. The message seems heavy-handedly obvious but does little to authenticate the episodes.

Loomis cites one of these quasi-religious instances: "A certain [potent] man, coming with his wife one Sunday to hear the divine services in the church of St. Clitaucus, lay with his wife on the bank of a stream not far from the church. After the sin was committed he could not become separated from her, remaining inseparably joined to his wife. He cried out to his companions loudly: 'Go to the tomb of the martyr Clitaucus, and promise that the meadow which I seized forcefully and without justice will be restored; I humbly beseech that he intercede for me.' When this was done [i.e. the promise made] he was freed immediately from the dreadful bond."[14]

Another very similar event, or the description of a supposed event, also comes from Loomis's brief article. For the translation of this passage I am indebted to my former colleague, Dr. Lester King:

> A certain seducer, one of the companions of King Clito, polluted the womb of a certain woman on the coffin of a venerable bishop. They copulated like dogs and then were unable in any way to become separated. At length they came to the attention of the glorious martyr Guignerus, and by the merit of Christ as witness and the intercessions of the faithful, they were freed.[15]

Whether there is any literary or anatomical significance in the fact that the first example refers to St Clitaucus and the second to King Clito is problematic. Were these not-so-subtle allusions to the clitoris?

Somewhat more convincing cases, chiefly because the accounts concern identified real individuals (inevitably, only the male participants!) Exist. This example was translated by Prof. Paul Potter:

> Such a case of cohesion once befell a certain well-known person by the name of Pierre Borel (1620–1689), who remained joined in coitus just in

the manner of dogs. This occurred either, as Borel himself thought, because of the excessive ardour of the swollen genital parts, or because these parts had been heated and irritated by *zybethus* [civet, in Rolleston], with which he, on the advice of a friend, had anointed his glans for the purpose of augmenting his pleasure. It was necessary to soften [relax] the said parts with frequent rectal injections, so that he could eventually be separated.[16]

Zybethus apparently was used as an aphrodisiac in earlier days. If Rolleston is correct in equating *zybethus* and civet, then the connection to modern aphrodisia is obvious: civet oil is a common constituent of perfumes. Christian Johann Lang (1619–1662) noted that a violent spasmodic affection of the female genitals results from excessive anointing of the glans penis with *zybethus*. This "... not only causes the male and the female to experience stimulation and joy, but also afterwards holds them bound so tightly together that they can hardly be pulled apart by force."[17]

A similar case was recorded by Daniel Ludwig (1625–1680). This was reported to him by a man who experienced vaginismus on his wedding night; afterwards he reported that "... not only his glans but also the foremost part of his penis had been most firmly seized."[18]

Saxo Grammaticus (?1150–1216) wrote that the inhabitants of Rügen, a German island in the Baltic Sea, are held together in coitus like dogs. He commented that it was no wonder these people feared the power of their gods, by whom they believe their debaucheries have often been thus punished. "If any males in that city of Carinthia used, in their cohabitation with a woman, to be caught together with her, and the two were unable by their own movement to pull themselves apart, both were hung up on poles from the opposite sides in order to afford, in their unusual connection, a mocking spectacle for the populace."[19]

Another brief example comes from the writings of Diemerbroeck, the 17th century anatomist: "When I was a student in Leyden I remember there was a young Bridegroom in that Town that being overwanton with his Bride had so hamper'd himself in her Privities, that he could not draw his Yard forth, till Delmehorst the Physician unty'd the Knot by casting cold Water on the Part."[20]

Finally, Rolleston cites Henrichsen, who recorded a case of vaginismus without any history of penis captivus. The spasm was relaxed by inserting the finger through the anal sphincter; Henrichsen went on to suggest that this procedure should be used in cases of penis captivus, but Rolleston had not found any case reported where this suggestion was put into practice. "According to Stoeckel even in the cases in which chloroform has been used, forcible introduction of the finger into the vagina is necessary to release the swollen and disco loured organ."[21]

Fictional Descriptions of Penis Captivus

In his searing novel of World War Two, *The Painted Bird,* Jerzy Kosinski portrays penis captivus in a brutal rape of a young Jewish girl who had been found, slightly injured, on the railway tracks. The man who found her was named Rainbow; after discussion in the town about her fate, Rainbow took her to his home for the night. Later, in his barn, Rainbow tears off the girl's dress:

> Rainbow sat at the girl's side and stroked her body with his big hands. His bulk hid her face from me, but I could hear her quiet sobbing broken

occasionally by a cry. Slowly Rainbow took off his knee boots and breeches, leaving on only a rough shirt.

He straddled the prostrate girl and moved his hands gently over her shoulders, breasts, and belly. She moaned and whined, uttering strange words in her language when his touch grew rougher. Rainbow breathed heavily. He lifted himself on his elbows, slipped down a little, and then fell on her with a thud.

The girl arched her body, screamed, and kept opening and closing her fingers as though trying to grasp something. Then something strange happened. Rainbow was on top of the girl, his legs between hers, but trying to break away. Every time he lifted himself, she screamed with pain; he also groaned and cursed. He tried to detach himself from her, but seemed unable to do so. He was held fast by some strange force inside her, just as a hare or fox is caught in a snare.

He remained on top of the girl, trembling violently. After a while he renewed his efforts, but each time the girl writhed in pain. He also seemed to suffer. He wiped the perspiration off his face, swore, and spat. At his next try the girl wanted to help. She opened her legs wider, lifted her hips, and pushed with her good hand against his belly. It was all in vain. An invisible bond held them together.[22]

There follows a description of the phenomenon in dogs. "From man's friend they became nature's practical joke."[23] The scene becomes increasingly violent between Rainbow and his victim. He cries for help, a crowd collects, and someone sent for a witch-midwife. When she arrived, she ". . . kneeled by the locked couple, and did something to them with the help of others. I could see nothing; I only heard the girl's last piercing shriek."[24] She was dead, and the next day her body was abandoned back on the railway tracks.

Does Penis Captivus Exist?

This is a question that arises naturally enough. That vaginismus occurs seems certain and unquestioned. James Ricci, in his text published in 1945 but reporting on gynecology in the 19th century, cites 130 references to vaginismus up to 1900.[25] But many writers have expressed the opinion that penis captivus is a suspect concept. This is evidently one of those areas of human existence that require personal experience — either as a victim or as medical attendant — to permit certainty.

A distinguished urologist, Earl Nation, doubts that penis captivus has occurred or can occur.[26] Nation indicates his agreement with Jacobsen, who asked: "Have the solemn recitals of such cases by professors of obstetrics and gynecology to convulsed and credulous students been anything but hokum? Has the human penis ever really been in captivity? We doubt it."[27] But Jacobsen's tone is so jocular that I cannot be certain that he was himself serious in doubting.

Altaffer has joined the ranks of the unconvinced; he wrote about the Davis letter and commented that most authorities agree that no documented cases have occurred in modern times.[28] He, in turn, seems to have relied chiefly on the opinions of Bondurant and Cappannari.[29] These authors discuss very briefly some of the historical descriptions before concluding: ". . . it is highly improbable for spasm of the pubococcygeus and bulbospongiosus to be severe enough after penetration to cause penis captivus. We also feel that the normal male response to a contraction of this type would be relaxation of the penis, allowing withdrawal."[30] Plainly there is a research project here crying out for study.

But penis captivus has its believers. Lachman concludes his article on the topic by stating that although Osler's case was fictitious, the occurrence itself is quite real, ". . . particularly to the victims and may lead to serious consequences. This was true in one particular case known to the author in which the male participant committed suicide two days after the event."[31]

Another even more tragic event took place in Poland about 70 years ago. In a thesis written in Paris in 1931, Pilz recorded:

> We remember a case of vaginismus with penis captivus which occurred in 1923 at Warsaw and ended by double suicide. It was in the spring, a couple of young students stayed behind in the garden after closing time. In the midst of their amorous sport a violent spasm occurred imprisoning the penis. The keeper alarmed by the desperate cries of the young man ran up. The doctor of the municipal ambulance after giving an anaesthetic to the woman separated the couple. The matter might have been forgotten, but the journalists in their greed for sensational facts did not fail to publish the adventure. The next day two revolver shots put an end to the mental sufferings of the two lovers.[32]

And note Rolleston's comment that "[a]t the present day administration of chloroform to the female partner is usually necessary to relax the vaginal spasm."[33] The wording suggests that the condition was known to Rolleston clinically. He further adds a postscript to the effect that a colleague has brought to his attention the Davis letter. The case, he says, ". . . though entirely fictitious so closely resembles those described by previous writers that it has been quoted in some standard works of sexology. . . ."[34]

Osler's Introduction to the Topic?

In the minutes of the regular meetings of the Montreal Medico-Chirurgical Society there is an entry germane to the subject of vaginismus. The relevant meeting took place on 16 February 1877, a Friday. Here are the pertinent portions of the minutes of this meeting:

> Dr. F.W. Campbell then read a very interesting case of Vaginismus in a young married lady. The patient was a lady of about aet 25 of good proportions and apparently in perfect health, who had been married for the space of three weeks, during which time the marriage had not been consumated [*sic*] notwithstanding vigorous and often repeated efforts on the part of her husband; each attempt being attended with excruciating pain. Dr. Campbell being consulted proposed an examination; and upon attempting to introduce the index finger well lubricated with warm oil found it utterly impossible to do so, owing to intense spasm of the sphincter vaginae. Assisted by Dr. Kennedy the patient was placed under chloroform (it taking over two ounces to produce complete insensibility). On examination the os uteri was found to be intensely congested and its mucous membrane exfoliating in places; the carunculae myrtiformes of the hymen, which had been previously ruptured by attempts at coition, were enlarged and congested having the appearance of raspberries; these carunculae were extremely sensative [*sic*] the slightest touch producing spasm of the sphincter even under chloroform. They were therefore carefully removed by scissors and the part touched with the solid stick of

silver nitrate. The patient was directed to use frequent injections of warm water, this was followed by injections of sulphate of zinc and the daily introduction of graduated metal bougies and in about 3 wks the patient was quite cured.

 Dr. H. Howard related a case in an insane lady in whom the spasm was so intense as not to admit of the introduction of a common probe; this patient afterwards confessed to having been addicted to masturbation and the Dr. gave it as his opinion that the disease was a very common result of that practice.

 Dr. Kennedy considered the carunculae as the cause of the trouble owing to their extreme irritability.

 Dr. Buller considered that the altered state of the secretions owing to nervous excitement might be the cause of the trouble.

 Dr. Trenholme mentioned that he had never had a case of vaginismus in his own practice but considered that the congestion &c might be produced by continuous excitement of the genital organs in a person of strong sexual desires.[35]

Among the list of attendees is the name of William Osler, then Professor of the Institutes of Medicine at McGill Medical College. Could this clinical information have been the spark for his E.Y. Davis letter in the Philadelphia *Medical News* on the same topic? Obviously, the subject matter in Montreal was vaginismus by Sims' definition, not penis captivus. But I find it easy to visualize some of the Montreal physicians chatting after the meeting, perhaps over cigars and brandy. The conversation about the evening's cases could easily have become ribald and Rabelaisian. There might have been speculation as to what would have happened to the newly married couple had the man successfully forced an entry and the woman's spasm then became acutely worse. Even if that conversation did not take place, there is no reason to suppose that the painful but titillating possibility would not have occurred to Osler spontaneously. That, at least, is my hypothesis.

However, I must attempt to deflect any criticism of my title. The reader may protest that one episode does not establish a "captivating penchant." Anticipating some concern over this question, I can state that the E.Y. Davis letter of 1884 is by no means the sole surviving instance of Osler's interest in the topic of penis captivus. There were at least two other instances, though neither of them was published by Osler.

In 1893, the Johns Hopkins medical faculty looked seriously at the propriety of issuing a clinical journal, tentatively named the *Archives of Medical Science*. As part of their planning, they had dummy issues prepared, with a contrived Table of Contents on the cover, though only blank pages inside. Of the Big Four, Welch, Halsted, and Kelly each invented a title for a non-existent article. Osler did not. But one Egerton Y. Davis contributed "Further researches of the maladie de Hildebrant."[36] You will recall that it was Hildebrandt who reported a case of penis captivus in the *Archiv für Gynecologie* in 1872, and that Theophilus Parvin quoted Hildebrandt in his seminal editorial.

The other mention of penis captivus occurred in 1911. Osler recorded the dreams he had had the night of 16/17 January. In one of these, he saw outside Christ Church ". . . a society lady's toy dog 'stuck' to a bitch about six times his size. Lady frantic. I helped her to get the dogs into a house near by."[37]

Some may feel that they now know more than they care to about our famous colleague. Personally, I take some pleasure in knowing that Osler had a slightly racy or salacious side. There is some discomfort in encountering the too-good person.

Endnotes

1. Egerton Y. Davis, "Vaginismus," *Medical News* [Philadelphia] 45: 673, 13 December 1884.
2. Harvey Cushing, *The Life of Sir William Osler*, Vol. 1, pp. 240–241. [NB: No mention of vaginismus *per se* only Parvin's interest ". . . in the action of the perineal muscles."]
3. W.W. Francis, "At Osler's shrine," *Bulletin of the Medical Library Association* 26: 1–8, 1937. [NB: No mention of vaginismus.]
4. William B. Bean, "William Osler: the Egerton Yorrick Davis alias," in: John P. McGovern and Chester Burns, (edits.) *Humanism in Medicine* (Springfield: Charles C Thomas, 1974, pp. 49–59.
5. J. Marion Sims, "On vaginismus," *Transactions of the Obstetrical Society* (London) 3: 356–367, 1862; see p. 362.
6. Max Huhner, *A Practical Treatise on Disorders of the Sexual Function in the Male and Female* 2nd edit. (Philadelphia: F.A. Davis Company, 1924), p. 183.
7. Charles G. Roland and Paul Potter, *An Annotated Bibliography of Canadian Medical Periodicals, 1826–1975* (Toronto: The Hannah Institute for the History of Medicine, 1979), p. 13.
8. Anonymous, "An uncommon form of vaginismus," *Medical News* [Philadelphia] 43: 602–603, 1884.
9. Harvey Cushing, *The Life of Sir William Osler*, Vol. 1, p. 241.
10. Anonymous, "An uncommon form of vaginismus," p. 603.
11. See William D. Tigertt, "An annotated life of Egerton Yorrick Davis, MD, an intimate of Sir William Osler," *Journal of the History of Medicine and Allied Sciences* 38: 259–297, 1983; see p. 263: Phineas should be Phinehas, Eleazr should be Eleazar, and the passage is from Numbers (25: 7–15), not Exodus.
12. *Ibid.*, p. 262.
13. William S. Kroger, *Psychosomatic Gynecology, Including Problems of Obstetrical Care* (Hollywood: Wilshire Book Co., 1962), p. 316.
14. C. Grant Loomis, "Three cases of vaginism," *Bulletin of the History of Medicine* 7:97–98, 1939. Translation by Dr. Lester S. King.
15. *Ibid.,* pp. 97–98.
16. Petrus Borel, *Historiarum et observationum med.-phys.*, 2nd hundred, 31st observation, p. 133; cited in D.M. Schurigius, *Spermatologia* (1737), pp. 314–315. Translation by Prof. Paul Potter, University of Western Ontario, 31 January 1997.
17. *Opera Medica*, vol. 2, Praxis, Chapter 23, page 145; cited in D.M. Schurigius, *Spermatologia* (1737), pp. 314–315. Translation by Prof. Paul Potter, University of Western Ontario, 31 January 1997.
18. Christian Paullini, *Cynograph. Curios.*, p. 54; cited in D.M. Schurigius, *Spermatologia* (1737), pp. 314–315. Translation by Prof. Paul Potter, University of Western Ontario, 31 January 1997.
19. Saxo Grammaticus (?1150–1216), cited by Johann Weier, *Opera Omnia*, Amsterdam, 1660, Part 1, Chapter 9, page 22; cited in turn by D.M. Schurigius, *Spermatologia* (1737), pp. 314–315. Translation by Prof. Paul Potter, University of Western Ontario, 31 January 1997.
20. Cited in J.D. Rolleston, "Penis captivus: a historical note," *Janus* 35: 196–202, 1935; see p. 200.
21. J.D. Rolleston, "Penis captivus: a historical note," *Janus* 35: 196–202, 1935; see p. 201.

22. Jerzy Kosinski, *The Painted Bird* (London: W.H. Allen, 1966), pp. 208; see p. 96.
23. *Ibid*, p. 97.
24. *Ibid*, p. 98.
25. James V. Ricci, *One Hundred Years of Gynaecology, 1800–1900* (Philadelphia: The Blakiston Co., 1945), pp. 551–553.
26. Earl F. Nation, "William Osler on penis captivus and other urologic topics," *Urology* 11: 468–470, 1973; see p. 469.
27. A.C. J[acobson], "Penis captivus: myth or actuality? With some notes on Sir William Osler's *Alter Ego*" *Medical Times* 73: 52–54, 1945; see pp. 52–53.
28. L.F. Altaffer III, "Penis captivus and the mischievous Sir William Osler," *Southern Medical Journal* 76: 637–641, 1983; see p. 638.
29. Sydney W. Bondurant and Stephen C. Cappannari, "Penis captivus: fact or fancy?" *Medical Aspects of Human Sexuality* 5: 224ˇ2D233, 1971.
30. *Ibid.*, p. 233.
31. Ernest Lachman, "Anatomy as applied to clinical medicine," *New Physician* 16: 301–303, 1967; see p. 303.
32. A. Piltz, Thèse de Paris 1931, No. 376; cited in J.D. Rolleston, "Penis captivus: a historical note," *Janus* 35: 196–202, 1935; see pp. 200–201.
33. *Ibid.*, p. 201.
34. *Ibid.*, p. 202.
35. Montréal, Québec, McGill University, Osler Library Archives 38/65/S/4/6/ Montreal Medico-Chirurgical Society. Minute Book. Vol. 1, 1865–1882.
36. This circumstance was described by Tigertt, "An annotated life of Egerton Yorrick Davis," p. 267.
37. Charles G. Roland (edit.), "Sir William Osler's dreams and nightmares," *Bulletin of the History of Medicine* 54: 418–446, 1980; see p. 431.

"A Calling, not a Business": William Osler's Call for Professionalism

 Herbert M. Swick, M.D.

William Osler's place in the pantheon of medical history is secure. His contributions to clinical medicine, exemplified by his textbook *The Principles and Practice of Medicine* and by various eponymous signs and diseases, are well known. So are many of his contributions to medical education, particularly his emphasis on the importance of bedside teaching. Less well known, perhaps, are his concerns about the state of medical practice in the late 1800s and its effect on the education of physicians as professionals. Yet throughout his career, Osler was keenly aware of the tensions that exist between medicine as a profession and as a business.

In his presidential address to the Canadian Medical Association in September 1885, Osler decried the proliferation of medical schools, many of which operated independently in a competitive environment, creating a situation in which "the schools degenerate into diploma mills, in which the highest interests of the profession and the public are prostituted to the cupidity of the owners."[1] This theme persisted. In an address to the Maryland State Medical Society four years later, in 1889, Osler noted that medical education still consisted largely of a series of repeated lectures given by faculty whose income related directly to the number of students. In his mind, this method had the tragic consequence of producing poorly trained physicians:

> It makes one's blood boil to think that there are sent out year by year scores of men, called doctors, who have never attended a woman in labor, and who are utterly ignorant of the ordinary everyday diseases which they may be called upon to treat, men who may never have seen the inside of a hospital ward, and who would know not Scarpa's space from the sole of the foot.[2]

This paper is based upon a presentation to the annual meeting of the American Osler Society, May 5, 1999, Montreal.

Many medical schools were structured as businesses that existed to make a profit for their owners, and Osler knew that "in the hurry and bustle of a business world, which is the life of this continent, it is not easy to train first-class students."[3]

William Osler's concern about the state of medical education reflected his concern about the state of medical practice. To become effective practitioners, Osler argued, students had to be educated in more than simply the science of medicine:

> As the practice of medicine is not a business and can never be one, the education of the heart – the moral side of man – must keep pace with the education of the head. Our fellow creatures cannot be dealt with as a man deals in corn and coal; "the human heart by which we live" must control our professional relations.[4]

His plea that patients not be dealt with as commodities, as corn and coal, became a recurrent theme—almost a leitmotiv—that echoed through many of his talks to medical students. He counseled students at the University of Toronto in October 1903 that "the practice of medicine is an art, not a trade; a calling, not a business; a calling in which your heart will be exercised equally with your head."[5] And in an address to students at St. Mary's Hospital, in London, in October 1907, he noted that medicine is "a calling, not a business. . . .Once you get down to a purely business level, your influence is gone and the true light of your life is dimmed."[6]

Osler worked at the juncture of two centuries, and it is certainly true that clocks ticking inexorably toward a new century seem always to measure out a time of volatility. In the past several years, especially in the United States, there has been an accelerating concern about the corporate transformation of medicine, two consequences of which are a sense that medical care has become nothing more than a commodity, and that medicine as a profession has suffered serious erosion. In all this angst about the state of medical practice, there is nothing new. Three centuries ago, in 1699, the British physician Samuel Garth lamented the fact that medicine had become a trade, not a science, when he penned this couplet:

> How sickening Physick hangs her pensive head
> And what was once a Science, now's a Trade.[7]

A century ago, the medical profession faced yet another period of volatility and uncertainty. There was a growing concern about the state of medical practice in both the United States and Canada. The countryside teemed with poorly educated physicians, while a plethora of charlatans and quacks sold nostrums to a gullible public.

The conflict between medicine as a healing profession and as a business recurred as a theme in many of Osler's addresses, not only to students, but also to practicing physicians and professional societies. Osler, in his address during the centenary celebration of the New Haven Medical Society in January 1903, noted that:

> Of medicine, many are of the opinion . . .that the ancients endeavored to make it a science and failed, and the moderns to make it a trade and have succeeded. Today, the cry is louder than ever, and in truth there are grounds for alarm; but . . .there are many more than 7000 who have not bowed the knee to this Baal, but who practice *caute caste et probe.*[4]

He took solace in the fact that many physicians had not succumbed to the business of medicine, the false idol Baal, but instead still practiced cautiously, purely and credibly.

Osler worried then—as many worry now—about an erosion of professionalism in medicine. In many settings, he called upon students and physicians to adhere to professional values and behaviors, in short, to practice professionalism, which he saw as an antidote to the business side of medicine.

William Osler recognized the critical importance of adhering to those values and behaviors that constitute professionalism. But what, exactly, comprises medical professionalism? This question has engaged the interest of a number of individuals and groups.[8–14] Briefly, medical professionalism comprises those behaviors that reflect medicine's long tradition as a learned and that represent physicians' commitments to meet their responsibilities both to individual patients and to the larger society in which they practice. This paper is not meant to offer an extensive discussion of the attributes of professionalism. Rather, it highlights certain of the key attributes of professionalism in the context of Osler's work.

The first attribute of professionalism is its central, fundamental element: professionalism entails subordinating one's self interest to the interest of others. It represents the fiduciary relationship that physicians hold to patients. In his centenary address to the New Haven Medical Association, Osler recognized this commitment as a sacred trust. He criticized the doctor who "is in the profession only for the money he can get out of patients without regard to the sacred trust to put himself in the best possible position to do the best that is known for them."[4] Today, that trust is too often in conflict with the physician's responsibilities to some business hierarchy, some set of rules imposed by a government regulatory body or a managed care organization.

Another key attribute of medical professionalism is that it responds to societal needs and reflects a social contract with the communities served. Osler was keenly aware of the social responsibility of physicians. In 1899, he stimulated medical students to address the public health challenges of tuberculosis, which was then rampant in Baltimore, by visiting patients and their families to educate them about the nature of the disease. Two women students did so and subsequently presented their findings regarding 190 families to the first meeting of the Laennec Society in 1900.[15]

To practice professionalism is to evince core humanistic values—values such as empathy and compassion, integrity and trustworthiness—and here Osler was an exemplar. Although he admitted that, at times, the practice of medicine was "a testy and choleric business"[16] nevertheless, as Lewellys Barker noted:

> his courtesy, his politeness, his kindness and his ability to make patients realize that he understood them, sympathized with them, and would leave nothing undone to help them, were inspiring.[17]

In the late 1930's, this author's mentor, David Barrett Clark, was a young neurologist at the University of Chicago. One afternoon, he saw in clinic a middle aged man, rather severely retarded, accompanied by his elderly mother, who was wearing a babushka and speaking broken English still heavily accented with her native Polish. She had cared for her son all his life. The mother remembered that, around the turn of the century, shortly after emigrating from Poland, she had brought her young son to see the doctors. She recalled that during the visit, a famous doctor examined her boy. She could not recall his name, but she remembered that he had a large mustache and that he had come by train all the way from Baltimore. When Dr. Clark asked what this famous doctor had told her, she could not remember any of the medical details, only that he had gently informed her that nothing much could be done. And her most vivid memory of William Osler, etched indelibly over the span of almost forty years, was that "he looked at me so kindly."

Medical professionalism commits the physician to strive always for excellence and to exhibit a commitment to scholarship. Osler encouraged physicians to be keen observers and to share with others the fruits of their learning, as he did throughout his career, from the time he was a young physician at McGill to his term as the Regius Professor at Oxford. He shared his scholarship not only through his bedside teaching and his publications, but also through his many presentations to learned societies. In his presidential address to the Maryland State Medical Society in April 1897, he commented that:

> A physician who does not use books and journals, who does not need a library, who does not read one or two of the best weeklies and monthlies, soon sinks to the level of the cross-counter prescriber, and not alone in practice, but in those mercenary feelings and habits which characterize a trade.[18]

The rather derogatory tone toward the "cross-counter prescriber" reflected Osler's disdain for the business side of medicine. Only by keeping current with the medical literature could a physician escape "those mercenary feelings and habits which characterize a trade."

Accountability—for oneself, for one's colleagues, and for medicine's specialized body of knowledge—is another important attribute of professionalism. Osler recognized that the profession had a responsibility to protect the public "against the depradation of ignorant graduates and of quacks."[2] While he acknowledged the importance of licensing by governmental agencies (a process that was in the latter years of the 19th century better developed in Canada than the United States), Osler also recognized the key role of the profession in maintaining accountability for its members:

> The principle is sound and well-founded; the united profession of a country or a province should be the guardian of its own honor.[1]

William Osler described medicine as "a science of uncertainty and an art of probability."[16] Medicine has always been practiced in an environment of uncertainty and complexity, and professionalism requires that physicians must be comfortable working in that environment.[19]

> The science on which [medicine] is based is accurate and definite enough; the physics of a man's circulation are the physics of the waterworks of the town in which he lives, but once out of gear, you cannot apply the same rules for the repair of the one as of the other. Variability is the law of life, and as no two faces are the same, so no two bodies are alike, and no two individuals react alike and behave alike under the abnormal conditions which we know as disease.[4]

Physicians must be reflective. Osler recognized the importance of keeping up to date with medical information: "We doctors do not 'take stock' often enough, and are very apt to carry on our shelves stale, out-of-date goods."[4] Given the rate at which biomedical knowledge is advancing, this is even more true today than it was a century ago. He recognized also the importance of maintaining the intellectual detachment that would enable physicians to escape for a moment the pressures of day-to-day work and hence to gain a deeper understanding of themselves. In his address to the Canadian Medical Association in September 1902, Osler noted that:

> there is possible to each of us a higher type of intellectual detachment, a sort of separation from the vegetative life of the work-a-day world – always

too much with us – which may enable a man to gain a true knowledge of himself and of his relations to his fellows.[20]

Osler's frequent attention to such essential attributes of medical professionalism served to frame his perspective on the practice of medicine. He recognized the need for practicing physicians to maintain the primacy of professional values over business values. In his address at the opening of a new building for the Medical Faculty at McGill University in 1905, he commented:

> We are only men. But we have ideals, which mean much, and they are realizable, which means more. Of course, there are Gehazis among us who serve for shekels, whose ears hear only the lowing of the oxen and the jingling of the guineas, but these are exceptions.[21]

William Osler's argument that medicine should be practiced as a profession rather than a trade, a calling rather than a business, is a message that the profession must heed today as it weathers the volatile changes that mark the end of another century. Physicians would do well to remember the clarion calls to professionalism made by Osler a century ago. We must remember his admonition that medicine is not a business and can never be one, lest, indeed, medicine loses its status as a profession and truly becomes—as Osler feared it might—a commodity in which physicians treat men as corn and coal.

References

1. Osler W: The growth of a profession. Can Med Surg J 1885; XIV:129–155.
2. Osler W: The license to practise. JAMA 1889; XII:649–654.
3. Osler W: The student life. In: Osler W: A Way of Life and Other Selected Writings of Sir William Osler. New York: Dover Publications; 1951. p. 171–193.
4. Osler W: On the educational value of the medical society. In: Osler W: Aequanimitas with other Addresses to Medical Students, Nurses and Practitioners of Medicine. 3rd ed. New York: McGraw-Hill Book Co.; 1932. p. 329–345.
5. Osler W: The Master Word in Medicine. Reprinted in: Roland CG: William Osler's The Master-Word in Medicine: A Study in Rhetoric. Springfield (IL): Charles C. Thomas; 1972.
6. Osler W: The reserves of life. St. Mary's Hospital Gazette 1907; 13:95–98.
7. Garth S: Dispensary; 1699. Cited in Osler W: On the educational value of the medical society [reference 4].
8. American Board of Internal Medicine: Project Professionalism. Philadelphia, PA: American Board of Internal Medicine; 1995.
9. Association of American Medical Colleges: Professionalism in Contemporary Medical Education: An Invitational Colloquium. Washington, D.C.: Association of American Medical Colleges; 1998.
10. Sullivan WM: What is left of professionalism after managed care? Hastings Center Rep 1999; 29:7–13.
11. Cruess RL, Cruess SR: Teaching medicine as a profession in the service of healing. Acad Med 1997; 72:941–952.
12. Relman AS: Education to defend professional values in the new corporate age. Acad Med 1998; 73:1229–1233.
13. Swick HM: Academic medicine must deal with the clash of business and professional values. Acad Med 1998; 73:751–755.

14. Swick HM, Szenas P, Danoff D, Whitcomb M: Teaching professionalism in undergraduate medical education. JAMA 1999; 282:830–832.

15. Cushing H: The Life of Sir William Osler. Oxford: Clarendon Press; 1926.

16. Bean RB, Bean WB: Sir William Osler. Aphorisms from his Bedside Teaching. Springfield (IL): Charles C. Thomas; 1961.

17. Barker LF: Time and the Physician; 1942. Cited in Fischoff EF: William Osler: Physician and Teacher. The Pearson Museum Monograph Series. Springfield (IL): Southern Illinois University School of Medicine; 1983.

18. Osler W: Presidential address to the Maryland State Medical Society, April 27, 1897. Cited in Cushing H: The Life of Sir William Osler [reference 8].

19. Southon G, Braithwaite J: The end of professionalism. Soc Sci Med 1998; 46:23–28.

20. Osler W: Chauvinism in Medicine. Address to the Canadian Medical Association, September 17,1902. Cited in Cushing H: The Life of Sir William Osler [reference 8]

21. Osler W: Teaching and Thinking: The Two Functions of a Medical School. In: Osler W: A Way of Life and Other Selected Writings of Sir William Osler. New York: Dover Publications; 1951. p. 194–294.

SECTION III

✥ Clinical Matters

Polycythaemia Vera: Osler-Vaquez Disease

 Marvin J. Stone, M.D.

The year 1999 marked the sesquicentennial of William Osler's birth. Osler (1849–1919) was regarded as the greatest and most respected physician of his era.[1,2] An outstanding clinician who emphasized bedside teaching and observation, he possessed extraordinary charm that inspired many disciples. As professor of medicine at four institutions in three countries, he exerted a profound influence on medical education. He was a prolific writer and his *Principles and Practice of Medicine*[3] became the most popular and widely read medical textbook in the world. He also was a medical historian, a classical scholar, and an avid bibliophile. In May 1999, a joint meeting of the American Osler Society, the Osler Club of London, and the Japanese Osler Society was held in Montreal to commemorate the 150th anniversary of Osler's birth. A new biography has appeared,[4] the first full-length account of Osler's life since Cushing's Pulitzer Prize-winning treatise published in 1925.[5] Thus William Osler remains one of the most famous and revered physicians of modern times.

Osler made contributions to many areas of internal medicine, including hematology.[6] He was one of the first to recognize the platelet as the third formed element in the blood and documented the importance of platelets in thrombosis.[7,8] His extensive experience with autopsies and the microscope made him knowledgeable about the natural history of disease and the importance of accurate diagnosis. He wrote on many subjects in hematology, but his name is particularly associated with polycythaemia vera.

Although plethora had been recognized by Hippocrates[9] and Maimonides[10], the term polycythaemia vera (PV) entered the medical literature only about a century ago. The purpose of this paper is to trace the evolution of knowledge about this disorder emphasizing the seminal contributions of William Osler.

Presented in part at the American Osler Society, May 6, 1998, Toronto.

Published also in: J. med Biog 2001 9:99–103. Reprinted by permission.

The First Patient

Louis Henri Vaquez (1860–1936) was born in Paris and was a pupil of Potain who described gallop rhythm.[11] An authority on disorders of the circulatory system, Vaquez's treatise *Diseases of the Heart* was translated into English in 1924 and became popular in America. Vaquez was a professor in the faculty of medicine in Paris, physician to the Hôpital de la Pitié, and a member of the Académie de Médicine. In 1892 he described cyanotic polycythaemia.[12] The first patient with the new type of polycythaemia was a 40-year-old man with a ten-year history of blue extremities and bulging veins. Three years before presentation, he developed breathlessness, palpitations, vertigo without fainting, and bleeding gums. The patient had cyanosis with dilated veins, intense redness of the face with marked conjunctival injection, and hepatosplenomegaly. Cardiac auscultatory signs and edema were absent. Examination of the blood showed 8,900,000 red cells; multiple determinations were performed, all of which were in excess of 8 million. Vaquez initially attributed the condition to congenital heart disease despite the absence of auscultatory signs. The patient died the following year of acute tuberculosis. Autopsy confirmed splenic (1800 gm) and hepatic (2800 gm) enlargement. Cardiac disease was absent. In his paper Vaquez noted recognized causes of an elevated red blood cell count, including high altitude and hemoconcentration. He also commented on other causes of cyanosis including congenital heart lesions. Vaquez cited three other patients with similar clinical findings and proposed that they might have had the same condition. He hypothesized that the persistent and exaggerated production of red blood cells was due to functional hyperactivity of hematopoietic organs, as supported by enlargement of the liver and spleen.

Osler's Cases

In 1903, Osler spoke on "Chronic cyanosis with polycythaemia and an enlarged spleen: a new clinical entity" at a meeting of the Association of American Physicians. His report was subsequently published in the *American Journal of the Medical Sciences*[13] (Fig. 1). Osler's paper described four patients with chronic cyanosis and polycythaemia (polyglobulism), two of whom had enlarged spleens. He cited Vaquez's case and four others from the recent literature. Osler's first patient was a 44-year old physician seen in 1901, at which time his red count was 9,952,000 and hemoglobin 120%. Several determinations were made, as it was thought there might have been a counting error. Evidence for heart disease and emphysema was absent. Subsequent papers in 1904 and 1908 provided a comprehensive clinical picture of the disease which has not been significantly amplified since.[14,15] Osler gave credit to Vaquez for his 1892 description and favored the term erythraemia. He discussed the "torpor, mental and physical" which characterized these patients and noted that the first patient looked "red as a rose and bursting with blood on a hot summer day" while in winter he became as "blue as indigo." He commented on the occurrence of vascular disease, erythromelalgia, and hypertension as well as intense bone marrow hyperplasia. He did not recognize the frequent association with leukocytosis or thrombocytosis. Osler made an analogy with leukemia: oversupply without corresponding demand. He favored treatment with repeated bleedings and possibly inhalation of oxygen and splenic irradiation. Osler discussed polycythaemia (polyglobulism)

CHRONIC CYANOSIS, WITH POLYCYTHÆMIA AND ENLARGED SPLEEN: A NEW CLINICAL ENTITY.

BY WILLIAM OSLER, M.D.,
PROFESSOR OF MEDICINE IN JOHNS HOPKINS UNIVERSITY.

THE group of cases here reported, with those collected from the literature, are worthy of careful study, as we have here in all probability " a definite clinical entity and one which is new to medical science," to use the words of Saundby and Russell in describing their case. The condition is characterized by chronic cyanosis, polycythæmia, and moderate enlargement of the spleen. The chief symptoms have been weakness, prostration, constipation, headache, and vertigo. A further analysis will be reserved until after the consideration of the cases :

CASE I. *Cyanosis for years, of unknown origin ; albuminuria ; rapid pulse ; polycythæmia ; high vascular tension.*—Dr. K., aged forty-four years, consulted me October 28, 1901, complaining of a rapid pulse and diffuse cyanosis. He has been a very healthy man, active and vigorous, of good habits ; has had no serious illnesses. He has been uneasy about himself, as he had detected a trace of albumin in the urine. For several years his wife has noticed that he has had a very congested appearance, and the eyes would often be deeply suffused. I have seen him at intervals for the past five years and have known him to be a very blue-faced man. He has been of a constipated habit. His eyes are somewhat prominent, but his wife says this is natural to him. He has constantly a feeling of fulness in the head, sometimes a sensation of vertigo, and for these symptoms he consulted me.

He was a well-built, well-nourished man ; the face much suffused ; the ears looked a little blue ; the conjunctivæ were injected, and the lips distinctly cyanotic. The tongue also looked cyanotic. The general surface of the skin looked suffused and the anæmia left after pressure of the hand on the skin was very marked and very slowly obliterated. The feet and hands were quite cyanosed. The radials and temporals were moderately sclerotic. Pulse 120, regular. Apex beat in fifth, just inside the nipple line ; sounds clear ; aortic second a little accentuated. There was no enlargement of the thyroid. No enlargement of the liver ; moderate enlargement of the spleen, the edge of which was palpable. The chest was well formed, not barrel-shaped ; the cervical muscles not prominent. Expansion of the chest good. No sign of emphysema. Expiration not prolonged. Once or

FIGURE 1 Osler's initial publication on polycythaemia vera (reference 13). He commented on Vaquez's case reported in 1892 and later suggested that the disorder be named "Vaquez's Disease."

of two types. One was relative and due to hemoconcentration; the other was true with persistent elevation of the red count. Secondary causes for the latter included high altitude, congenital heart disease and emphysema, but red cell counts in patients with these conditions typically were not as high as in Osler's cases. Osler thought the patients he described represented a new clinical entity, but that additional investigation was required for confirmation. He concluded by stating that the "clinical picture is certainly very distinctive; the symptoms, however, are somewhat indefinite, and the pathology quite obscure."

Osler's 1907 clinical lecture on erythraemia[15] was delivered at the Radcliffe Infirmary, Oxford and began with the following words:

"Gentlemen, —it is interesting to follow the stages in the recognition of a new disease. Very rarely does it happen that at all points the description is so complete as at once to gain universal acceptance. Albuminous urine and its association with dropsy had been noted before Bright studied the changes in the kidneys and drew with a master hand the picture of the disease which we now know so well. Complete as was Addison's monograph it took a good many years before we recognized fully the relation of the suprarenal bodies to the disease that now bears his name. The original description of the simultaneous disease of the lymph glands and spleen by the distinguished old Quaker physician, Hodgkin, had not attracted any more attention than had his equally remarkable contribution on insufficiency of the aortic valves (which antedated by several years Corrigan's account) until Wilks, the "grand old man" to-day of British medicine, drew attention to the condition. And so it was with myxoedema, which was well known for years in England before our continental brethren recognized its existence. First a case here and there is reported as something unusual; in a year or two someone collects them and emphasizes the clinical features and perhaps names the disease. Then in rapid succession new cases are reported and we are surprised to find that it is by no means uncommon. This has been the history of a very remarkable malady of which the patient before you is the subject."

Later in the lecture, Osler stated:

"A word about the name, always a difficulty in connexion with a new disease. The choice lies between an eponymic, an anatomical, or a symptomatic name. The one suggested by Parkes Weber—splenomegalic polycythaemia—has been adopted in this country. In France it has been called maladie de Vaquez, or Vaquez-Osler, and in the United States some of my friends have been kind enough to associate my name with it. But the priority of description rests with Vaquez and if a name is to be associated with the disease it should be that of our distinguished French colleague."

Osler's lecture on erythraemia provided a comprehensive clinical picture of the disorder which has not been surpassed.[16] His presentation was a striking example of Osler's method of bedside teaching—integration of clinical observation and laboratory findings with pathophysiological concepts.[6] In the 7th edition of his textbook, Osler described the condition as "splenomegalic polycythaemia with cyanosis (Vaquez's Disease)."[17] The chronic disorder was associated with red blood cell counts of 9–13 million/cu mm. Headache, giddiness, and constipation were common symptoms. Patients were said to have a brick-red color, or when cold marked cyanosis. At autopsy, extreme bone marrow hyperplasia was found. Osler suggested that the disorder was the red cell counterpart of leukemia. Finally, he noted that polyglobulism without an enlarged spleen occurred in many other conditions, especially congential heart disease and exposure to high altitudes.

Terminology and Synonyms

The term *polycythaemia* refers to a higher that normal number of red blood cells. *Relative* polycythaemia indicates a reduction in plasma volume (haemoconcentration). *Erythrocytosis* denotes polycythaemia which occurs in response to some identifiable stimulus (pulmonary or congenital heart disease, high altitude, certain abnormal hemoglobins, erythropoietin-producing tumors). *Polycythaemia vera*, *polycythaemia rubra vera*, and *splenomegalic polycythaemia* refer to the idiopathic disorder (now included in the myeloproliferative group) described by Osler. He preferred the term erythraemia.

Polycythaemia Vera after Osler

Milestones in the history of PV are listed in Table 1. Parkes Weber emphasized that hypertension was unusual in erythraemia despite increased blood viscosity.[18] He also recognized the frequent elevation of the white blood count in peripheral blood and remarked that "the increased activity of the bone marrow is in its results practically equivalent to a gradual persistent transfusion of blood into the vessels." By 1912, 181 cases were cited by Lucas,[19] who pointed out that although a few cases of the disease had been reported, it was not until Osler's papers that the condition was widely recognized. Minot and Buckman[20] considered PV a neoplasm closely related to chronic myelogenous leukemia. They called attention to the elevated platelet counts and increased marrow megakaryocytes that were prominent features of the disorder. Minot and Buckman also described the late occurrence of anemia and massive splenomegaly in some patients. Patients with untreated symptomatic PV had a median life expectancy of eighteen months after diagnosis.[21] The introduction ^{32}P therapy by Lawrence in 1938 produced sustained remissions in many patients.[22] Because of the generalized nature of blood and marrow involvement, Dameshek incorporated PV into his concept of the myeloproliferative disorders.[23] The Polycythaemia Vera Study Group was organized in 1967 by Wasserman to accurately delineate the criteria for diagnosis, natural history, and optimal treatment of the disease.[24] In 1976 Adamson et al provided direct evidence that PV was a clonal stem-cell disorder.[25]

Numerous variations on the theme of bloodletting have been used in the treatment of PV since it was first described.[24,26] Venesection (phlebotomy) was employed as a panacea for varied conditions dating back to ancient Egyptian civilization,[27,28] but proved effective for many patients with PV and is still used. Radiophosphorus therapy often produced prolonged remissions, but led to a controversy regarding its leukemogenic effect. Chlorambucil, an alkylating agent of the cytotoxic chemotherapy type, also proved leukemogenic as revealed by the results of the Polycythaemia Vera Study Group. In recent years the antimetabolite, hydroxyurea, has been employed as it is less leukemogenic than radiophosphorus or alkylating agents. Interferon, which had been shown to be active in chronic myelogenous leukemia and other myeloproliferative disorders, has been utilized in PV. The thrombocytosis associated with PV has responded to anagrelide.[26]

The principal complications of PV include thrombosis (18 to 61%),

Table 1. Polycythaemia Vera (PV): Milestones

1892–Original description (Vaquez)
1903–Osler's 4 cases
1907–Osler's lecture on erythraemia
1908–Splenomegalic polycythaemia (Weber)
1912–181 cases of polycythaemia, 125 erythraemia (Lucas)
1923–Neoplastic nature of PV, thrombocytosis (Minot & Buckman)
1938–Radiophosphorus therapy (Lawrence)
1951–PV a myeloproliferative disorder (Dameshek)
1967–PV Study Group formed (Wasserman)
1976–PV a clonal stem-cell hematopoietic disorder (Adamson et al)

bleeding, (4–35%), and transformation to acute leukemia or myelofibrosis.[26] Surgery in patients with uncontrolled PV is associated with significant increases in morbidity and mortality.[29] Improvement in duration and quality of life for patients with PV occurs with effective therapy. It is possible to live for many years with adequately treated PV. The composer Igor Stravinsky remained creative and productive into his 80's with PV controlled by treatment.[30]

Two recent reports have added to our understanding of PV. Autonomous erythropoietin-independent cells derive from monoclonal progenitors in PV. Silva et al have identified high levels of Bcl-x protein in erythroid precursor cells from PV patients.[31] This protein inhibits programmed cell death (apoptosis) allowing erythroid progenitors in PV to bypass the need for their growth factor, erythropoietin. In addition, Moliterno et al have shown that platelets and megakaryocytes from PV patients have absent or reduced thrombopoietin receptor.[32] Thus megakaryocytes in PV are independent of their growth factor—analogous to the circumstance with erythroid precursors and erythropoietin.[33] The results of these studies explain why endogenous erythropoietin levels are low in PV. This finding is in contrast to secondary polycythaemia in which they are uniformly elevated, or in tumor polycythaemia where erythropoietin is produced by various neoplasms.[24]

Eponyms: Pro and Con

Which eponym should be used for PV? Possibilities include Vaquez Disease, Osler Disease, Vaquez-Osler Disease, and Osler-Vaquez Disease. All exist in the literature. As noted, Osler himself suggested that it be called Vaquez Disease.[15,17] In the recent articles regarding PV growth factor-independence described above, no eponym was used.[31–33] Some authors no longer favor the use of eponyms to describe diseases. Journal editors are particularly likely to omit eponyms as they take up valuable space. In addition, it is noteworthy that Osler-Vaquez Disease is not used to describe PV in contemporary textbooks of medicine and hematology.[34, 35]

McKusick has recently considered the use of eponyms in naming clinical disorders.[36] He notes that eponyms remind us of the nosologic history of the condition and contribution of a previous investigator. For diseases with geographic or ethnic designations, eponyms help us remember the population distribution. McKusick favors the use of eponyms, but strongly recommends the use of the nonpossessive form.

It seems fitting that both Vaquez and Osler receive recognition for their contributions to the history of PV. Vaquez described the first patient and this was acknowledged by Osler. However, Osler's superb clinical description of the disorder led to its widespread recognition and definition as a new entity. Osler's own perspective seems pertinent in this regard: "In science the credit goes to the man who convinces the world, not to the man to whom the idea first occurs."[37] All things considered, "Osler-Vaquez Disease" appears to be the most appropriate eponymic designation for PV.

Acknowledgment

Supported in part by the Edward and Ruth Wilkof Foundation. I thank Amanda Boyd for expert assistance with manuscript preparation.

References

1. Bailey I. Sir William Osler (1849–1919): physician, teacher, historian, biographer, bibliophile. J. Med Biography 1993; 1:2–10
2. Stone MJ. The wisdom of Sir William Osler. Am J Cardiol 1995; 75:269–276
3. Osler W. *The Principles and Practice of Medicine.* New York: Appleton, 1892
4. Bliss M. *William Osler. A Life in Medicine.* Oxford: Oxford Univ Press, 1999
5. Cushing H. *The Life of Sir William Osler.* Vol 1 and 2. Oxford: Clarendon Press, 1925
6. Robb-Smith AHT. Osler's influence on haematology. Blood Cells 1981; 7:513–533
7. Osler W. Cartwright Lectures: on certain problems in the physiology of the blood corpuscles. Med News 1886; Apr 3, 10, 17
8. Robb-Smith AHT. Why the platelets were discovered. Brit J Haematol 1967, 13:618–637
9. Coar T. *The Aphorisms of Hippocrates: With a Translation into Latin, and English.* London: AJ Valpy, 1822 (Classics of Medicine Library edition, Birmingham, Alabama, 1982)
10. Rosner F, Muntner S. *The Medical Aphorisms of Moses Maimonides.* New York: Bloch Publishing Co Vol II, p. 127
11. Major RH. *Classic Descriptions of Disease.* 2nd edit. Springfield: Charles C. Thomas, 1939, pp 419–21
12. Vaquez H. Sur une forme spéciale de cyanose s' accompanant d'hyperglobulie excessive et peristente, Compt rend Soc de biol 1892; 4:384–88 and suppl. note, Bull et mém. Soc. méd. d'hôp. dc Paris, 3 ser., 1895, 12:60.
13. Osler W. Chronic cyanosis with polycythaemia and enlarged spleen; a new clinical entity. Am J Med Sci 1903; 126:187–201
14. Osler W. Chronic cyanotic polycythaemia with enlarged spleen. Brit Med J. 1904; 1:121–122
15. Osler W. A clinical lecture on erythraemia (polycythaemia with cyanosis, maladie de Vaquez). Lancet 1908; 1:143–146
16. Wintrobe MM. Osler's chronic cyanotic polycythemia with splenomegaly. Bull Johns Hopkins Hospital 1949, 85:74–86.
17. Osler W. *The Principles and Practice of Medicine,* 7th edit. New York: D. Appleton, 1909, p 762–3.
18. Weber FP, Polycythaemia, erythrocytosis and erythraemia., Qtr J Med 1908; 2:85–134
19. Lucas WS, Erythraemia, or polycythemia with chronic cyanosis and splenomegaly. Arch Intern Med 1912; 10:597–619
20. Minot GR, Buckman TE. Erythremia (polycythemia rubra vera). Am J Med Sci 1923; 166:469–89
21. Chievitz E, Thiede T. Complications and causes of death in polycythaemia vera. Acta Med Scandinav 1962; 172:513–23.
22. Lawrence JH, Nuclear physics and therapy: Preliminary report on a new method for the treatment of leukemia and polycythemia. Radiology 1940; 35:51–60
23. Dameshek W. Some speculations on the myeloproliferative syndromes. Blood 1951; 6:372–75
24. Wasserman LR, Berk PD, Berlin NI eds. *Polycythemia Vera and the Myeloproliferative Disorders.* Philadelphia: W.B. Saunders, 1995
25. Adamson JW, Fialkow PJ, Murphy S, et al. Polycythemia vera: stem-cell and probable clonal origin of the disease. N Eng J Med 1976; 295:913–16

26. Berlin NI, ed. Polycythemia vera: Semin Hematol 1997; 34:1–80

27. Wintrobe MM. Milestones on the path of progress. In: Wintrobe MM (ed). *Blood, Pure and Eloquent.* New York: McGraw-Hill, 1980, 1–31

28. Hoffbrand AV, Fantini B. Achievements in hematology in the twentieth century: an introduction. Semin Hematol 1999; 36 (suppl 7): 1–4

29. Wasserman LR, Gilbert HS. Surgery in polycythemia vera. N Engl J Med 1963; 269:1226–1230

30. Weinstein IM. Clinical Manifestations. In Klein H ed. *Polycythemia Theory and Management.* Springfield: Charles C. Thomas, 1973, p. 95

31. Silva M, Richard C, Benito A, Sanz C, Olalla I, Fernandez-Luna JL. Expression of Bcl-x in erythroid precursors from patients with polycythemia vera. N Engl J Med 1998; 338:564–71

32. Moliterno AR, Hawkins WD, Spivak JL. Impaired expression of the thrombopoietin receptor by platelets from patients with polycythemia vera. N Eng J Med 1998; 338:572–80

33. Schwartz RS, Polycythemia vera – chance, death, and mutability. N Eng J Med 1998: 338:613–15

34. Spivak JC. Polycythemia vera and other myeloproliferative diseases. In: Fauci AS, Braunwald E, Isselbacher KJ, Wilson JD, Martin JB, Kasper DL, Hauser SL, Longo DL (eds). *Harrison's Principles of Internal Medicine.* 14th edit. New York: McGraw-Hill, 1998, pp. 679–81

35. Means RT. Polycythemia vera. In: Lee GR, Foerster J, Lukens J, Paraskevas F, Greer JP, Rodgers GM (eds). *Wintrobe's Clinical Hematology.* 10th edit. Baltimore: Williams & Wilkins, 1999, v2, p 2374–89

36. McKusick VA. On the naming of clinical disorders, with particular reference to eponyms. Medicine 1998; 77:1–2

37. Bean RB, Bean WB (eds). *Sir William Osler. Aphorisms from His Bedside Teachings and Writings* (2nd printing). Springfield: Charles C. Thomas, 1961:112

William Osler and the First Opioid Epidemic

 David F. Musto, M.D.

One of the elements in the rise of modern medicine last century was a series of achievements by organic chemists. Among these was the isolation from natural sources of purified active ingredients like morphine, codeine and cocaine and the synthesis of diacetylmorphine, or heroin. Never before had these pure chemicals been at the service of physicians—and everyone else, for that matter. Furthermore, in mid-century the hypodermic syringe was perfected, adding a simple way to introduce these chemicals into the body's tissues in a measured quantity.

The nineteenth century also witnessed the rise in problems associated with the widespread use of these substances and the first attempts to control them by education and legal sanction. The popularity of these new drugs could be gauged by the rise in use of opium and opiates in the United States. For a variety of disparate reasons, this nation allowed an open market for morphine, cocaine and heroin at their earliest availability.

In the decade of Osler's birth, the 1840s, per capita consumption of opium in the United States was about 12 grains. Fifty years later that individual average had increased to 52 grains, an increase of over 400%. Although the consumption on an individual basis had diminished somewhat by 1915, the first year of the Harrison Narcotic Act, a widely-held conviction that physicians were responsible for at least half of the addicts in the country was shared not only by critics of the medical profession, but by experts within the profession itself. By 1919, the year of Osler's death, the problem of drug addiction dominated the presidential address to the American Medical Association. The President, Dr. Alexander Lambert, urged tight control over physicians writing narcotic prescriptions in order to stop "a few renegade and depraved members of the profession who, joining with the criminal class, make it possible to continue the evil and illicit drug trade." (Lambert 1920:1767).

Gradually the number of those addicted to opiates declined, especially

Presented at the American Osler Society, May 12, 1993, Louisville, Kentucky.

the middle-class addicts. From an estimate of a quarter-million in 1900, in 1924 (Kolb and DuMez 1924) the number had fallen to about half that amount. In these estimates I am choosing the most calm and professional investigators and excluding the gross exaggerations proclaimed at times by the government and independent anti-narcotic crusaders.

It is evident, then, that William Osler's life spanned the early rise in opiate addiction, its peak, and early stages of what was to be a gradual and lengthy decline that continued until the 1950s.

***

The first reference I find regarding morphine in Osler's publications is a short autopsy note published in the *Montreal General Hospital Reports* for 1880. In spite of its brevity, it is an historic description of a phenomenon that has become commonplace in our day. In mid-December, in an out-building, a forty-year-old man was found at the bottom of his sleigh. At the autopsy morphine was found in his stomach. Osler took an interest in his lungs. "I had never before seen," Osler wrote, "an organ so infiltrated with bloody serum" (Osler 1880:292). He also noted that the "bronchi contain frothy serum" (291). This finding, of oedema and frothing, is characteristic of deaths in the drug shooting-galleries and other places where victims of opiate overdose are found. To my knowledge, Osler was the first to call attention to this curious aspect of deaths from opiates.

In trying to trace Osler's subsequent response to the first drug epidemic, I have chosen to follow his description of opiate addiction in *The Principles and Practice of Medicine* (1892:1005–07). The great book's appearance coincided with the peak of opiate consumption in the United States. Osler's attitude toward the problem is valuable not only as the distillation of the thought of a great physician who grew up, so to speak, with the rise in drug use last century, but even more as an influence on physicians who took from the textbook an authoritative account of drug addiction—its causes, characteristics, course, treatment and prognosis. I have found it fascinating to put Osler's entry on the "Morphia Habit" into the social and legal context in which it appeared.

Osler placed morphinism just after alcoholism among the intoxications. The cause was simple prolonged use of morphia. In 1892, heroin was still six years away. The first use of morphia arose from seeking pain relief, not from what we would now call "recreational" use. Osler added that the use of smoking-opium in Asia "where opium-smoking is as common as tobacco-smoking with us," had ill-effects that were "not so striking." I assume Osler drew this opinion from some articles in British medical journals which served to justify British export of Indian opium to China during the last century. A similar opinion also concluded an 1895 Royal Commission report on the opium situation in India. An opposite opinion on opium smoking would lead in the first decade of this century to a vigorous attack on opium-smoking by the Chinese Empire.

Osler singled out two groups where morphinism could most frequently be found: women and physicians. Women were probably the largest group of addicts in the late 19th century. In David Courtwright's fine study of opiate addiction in America, the model addict of that time was "a native Southerner, possessed of servant and property, once married, now widowed and homebound . . addicted since middle age" by her physician (Courtwright 1982:42). A contemporary implication of physicians as the other great class of addicts was given in 1899 by an eminent expert on the subject, Dr. T.D. Crothers, editor of the *Journal of Inebriety*. He reported that six to ten per cent of physicians in the United States were "opium inebriates" (Crothers 1899). The culprit here, Osler warned, was the hypodermic syringe, particularly in the instance of chronic pain such as sciatica.

Osler's description of morphinism is, from today's vantage, both exaggerated and less alarmist. He grants that large amounts may be taken for years without deterioration of "mental or bodily functions." But the usual course is one of gradually increasing doses to ward off withdrawal symptoms. Incidentally, he described withdrawal symptoms fairly mildly, as lassitude, mental depression, slight nausea and epigastric distress, and occasional profuse sweats. He gives no drastic depiction of going "cold turkey," nor does he claim that death could result in the process, a warning often asserted until the 1920s. The addict can be recognized by a "sallowness of the complexion which is almost pathognomonic," emaciation, graying and premature aging. "Finally," Osler concludes, "a condition of asthenia is induced, in which the victim takes little or no food and dies from extreme bodily debility." This sounds more like the end stage of alcoholism than of opiate addiction. Today the death of addicts is more often from overdose, hepatitis, septicemia, and, of course, AIDS.

Osler also comments on the mental effects of addiction. Persons addicted to morphia," he wrote, "are inveterate liars, and no reliance whatever can be placed on their statements."

Here I would like to introduce William Stewart Halsted, one of Osler's patients. It is now common knowledge that Halsted became catastrophically reliant on cocaine while self-experimenting in the mid-1880s. Peter Olch's research revealed that Halsted, having worked his way free from cocaine, became addicted to morphine and remained so to the end of his life.

Osler's account of Halsted was not released until 1969 in an article by Wilder Penfield. The accepted history of Halsted's drug problem was that he could not be taken on permanently at the Hopkins until he had broken his tie to cocaine, that he did so and then established his distinguished career. Without going into detail, I believe Osler's account of Halsted's continued use of morphine illustrates some of the characteristics of opioid dependency that have once again—in our second drug epidemic—become familiar.

Osler's "secret history" was written, according to Penfield, about 1893 and certainly before 1899. In it Osler states that Halsted could not get the morphine below three grains daily. In a later note, Osler wrote that Halsted did reduce the dose in 1898 to one and a half grains and "of late years (1912) has possibly got on without it." Whether morphine, heroin or methadone, there is commonly a floor below which the patient can go only with the greatest difficulty. Why this exists for some users, I cannot explain. Halsted seems to be one of those persons who can come down almost, but not quite all the way from a high daily dose. It is extremely frustrating, and I have wondered whether Halsted's summer trips to Europe where he lived incommunicado were arranged so he could try to wean himself from the tenacious opiate.

In 1898 when, Osler wrote, Halsted had reduced his daily dose to one and a half grains, Osler added one new sentence to his third edition's entry on morphinism. It reads: "An increase in the dose is not always necessary, and there are *habitués* who reach the point of satisfaction with a daily amount of 2 or 3 grains of morphia, and who are able to carry on successfully for many years the ordinary business of life" (Osler, 898:385).

Osler faced the treatment of addiction frankly and offered no hopeful prognosis. First, he warned off the general practitioner who might try to cure a confirmed addict. The essential requirements are isolation, systematic feeding and gradual withdrawal of the drug. Isolation was required because the patient would obtain morphine in the most ingenious ways. "Even under the favorable circumstance of seclusion in an institution," Osler warned, "and constant watching by a night and a day nurse, I have known a patient to practice deception for a period of three months."

Osler took a middle road on how best to respond to the regular doses of morphine. Eduard Levinstein, a Berlin specialist on addictions, had published in 1875 an extensive account of his experience. He concluded that abrupt cessation of the drug was preferable to gradual withdrawal which he likened to cutting off a dog's tail one slice at a time. In the other corner was the view that no reduction was necessary, a view more fully developed in the decade before the First World War. Its proponents argued that addiction caused a permanent pathological change in the body that required a certain daily dose for normality. Too little and the patient would slide into withdrawal; too much and the patient would get "high", to use a modern term. This hypothesis fell into disfavor in the 1920s, but was revived by Drs. Dole and Nyswander in the 1950s and is a foundation of methadone maintenance.

Osler's description of withdrawal in an institution is much more severe than that he gives for the user in everyday life. It is, of course, the fear of withdrawal that makes an injection of morphine the user's highest priority. Withdrawal sufferings are "usually very great," Osler wrote, "more particularly the abdominal pains, sometimes nausea and vomiting, and the distressing restlessness." This is what Halsted would undergo as he tried to reduce his dose below the two or three grains a day.

Perhaps it explains a passage in the recently published H.L. Mencken *Diary* (1989). In an entry in 1931, Mencken quotes Dr. Joseph C. Bloodgood as saying that when he was a surgery resident at the Hopkins, 1893 to 1897, he had to do a great deal of Halsted's work. Halsted would begin an operation and then have to stop, saying his heart was thumping due to excessive smoking, an explanation Bloodgood seems to have accepted (p. 10). Another cause, however, may have brought on Halsted's distress. One can imagine the difficulties Halsted faced each day.

Osler described morphinism in 1892 as a condition that "has become so common, and is so much on the increase, that physicians should exercise utmost caution in prescribing morphia, particularly to female patients." As I have mentioned, he was writing at the peak of opiate consumption and at a moment when growing alarm at addiction would begin to drive down per capita consumption. Laws would also be enacted to restrict morphine to a physician's prescription. Anticipating a further restriction, now hotly debated in state legislatures, Osler urged that only physicians, not nurses nor anyone else, should employ the hypodermic syringe, "this dangerous instrument."

Reading Osler reveals the image of addiction that led to severe laws intended to curb the easy availability of habit-forming drugs in the United States. Unlike Britain and other European nations, the US lacked national medical or pharmacy laws. We were stymied by the Federal Constitution's reservation of the relevant police powers to the individual states. State after state enacted controls over morphine, but the momentum for a national law was so strong that eventually the Harrison Act, based on the Federal power to tax, was enacted 1914. In the meantime the United States had started the world anti-narcotic movement, presided over the world's first Conference on Opium, at the Hague in 1912, and drafted an international treaty that would become the basis for action by the League of Nations and the United Nations. Interestingly, the person who had the idea for an international meeting and who chaired the Hague Opium Conference was a fellow graduate of Trinity

College School and the University of Toronto, Bishop Charles Henry Brent. Together, these two Canadians encompassed the drug problem.

We should be forthright in recognizing some questionable themes in Osler's perspective. When we consider the trepidation with which many physicians prescribe—or should I say *underprescribe*—pain medication, we should look at the passage in the first edition of the great textbook to see how this fear was expressed and was transmitted by the most authoritative voice among English-speaking physicians.

Do we feel that ascribing moral degradation to addicts is a prejudice that interferes with treatment? If so, consider that the statement that morphia addicts are "inveterate liars" still appeared at least as late as 1944 in the fifteenth edition of the textbook (Christian 1944).

From the perspective of today, one of the lessons to be drawn from Osler's textbook is that alarm, fear and disgust at addiction was not the result of some legislative action such as the Harrison Act. Rather, the extremely negative perception of addiction arose from the widespread use of the drugs themselves and direct experience with the consequences.

***

A century has passed since Osler's text appeared. The wave of drug use he witnessed eventually receded, only to flow over us again. What I draw for our time from Osler's experience is the importance of patience, tolerance and personal responsibility in that prolonged battle.

References

Christian, Henry A., *Principles and Practice of Medicine, Originally Written by Sir William Osler . . .* , 15th ed., New York: Appleton-Century (1944).

Courtwright, D., *Dark Paradise, Opiate Addiction in America before 1940*, Cambridge: Harvard University Press, (1982).

Crothers, T.D., "Morphinism among Physician," *Med. Rec.* 55:784–6 (1899)

Kolb, L. and DuMex, A.G., "The Prevalence of Drug Addiction in the United States and Factors Influencing It," *Pub. Hlth. Rpts.* 39:1202–1203 (23 May 1924).

Lambert, A., "Address of the President-Elect," *JAMA* 72: 1767 (1920).

Levinstein, E, Morbid Craving for Morphia, trans. C. Harrer, London: Smith, Elder (1878).

Mencken, H.L., *Diary,* ed. by Charles A. Fecher. (1989)

Osler, W. "Oedema of Left Lung—Morphia Poisoning," *Montreal General Hospital Reports,* 1:291–292 (1880).

Osler, W., *Principles and Practice of Medicine*, Edinburgh, London: Young, 1982.

Osler, W., *Principles and Practice of Medicine*, 3rd ed., New York: D. Appleton and Co., (1898)

Penfield, W., "Halsted of Johns Hopkins: The Man and His Problem as Described in the Secret Records of William Osler," *JAMA* 210: 2214–8, (1969)

Report of the Royal Commission on Opium (1894–1895) 7 vols. London: HMSO.

Osler the Microscopist: Teaching, Research, and Practice; Part 1: The Canadian Years

 Alvin Eli Rodin M.D., F.R.C.P.C.,
Jack D. Key M.A., M.S.

Summary

William Osler's introduction to the microscope began when he was 16. His interest continued in medical school, resulting in a graduation thesis on microscopy accompanied by 33 slides. As professor of the institutes of medicine at McGill University, Osler started a course in microscopy, developing a manual using material from both human and veterinarian autopsies. He continued gross and microscopic studies while professor of medicine at Philadelphia, despite opposition from pathologists. His research topics were platelets and malaria. His "Principles and Practice of Medicine" includes at least 60 histologic descriptions of disease with discussion of their significance. Osler's activities related to microscopy reveal him to have been a leader in its development as a tool for medical education, research, and practice.

Sommaire

William Osler a été initié au microscope à l'âge de seize ans. Même à la faculté de médecine, il a continué à s'intéresser au microscope, d'ailleurs, il a

Presented at the American Osler Society, April 11, 1991, New Orleans.

Published by permission of The Royal College of Physicians and Surgeons of Canada.

rédigé une thèse sur le microscope accompagnée de 33 diapositives. En qualité de professeur aux instituts de médecine de l'université McGill, Osler a lancé un cours sur le microscope et préparé un manuel faisant appel aux données tirées d'autopsies d'humains et d'animaux. Alors qu'il enseignait la médecine à Philadelphie, il a effectué des études macroscopiques et microscopiques en dépit de l'opposition des pathologistes. Il s'est consacré à la recherche sur la malaria et les platelettes. Son ouvrage Principles and Practice of Medicine compte au moins 60 descriptions histologiques de maladies ainsi qu'une discussion de leur signification. Osler se révèle un chef de file qui a su imposer le microscope comme outil d'enseignement, de recherche et de pratique en médecine.

Introduction

Sir William Osler was an outstanding physician whose career as an internist straddled the turn of the century. Born in Canada in 1849, his medical activities began there, continued in the United States, and ended in England, where he died in 1919. Biographers have stressed his humanistic and clinical attributes. Not as well known is the extent of his contributions to the then newly developing science of medical microscopy.

Introduction to Microscopy

Osler began his involvement with microscopy at the age of 16, when he entered a private boarding school in Weston, Ont., in 1866. He came under the tutelage of the Rev. W. A. Johnson, who introduced him to the microscope.[1] Osler's earliest microscopic studies included fresh water diatomaceae, such as polyzoa.

On transferring to Trinity College in Toronto in 1867, Osler continued histologic studies. Such studies were encouraged at Trinity by a physician, James Bovell, who had studied pathology, among other disciplines, in Edinburgh. Osler's first publication was titled "Christmas and the Microscope,"[2] published in 1869, the year of his enrolment in medical school. It is an account of his search in the Canadian woods for water from unfrozen streams. Finding some algae, he returned home. "Upon putting a slide under the microscope before I had properly focused, I saw the dim outline of some little creature kicking and struggling as though it were in a net. It turned out to be one of the Tardigrada, or little water-bears, that had gotten entangled in the gelatinous tube of Encyonema prostratum."

In 1870, while at the Toronto medical school, Osler published an account of the microscopic appearance of diatomaceae.[3] He gave a detailed description of these one-celled creatures, including their method of reproduction and development. Typical of Osler's painstaking of endeavors, both research and clinical, is the inclusion of a list of 31 genera with 110 species. Similar studies continued even when he was a McGill professor. For example, in 1881, he made a presentation to the Natural History Society of Montreal on fresh-water polyzoa.[4] Included were three species, Cristatella, Plumatelidae, and a new one. A more extensive account was delivered to the society in 1883, including detailed descriptions of structure and life history.[5]

Medical Student Days

In 1869, as a neophyte medical student at the Toronto medical school, Osler expanded his microscopic studies by investigating the histology of the mouse trachea.[1] In January and February 1870, while dissecting a cadaver, he saw minute cysts of trichinae throughout the muscular system of a cadaver. There is no record that he studied them microscopically.[6]

In the summer of 1870, Osler transferred from Toronto to McGill, largely because of the wider range of clinical activities (Figure. 1). According to the December 1870 records of the Montreal Medical-Chirurgical Society: "Professor Howard Exhibited under the microscope very beautifully stained sections . . . executed by Mr. Osler, one of the students of the McGill Faculty." According to Maude Abbott: "His interest in the postmortem room and his free use of the microscope, are among the most conspicuous acts in his history, revealing as they do, the quick grasp of essentials which was the outstanding feature of his genius. Already, in 1872, we find him, while still a student, assisting his Chief at the Medico-Surgical Society by the demonstration of pathological material, and publishing from a student-pen, his first classic case reports, with autopsy findings."[7]

In 1872, Osler published a report on a patient with carcinoma of the

Figure 1. Building of the McGill medical faculty, Montreal, 1871.[56]

breast, including not only the history and physical examination, but also gross and microscopic descriptions of the surgical specimen.[8] In his words: "The microscopical structure agreed in the main with that of schirrhus, the cells were however very much broken down, especially those of the cysts, and the arrangement of the stroma and contained cells presented a greater irregularity than is common."

Osler's last microscopic effort as a medical student was his graduation thesis. According to the report of the 1872 McGill University convocation: "the faculty has in addition this session awarded a special prize to the thesis of William Osler, Dundas, Ont., which was greatly distinguished for originality and research and was accompanied by 33 microscopic and other preparations of morbid structure kindly presented by the author to the museum of the faculty."[9] The prize was a set of books, among which he particularly valued Klein and Sanderson's "Handbook for the Physiological Laboratory," an indication of his propensity towards research early in his career.

Osler's graduation thesis is unpublished, and only the first three pages of the draft for the introduction are extant.[10] These contain, however, insights into his orientation to microscopy (Figure 2), for example, ". . . to interpret aright the pathological changes, and to appreciate as well the courser lesions observed by the natural senses, as those more delicate deviations from the standard of health revealed to us by the Microscope, requires qualities such as few possess." He writes that he was "fortunate enough to possess that amount of microscopical skill necessary for the preparation (sic) of specimens." Osler was aware that he had "a predilection for Pathological Anatomy," which was to place him in the forefront of the developing orientation of clinical medicine to the scientific study of disease.

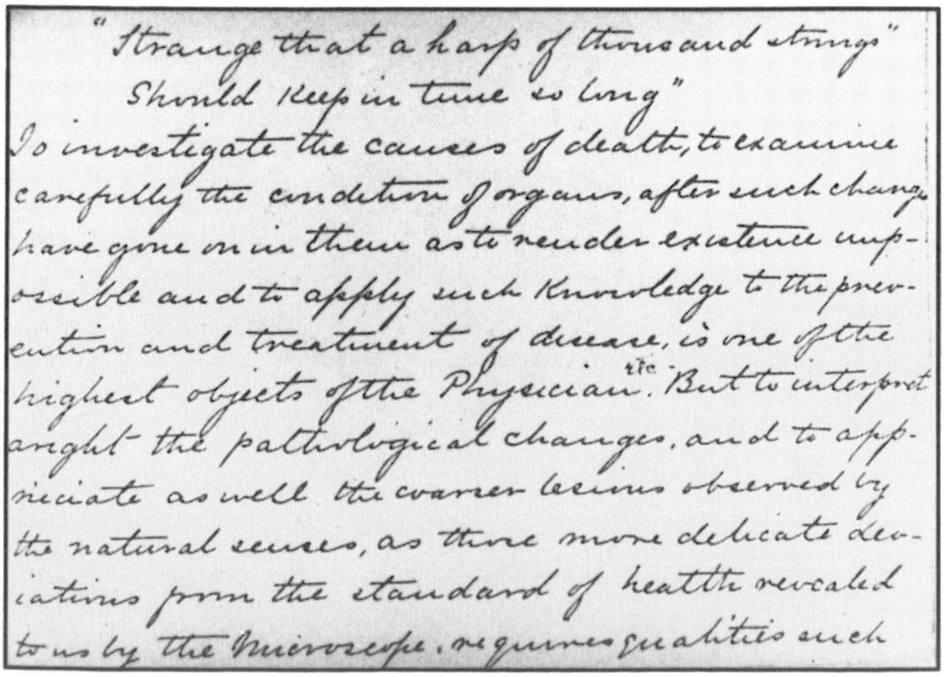
"Strange that a harp of thousand strings"
Should keep in tune so long"
To investigate the causes of death, to examine
carefully the condition of organs, after such changes
have gone on in them as to render existence impossible and to apply such knowledge to the prevention and treatment of disease, is one of the
highest objects of the Physician. But to interpret
aright the pathological changes, and to appreciate as well the coarser lesions observed by
the natural senses, as those more delicate deviations from the standard of health revealed
to us by the Microscope, requires qualities such

Figure 2. From the introduction to Osler's handwritten graduation thesis, 1872;10:2.

Postgraduate Training

After graduation in 1872, Osler continued his microscopic work in experimental physiology. A year was spent in the laboratory of Sir John Burdon-Sanderson at the University College Hospital in London, England.[1] This relationship may have intensified Osler's commitment to microscopy, because his mentor had shown interest in the area as early as 1861, when he "asked permission to give microscopical demonstrations" at St. Mary's Hospital.[11] In 1878, Osler, as a member of the Microscopic Club, gave a demonstration of "the various modes of illumination under high and low powers" of the microscope at a meeting of the Natural History Society of Montreal.[12]

While doing microscopic studies in his blood in London, Osler noted some peculiar globoid bodies.[13] The result was an article in 1873, "On the Action of Certain Reagents . . . on the Colorless Blood-Corpuscles" (Figure 3).[14] His report is one of the first observations of platelets in the circulating blood, which he first labelled as "certain organisms."[15] He described them as "round disks, devoid of granules and with well-defined borders," being "from one-eighth to one-half the size of a red blood corpuscle." He also observed that platelets do not adhere to each other while in blood vessels.[16] Osler's studies of platelets, including those in rat blood, led him to conclude that their significance in disease, their influence in chronic infections, and their relation to bacteria were unknown. These austere conclusions were contrary to the statements of other observers. Osler continued his studies on platelets throughout his career in Montreal and Philadelphia.[17]

After these studies, Osler travelled to Europe. In Berlin, he observed Rudolph Virchow's teaching of pathology, including pathological histology.[18] His exposure served as an enhancement for his microscopic orientation. It was Virchow's book "Cellular Pathology"[19] that established this method of investi-

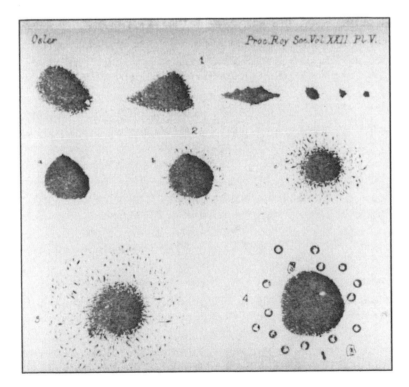

Figure 3. Osler's drawings of colorless blood corpuscles in 1873.[14]

gation as a practical medical discipline. Osler admired Virchow to the point of adulation. In remarks at the Fest for Virchow at Johns Hopkins in 1891, Osler said that "Virchow's life-work has been the study of the processes of disease, and in the profession we revere him as the greatest master that has appeared among us since John Hunter."[20]

In Vienna, Osler visited another well-known pathologist, Rokitansky, but was unimpressed. The "post-mortems here . . . are performed in so slovenly a manner, and so little use is made of the material."[21] While in Vienna, Osler bought a book by Billroth entitled "Coccobacteria Septica." It contained plates depicting bacteria under the microscope.[22] Osler than spent another month in London. In all, his postgraduate experiences enhanced his expertise in medical microscopy.

McGill Professor

Osler returned to Montreal in May 1874. He had spent almost two years overseas, a large part of the time being devoted to microscopic studies. In Montreal, Osler opened a private office for the practice of medicine, but he soon joined the medical faculty at McGill.[1] He began as an instructor, and within a year became professor of the institutes of medicine.

In the 19th century, the institutes of medicine referred to the principles of medicine, including histology, physiology, and some pathology.[23] The name was taken from the University of Edinburgh and used at McGill for a course taught by William Fraser from 1849 until his death in 1872. Only once was a microscope seen in Fraser's course. He borrowed one from the Montreal General Hospital to demonstrate the circulation of blood in a frog's foot. Osler introduced the instrument in practical laboratory work to augment teaching by lecture and textbook. The course on the institutes of medicine lasted until Osler left McGill in 1884, at which time the three subjects were taught by three faculty members.[23]

The contents of Osler's course are described in the annual announcement of the faculty of medicine at McGill University for 1877–1878.[24] "This course comprises histology, physiology, and general pathology. The lectures are illustrated by apparatus, diagrams, plates, and microscopic preparations of the various tissue, and by Pathological specimens from the museum." For the first five years, the course was held in makeshift quarters, including the chemical laboratory and the student's cloakroom.[25]

Osler's dedication to microscopy is shown by the purchase, with his money, of 12 Hartnack microscopes from Paris for student use, at $45 each (Figure 4).[26] His reasons for choosing this particular type indicate an extensive experience with microscopes. "Hartnack's students' microscope . . . is small and easily carried about, not burdened with stage movements, . . . and so not liable to get out of order. The object glasses are very superior, possessing a clearness of definition and power of penetration excelled by few, if any English lenses . . ."[26] These were manufactured by E. Hartnack et Cie, Place Dauphine 21, Paris.[27]

The first use of the microscope in a medical school was in Europe by Alfred Donné in 1844.[28] Osler was not even the first to use a microscope for teaching in Canada. Queen's University, Kingston, Ont., had two British microscopes, which were used in 1854 for the teaching of histology to medical students, and within a few years, pathological physiology.[29]

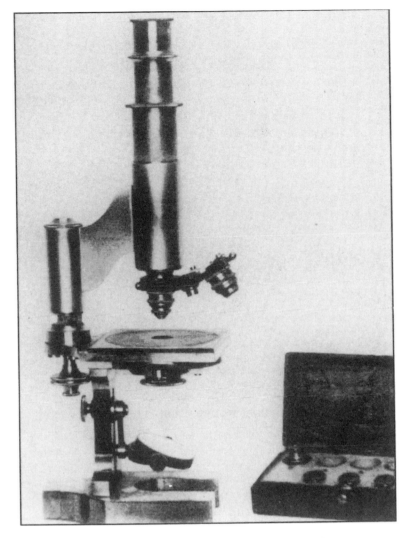

Figure 4. A compound monocular microscope made before 1870 by E. Hartnack and Co., Paris, France.[27] This is likely the model bought by Osler for McGill medical students.

The first class in microscopy at McGill was organized by Osler. "It was a voluntary class held on Saturday afternoons in the cloak-room in the basement of the medical building. I think every member of the class of '77 joined.[30] His method of teaching microscopy began with the practical basis. We were given bits of tissue which we embedded in little paper boxes in wax . . . and then cut our own sections with a razor. After we became somewhat familiar with the normal tissue, we were given abnormalities and we then laid the foundation of our knowledge of pathology."

Osler also joined the Microscopical Club, which was formed by younger members of the Natural History Society, before which he demonstrated newer methods of microscopic illumination in 1878.[1] He promoted histology by writing a manual of normal histology for students. This was the text for his 25 lessons in practical histology.[31] The manual begins with a description of the microscope, a section on the preparation of tissues, and a page on artifacts such as air bubbles, oil drops, granules, fibres, dust, and starch. An indication of Osler's histologic techniques can be obtained from his manual. Fixation methods mentioned include freezing, bichromate of potash, Müller's fluid, chromic acid, alcohol, picric acid, and osmic acid. Stains recommended were carmine, log wood, aniline blue, silver nitrate, gold fluoride, and osmic acid.

The synopsis of his microscopy course, as given by Abbott, indicates how well versed Osler was in the status of microscopy (Table 1).[7] Chapters of his manual deal with cells, fungi, blood, epithelium, and connective tissues, and contain a histologic description of each organ system. His practical approach to microscopic studies of diseased conditions is given in introductory remarks for his course.[26] "As practical Physicians a knowledge of its (microscope) use will be most advantageous, and limited indeed must that practice be which does not afford some cases upon which the microscope would throw light . . . Here (renal disease) we may not only date the commencement of the affection, and follow it in its progress, but also, very often obtain tolerably certain evidence of the nature of the changes going on in the kidneys."

Osler also refers to the diagnostic value of the microscope in examining vomit, alvine discharges, and sputum. He mentions its use in the diagnosis of tumors, but adds a note of caution about the degree of precision possible. The breadth of his orientation to microscopy is evident by its inclusion in medico-legal inquiries, for example, to identify blood and human stains, and to distinguish between human and animal hair. He also mentions the use of the microscope in distinguishing diseased from healthy meat for human consumption. In 1877, he offered an extra-curricular course on "The Microscope in Medicine."

Osler also applied his knowledge in pathology to the teaching and practice of medicine.[1] In 1876, he was appointed pathologist to the Montreal General Hospital in addition to his other duties. This was suggested by his willingness to perform autopsies for his colleagues at the hospital. It was a position created for him; before 1876, autopsies had been performed by physicians on their own cases. Osler continued to do all autopsies, and some with microscopy, even after his appointment as physician to the hospital in 1879. It was not until 1892 that a chair in pathology was created, first occupied by George Adami.

TABLE 1 SYNOPSIS OF THE COURSE DEMONSTRATIONS

1. General description of the Microscope. How to clean it. How to tell a magnifying power. How to draw with it. Examination of dust, cotton fibres and air-bubbles.
2. Protoplasm. Amoeba. Cyclosis in Anatchris. White blood corpuscles.
3. Red blood corpuscles of Frog, Fish, Bird and Man. Haemoglobin crystals from Rat's blood. Haemia crystals. How to examine blood stains.
4. Epithelium: squamous, cylindrical, glandular, ciliated.
5. Connective tissues. Corpuscles. White fibrous and elastic tissues, Adipose tissue. Pigment.
6. Tendon, Cartilage, Bone and Teeth.
7. Muscle, voluntary and involuntary.
8. Blood vessels. How to inject.
9. Method of hardening tissues. How to cut sections.
10. Lung.
11. Alimentary Canal.
12. Kidney.
13. Lymphatic Vessels. Skin.
14. Nerves, Fibre Cells, Central Organs.
15. Examination of sputum and vomit, discharges from uterus and vagina.
16. Pus and Tubercle.
17. Examination of Urine. Casts.
18. Examination of Urine. Inorganic Deposits.
19. Morbid Growths. Cancer Cells.
20. Parasites. Animal and Vegetable.

At least 786 autopsies were performed by Osler while he was pathologist to the Montreal General Hospital from 1876 to 1884. These were in addition to his duties as physician to the hospital, registrar for McGill medical school, and professor of the institutes of medicine.[32] Even more remarkable is the use Osler made of the material. These included teaching, preparation of museum specimens, pathology reports of the Montreal General Hospital, presentations to medical societies, publication of papers, and writing a textbook of medicine. Although some of his autopsies included histologic studies, the number is unknown. He kept records of these separate from the gross descriptions in his autopsy protocols, and none can be found today. Fortunately, several examples are included in his two collections of autopsy descriptions of 1878[33] and 1880.[34]

In the first pathological report, there are detailed microscopic reports of cirrhosis of the liver, gumma of the liver, and of many organs from a case of pernicious anemia.[33] The histology of cirrhosis is extensive, being almost two pages long. Described is bile pigment in relatively normal liver cells, lobules of which are surrounded by connective tissue. There is evidence of a minute study of the slides. "The method of invasion can be traced in all its stages, the new growth creeping in, as it were, from the periphery between the cells, sometimes separating them in rows, but frequently surrounding individual cells or groups of two or three." Osler describes the blood and bone marrow in a patient with pernicious anemia, stressing the presence of large nucleated red blood cells, the megaloblasts found in this condition.

The second pathological report is even richer in miscroscopic descriptions.[34] In a case of endarteritis and aneurysmal dilatation of the basilar arteries with rupture, Osler said that "on microscopic examination there were no special features in the diseased arteries which would warrant that the process was syphilitic." He also used the microscope to do a comprehensive study of the heart of an 11-year-old patient who had died of diphtheria. "Muscle substance of fairly good colour, but when examined with the microscope is found in a state of advanced degeneration. Very many of the fibres appear made up of closely set, dark, fat granules, no trace of contractile substance remaining. . ." The microscopic appearance of a "sarcoma" of the kidney was described: ". . . the softer portions of the tumor are found to be made up of large, irregular cells, with distinct nuclei. Many of these are exceptionally large, somewhat flattened, and with one or two central nuclei. In sections, the softer parts appear made up entirely of closely packed cells with very little stroma." This passage indicates an adeptness with microscopic study.

In addition to microscopic descriptions in Osler's pathological reports from the Montreal General Hospital, others are contained in published case reports.[35] Included are conditions that he investigated while a McGill faculty member from 1874 to 1883. Their calibre is evident from a sampling of Olser's articles, written when microscopy of pathologic conditions was in its infancy (Table 2).[7] Of importance is Osler's description in 1881 of micrococci in the vegetation of endocarditis.[36] He described them as "minute retractile granular spherules, which behave with reagents like micrococci." Credit for the early observation of micrococci in endocarditis was given to Klebs, Koster, and Osler by Coats, in his "Manual of Pathology."[37]

According to a student, in 1882, Osler helped a pathologist to make a microscopic examination of the brain of a criminal who had been hanged in Montreal.[38] "In his inimitable way, he led the pathologist with microscope to a better light." However, his two publications on the brains of murderers, published that year, contain only gross descriptions, measurements and analyses of the external surface of the brains.[39]

TABLE 2 MICROSCOPY IN OSLER'S ARTICLES (1874 TO 1884)

Chorea with Endocarditis: a soft spot in the corpus striatum had "much granular matter, nerve fibres and large granular corpuscles."

Insular sclerosis: In firm patches in the brain "fibres seem larger."

Syphilitic Aortitis: in the media there is "fragmentation of the elastic fibres" and "giant foci of round-celled infiltration containing giant cells and areas of necrosis."

Obliteration Inferior Vena Cava: the central portion was "composed of closely-compressed bundles of connective tissue."

Encephaloid Disease of Stomach: "The appearance suggested to me a diffuse carcinoma, and, on examining some sections microscopically, I was still more inclined to this view."

Carcinoma Mammae: The surgical specimen, "contained cells presented (sic) a greater irregularity than is common."

Myelogenous Leukemia: ". . . the proportion of white corpuscles is about 1 to 15 or 20 red corpuscles [and] the presence of Ehrlich's myelocytes . . . derived from the marrow but do not occur in the normal blood."

Infectious Endocarditis: Tricuspid valve-"dense fibrin, granular matter, spherules which behave with reagents like micrococci."

Neuroma of Brain: "small corpuscles, fibrils, ganglion like cells with processes, large vesicular nuclei."

Myosarcoma Kidney: "elongated spindle cells, striped muscle fibres."

Pleuro-Pneumonia: "air vesicles completely filled with pus cells.

Tonsils: There as "a network of fibres with numerous round cells, leucocytes and granular debris. Here and there groups of micrococci were met with."

Microscopic descriptions are also included in some of Osler's review articles. In "On the Pathology of Miner's Lung," there are detailed microscopic descriptions of four lungs with anthracosis.[40] Because of the extensive fibrosis described, it is likely that silicosis was also present, although it had not been delineated in 1875. Osler was also knowledgeable about advances in bacterial diseases, including microscopic study. Four months after Koch published an account of his discovery of the tubercle bacillus, Osler showed this microorganism to medical students,[41] and again at a meeting of the American Association for the Advancement of Science, on April 10, 1882.[1]

Osler's histologic studies while at Montreal were also applied to animals at the Montreal Veterinary College, at which he had an appointment as lecturer in physiology and helminthology.[1] Still in existence at McGill is the gross specimen of the jaw of a cow with actinomycosis; it was accompanied originally by microscopic slides containing the fungus.[42] As part of Osler's study on miner's lung, he injected India ink into the axilla of a kitten to show that the ink entered into the local white blood cells, lymphatics, alveoli and lymph glands.[40] These studies were published in 1875, eight years before Metchnikoff's first paper on phagocytosis.[43] In 1889, while at Philadelphia, he presented a lecture on phagocytes to the alumni association of Bellevue Hospital, New York, including a review of the contributions of Metchnikoff and others.[44] Described is the phagocytosis of carbon in the sputum and lung of cigarette smokers, distributed in the latter much as he had found India ink in the lungs of kittens.

Curiosity and keen observation were also shown by Osler in the microscopic study of parasites in animals, including parasites in the blood of frogs. In the winter of 1881–1882, during a class in practical histology, he "noticed in one of the slides a remarkable body like a flagellate infusorian."[45] These were also seen in the slides of several students. Osler did not let it pass. "On looking up the subject I found that the little organism was the Trypanosoma sanguinis which had been originally described by Gruby . . ." Osler studied the movements of this parasite, and included his sketches of its variable appearances in his article.

The internal structure of helminths in verminous bronchitis of pigs and dogs was investigated by Osler in 1877.[46] He could not find any published descriptions of nematodes with the same characteristics, and called it Strongyloides canis bronchalis. In 1879, it was labelled as Filaria osleri by Cobbold, but in 1921, Hall considered it to be a new genus, which he called Oslerus. Osler's name is now used for the species osleri in the genus Filaroides of the order Strongyloidea. Filaroides osleria is of rare occurrence, being found in America, England, India, South Africa, and New Zealand. Osler also used the microscope for more utilitarian purposes, such as identification of blood stains and hairs as being either human or animal, and distinguishing diseased from healthy animal meat for human consumption.[32]

Osler continued his study of blood platelets, begun in London, when he returned to Montreal. In 1883, he published "The Third Corpuscle of the Blood" stating that "there is evidence to show that [it] plays an important role in coagulation."[16] Osler gives credit to Donné of France for the first description of these structures in 1842, although Dreyfus credits Hayem.[28] In 1878, Haymen found that platelets play a role in the clotting of blood. The aggregation of blood platelets, which occurs on removal of blood from the body, is known as "Osler's phenomenon." "I was the first to observe, in 1881, that in the most superficial part of the white thrombi, the blood-plaques were present."[34]

Osler's interest in platelets did not stop when he left McGill in 1884. Three Cartwright lectures on platelets were published in 1886, using names such as globules, plaques and blood plates,[17] the latter being the source of their modern name as platelets. It was in Philadelphia, however, that his studies expanded to include a variety of diseases such as endocarditis and malaria.

(Part Two of this article will look at Osler's microscopic activities at Philadelphia and Baltimore, and will contain an assessment of his contributions. The list of references can be obtained by writing the first author.)

References

1. Cushing H.: *The Life of Sir William Osler:* London, Oxford U. Press, 1940.
2. Osler, W.: Christmas and the Microscope: *Hardwicke's Science-Gossip,* 5:44, 1869.
3. Osler, W.: Canadian Diatomaceae: *Can Naturalist & Q J Sci,* Montreal, 5(n.s.):142–145, 1870–71.
4. Osler, W.: Supplementary Note on Canadian Fresh-Water Polyzoa: *Can Naturalist,* 9(n.s.): 473, 1881.
5. Osler, W.: On Canadian Fresh-Water Polyzoa: *Can Naturalist,* 10(n.s.): 399–406, 1883.
6. Osler, W.: Trichina spiralis: *Can J Med Sci,* 1:134–135, 175–176, 1876.
7. Abbott, M.: The Pathological Collections of the Late Sir William Osler at McGill University: in *Sir William Osler Memorial Number,* Bull. IX, Internat. Assoc. Med. Museums, 1926, pp. 190–92.
8. Osler, W.: Carcinoma Mammae. Removal by Excision: *Can Med J,* 8:107–109, 1872.
9. *Can Med J,* 7:473–474, 1872.
10. Osler Library, McGill University, Montreal.
11. Cope, Z.: *The History of St. Mary's Hospital Medical School:* London, William Heinemann, 1954, p. 34.

12. Natural History Society, 4th Monthly Meeting, February 25th, 1878: *Can Naturalist,* (n.s.):144, 1878.

13. Robb-Smith, A.H.T.: Why the Platelets were Discovered: *Br J Haemat,* 13:618–637, 1967.

14. Osler, W.: On the Action of Certain Reagents, Atropia, Physostigma and Curare on the Colourless Blood-Corpuscles: *Q J Microsc Sci,* 13(n.s.): 307–309, 1873.

15. Osler, W.: An Account of Certain Organisms Occurring in the Liquor Sanguinis: *Proc R Soc* (London), 22:391–398, 1873–74.

16. Osler, W.: The Third Corpuscle of the Blood: *Med News* (Phila), 43:701–702, 1883.

17. Osler, W.: On Certain Problems in the Physiology of the Blood-Corpuscles: *Med News* (Phila), 48:365–370, 393–399, 421–424, 1886.

18. W. O. [Osler]: Berlin Correspondence: *Can Med Surg J,* 2:308–315, 1873–74.

19. Virchow, R.: *Die Cellularpathologie:* Berlin, August Hirschwald, 1859.

20. Osler, W.: Rudolph Virchow, the Man and the Student: *Boston Med Surg J,* 125:425–427, 1891.

21. W. O. [Osler]: Vienna Correspondence: *Can Med Surg J,* 2:451–456, 1873–74.

22. Garrison, F. H.: *An Introduction to the History of Medicine:* Philadelphia, W. B. Saunders, 4th ed., 1960, p. 592.

23. Hanaway, J.: *History of the Faculty of Medicine of McGill University 1829–1885:* Montreal, McGill-Queen's U. Press, in press, 1991.

24. McGill University: *Annual Announcement of the Faculty of Medicine, Session 1877–78:* Montreal, J.C. Becket, 1877.

25. Cushing, H.: Laboratories: Then and Now: *Can Med Assoc J,* 13:59–61, 1923.

26. Osler, W.: Introductory Remarks to, and Synopsis of, Practical Course on Institutes of Medicine: *Can Med Surg J,* 4:202–207, 1875–76.

27. Blumberg, J. M., Smith, B. H., Leeper C. K. et al: *The Billings Microscope Collection of the Medical Museum Armed Forces Institute of Pathology:* Washington, DC, Amer. Registry Path., 1967, pp. 61–62.

28. Dreyfus, C.: *Some Milestones in the History of Hematology:* N.Y., Grune & Stratton, 1957.

29. Travill, A. A.: *Medicine at Queen's 1854–1902.* A Peculiarly Happy Relationship: Kingston, Ont., Canada, Hannah Institute for Hist. Med., 1988.

30. Armstrong, C. E.: Student Reminiscence-Montreal Period: In *Sir William Osler Memorial Number,* Bull. IX, Internat. Assoc. Med. Museums, 1926, p. 175.

31. Osler, W.: *Student Notes. I. Normal Histology for Laboratory and Class:* Montreal, Dawson Bros., 1882.

32. Rodin, A. E.: *Oslerian Pathology. An Assessment and Annotated Atlas of Museum Specimens:* Lawrence, Kansas, Coronado Press, 1981.

33. Osler, W.: *Pathological Report, Montreal General Hospital for the Year Ending May 1, 1877:* Vol. I, Montreal, Dawson Bros., 1878.

34. Osler, W.: *Montreal General Hospital Clinical and Pathological Reports:* No. II, Oct. 1877 to Oct. 1879: Montreal, Dawson Bros., 1880.

35. Abbot, M. E.: *Classified and Annotated Bibliography of Sir William Osler's Publications:* 2nd ed., Montreal, Medical Museum, McGill U., 1939.

36. Osler, W.: Infectious (So-called Ulcerative) Endocarditis: *Arch Med,* 5:44–68, 1881.

37. Coats, J.: *A Manual of Pathology:* Philadelphia, Henry C. Lea's Son, 1883, pp. 308–309.

38. Smith, E. W.: Student Reminiscence-Montreal Period: in *Sir William Osler Memorial Number,* Internat. Assoc. Med. Museums, 1926, p. 184.

39. Rodin, A. E. & Key, J. D.: Osler's Brain and Related Mental Matters: *Southern Med J,* 83:207–212, 1990.

40. Osler, W.: On the Pathology of Miner's Lung: *Can Med Surg J,* 4:145–168, 1875–76.

41. Parfitt, C. D.: Osler's Influence in the War Against Tuberculosis: *Can Med Assoc J,* 47:293–304, 1942.

42. Rodin, A. E.: Contributions of William Osler to our Knowledge of Respiratory Disease: *Chest,* 74:85–87, 1978.

43. Metchnikoff, O.: Life of Elie Metchnikoff, 1845–1916: *Can Med Assoc J,* London, Constable, 1921, p. 120.

44. Osler, W.: On Phagocytes: Med News, 54:393–396, 421–425, 1889.

45. Osler, W.: On Certain Parasites in the Blood of the Frog: *Can Naturalist,* 10(n.s.):406–410, 1883.

46. Osler, W.: Verminous Bronchitis in Dogs: *Rept Veterinarian,* 1:158, 1877.

47. Clark, J. H.: The Development of a Pathological Laboratory at Blockley: *Med Life,* 40:237–252, 1933.

48. Landis, H. R. M.: The Pathological Records of the Blockley Hospital: in *Sir William Osler Memorial Number,* Bull. IX, Internat. Assoc. Med. Museums, 1926, pp. 232–237.

49. Middleton, W. S.: William Osler and the Blockley Dead House: *J Okla State Med Assoc,* 69:387–397, 1976.

50. Osler, W.: The Gulstonian Lectures on Malignant Endocarditis: *Br Med J,* 1:467–470, 522–526, 577–579, 1885.

51. Levy, D. M.: Centenary of William Osler's 1885 Gulstonian Lectures and Their Place in the History of Bacterial Endocarditis: *J R Soc Med* 78:1039–1046, 1985.

52. Osler, W.: Chronic Infectious Endocarditis: *Q J Med,* 2:219–230, 1908–9.

53. Dock, G.: Dr. William Osler in Philadelphia 1884–1889; in *Sir William Osler Memorial Number,* Bull. IX, Internat. Assoc. Med. Museums, 1926, pp. 208–212.

54. Osler, W.: An Address on the Hematozoa of Malaria: *Br Med J,* 1:556–562, 1887.

55. Welch, W. H.: Remark's of William H. Welch: *Johns Hopkins Alumni Mag,* 11:302–311, 1920.

56. McCrae, T.: The Influence of Pathology in the Clinical Medicine of William Osler: in *Sir William Osler Memorial Number,* Internat. Assoc. Med. Museums, 1926, pp. 37–41.

57. Bunting, C. H.: Osler as a Pathologist: *Bull Hist Med,* 23:336–340, 1949.

58. Opie, E. L.: Osler as a Pathologist: *Bull Hist Med,* 23:321–326, 1949.

59. Malkin, H. M.: The Influence of William Osler on the Development of Clinical Laboratory Medicine in North America: *Ann Clin Lab Sci* 7:281–297, 1977.

60. Osler, W.: Clinical Microscopy at Johns Hopkins Medical School, Baltimore: *Br Med J* 1:69–70, 1899.

61. Osler, W.: *The Principles and Practice of Medicine:* N.Y., D. Appleton, 1892.

62. Osler, W.: On the Amoeba Coli in Dysentery and in Dysenteric Liver Abscess: *Johns Hopkins Hosp Med Bull,* 1:53–54, 1889–90.

63. Beale, L. S.: *How to Work the Microscope:* 3rd ed., London, Harrison, 1865.

64. Warner, D. J.: *Microscopes and Medicine in the United States, 1840–1860:* Hastings-on-Hudson, N.Y., Rittenhouse, 4:19–29, 1989.

65. Strümpell, A.: *A Text-Book of Medicine for Students and Practitioners:* trans. from 2nd & 3rd German eds. by H. F. Vickery & P. C. Knapp, N.Y., Appleton, 1892.

66. Rhea, L. J.: Osler and Pathology: in *Sir William Osler Memorial Number,* Bull. IX, Internat. Assoc. Med. Museums, 1926, pp. 12–13.

SECTION IV

 Societies

The Formative Years of the American Osler Society

 Charles G. Roland, M.D.

The American Osler Society held its first formal meeting in 1971, an event that will represent not the beginning of this paper but, rather, almost the end. Though some portion of the founding story has been told by Alfred Henderson,[1] and again by Henderson and McGovern,[2] I believe that there is a duty for any society—particularly an historical society—to record its own origins as thoroughly as possible while the principals remain on the scene.

This paper is based on my personal involvement in the founding and the early years, on interviews or correspondence with other founders, and on examination of the limited published material. The contributions of the two primary movers, John P. McGovern and Alfred Henderson, will be documented. Some information is available about the process whereby the original contingent of Oslerians was selected, the constitution created, and the meeting arrangements made.

* * * * * *

Zeitgeist is defined as a pattern of thought or feeling characteristic of a particular period or time. In the 1960s, the North American medical zeitgeist was such that the desirability and need for an international Osler society expressed itself in several minds more or less simultaneously. One factor helping to fashion this zeitgeist was increasing concern among thoughtful physicians — and non-physicians — about the growing sterility induced by the prevailing emphasis on science in medical education. The concern was not a reaction against science but rather with the apparently concomitant loss of humanity and humaneness in our profession. Technology threatened to substitute for caring. A humanist role-model was needed, and who better than William Osler?

The two minds most productively tuned to the desirability of creating a society were those of John P. McGovern, in Houston, Texas, and Alfred Henderson, in Washington, DC. Neither man remembers, now, exactly when the initiating thought began to flower in his mind. McGovern recalls discussing

Based on a paper presented at the American Osler Society, May 7, 1999, Montreal.

the topic with Grant Taylor while both men were attending scientific meetings in the mid-1960s. Henderson, in 1966 and 1967, ". . . brought the subject up to a number of Oslerians, including Wilburt C. Davison and Wilder Penfield. . . . All were of one accord — that such an organization was, indeed, overdue."[3]

Dean Davison played a pivotal role here. He was Jack McGovern's professional mentor and hero, and close friend, and Jack had already discussed his idea with Davison. Thus when Henderson called, Davison promptly suggested a meeting between the two men.

McGovern had occasion to attend a medical meeting in Washington in October 1967; there, at Davison's suggestion, he met Al Henderson for the first time. Al was then at the Smithsonian Institution, where they met.[4] The two men quickly established the existence of mutual aims. They agreed to work together toward creating an Osler society. As it turned out, Houston, Texas, was to be the birthplace and Jack McGovern the presiding man-midwife. Those who know McGovern, his enthusiasm for William Osler, and his boundless, restless energy, three decades ago, will not be surprised to learn that he devoted this energy to the cause unceasingly.

In the last half of 1969, Henderson twice traveled to Houston to meet with Jack and to discuss how to set up the society. (See Figure 1) The process was very much a "smoke-filled back-room" operation (though without the

Figure 1: John P. McGovern and Alfred Henderson, Houston, Texas, August 1970: planning the American Osler Society. (Courtesy Al Henderson; photograph by Kathy McGovern.)

fumes since none of the founders smoked). Jack had been part of the establishment of another society and had come to believe that the initial planning should be done by the smallest possible group. He functioned as the nucleus of the AOS group.

McGovern and Henderson and, on one occasion, Tom Durant, spent time together in Houston trying out ideas and making decisions. (See Figure 2) At other times Jack, with regular consultation with Henderson and others, moved the planning and organization along. Various decisions and suggestions were tested on a few others, including Dean Davison, Grant Taylor, and myself.

A slate of officers was an early requirement. McGovern would have been happy to see his hero, Davison, as the first president, but the Dean urged that someone younger was needed. The then apparently unanimous choice was William B. Bean, at the time the Sir William Osler Professor of Medicine at Iowa City (See Figure 3). That invitation epitomizes the process of our founding. On Sunday 30 November 1969, Jack McGovern called Iowa City and traced Bean to Clinton, Iowa, and to — not surprisingly — a tennis court.[5] A call to the clubhouse brought Bill breathlessly away from his game. Jack explained what was happening, because at this stage Bean was unaware the society was being created. McGovern extended the invitation, Bean accepted, and returned to finish his set.

McGovern asked Henderson to nominate an officer and Henderson suggested Tom Durant, whom Jack didn't know. Durant had taught Henderson at Temple. And Durant was interested enough to attend and participate in the second meeting between McGovern and Henderson; he was very positive about the new society, and he ultimately was named 2nd Vice-President. McGovern wanted to have well-known physicians among the first set of officers, to provide a cachet to the Society; in recent interviews he has been can-

Figure 2: Henderson, Tom Durant, McGovern, Houston, Texas, 21 February 1970. (Courtesy J.P. McGovern; photograph by Kathy McGovern.)

Figure 3: William B. Bean, first president, American Osler Society. (Courtesy Bill Bean.)

did about this—the aim was to find an initial slate of people who would do the job but who were also prominent in American medicine.[6] So as well as Bean and Durant, George Harrell was invited to be an officer—vice-president (and thus president-elect) (See Figure 4)—and Ed Rosenow Jr to be Secretary-elect. McGovern was the first Secretary, Henderson the Treasurer-Historian. (See Figure 5) The last was to be an ongoing position, in 1974 transformed into the current Secretary-Treasurership; the other positions rotated upwards annually, secretary to second vice-president, and so on.

George Harrell was on the original slate of officers, having been invited both to join and to serve by Jack McGovern. Because these initial contacts were all made by telephone, documentary support is minimal. Harrell later recalled that at the time he joined, he had not thought of Osler in an historical sense[7] — at least, I think that is what George recalled: one of the challenges of historical research is interpretation! (Figure 6) Of course, George soon became a major laborer in the Oslerian vineyard.

This is perhaps the proper place to mention my own modest rôle in these formative days. I had met Jack McGovern on a trip to Houston in about 1965, soon after I had joined the editorial staff of *JAMA*. It was the editor, John Talbott, knowing of my interest in Osler, who suggested that I should meet McGovern. Sometime in 1967 we agreed to work on a project relating to Osler, the end prod-

Figure 4: George Harrell, ca 1970. (Courtesy George Harrell.)

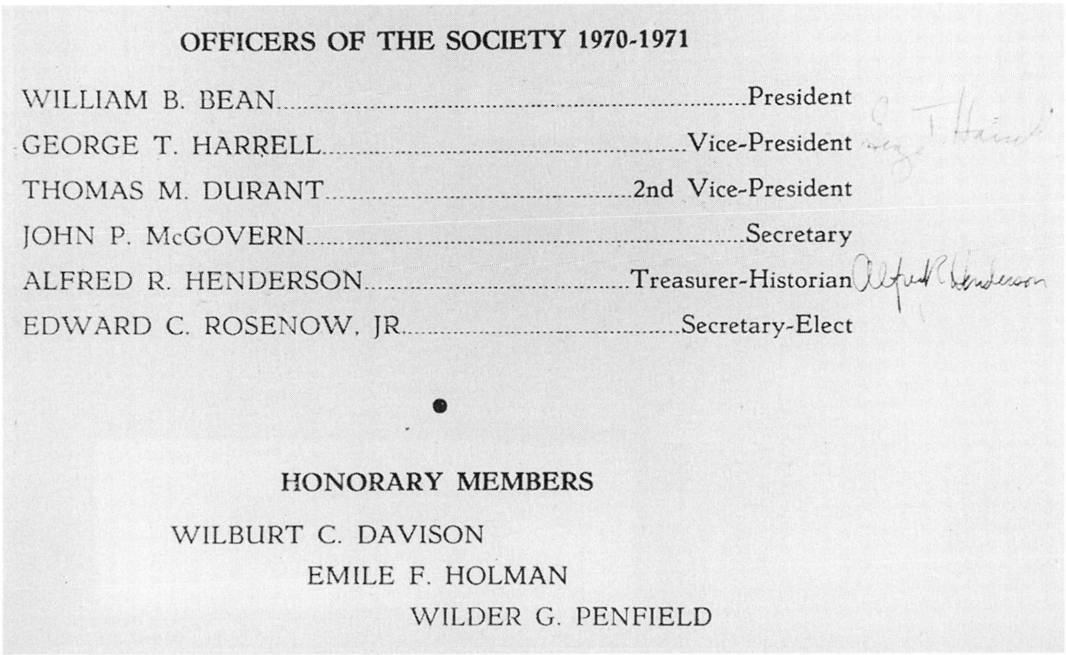

OFFICERS OF THE SOCIETY 1970-1971

WILLIAM B. BEAN..President

GEORGE T. HARRELL....................................Vice-President

THOMAS M. DURANT...........................2nd Vice-President

JOHN P. McGOVERN......................................Secretary

ALFRED R. HENDERSON.................Treasurer-Historian

EDWARD C. ROSENOW, JR..........................Secretary-Elect

•

HONORARY MEMBERS

WILBURT C. DAVISON

EMILE F. HOLMAN

WILDER G. PENFIELD

Figure 5: First slate of officers, AOS, 1970–1971.

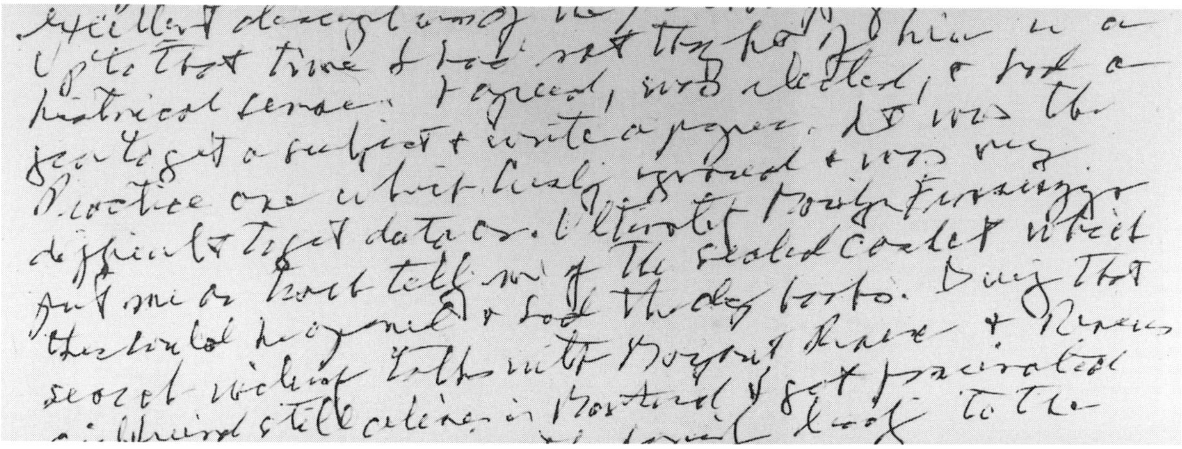

Figure 6:   Sample of Harrell's handwriting from letter to the author, 7 June 1994.

uct of which was the book, *William Osler: The Continuing Education,* published in 1969.[9] Thus we were in regular correspondence and met frequently about the book while the Osler Society began to take shape. Also I was organizing what became the special issue of *JAMA* for 22 December 1969, commemorating the 50th anniversary of Osler's death. Among those whom I invited to contribute an article was Jack McGovern. It was this connection that led McGovern to put my name forward not only as a Charter Member but also as a member of the initial Board of Governors. Moreover, McGovern and I talked on the telephone, frequently and at length, about various aspects of the new organization, the form it should take, who should be approached to join, and similar questions. So I was not among the very small group that met once or twice in Houston but was fully aware of what was happening, and I provided some input into the process.

An informal division of labor seems to have been worked out between McGovern and Henderson. McGovern, from the functional center of operations in Houston, played the larger role in contacting potential officers, governors, and Active Members, arranging for incorporation, and planning the Galveston meeting that became a sort of informal first meeting of Oslerians in advance of the Osler Society. Henderson began to draft a statement of purpose, design a logo, arrange for the printing of membership certificates and programs — his father-in-law was a printer — and other similar tasks (See Figure 7). This division was not absolute and never formal.

The officers and the members of the first Board were invited by telephone; no letters. Charter Members were largely invited by letter. For example, I invited Earle Scarlett, Earl Nation, Bill Gibson, Ray Pruitt, Tom Keys, R. Palmer Howard, and Edward H. Bensley.[9] All except Bensley accepted promptly and happily.[10] Edward Bensley informed us that he had just discovered he belonged to 40 societies and had vowed to cut down. Characteristically, given this, and despite his great interest in Osler, he felt obligated to decline.[11]

The statement of purpose of the fledgling organization was as follows:

The purpose of the Society is to unite, into an organized group, physicians, and others allied to the profession, with a common interest in memorializing and perpetuating the lessons of the life and teachings of William Osler; to meet periodically for the purpose of presentation and discussion of papers on the life and influence of Osler upon the profession, and to publish these essays as a Proceedings of the Society; to continually place before the profession a reminder of the high principles of life and

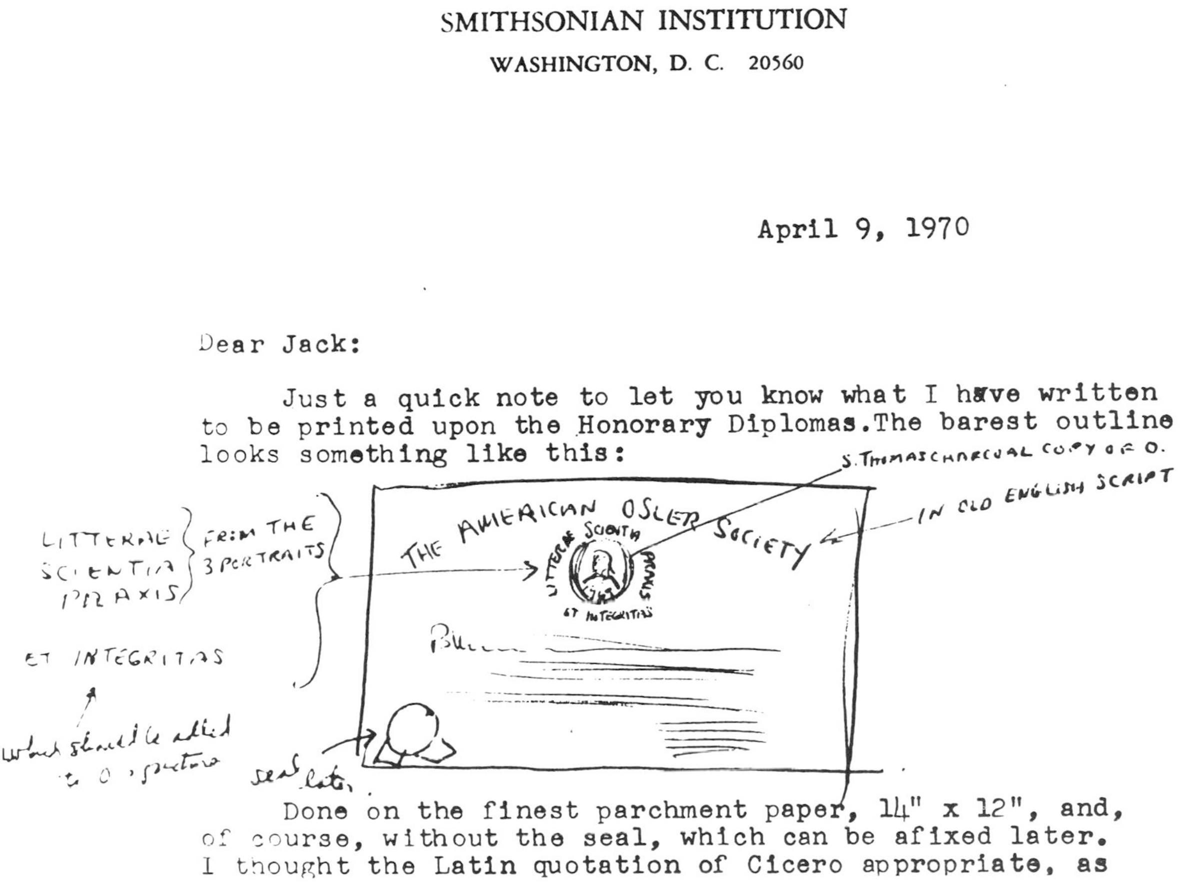

SMITHSONIAN INSTITUTION
WASHINGTON, D. C. 20560

April 9, 1970

Dear Jack:

Just a quick note to let you know what I have written
to be printed upon the Honorary Diplomas. The barest outline
looks something like this:

Done on the finest parchment paper, 14" x 12", and,
of course, without the seal, which can be afixed later.
I thought the Latin quotation of Cicero appropriate, as

Figure 7: Henderson's sketch of AOS membership certificate, from letter, Henderson to McGovern, 9 April 1970.

humanism in practice of Osler, and to introduce these things to those entering the profession.[12]

Here I must interject myself again. One of my suggestions was that we *not* establish a journal. My reasoning was explained in a letter to Jack: "I would like to suggest an alternative procedure for the dissemination of the papers which might be presented at meetings of the group. I assume that the purpose of publication is to spread the gospel to those who are not as familiar with Osler as some of us. If this is the case I would suggest that this could be more effectively done by arranging to have the articles published in a variety of different journals in this country and perhaps abroad also. Inevitably a separately published Proceedings would have a small circulation and would not be seen by those we are trying to reach."[13]

This suggestion was followed and, therefore, the AOS does not have a journal. Perhaps ironically, though, we have published two volumes of *The Persisting Osler*, with a third being planned. This is a type of Proceedings — and I am one of the editors, with Jerry Barondess and, for Volume One, Jack McGovern. Volume three is in process.

Among the original members of the AOS, some had, in 1969, a basically passive interest in Osler, admiring him as a role model but not doing research or writing about him. Examples would be Bill Beatty, George Harrell, Ray Pruitt, or Chauncey Leake. Of course, most or all of these became heavily involved in the ensuing years. Others had already taken a more active interest, including Jack McGovern, Bill Bean, Earl Nation, and myself.

Many of these original members were unacquainted. One instance of how the informal nomination process worked is that of Earl Nation. Earl, in a recent letter, has recorded some mystery about his involvement as a charter member. He wrote: "I am one of the fortunate ones, [although] not present at the formative meeting of the Osler Society, to have been selected to be a charter member. To this day I do not know how this came about."[14] Nation goes on to say that his sole Oslerian contribution before this time was his compilation and publication of Osler's "Men and Books" items in the *Canadian Medical Association Journal* as a small book. But that book is the clue to the explanation. I had read of the book and had obtained a copy from Nation, while I was still in general practice, and thus was very much aware of him. When Jack McGovern asked for suggestions for names of potential members in the new society, Nation's was one of those I put forward. Once the officers agreed, sometime towards the end of 1969 I called Nation in Pasadena and invited him to become one of us. Happily for the organization, he agreed. Needless to point out, this is the well-recognized "Old Boys" system.

Palmer Futcher was another Charter Member. He recalls that he played no rôle in setting up the Society: "I just suddenly found myself a Charter Member — by heredity!"[15] I should elucidate Palmer's jocular comment: his grandfather, R. Palmer Howard, was Osler's mentor at McGill; his mother was Marjorie Palmer Futcher, and his father was Thomas B. Futcher, MD, Osler's resident and then faculty associate at Hopkins.[16] If his inclusion was due to heredity, it certainly was remarkably solid Oslerian heredity.

Among Palmer's inherited Osleriana was one of the original latch-keys to 1 West Franklin Street, the Osler home in Baltimore. The key was given to Tom Futcher when he with other residents lived at 3 West Franklin, so that they could have access to Osler's library at will. And it is that original key that served as the model for the large-scale key that adorns the neck of the current President on formal occasions, and that, in miniature, appears on many jacket lapels today, and as a motif on the Society tie.

Another Charter Member, William C. Gibson, in a recent somewhat cryptic postcard, said, "I think you . . . thought I should be the anchor (a poor one) on the Pacific. Your idea is a good one but St. Alzheimer may be in the ascendant here!"[17] Relative to Gibson's last comment, referring jocularly to himself in 1969, I should just point out that in 1998 — just short of three decades later—he had not one but two books published. Alzheimer indeed.

A word should be said here about the name of the organization. One possibility discussed was the William Osler Society of America.[18] Though a serious suggestion, by the time it surfaced the organization had become a legal entity under our present name. Another proposition was the North American Osler Society, a move that might more fully have recognized the always strong Canadian presence in a society honoring a man who remained a Canadian citizen all his life. But this — obviously — did not happen either.

Jack McGovern arranged for the Society to be incorporated in the State of Texas. This acquired legal validity on 6 February 1970, with the document naming the initial five officers as a Board of Trustees, and signed, as incorporators, by Jack and two other (non-Oslerian) residents of Houston. (Ultimately incorporation was revoked because the annual fee was not paid by the then Treasurer.[19] In 1974 I took over as Secretary-Treasurer and re-incorporated the AOS in Minnesota.)

On 22 February 1970, the Board of Trustees had its first meeting. It was at that time that the Board of Governors and the Charter Members all were formally elected.[20] A constitution was drawn up at this time. And the three

Rhodes Scholars who had been Osler's students at Oxford—Davison, Holman, and Penfield—were named Honorary Members, though the formal announcement of this was postponed until it could be done with them present, at the April symposium in Galveston, Texas.

The 1970 Galveston meeting on Humanism in Medicine was seen by McGovern, Henderson, Davison, and others as a "trial run" for an Osler Society. Planning had begun in November 1968, when Jack McGovern and Grant Taylor decided to organize a symposium; originally it had been scheduled for Houston for late 1969, to be part of the commemoration of the 50th anniversary of Osler's death in 1919. For various reasons this timing did not work out. But McGovern had been discussing the concept of a meeting with Chester Burns and Truman Blocker, at the University of Texas Medical Branch at Galveston. When the Houston plans foundered, President Blocker suggested coming to Galveston.[21]

The speakers who were selected for Galveston were seen as a potential core of members for the new society. This meeting played a significant rôle in the organizational Zeitgeist; at least one aspect of this was the opportunity of many members and prospective members to meet or to become better acquainted with the three men who were our initial Honorary Members—Drs Wilburt Davison (See Figure 8), Emile Holman (Figure 9), and Wilder Penfield (Figure 10).

Figure 8:   Dean Wilburt C. Davison, ca 1960. (Courtesy J.P. McGovern.)

Figure 9: Dr Emile Holman, 23 March 1970. (Courtesy Emile Holman.)

Figure 10: Dr Wilder G. Penfield, 1963. (By permission of the Curator, Penfield Collection, Montreal Neurological Institute, item 63–0756.)

All three achieved prominence in medicine. All had been Rhodes Scholars and Osler's students. And they all revered the man, even into their eighth decades. Penfield has described himself as ". . . one of the hardy perennials who knew him in student days. . . . "[22] As Jack McGovern wrote, in this case regarding his relationship with Davison: "This influence of teacher upon student may well be the most realistic avenue to immortality — not an immortality of mere name but rather of spirit and philosophy."[23]

Dean Davison knew Osler well; he saw him frequently between 1913 and 1915 and then, as his intern, essentially daily, 1915 through 1916.[24] Davison has written about his first meeting with Osler, in Oxford. He had been sent to Sir William to present his unusual request for an heretical alteration in an Oxonian tradition. Of course, Osler was supportive. Davison's trepidation vanished as he found the Oslers "so charming and friendly that I soon felt I had two friends at Oxford. My awe immediately turned to adoration and devotion."[25] That feeling never disappeared.

The initial formal meeting of the AOS was held in Denver on 1 April 1971. (See Figure 11) Bill Bean, the first and outgoing president, presided; nine of the original thirty members attended. Membership diplomas were presented at the business meeting, at which A. McGehee Harvey was elected secretary.

These sessions and dinner were followed by an open meeting attended by about sixty interested members of the American College of Physicians. Bill Bean and Chauncey Leake both spoke, very well, and my journal closes, "All in all, a good first session."[26] This early, though completely informal, relationship with the American College of Physicians provided a nurturing environment. Our initial Secretary-Elect, Ed Rosenow, who was then the chief executive officer of the ACP, assisted greatly in establishing this ongoing relationship.

The next year we met in Montreal in conjunction with the American Association for the History of Medicine. The ACP and the AAHM have continued to be friendly neighbors for the AOS. And as the Montreal program of 1972 shows, we had already begun to grow. Instead of two papers there were four, including Harrell's presidential address on Osler's practice in Baltimore. Obviously, Harrell had begun to look at Osler historically.

In 1961, Robert Merton published a magisterial study of multiples — instances in the humanities, the arts, and science, where two or more people discover the same thing simultaneously and independently.[27] The impetus to create the American Osler Society seems to be yet another instance of this phenomenon.

Both Al Henderson and Jack McGovern participated fully in the early deliberations that resulted in the healthy birth of the American Osler Society.

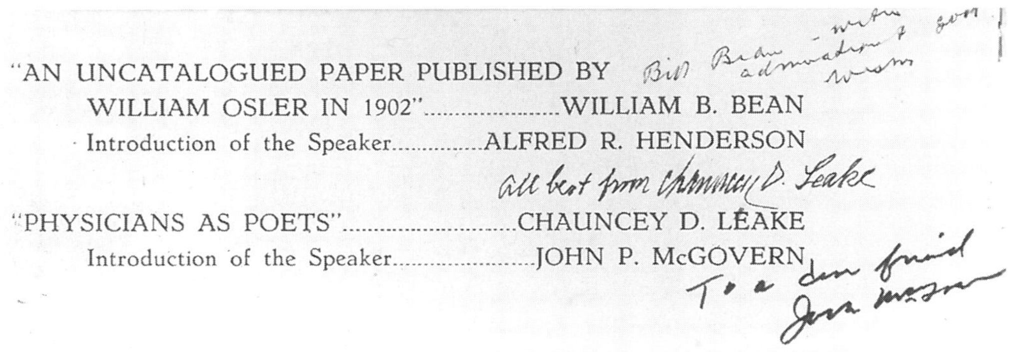

"AN UNCATALOGUED PAPER PUBLISHED BY
WILLIAM OSLER IN 1902".....................WILLIAM B. BEAN
Introduction of the Speaker..............ALFRED R. HENDERSON

"PHYSICIANS AS POETS"...........................CHAUNCEY D. LEAKE
Introduction of the Speaker....................JOHN P. McGOVERN

Figure 11: Program for the first meeting of the American Osler Society, Denver, 1971.

The record amply supports this observation. But I would go one step further and suggest that the key might well be Jack McGovern's boundless energy and focus, and, administratively, the dedication of his facilities in Houston—telephones, secretaries, meeting space, and so on—that made the creation happen. Without that drive we might well have remained merely a good idea unrealized. This opinion is widely supported, one of those in agreement being the other original planner, Al Henderson, who, in discussing the creation in a recent letter to me, stated that its existence was "... much more to John McG.'s credit than mine. . . ."[28] The weight of the documentation is convincing: John P. McGovern was indeed the principal founder of the American Osler Society.

Endnotes

1. Alfred R. Henderson, "Comments on the American Osler Society and an introduction of William B. Bean," *Johns Hopkins Medical Journal* 129: 343-345, 1971.
2. Alfred R. Henderson and John P. McGovern, "The American Osler Society: Its Occasion for Being and its Origin," *Southern Medical Journal* 67: 1209-1211, 1974.
3. *Ibid*, p. 1209.
4. *Idem.*
5. Bill Bean, TLS to J.P. McGovern, 19 December 1969.
6. John P. McGovern interview by C.G. Roland, Naples, Florida, 29 March 1995, pp. 18–19.
7. George Harrell, ALS to C.G. Roland, 7 June 1994.
8. John P. McGovern and Charles G. Roland (eds.), *Wm. Osler, the Continuing Education* (foreword by Wilburt C. Davison), (Springfield, IL: Charles C Thomas, 1969), pp. 365.
9. C.G. Roland, TLS to J.P. McGovern, 7 January 1970, p. 1.
10. C.G. Roland, TLS to J.P. McGovern, 28 January 1970, reported the acceptances by Nation, Howard, Scarlett, and Gibson. Keys and Pruitt had expressed their acceptance in person.
11. C.G. Roland, TLS to J.P. McGovern, 5 February 1970.
12. John P. McGovern, TLS to Willard E. Goodwin, 9 December 1969.
13. C.G. Roland, TLS to John P. McGovern, 7 January 1970, p. 1.
14. Earl Nation, ALS to C.G. Roland, undated but June 1994.
15. Palmer H. Futcher, ALS to C.G. Roland, 6 June 1994.
16. Palmer H. Futcher, "Oslerian mementos," MS memoir, 26 September 1994, in possession of the author; p. 1.
17. W.C. Gibson, ALS to C.G. Roland, 8 June 1994.
18. John P. McGovern, TLS to C.G. Roland, 11 February 1970.
19. Secretary of State, Austin, TX, Determination of Forfeiture, 1597-D, 8 May 1972.
20. The plans for this meeting were discussed in John P. McGovern, TLS to C.G. Roland, 11 February 1970.
21. Grant Taylor, "Preface," *Humanism and Medicine* John P. McGovern and Chester R. Burns (eds.), (Springfield, IL: Charles C Thomas, Publisher, 1973, p. ix.
22. Wilder Penfield, "Osler's voice," *Humanism and Medicine* John P. McGovern and Chester R. Burns (eds.), (Springfield, IL: Charles C Thomas, Publisher, 1973, p. 35.

23. John P. McGovern, "Wilburt Cornell Davison: apostle of the Osler tradition," in: Jeremiah A. Barondess, John P. McGovern, and Charles G. Roland, *The Persisting Osler: Selected Transactions of the first ten years of the American Osler Society* (Baltimore: University Park Press, 1985), p. 265.

24. Wilburt C. Davison, "Osler's opposition to 'Whole-time clinical professors,'" in: *Humanism and Medicine* John P. McGovern and Chester R. Burns (eds.), (Springfield, IL: Charles C Thomas, Publisher, 1973, p. 30.

25. W.C. Davison, "Reminiscences," *McGill Med. J.* 16: 157–182, 1947

26. C.G. Roland, manuscript journals, entry for 2 April 1971.

27. Robert K. Merton, "Singletons and multiples in scientific discovery: a chapter in the sociology of science," *Proceedings of the American Philosophical Society* 105: 470-486, 1961

28. Alfred R. Henderson TLS to Charles G. Roland, 8 February 1997, p. 1.

History and Activities of the Japan Osler Society

 Shigeaki Hinohara, M. D.

The Japan Osler Society was established in 1983, 13 years after the American Osler Society came into existence. The Japan Osler Society started with 43 founding members, with a membership of 169 physicians, 23 nurses, 48 medical students, and 42 non-professionals, all of whom shared Osler's way of thinking.

The objective was to contribute towards betterment of medical care and education in Japan through propagation of the Osler spirit among the Japanese people. In this sense, the Japan Osler Society had a slightly different start from the American Osler Society, which had a closed membership, consisting only of academic researchers on Osler and medical historians.

Japanese Medicine Before and After World War II

During the Edo period (1603~1867), Dutch medicine was imported to Japan. Under its influence, several small private medical schools were established in various parts of Kyushu Island around 1858. Then after the Meiji Restoration in 1868, after long deliberation the Japanese Government decided to adopt German style medicine, rather than English style. Thereafter, many German medical scientists and professors were invited to Japan, and simultaneously, many Japanese medical school professors studied medicine abroad in Germany. For the most part they carried out fundamental medical research, to provide the basis for the newly established Japanese medicine.

When I entered the Faculty of Medicine at Kyoto Imperial University in Kyoto, Japan in 1932, the textbooks used there were all in German, for both basic and clinical medicine. Such German-oriented Japanese medical education persisted until the end of World War II. Medical students were even directed to write the patients' medical records in German.

Presented at the American Osler Society, May 7, 1999, Montreal.

Because of such government policies, Japanese physicians rarely studied in the United States during the Meiji period (1868–1912). Only one, Dr. Ri'ichiroh Saiki (1862–1958), went to the United States to study medicine, during which he was exposed to the influence of Osler.

He was born in 1862, and studied in a private medical school in Kyuhshuh. Upon graduation he became a military medical officer in the Japanese Imperial Navy. Then in January 1887 at age 25, he sailed to the United States to study at the University of Pennsylvania until April, 1888 for a year and a few months. There, he received teachings from Osler.

Subsequently, Dr. Saiki went to Germany and specialized in gynecology. Upon return to Japan, he worked for a while at a hospital and a nurse-training school managed by Dohshisha School, then a Christian mission in the city of Kyoto. He left no record of his encounter with Osler. However, Dr. Wilburt C. Davison, a disciple of Osler and then Dean at Duke University Medical School, visited Kyoto in 1946, two years after the end of the war. At this time Dr. Davison met with Dr. Saiki, who was then an 86-year-old medical practitioner. Dr. Davison heard from Dr. Saiki the episodes of receiving guidance from Osler when he was a foreign student at the University of Pennsylvania.

According to Dr. Davison's writing titled Humanism in Medicine (Charles C. Thomas, 1973), Dr. Saiki's reminiscence went as follows:

> Osler spent most of his time at the Blockley Hospital with students and interns, using his methods of careful history taking, painstaking examination, systematic recording of progress notes, the regular use of the laboratory in the study of the patient, and the introduction of the student into the wards and outpatient department, which later established his reputation and that of the Johns Hopkins Medical School and Hospital.

After his encounter with Osler, Dr. Saiki eventually returned to Japan and practiced medicine as an obstetrician and gynecologist. He passed away in 1953 at the age of 91. Most of his life, he managed a training school for midwives and ran a maternity clinic, contributing much to primary care of the community people. Because he was not involved with medical education at any medical schools in Japan, no opportunity arose for Osler's teaching methods to be introduced to Japan.

In 1941, I started working as an internist at St. Luke's.

International Hospital

The American Episcopal Church Mission originally built this hospital. The late Dr. Rudolf B. Teusler was its founder. When the Pacific War ended in 1945, the Allied forces requisitioned it for use as one of their army hospitals. It was through this that I got to know Dr. Warner Bowers, then the Head of the army hospital. He was one of the medical officers of the American Forces. It was most kind of him to permit me to use their medical library. As I read numerous American medical textbooks and journals there, I noticed the name "Osler" mentioned here and there in the articles, and I became interested in Dr. Osler. One day I said to Dr. Bowers that I wanted to read Osler's book *Aequanimitas with Other Addresses to Medical Students, Nurses and Practitioners of Medicine.* And then and there, Dr. Bowers gave me the book. He told me that he had read it himself every night in the hospital ship during the Pacific War. It was the 1932 edition, donated to him by Lilly.

On the other hand, when the Allied forces requisitioned St. Luke's International Hospital, we had to carry out our own holdings of medical books from the library. Included there was the collection which belonged to Dr. Teusler. In his collection, I found a biography of Osler: *The Life of Sir William Osler*, as well as Osler's *Textbook of Medicine*, the second edition. I read them all, and I was deeply impressed. I decided then that I would introduce Osler's humanistic thought and bedside medical teaching to the Japanese medical students. In particular, I wanted to introduce to the Japanese students Osler's way of residency training.

In July, 1946, as the editor-in-chief, I started publishing a medical journal titled: *American Medicine*. Then from volume 2, number 5, I started publishing serial installments titled: "A Portrait of a Physician: Dr. Osler's Life" which continued for 9 months. In April 1948, two years and 8 months after the end of the Pacific War, I published a 299-page book, titled *The Life of Osler—The Pioneer of American Medicine*, a small biography of Dr. Osler. I dedicated this book to the Japanese medical students, because I wished to convey Osler's spirit and the story of his life to the Japanese rising generation.

Then six years after the end of the Pacific War in 1951, a Peace Treaty was concluded. Immediately after this, in September 1951, I left Japan to study internal medicine as well as American medical education at Emory University Medical School in Atlanta, Georgia, for a full year. On my way back to Japan, I stopped at Duke University in North Carolina, which was the Alma Mater of my father, a minister of the Methodist church, who graduated from Trinity College, now called Duke University, in 1904. At the dean's office of Duke Medical School I met with Dr. W. C. Davison. Dr. Davison was extremely busy, but he kindly gave me time and discussed Osler. When I visited the United States for the second time in 1974, I had an opportunity to visit Dr. E. Holman, another disciple of Osler. Dr. Holman then was a Professor of Internal Medicine at Stanford University. I visited his home, and he told me about Osler's ward-rounds when Osler was a Professor of Internal Medicine at University of Oxford. He gave me his words and signature on the book, "Aequanimitas" which was given by Dr. Bowers.

Sixteen years ago in 1983, together with Professor Hisae Niki, I published a book called *Heisei no Kokoro*. "Heisei" means "serenity" and "kokoro" means "heart" or "mind" in Japanese. This is a collection of Osler's lectures contained in his *Aequanimitas with Other Addresses to Medical Students, Nurses and Practitioners of Medicine*. The book contained additional lectures, which he gave in his late years. Professor Niki and I translated them into Japanese with comprehensive annotations. Since then these annotations accounting to 1520 have been translated into English, and the book is now in the process of publication from an American University Press, thanks to kind support given by Dr. John McGovern of Duke University.

Aside from this, I published in 1993 another detailed biography of Osler in Japanese.

Now let me tell you about my involvement with the American Osler Society. It was from Dr. Grant Taylor and Dr. John McGovern of Houston, Texas, both of whom graduated from Duke, that I heard about the establishment of the American Osler Society in 1971. At the encouragement of Dr. Irving A. Beck (1911 ~) of Rhode Island, I started attending the annual meeting of the Society.

In 1983, I was chosen as the first Asian honorary member of the Society. I cannot express how moved I was at that time. With such experiences, I resolved to found an Osler Society in Japan. The Japanese physicians, who read my books on Osler and became friends of mine, supported me. So I was able to start the Japan Osler society in 1983, with 43 founding members.

Dr. Masakazu Abe, one of the founders, was a professor of medicine of Tokyo Jikeikai Medical College from 1964 to 1984. During these 20 years, whenever he conferred a Ph.D. degree on a graduate student in internal medicine, he gave out a medal with a portrait of Osler, along with the engraved phrase: "Listen to the patient, he is telling you the diagnosis."

Dr. Tsutomu Sasagawa, the honorary Director of Niigata Municipal Hospital, erected a bust of Osler at the entrance of the hospital in 1985, before his retiring from the position of a director.

When the Japan Osler Society was founded, its objective was as follows:

> The members will learn from a wide variety of writings of Osler, which conveys Osler's life and thought, the following: Osler's personality and knowledge; his method of education for physicians and other medical professionals; the health-promoting activities, which Osler carried out in the local area. The members will propagate Osler's humanistic spirit in practicing medicine, as well as his scientific curiosity, to the younger generation of the Japanese medical professionals. The members will also transmit Osler's humanistic spirit to the people of the various strata of Japanese society.

Thereupon we decided in the constitution that whoever agrees with the above objectives of the Society would be accepted as a member. Of the objectives, the most important of all is the transmission of Osler's spirit to the next, younger generation. This aim corresponds to the following passage, written by Dr. Davison for the article titled "The Basis of Sir William Osler's Influence in Medicine," which was published in *Annals of Allergy,* volume 27, 1969, from page 366 to page 372.

"No one has taken Osler's place. We must demonstrate to this generation not only what he was and meant to us, but what he did for them and for medicine, and can continue to do if the medical youth will try to emulate him as we attempted to do. He embodied, applied, transmitted all that is finest and best in a physician." The current membership is 186, of whom 144 are physicians, 5 are nurses, 2 are medical students and 35 are supporting members. Since the establishment in 1983, we have published regularly *The Japan Osler Society News,* 8 to 12 pages long, two to three times a year. The most recent issue is number 35. To date, the Japan Osler Society has held 18 annual meetings. At each of the meetings, an Oslerian from either outside or inside Japan was invited. Those invited from overseas were recommended as honorary members. They are listed as follows:

1. Dr. Robb-Smith was invited from Oxford University in the United Kingdom in 1984.

2. Dr. Alex Sakula, the President of London Osler Club of the United Kingdom, was invited in 1984.

3. Dr. Robert E. Rakel was invited from Baylor College of Medicine in 1985.

4. Dr. Charles Roland was invited from McMaster University in 1986.

5. Dr. W. B. Spaulding was invited from McMaster University in 1987.

6. Dr. Chester R. Burns was invited from the Medical Branch, University of Texas in 1988.

7. Dr. Richard L. Golden, the President of American Osler Society, was invited in 1989.

8. Lord Walton of Detchant was invited from Green College, United Kingdom in 1990.

9. Dr. Frederick B. Wagner, Jr. was invited from Thomas Jefferson University in 1991.

10. Dr. John D. Stoeckle was invited from the Massachusetts General Hospital in 1994.

11. Dr. Om P. Sharma was invited from the University of Southern California in 1995.

12. Dr. Billy Andrews was invited from University of Louisville in 1997.

13. Dr. John McGovern, President of the John P. McGovern Foundation, was invited in 1998, however, he could not attend the meeting.

Let me add that at the 15th Annual Meeting of the American Osler Society, which was held in San Francisco, California, I gave a presentation titled: "Dr. Osler's Theory on Habits." Subsequently, 13 members from the Japan Osler Society attended the 20th Annual Meeting of the American Osler Society, held in Baltimore, Maryland. There, I gave a presentation titled: "Dr. Osler's Thanatology." In 1994, the 24th Annual Meeting of the American Osler Society was held in the United Kingdom. For this occasion the members from the London Osler Club and the Japan Osler Society joined. As the result, 14 members attended the meeting from Japan.

At this Annual Meeting in 1999, which commemorates the 150th year since the birth of Dr. Osler, 22 members came from Japan to participate at the meeting.

It has been a great honor to have the opportunity to discuss the birth of the Japan Osler Society in 1983, and its activities. Thank you very much for your attention.

The Osler Club of London, 1928–1938: Young Medical Gentlemen, Their Heroes, Liberal Education, Books, and Other Matters

 Joseph W. Lella, Ph.D.

As Philip Teigen has noted, Sir William Osler has been "the subject of a mountain of secondary literature (more than 1,600 items recorded to date), and the posthumous presence in the *Science Citation Index*, [has] cited him an average of 120 times per year between 1955 and 1984." Teigen has rather sardonically labeled much of this activity the "Osler industry."[1] And yet, even for Teigen, it hasn't all been said. During his lifetime (1849–1919) and since, Osler achieved much, and perhaps more importantly has come to represent "important values and ideals for twentieth century physicians and biomedical scientists."[2] His achievements may not seem extraordinary[3]—debatably, perhaps, the most important line in his *"C.V.,"* the *Principles and Practice of Medicine,*[4] is considered the first comprehensive textbook of medicine in the modern era, and a most influential one. He wrote many scientific papers, founded a number of professional associations, was an early fighter for public health and defensible scientific standards in medicine. He was one of the founding "fathers" of Johns Hopkins School of Medicine the leading U.S. exponent at the time of the link between university science, medical teaching and clinical practice. He was knighted and finished his career as Regius Professor of Medicine at Oxford, continuing his medical work, rare book collecting and writing in the history of medicine. But perhaps most importantly, Osler was considered *the* respected

Presented at the American Osler Society, 5/10/94, London.

Previously published in Can Bull Med Hist 1995, *12:* 313–338. Reprinted with permission.

and beloved mentor and teacher by innumerable colleagues, residents and medical students.[5] The record of what he meant to them is abundantly available both in the literature noted above, but also in his own published "lay sermons" which continue to be consulted today.[6] In these, he enunciated a range of humanistic ideals and values for the profession. The interpretation of these ideals and values continues to evolve. Teigen continues, "[w]hat meanings he embodies and how he and the Osler industry interact is not yet clear, but the complexity of this social process . . . should make Osler and the Osler industry of considerable interest to social historians."[7]

The Osler Club of London was among the first organisations to be founded in Osler's name. It was one of the first expressions of "the Osler Industry." Understanding the source, process and outcome of its evolution could promote a deeper understanding of what Osler offers to modern medicine, but also what has been made of him and why. It also promises some clues concerning what Osler could offer, to the world of modern medicine. Indeed, the later work of one of the founding and central figures of the Osler Club of London, the pediatrician, Alfred White Franklin offers hints of an expanded vision. All of this, I shall argue, points toward a revivified Oslerian legacy in today's highly technical, specialised and bureaucratized medical world.

The Medical Gentleman

Focusing on what the Osler Club of London "made of" the Oslerian legacy implies somehow that our Canadian hero returned to Britain to bequeath something of his North American character. But this is misleading, for the club which these young physicians and surgeons founded was marked primarily by the background and traditions of these young men themselves. In short, in founding the Osler Club of London, these British medical neophytes were largely acting on an ancient European and British ideal, that of the gentle life enhanced by a broad education,[8] the life of the 19th century "gentleman;"[9] more particularly, the life of the 19th century "medical gentleman."[10] For them, it was because Osler so completely embodied what they made of this ideal, that he was chosen as the Club's "Patron Saint." In a sense, then, as I shall briefly suggest in a post-script to my discussion of the Club, Sir William inherited this ideal from his British forebears and teachers, made it his own and returned it to Britain where it became newly incarnate in the Osler Club of London. But this is to get ahead of our story. What about the Club?

The Club and Its Founding

On the evening of Monday, April 30, 1928, six medical students and a medical historian, Dr. Charles Singer, along with Mr. L.W.G. Malcolm, Conservator of the Wellcome Historical Medical Museum, sat around a fire in the drawing room of 27 Wimpole Street in "Harley Street," the heart of medical London, to hear a paper by one of their number on the "Life and Work of Louis Pasteur." It was the first meeting of the Osler Club of London. The very date and circumstances of its founding are interesting since it seems to have been the first organisational manifestation of what at least one of its members would call 'oslerolatry'[11] in Britain.[12] The Club had been started with the blessings both of

Lady Osler, and of Dr. W.W. Francis, Sir William's literary executor and nephew. The latter was then living in Oxford, attempting to complete the *Bibliotheca Osleriana,* while planning his move to Montréal to install McGill's new Osler Library.

Over the next 10 years, the Club would meet a total of seventy one times. By 1933, there were 22 members who with friends and occasional guests contributed to an average attendance at meetings (from 1928 through 1934) of 17 persons.[13] During the Club's last four years it underwent a decline in vigour if not in membership, dipping from four meetings in 1935 to only one in 1938. The Club did not meet for the duration of the war, but has resumed since with a different sort of activity and much enlarged membership.

Alfred White Franklin, along with W. R. Bett, was the prime mover behind the Osler Club of London. He was its Secretary, kept impeccable minutes, and organised most of its functions for all but one of the ten years with which we are concerned. In 1928, Franklin lived with his father, Philip Franklin, a "Harley Street" surgeon.[14] Alfred had been a student of the classics before entering Clare College, Cambridge, with a scholarship to his B.A. While at Clare, he became a member of the Cambridge University Medical Society which, in the summer of 1926, sailed the Atlantic for a brief tour of university medical centers in Canada and the United States. They were greeted and feted by university faculty and students in Washington, Baltimore, Philadelphia, New York, New Haven, Boston, Montreal, Kingston, and Toronto. Franklin published a brief description of the tour in a Cambridge periodical on his return. Based on notes in his journal, it describes the beauty of the trip, but more importantly its "supreme value . . . it is only upon the basis of such individual contacts and understandings that there can be built up and maintained . . . sympathy and cooperation between the English-speaking peoples that is so essential for international peace."[15] Because of this tour "a few young men, in Philadelphia, in Baltimore, and above all in Montreal, met the spirit of Osler and felt the influence of that spirit on the men and in the places that he had known."[16]

Franklin had become fast friends with T.F. McNair Scott, G.W. Pickering, H.E. Mansell, and C.F. Watts, who along with Bett and himself would be the Club's founding members. Scott, Watts and Pickering were also public school educated and Cambridge men, the first two at the traditional medical College, Caius, the third at Pembroke. Mansell was a scholarship student at Oxford. Each of these men had already built distinguished student careers receiving various honours in University. They went on to equally distinguished work in their further medical studies before qualifying as physicians and surgeons. Scott became a student at St. George's Hospital, was awarded the Medical Brackenbury Prize and considered a strong candidate for the consultancy staff before leaving for the United States where he continued his career. From Cambridge, Watts entered St. Bartholomew's Hospital, familiarly known as "Bart's," where he won prizes in pathology and surgery. Pickering qualified at St. Thomas's hospital where he had won an entering scholarship. Mansell entered St. George's (his father's old hospital) and held successive junior positions at other hospitals.[17]

Walter Reginald Bett was born in Latvia, of German ethnic background. Coming to London at the end of the first world war, he was enrolled in St. Paul's School. Franklin had met Bett in 1927 when they were both medical students at Bart's. Franklin describes Bett and his influence on the founding of the Club.

> [w]e were idle fellows then, he persuaded me that together we should found
> a students' club for the study of medical history. As a good Cambridge man
> my obvious choice for Patron Saint was Sir Clifford Allbutt. But Bett had
> other views. The Osler Club? . . . then we went down to Oxford [and Osler's

former home, 13, Norham Gardens]. . . Here Dr. Francis showed us the
books, and he talked, how he talked, of them and of the Catalogue and of
his kinsman hero, William Osler. . . .During that morning I was infected, as
Bett had planned, with the virus of Oslerolatry. . . . After that morning there
was no more talk of what The Osler Club should be called. [18]

Harley Street and environs has achieved popular renown at least from
mid-Victorian times to the present day, as the center of fashionable medical
London. Then, it contained the consulting rooms *and* homes of some of the
nation's most highly qualified physicians and surgeons. Before and since the
days of the National Health Service, it has been known as the area where the
most costly practitioners are to be found, some of dubious qualifications, who
cater to the "rich and famous."[19] That A.W. Franklin lived there, his father
practised there, and the Club met and dined there is at least an initial indication that the Club might be oriented to a medical elite.

The educational backgrounds of its founders and initial members as well
as the circumstances of its founding also indicate this. Although graduation
from these universities was no longer a requisite for qualification as a physician, Oxford and Cambridge had long been considered important sources of
the Capital's most prestigious physicians. Until early in the nineteenth century, Fellowship in the Royal College of Physicians and hospital consultancies
had been almost exclusively reserved to its graduates who went on to train at
the London hospitals. Throughout that century, access to wealthy patients
tended to be achieved (though not exclusively so) through hospital ties to
wealthy patrons, and through the network of relationships developed and
maintained through family and an Oxbridge-old-London-hospital education.
A public school, and university classical education was considered key to a
physician's education not only, or even primarily because it gave him access to
the medical classics of Hippocrates, Galen and later writers in Latin, but
because it was key to his moral development, his acceptance as a gentleman
and to the maintenance of relations with gentlemen.[20] Thus, Peterson cites Sir
Henry Acland, F.R.C.P. and Regius Professor of Medicine at Oxford late in the
19th Century, who in an address to the BMA in 1869, argued that a liberal education served to "discipline the faculties and gave the professional man the
benefits of the "light of general culture." Because this 'general culture' facilitated relations with gentlemen it also helped gain him access to a much higher
income and standard of living than that of the general run of the medical profession. Peterson goes on to note that

> Hospital posts introduced physicians and surgeons to eminent City officials,
> merchants, businessmen, and the aristocracy that gave their names time and
> favor to medical philanthropy. Senior medical men in the hospitals and
> royal Colleges in turn often helped their young successors build their
> practices and advance their careers.[21]

She states further that "medical men in the consulting ranks had, in a few
instances, sizable fortunes and in a number of cases substantial financial
resources."[22]

In discussing the process from university or College through hospital
education, Peterson notes that, of course, medical training involved learning
occupational skills. But it also established and extended "personal and professional connections—those "useful and interested friends" that could contribute to a man's future career. . . .

> [C]ourse work, clubs, prizes and service also brought students into the
> process that socialized them to the profession of medicine. . . . [Y]ears at

medical school, whether at Guy's or Bart's or Charing Cross, were years when the student came under the discipline and control of the elites of the medical schools. Out of the shared experiences of living and working together a new professional identity was being forged.[23]

As noted above, crucial to the definition of that identity was that of the "gentleman" as applied to medicine. Thus, the ideal member of the Oxbridge-London Medical elite was the "medical gentleman."

An Ideal for the 19th Century Doctor: The English Gentleman

Throughout the 19th Century, medicine in Britain struggled to incorporate newly emerging scientific ideas and practices. As these apothecaries, practitioners of 'physic,' and surgeons wrestled with new organizational forms to fit new social realities, the ideal of the Doctor as Gentleman was regularly invoked by representatives of the Royal Colleges of Physicians and Surgeons as a basis for their claims to recognition, status and associated social and professional privileges. This ideal continued to be asserted, often if only implicitly, well into the 20th Century both in the lives of individuals and of interesting and sometimes significant groups of British medical men. The Osler Club of London was one of these groups. In order to understand the Osler Club, then, it is important to appreciate this ideal. And it is impossible to do this without relating it to the ideals of both liberal pursuits in general and liberal education in particular.

John Henry (Cardinal) Newman's series of lectures, *The Idea of a University*,[24] incorporated classic statements of these ideals, and that of the "gentleman" which rested upon it. For Newman, a liberal activity was an activity worth pursuing for its own proper enjoyment, worth pursuing in its own right—not for its utility or for what it will bring beside itself. Indeed it is seen to be pursuable only if "material cares are. . .if not altogether banished, at least not . . . too consuming."[25] Liberal education involved the pursuit and acquisition of knowledge worth having for its own sake and also learning *how* to pursue and acquire such knowledge. Moreover, all this was related not only to learning and acquiring facts, but facts in "philosophic" perspective, i.e. learning to see the important as important, and the less as less, to place all in proper context. The presence of multiple disciplines in the university facilitated this. For Newman, liberal education produced a cultivated and cultivating intellect and this helped produce a person who possessed the attributes of "a gentleman . . . to have a cultivated intellect, a delicate taste, a candid, equitable dispassionate mind, a noble and courteous bearing in the conduct of life; these are the connatural qualities of a large knowledge; they are the objects of a university.[26]

According to Newman, the social life of the university or college facilitated making the gentleman. Based on his own experience, he felt that in British universities and scholastic establishments men from widely different backgrounds associated with and taught each other as well as learning from their teachers. All of this formed a local tradition, a *genius loci*, an ethically sensitive, intellectual community.[27]

Newman's classic and oft quoted definition of the gentleman embodies what he sees as the distillates of liberal pursuits, and most especially that of liberal knowledge and education in a system such as that of the British university:

> . . . it is almost a definition of a gentleman to say he is one who never inflicts pain. . . . His benefits may be considered as parallel to what are called comforts or conveniences in arrangements of a personal nature: like an easy

chair or a good fire, which do their part in dispelling cold and fatigue . . .
The true gentleman in like manner carefully avoids . . . all clashing of
opinion, or collision of feeling. . . his great concern being to make everyone
at their ease and at home. . . . . [H]e is seldom prominent in conversation,
and never wearisome. He makes light of favours while he does them, and
seems to be receiving when he is conferring.[28]

The Osler Club of London

Starting Out in the Medical Elite

It is clear that A.W. Franklin, friends and colleagues had the background to
enter the London medical elite and were, in actuality, taking their first steps
into it. The trip to North America and Franklin's description of it illustrate that
love of "liberal" experience, of broad learning and the quest for perspective
that Newman describes as well as the habit of association with their fellows, the
habit of learning from them. It also illustrates their general association with a
broad international medical elite and the ease of their association with it. Their
work with the Osler Club of London was, however, a part of their entry into a
more local elite. Their choice of Osler as a patron, their contacts with W.W.
Francis, their espousal primarily of Medical History as a topic for the Club, the
way in which they organized and pursued its activities, indicates that they were
pursuing activities which qualified them as a specific sort of "English medical
gentleman" which would have a profound influence on their construction of
the Osler legacy.

Despite their youth, the founders were no babes in the wood launching
their club. Franklin and Bett's initial visit to Dr. Francis at Osler's former
Oxford home, 13, Norham Gardens, illustrates a familiarity with Sir William's
social network. Indeed, one of their companions from the Cambridge tour of
North America "Hal" Mansell "had been in Lady Osler's circle" in Oxford.[29]
This mutual acquaintance may have facilitated their reception. As young
physicians and novice members of the Oxbridge-London medical group, however, the Club's first five meetings indicate that they had little difficulty in
achieving other important contacts—in the network established by Osler during his life time, in the world of the history of medicine and in the Oxbridge-
London medical elite. These social worlds seem to have overlapped, to form
a special segment of the medical elite to which I referred above. These meetings also illustrate the privileged physical circumstances, peculiar relationships and ideology of this segment, an evolved version of those of the 19th
century medical gentleman. All of this would continue and be further developed over the ten year period in question. The club's early activities, its statement of goals, and initial meetings give something a flavour of the later years
of this period, which will be treated in summary.

Early Meetings and Goals

A.W. Franklin, who served as recording Secretary, took minutes in a long, lined
ledger, its spine and corners bound in leather, its paper substantial. Members,
honourary members and friends were signed-in in the first few pages which
were left empty for that purpose. Each of the meetings was assigned a new
page, with a title and roman numeral indicating the theme and number of the
meeting. Each meeting's page provided space at the top for signatures, on the

left, for guests, on the right, for members, honourary members and friends. The minutes though short were meticulously recorded in Franklin's exact and highly legible hand. Franklin was the cultivated gentleman at work, facilitating the operation of the Club, its orderly and continuing process.

Twenty one years later, Franklin described the Club's initial goals as encouraging the study of medical history among medical students and keeping "green the memory of Sir William Osler." This study was to be "an introduction to modern medicine." Historical understanding was to be a background for a "true and full perspective of present changes and of the future" and also to teach a "humanistic approach to man and his medical problems,. . . saving grace in a materialist world of dissolving values and of lost beliefs. Great lessons are to be learned in history's pages, from the story of the slow triumph of the minds of men over the problems set by pain, disease and death."[30]

Although this was "implicit" some of it was explicit. An early, unofficial statement of the ideals of the Club, composed by Bett at Franklin's instigation and circulated to the membership (though never voted upon) proposed as ideals: to cultivate and carry into our daily work the Historical Spirit, exemplified in the life and works of our Patron Saint, William Osler; to study the History Of Medicine as exemplified in the life and works of those who have built up the Medical Profession; to promote a sense of universal fellowship in the spirit of Osler. An indication of the seriousness with which these ideals were taken were the requirements for membership (which seem to have been adhered to at least in the Club's early days); new members were required to "undergo an apprenticeship of three months, during which time he should communicate one paper on a medico-historical subject, he should take part in at least one discussion, and he should show his interest in the activities of the club, e.g. in the Library by augmenting its volume or by increasing the utility of its contents." Bett explains these requirements. They are an attempt to ensure a membership "with a taste for the salt of serious medico-historical study, with the savour of Oslerian informality. The approach to these Elysian Fields must be closely watched." Provision was also made for Honorable Members, Friends, and Corresponding Members in foreign countries. The statement also includes the provision that the Club have an "Hon. Sec. and keeper of the Library, and an Hon. Sec. for Foreign Affairs." All of this was to "do our share of work for international peace. By introducing the work of foreign historians and scientists to the profession in general, by inviting them to visit this country to address us, by entertaining them when they do visit this country, by traveling abroad as a body of intelligent, broad-minded sympathetic Englishmen, in many ways we can be useful."[31]

These goals and their moral character exemplify Newman's view of the operation of the gentlemanly fruits of a liberal education in medicine. The usual functioning of the Club in its early days also embodied this. Franklin recalls the setting and ambiance in "the L shaped drawing room in my father's house" at 27 Wimpole Street where most of the meetings took place

> The members and their guests would sit in armchairs, on sofas, on the floor. . . . the short minutes were read by the Secretary and the meeting started. . . . Usually pictures and books were passed round to illustrate the subject, and a historical exhibit with recent accessions to the library of papers by members, Osleriana, presents of medico-historical books from friends were shown on the top of the grand piano. The meeting was usually long and the discussion free. J.D. Rolleston could be relied on for a characteristic Rabelaisian touch (there were no lady members) . . . . And then before the meeting adjourned for refreshments, a finale from Foreign Secretary Bett, a queer mixture of

confession, invocation and medical history, studded with odd allusion, half song, half sermon, brought the meeting to a close.[32]

Their first meeting was attended by Dr. Charles Singer, Lecturer in Medical History at the University of London, and Dr. L.W.G. Malcolm, then Curator of the Wellcome Historical Medical Museum.[33] Singer's career in the history of medicine had been if not initiated, then facilitated and stimulated through the kindness of Osler at Oxford in 1914. He had already published several volumes and, in 1928, was well on his way to intercontinental, scholarly celebrity in the Anglo-Saxon world.[34] Franklin's minutes note that "G.W. Pickering read a paper on Louis Pasteur, his life and his work;" some reproductions of Pasteur's youthful drawings were shown; there was an informal discussion of Pasteur's predecessors, Redi, Paracelsus and Leeuwenhoek; and that "Pasteur's classical works were displayed, and an interesting collection of photographs relating to the Pasteur Institute and the Pastoriens."

W.R. Bett produced a brief paper not noted in the minutes, but entitled "The Osler Club-Pasteur Meeting, 30. IV. 28," in which his noted florid language, combined with the idealism noted above were generously displayed:

> The Osler Club has honoured itself by honouring so graciously the memory of its Patron Saint in a special soirée devoted to a man who in Osler's words had opened a new heaven in medicine and a new earth in surgery. . . . With what joy would we not have welcomed him here tonight, with his almost bloodthirsty interest in the history of his Art, his unmeasured friendliness towards those of a younger generation. One who breakfasts on Aequanimitas, lunches on the Alabama Student, and dines on the Biography, is conscious of him coming up the stairs with his curiously alert carriage and his notably light tread.

The second meeting, also at 27 Wimpole Street was entitled the Lymphatic Meeting. Bett read a paper on the early history of lymphatics emphasizing the life and work of Aselli and Pacquet and other short communications continued the theme through to the present day. "Important books and pictures relating to the History of the Lymphatics and Lymphadenoma were displayed" and distinguished new members and friends welcomed. Along with Geoffrey Keynes who presented "two books to the library" and who will be discussed later,[35] Prof. leGros Clark was present, cited in the Medical Directory of 1933, as Professor of Anatomy and Examiner for the B.Sc., University of London, an Examiner for the primary F.R.C.S., and Fellow of the Royal Anthropological Institute with publications in the Journal of the Royal Anthropological Institute, and the Journal of Anatomy. Professor Arturo Castiglioni, recognized as an authority in the history of Italian medicine,[36] was also there. During this era, he enjoyed a career which included the positions of the Professor of the History of Medicine, University of Padua, and Lecturer on the History of Medicine at Yale University. He would be Noguchi Lecturer, Johns Hopkins University, in 1933 and elected Honorary Member of the History of Medicine Section of the Royal Society of Medicine in 1932.

The third meeting was held in the library of Sir D'Arcy Power who, as we shall see, was not the only titled physician or surgeon to grace the Club with his presence.[37] He was "welcomed as a friend" at this meeting and "displayed a selection of important medical books from his shelves. The members fell to and endeavoured to carry out their host's exhortation 'to see, handle and smell but not lick them.' " That very afternoon, Club was also "honoured" by Mr. Francis R. Packard's acceptance of corresponding membership status for the United States of America. Packard who held a chair in the history of medicine in Philadelphia was editor of the *Annals of Medical History* published in New York and considered the leading American periodical in the area.[38]

The fourth meeting saw the Club return to 13, Norham Gardens in Oxford with two young men added to the original six. H.J. Burroughs was also a Cambridge-Bart's man and J.F. Fulton, the Harvard graduate (and ex-Rhodes Scholar). Fulton was a neurophysiologist who had been with Harvey Cushing at the Peter Bent Brigham Hospital in Boston. He was currently a fellow at Magdalen College Oxford. They were all received by Dr. W.W. Francis who was made "Friend" of the Club and "Dr. A.G. Gibson [a long time friend and colleague of Osler's at Oxford[39]] and Dr. R.T. Gunther [another Osler colleague and Magdalen College Science Tutor] who honoured the club by becoming honorary members."[40] Dr. Gibson read and commented upon some of his letters from Osler, and members then "browsed over a selection of books from the Bibliotheca Osleriana." The next day, "some members . . . visited the Almshouse at Ewelme where they saw the muniments rescued from damp & decay by their Patron Saint."[41] In the afternoon, "they were shown round the Bodleian Library by Mr. F.R. Needham." The next day, Dr. R.T. Gunther showed them the "Lewis Evans Collection of Scientific Instruments at the old Ashmolean, where there is one case dedicated to the memory of Sir William Osler."

The Club's fifth meeting was back at 27, Wimpole Street, on the evening of July 12, 1928. It featured what the Club entitled the "First Osler Oration" the first in a series to commemorate Osler's birthday. The minutes for that meeting are headed "The Seventy ninth Anniversary of Sir William Osler's Birthday." Both *The Lancet* of July 21st and *The British Medical Journal* of that same date carried detailed descriptions of the meeting. Following a pattern that would be usual, the attendance was greater than usual[42] and there were a number of distinguished guests and speakers. The report in *The Lancet*, bears a striking similarity to that in the *B.M.J* and has the air of press release composed by a member of the club.

> Sir Wilmot Herringham . . . spoke of Osler's love of rare cases, not because they represented extremes of normal physiology, but because their rarity appealed to him as an artist. . . . Dwelling happily on Osler's personal charm and affectionate nature, Sir Wilmot closed a speech of genuine feeling.

> Dr. E.O. Meynen, .. wished particular success to the club as an agency for the promotion of international goodwill, under a patron saint whose name was held in reverent esteem in Germany.

> Sir Humphry Rolleston then spoke of "Osler as a Human Being," showing that it was the combination of so many different personalities in one body that made Osler the beloved man that he was.[43]

Prof. D. Fraser-Harris, spoke of Osler as a physiologist; Dr. H.H. Scott saw him as a naturalist and comparative pathologist; Dr. Andrew Balfour treated his interest in tropical medicine; Sir Squire Sprigge considered him a great man of letters; Sir Walter Fletcher discussed Osler as a friend; Dr. Franklin Martin (President Elect of the American College of Surgeons) on Osler as an organizer; J.D. Rolleston (brother of Sir Humphry) as an epidemiologist.[44]

> Dr. Ernest Jones brought the symposium to a delightful conclusion with some personal reminiscences. The exhibition of a selection of Osler's writings, literary and scientific, of biographical appreciation's, and of books inspired by him, bore further witness to the breadth of the man and to the

many-sided nature of his interests and enthusiasms. Among other guests of the club were Sir Thomas Lewis, Dr. Burton Haseltine of Chicago[45], Messrs. Geoffrey Keynes. . . , Dr. Henry Viets of Boston, and Mr. Philip Franklin.[46]

Three of the four titled speakers were Cambridge and Bart's or St. George's physicians or surgeons and the fourth was an Oxford-Barts man. Sir Wilmot and Sir Humphry and Sir Walter had been friends of Osler and distinguished practitioners in their own right. Sir Squire Sprigge was editor of *The Lancet*. The other guests and speakers were also distinguished medical-surgical men.

It had been easily done. Calling upon existing family, school, and professional relationships, Franklin and Bett quickly established the Club within the network of Osler's friends and acquaintances, and in a corner of the world of elite British medicine generally as a focus of activity for those interested in the history of medicine and in perpetuating Osler's memory. The Oxbridge-London-Harley Street network would continue to be important in supplying members, speakers, participants, sponsors and places for the Club's activities. More significantly, perhaps, this network seems to have provided the framework within which the Club's definition of Osler, and his legacy was taking shape.

The Club was developing its ideals and activities in a way that was congenial to those of the 19th Century medical gentleman. Osler was construed as a model for their life and their behaviour in a very broad way. He was seen as providing an approach to the history of medicine which allowed the modern doctor to study and to define a humane and informed view of medical activity. The great physician-surgeon scientists of the past were held up as individuals to emulate. The great discoveries of the past were seen as sign-posts toward the future. Osler was seen as an abiding role model in his interest in the history of medicine, and in his humanism, his broad interest in people and in literature.

All of this can be seen more completely in the following analysis of Club members and their activities.

Members, Mentors and Activities: Emerging Patterns

Members. I have noted above that there were 22 members of the club during the period under consideration. 18 of these joined or had been admitted before 1933. Of these, 7 were graduates of Cambridge University, 5 of Oxford, (59%) and 6 of the University of London (27%). Among the others, one was a graduate of Harvard (more of him later). I was unable to discover the educational backgrounds of three of them. Hospitals at which members of this group trained were: 9 at St. Bartholomew's (Bart's), 4 at St. Thomas's, 2 at St. George's, (68%) and 7 for whom this was unknown. There were at least 2 non-physicians in the group which was composed wholly of men. [Indeed, I am unaware of any female who ever attended a meeting of the group.] Members of the club tended to be rather youthful.[47] Of the 18 who had done medical studies in England for whom we have information and for whom this statistic is relevant, 16 either had achieved membership in one or both of the Royal Colleges (of Physicians or Surgeons) in 1926 or later, or had not yet achieved it. Thus, the founding members (and later additions) were either completing their studies or at the beginning of their medical careers and were largely neophyte members of the Oxbridge-London central teaching hospital elite.

Other Participants and Mentors: for the 71 meetings that took place between

1928 and 1938 (at which there were 113 presentations), 17 presenters and or discussants were listed in the minutes as titled. Although a number of the elder participants could be called mentors to the Club, especially active were Sir D'Arcy Power, medical historian and senior surgeon at Bart's, and Geoffrey Keynes, also a Bart's surgeon, and bibliographer. D'Arcy Power gave two presentations to the Club during this period; as well, three meetings were held at his home, 10A Chandos Street, also in the Harley Street area, and emblazoned "Medical Society of London Founded A.D. 1773." He appears as discussant in the Club's minutes no fewer than 12 times during the ten-year period. Sir D'Arcy was himself, the eminent surgeon son of an "eminent ophthalmic surgeon," [48] an Oxford, Bart's man and widely published in surgery, the history of medicine, medical biography and bibliography. In 1928, he was 73 years of age. Geoffrey Keynes, knighted in 1955, a Cambridge-Bart's man, was often prominent in the meetings of the Club. In 1928, he was 41 years old and well launched on a distinguished career in surgery. He had published on blood transfusion, and somewhat controversially on carcinoma of the breast. Brother of the great English economist, John Maynard Keynes, he was becoming perhaps *the* liberally educated and active, medical gentleman scholar of his time. In the early days of the club, he was becoming noted for his bibliographic, editorial and biographic work on literary, artistic and scientific figures, including William Blake, Sir Thomas Browne, John Donne and Robert Boyle.[49]

Of the 14 titled participants on whom data concerning medical education and career could be found (the other three were probably not physicians) our information confirms their participation in the London medical elite to which we referred above. 5 were Cambridge graduates, 4 Oxford, 4 London and one other. Nine of them had been trained at Bart's, 2 at St. Thomas's, 1 at St. George's and 1 at another hospital. Most of these individuals had addresses in the Harley Street or adjacent London areas. Several were or had been listed as physicians to His Majesty the King. They had numerous consulting positions in a range of prestigious London hospitals, private, charitable, professional and governmental organisations as well as ranking academic appointments (including two Regius Professorships of Medicine) and many scholarly and professional publications.[50] A perusal of the names of non-titled, occasional participants in the Club's meetings indicates a similar roster of London medical, surgical and medical historical luminaries.

Aside from Sir D'Arcy, these titled individuals attended only one meeting apiece and the meetings which they did attend tended to be special affairs. Eight of the titled participants attended special Osler Oration meetings. Four others were special commemorative meetings, including: the first anniversary of the Club's existence; a special session on the 50th anniversary of Koch's discovery of the tubercle bacillus and another celebrating the centenary of the birth of Richard Von Volkmann, a noted Prussian surgeon and humanist. The Club was quite skilled at persuading notables to grace its special meetings and some of these seem to have been rather lavish and formal affairs. Later in the period, for example, the Club's Annual "Osler Oration" meetings (on July 12, Osler's Birthday) were held at the Langham Hotel, in its heyday the most prestigious London hotel and a short walk from Harley Street. Special menus were printed and invitations sent. These meetings were the most well-attended, averaging close to 27 participants. (The average meeting during the Club's prime attracted 10 fewer, a number, it would seem, much more appropriate to the drawing room discussions which were the Club's usual fare.) Of the 52 ordinary meetings on which information was available an average of 65% or 10 of the average 16 attendees were club members. Among the regulars were, of course, Franklin and Bett and several of the later youthful additions, but a considerable number of senior medical people attended along with others interested and well-placed in the history of medicine.

But the Club was not all meetings. In 1929, the Club (probably Franklin, as Secretary) compiled a list of "Published papers and press notices relative to the first 16 meetings of the Club.— April 30, 1928- July 12- 1929." Another compilation lists similar publications up to November, 1931.[51] Also in 1929, W.R. Bett corresponded with the Oxford University Press concerning the possibility of launching a *Quarterly Journal of Medical History*. Possibly because of its expense, the project was not completed. Among the more significant activities, in 1930, one of the club's youthful members, Alastair Robb-Smith, proposed a *Festschrift* to celebrate D'Arcy Power's 75th birthday. In January

> a special copy of his own *Selected Writings*, published by the Oxford University Press was presented to him by Lord Moynihan in the Great Hall of St. Bartholomew's Hospital. The book was edited by members of the Club, who had also prepared for inclusion a hand list of the titles of over six hundred books and papers by the man they honoured."[52]

Were all these *merely* activities "establishing and extending personal and professional connections"—those "useful and interested friends" that could contribute to a man's future career and income?[53] A firm answer, of course, would entail study in greater depth, and over a longer time period. But I would venture a tentative "No." Of the founding four, all, except Bett at the time, were well on their way to successful careers in medicine whether in practice or scientific-academic work or a combination of both. George W. Pickering perhaps was to be the most successful, making significant contributions to the understanding of hypertension and becoming a successor to Osler as Regius Professor of Medicine at Oxford.[54] Bett later pursued a career in the U.S.A., for which he seems to have benefited from his contacts in the Club. Franklin notes that Bett's first position in the U.S. as Medical Librarian, Columbia University was obtained through the good offices of J.F. Fulton, the Harvard graduate noted above as participant in the Club's early meetings.[55] Fulton, while in England, was a Rhodes Scholar at Oxford, and Christopher Welch Scholar and Demonstrator in Physiology. He later became Sterling Professor of Physiology, and historian of medicine at Yale University.[56] But all of these or similar accomplishments could have been achieved (and were by many) outside the orbit of Osler and the history of medicine. Although I would not deny that "connections" in the club, may have helped, these could have been made outside in other, similar circles. No, whatever else it may have been, the Osler Club of London was about weaving more subtle threads into the whole cloth of a medical life, a medical identity; it was about living the life of the liberally educated, and well-endowed,[57] medical gentleman. Although this sort of life had been, perhaps, on the wane since the early 19th century through the democratization of the profession with the admission of general practitioners as colleagues, the rise of prestige and authority based upon scientific expertise, and the smaller and smaller proportion of the whole that linked an Oxbridge education with prestigious consultancies in the London hospitals,[58] it was still alive and kicking in the Club. It was about companionship in the profession and in scholarship, and it was about rejoicing in medicine, in its past, its heroes, sacred events and relics, especially its rare books. It is noteworthy that of the 113 presentations made at meetings during this period, 55, or close to half, were made by members of the Club itself.

At D'Arcy Power's birthday-presentation ceremony, Lord Moynihan, arguably the most notable surgeon of his era, celebrated his Bart's colleagues as "men of distinguished character—great even in truancy—who have added to the renown and respect of our profession." He noted how "significant and delightful [it was] that the initial impulse and the sustaining power of this project came from the younger men, and is associated with the energies of the Osler Club, and I may perhaps be permitted to mention the names of W.R. Bett and A.W. Franklin." He continued

> . . . when the name of D'Arcy Power comes to my mind, or his familiar image to my eye, I recall on the instant, not his career as a surgeon, not even his unrivaled knowledge of surgical history, from which the *British Journal of Surgery* has continuously and greatly benefited, but his friendliness, his cheery disposition, and his beauty of character. When we call to mind the names and services of our professional friends, we judge them, I think, not by the size of their practice, nor the money they have with so great difficulty accumulated, nor by their contributions to the science, the craft or the lore of medicine, but by their character and their influence upon the younger members of their calling, through whom they earn immortality. . . . D'Arcy Power has been one of the greatest influences in medicine in our day. He has been prudent in counsel, wise in action, eloquent in word written or spoken, imperturbable and resolute in time of challenge and difficulty, a staunch, loyal, happy friend whom all men have welcomed and trusted and loved.[59]

Meetings and their Subject Matter. Morrell and Thackray's monumental work, *Gentlemen of Science: Early Years of the British Association for the Advancement of Science,* clearly outlines the centrist, political and scientific orientations linked to the social status of these early-mid 19th century scientists as gentlemen of leisure, of the University, and or Anglican churchmen. "The core members had a definite meliorist, centrist, reforming political attitude . . . Temperamentally they were conservative, piece-meal reformers, opposed to the political claims of both die-hard Tories and fierce democrats."[60]

Similarly, the subject matter and style of the Osler Club of London in this early period were those of elite practicing physicians and embodied their status and aspirations within the profession. We have witnessed their joy at the companionship and scholarship the profession offered, a celebration of their ancestors' individual scientific, and clinical achievements. There was a broader interest in the humanities, but the humanities oriented to individual edification, personal-intellectual and/or moral benefit. By contrast, as Philip Teigen notes, Osler the historian "was chiefly preoccupied with collectivities such as the profession, local medical societies, and medical science as an institution." He notes Osler's desire that "the unity, peace and concord of the medical profession . . . transcend the economic and political desires of individual physicians."[61] Although Osler's view was that of the 19th century Social Darwinist, tending to see unremitting progress in medicine and medical science, Osler kept his eye on medical institutions and the broad sweep of medical history, and especially in his early days was sharply critical of those of his colleagues whom he saw as self-interestedly standing in its way.

Among the writings and topics of these early years of the Osler Club of London, I have found little, if any, reflection on medicine as a collectivity, as a profession, and on the evolution and future of its institutional arrangements. I have found still less critical reflection on that profession. This is perhaps surprising in an era in which the rise of specialism was being widely discussed and debated, in which various medical insurance schemes were being discussed and tried out,[62] indeed, in which socialized medicine was being implemented in the newly born Soviet Union.[63]

A.W. Franklin and the Gentleman's Legacy

Although space forbids elaborating this analysis, some of A.W. Franklin's later comments do as well. In them, one sees a critical and reflective social consciousness asserting itself, perhaps nostalgically, over an era of lost and privileged innocence. In 1975 he wrote of a visit to Italy in which he viewed a statue commemorating the Latin poet, Virgil. Franklin remembers his schooldays and pays "homage to the man whose flowing hexameters first taught me the beauty of the sound of words." He reflects on the statue's theme, a celebration of the values of home, family and military victory in defense of one's country. The poet blesses a victorious warrior, foot planted on a defeated enemy.

> The eye is caught by the central figure of the poet, laurel crowned. But the heart is caught by that poor prostrate victim. Ours is an age when the loser wins. The warrior has no right to put his foot upon another man. The copy book virtues, along with the cult of goodness, truth and beauty, have lost their hold upon the human spirit. Renaissance man, the measure of all things and their vaunted master, has fled, leaving behind the mass of pollution created by his pride, his cruelty and his greed. And leaving us, his successors to expiate his guilt. It is with the deprived and the underdogs that we identify. Moved by compassion, the able bodied have tried to lift the burden of the victims on to their shoulders. It is a heavy load, when there are so many. . . .[64]

Franklin then speaks of the social responsibilities thrust upon modern medicine and the physician, especially in his own domain of pediatrics. Noting that science has given us many choices and social-ethical temptations, he states his faith that "Science . . . is not the enemy of the spirit of man." However, if forced as he had been when a student participant in a Cambridge debate, to choose between scientific technology, and a more literary expression of the spirit of man: if he had now to choose between doing without "Virgil or the electric light," Franklin would now, in contrast to then, opt for "keeping Virgil . . . "[65] Such critical, social commentary is nowhere in evidence in the earlier Franklin, nor among the earlier writings of the Osler Club that I have examined.[66]

In another place, Franklin again gives evidence of an awakened social conscience going so far as to mildly criticise his patron Saint. He notes that Osler,

> had a kindly regard for the less privileged person but, [as] a man of his time, . . . had no general sympathy for the poor who are always with us, to excite pity and solicitude but not to be inspirers of social action. . . . His privileged position in a secure society allowed him to surround himself with books, concentrating on those important in the history of science and of medicine. . . .[67]

Franklin goes on to discuss what was missing in the triptych of Osler's heroes, "Linacre, Harvey and Sydenham—letters, science and practice; teaching research and service to patients—from these three strands the personal physician weaves his professional career. . . . but there is a fourth strand, of preventive medicine."[68] Although he recognizes that Osler appreciated the need for preventive medicine, Franklin suggests that he did not stress it enough.

If not as great a man as Osler, Franklin seems to have grown beyond what his Club made of Osler in those early days and, in a crucial way, beyond Osler himself. In 1972, in those still early days of the National Health Service and before the neo-conservative reaction against it and its broad social concerns, Franklin glimpsed the need for his colleagues to expand the perspective of the liberally educated, gentleman physician to include critical reflection upon the social position of the physician him/herself, and upon his/her profession in the broad sweep of history. At this time, he himself was at the height of a successful career as a London paediatrician. After becoming one of England's early neonatologists at the Queen Charlotte Hospital, Franklin had become physician in charge of the department of child health at Bart's. He later became member of the Council of the Royal College of Physicians of London, president of the British Paediatric Association, of the British Society for Medical History, and of the International Society for the Prevention of Child Abuse and Neglect. When he wrote the above lines on Virgil, he had been deeply involved in a range of clinical and preventive matters having to do with child health.[69] After his death in 1984, his biographers noted in that in working toward the prevention of child abuse he

> was instrumental in holding together the various professions, doctors, social workers and lawyers, whose collaboration was essential if problems were to be resolved in the best interests of the child, the family and the State. Alfred recognized that it was necessary for paediatricians to become knowledgeable and active in their diagnosis of children suffering from abuse and neglect and to seek ways of preventing it.[70]

It remains for further study to determine whether and how these perspectives of Franklin and Osler's broader interests did or did not become incorporated into the agenda of the post World War II Osler Club of London.

Sir William's British Legacy.

This legacy, we have seen, was present in Britain all along. Sir William reminded the young Franklin, Bett and their colleagues of the heritage which they themselves had received in public school and university, the heritage of the liberally educated gentleman as applied to medicine. In reminding them of this, Osler handed back what he himself had received through letters, and books, from his Uncle Edward so long ago while being raised in that frontier Canadian parsonage. Cushing and much later, Anne Wilkinson (Sir William's grandniece) tell us something of Edward, himself parsonage educated, and later a Guy's trained surgeon, member of the Royal College who reveled in the liberal interests of the gentlemen surgeons whom he met in London in 1818, some thirty years before his famous nephew's birth. Wilkinson cites Edward's letter to his father.

> . . . I shall feel some regret at leaving London. . . . I can never hope to experience more kindness than I have received from . . . my friends in town. To the Literary Society I must in a great degree bid good-bye and perhaps few have enjoyed that more than myself. Almost invariably I have gone home with Mr. Travers (surgeon at Guy's Hospital) and Mr. Allen after their lectures and have learnt as much from their conversation as from the lectures themselves. . . .
> Under the loss of this kind of Society I must console myself with the resolution that instead of being a second I will be a principal, so that a few years hence instead of being invited to a party that I may be honored with the company of a distinguished author, my friends will invite their acquaintance. . . that they may say that they have been in company with me . . .

> There is a bill now going through the House to regulate the practice of surgeons. . . Its main object is to prevent any persons practicing in future as surgeons except Members of the College [and includes] clauses calculated to increase the respectability [of the profession]. . .[71]

Edward Osler did become a most respectable and liberally accomplished gentleman. His life is recorded in the *Dictionary of National Biography* which cites his most notable works in natural history, theology and biography. His nephew Willie recollects:

> As a boy in a backwoods settlement in Upper Canada, the English post would bring letters from an Uncle Edward for whom we cherished an amazing veneration; for on the shelves in Father's little study were there not actually books written by him, and poems, and mysterious big articles with drawings about shells, and now and again did we not sing in church one of his hymns? The reputation of the family seemed to circle about this uncle whose letters were always so welcome and so full of news of the old home and so cheery. We boys could read the difference in our father's face when the post brought a letter from Uncle Sam, the black sheep of the family.[72]

Cushing notes that in Edward "as physician, naturalist, and author may be recognized many marks of resemblance to . . .the nephew with whose traits this memoir is primarily concerned."[73] In his youth and early adulthood in Canada, Osler studied with two individuals, educated in Britain, whose gentlemanly character and interests were similar to those of Uncle Edward Osler's and whose influence upon the young Willie was perhaps much greater. The Rev. W.A. (Father) Johnson (an Anglican Clergyman), and Dr. James Bovell (a physician), both naturalists who were theologically inclined, remained father figures to Osler throughout his life.[74] And so, in the Osler Club of London, the legacy came home, and in Alfred White Franklin was modestly received and somewhat broadened.

Some Conclusions

Charles Roland has noted that Osler's primary legacy was his humanism. He cites A.W. Franklin.

> Osler had done more than his share of diminishing the art and strengthening the science of medicine. Yet he was intensely aware of the need for doctors not to become technologists but to remain human practitioners of a most human art. Bacon's ideal man, streamlined to technical efficiency, powerful for good and evil beyond any seventeenth-century dreams, has become a danger to the world about him and to himself. In the evolution of his attitudes he is losing touch with this moral nature.[75]

Osler never lost touch with his moral nature. Perhaps it is this more than anything that could help revive his memory among modern physicians and their students, who, as Franklin indicates, may feel that they work in a moral wasteland. But Osler's moral nature was exercised not only in practising and teaching his art for the benefit of other individuals, but working too as member of an historically rooted social group, a profession, called to benefit society as a whole. Thus, throughout his life, he remained the liberally educated, medical gentleman, pursuing knowledge worth having for its own sake, acquiring medical facts, and doing medical deeds, but all in "philosophic" perspective trying to see the important as important, and the less as less, trying to place all in proper context and not only in individual but social context.

During its initial years, the Osler Club of London constructed and emulated an individually oriented Osler. During his later years, A.W. Franklin, a founder of the Club, appreciated the more complete Osler. Indeed, he began to glimpse ways in which the Oslerian legacy itself could become more complete by focusing more fully on preventive medicine especially among the deprived and neglected of society.

*This paper was presented in a preliminary version to a joint meeting of the American Osler Society and the Osler Club of London, May, 1994. The author gratefully acknowledges officers and members of the Osler Club of London for their assistance: especially helpful were Drs. Alex Sakula, and Gordon Cook, and Mr. Richard Osborne, archivest. Mr. Geoffrey Davenport, Librarian of the Royal College of Physicians of London was also most helpful. He also would like to thank Dr. Laurence Longo of the American Osler Society for his comments.

Endnotes

1. Philip M.Teigen, "William Osler as Medical Hero," *Bull. Hist. Med.*, 1986, 60: 573.
2. *Ibid.*
3. Roland notes, ". . . sceptics have suggested that Osler really did little or nothing to deserve his immortality." Charles Roland, "The Palpable Osler: A Study in Survival," *The Persisting Osler*, J. A.(Barondess, J. P. McGovern, and C. Roland, eds.). Baltimore: University Park Press, 1985, p. 3. See, also: H. Bloch, "William Osler, MD (1849–1919): Myths, Images, Realities" *Journal of the National Medical Association*, 1986, 78, No. 2: 153–155; and, P.K. Bondy, "What's So Special about Osler," *Yale J Biol Med*, 1980; 54:418–447.
4. William Osler, *The Principles and Practice of Medicine*, New York: D. Appleton and Company, 1892.
5. See, for example, "Sir William Osler Memorial Number: Appreciations and Reminiscences," *Bulletin No. IX of the International Association of medical Museums and Journal of Technical Methods*, Montreal: Privately issued at 836 University Street, 1926.
6. See, for example, J.P. McGovern, , and C. Roland (eds.), *The Collected Essays of Sir William Osler. Vol. I: The Philosophical Essays*, Birmingham, Ala.: The Classics of Medicine Library, 1985.
7. Teigen, *Ibid.*
8. See Fritz K. Ringer, *Education and Society in Modern Europe.* Bloomington and London: Indiana University Press, 1979. See, especially, pp. 206ff.
9. Robert E. Proctor, *Education's Great Amnesia.* Bloomington, Ind.: Indiana University Press, 1988, pp. 103 ff.; and, more generally, Pierre Bourdieu, *Distinction: A Social Critique of the Judgement of Taste.* Cambridge, Mass.: Harvard University Press, 1984, p. 2–7 and *passim.*
10. A.M. Carr-Saunders and P.A. Wilson, *The Professions.* Oxford at the Clarendon Press, 1933, pp. 65–75; A. J. Youngson, *The Scientific Revolution in Victorian Medicine,* London: Croom Helm, 1979, p. 15.
11. A.W. Franklin, "The History of the Osler Club of London," *St. Bartholomews Hospital Journal, March, 1961, p. 53.*

12. There were precedents in North America. The Osler medical Historical Society at the Mayo Foundation in Rochester, Minnesota and the Osler Memorial Association of Los Angeles had both been established, in would seem, in 1920. An historical club had been established by Osler at his home, at Johns Hopkins and this later became the Osler Historical Club (1929). The Osler Reporting Society had been formed about 1920 in Montreal at the Royal Victoria Hospital and, there was an Osler Society at Queen's University, Kingston, Ontario dating at least to Jan. 13, 1916. See: Ruth J. Mann, and Jack D. Key, "The Osler medical Historical Society: Mayo Foundation "Chapter," August 28, 1920-July 3, 1925," in Barondess, McGovern and Roland, (eds.) *The Persisting Osler:Selected Transactions of the First Ten Years of the American Osler Society* . . . pp. 291–99.

13. The factual assertions in this paper which are not supported with references to published materials have been largely based on materials in the archives of the Osler Club of London, most especially its minutes which recorded: date and place of each meeting; members, honourary members, friends and visitors in attendance; presenters and topics of papers, names of those intervening in discussions, and occasionally the gist of discussions. Other archival references are generally referred to in the text.

14. Actually, Alfred's father, Mr. Philip Franklin a consultant otolaryngologist and surgeon, lived at 27 Wimpole Street which is in the Harley Street medical area. See:Harvey Graham, *A Doctor's London.* London: Allan Wingate, 1952, p. 27; also, C.P. Bryan, *Roundabout Harley Street,* London: John Bale and Sons and Danielson, Ltd., 1932.

15. A.W. Franklin, "Cambridge University Medical Society Tour To America, 1926."

16. A.E. Franklin, "Proem for the Osler Club of London," reprint of a talk "given at the joint meeting of the Osler Club of London and the American Osler Society at the Royal College of Physicians on Tuesday, 5 September 1972, during the XXIII International Congress of the History of Medicine."

17. *Ibid.* See also citations for these men (except for Watts, who died in 1930) in *The Medical Directory: 1933.* London, J.& A. Churchill, 1933.

18. A.W. Franklin, toast to the health of Dr. and Mrs. Bett at a dinner in their honour given by The Osler Club in the Council Chamber of the Royal College of Surgeons, London, on November 5, 1959. Mimeographed and "circulated to members with Dr. Bett's compliments."

19. See: *Op. Cit.* Graham, and Bryan, as well as E.S. Turner, *Call the Doctor: A Social History of Medical Men.* London: Michael Joseph, 1958, *passim.*

20. See: M.J. Peterson, *The Medical Profession in Mid-Victorian London.* Berkeley: University of California Press, 1978, especially Chapter II, "Education for a Profession," pp. 40–89. A classic Victorian exposition of this ideal is W. Macmichael, with additions by Dr. William Munk, *The Gold-Headed Cane: A reprint of the Edition of 1884,* London: Johnson Publications, Ltd., 1965.

21. *Ibid,* p. 154.

22. *Ibid.,* pp. 208–209.

23. *Ibid.* p. 88.

24. Newman, John Henry Cardinal, *The Idea of a University,* Garden City, New York: Image Books, Division of Doubleday and Company, Inc., 1959. The original was published in 1852.

25. See: J.J. Cameron's comments on Newman's work In his *On the Idea of a University,* Toronto: University of Toronto Press, 1978, p. 9.

26. *Ibid.*, pp. 144–145.

27. *Ibid.*, pp. 166–167. This is, of course, a highly idealized view of the gentlemanly, British Public School-Oxbridge University sub-culture. Others are less sanguine and point out some less than ideal patterns of behaviour and belief among its members. See, for example, Ponsonby, Arthur, M.P., *The Decline of Aristocracy.* London: T. Fisher Unwin, 1912 and Martin Green, *Children of the Sun: A Narrative of "Decadence" in England after 1918.* New York: Basic Books, 1976.

28. *Ibid.*, pp. 217–219.

29. A.W. Franklin, "Proem for the Osler Club of London," *Op. Cit.*

30. Reprint from A.W. Franklin, "The Osler Club of London," *The Medical Press,* July 13, 1949, Vol. CCXXII, No. 5749, pp. 3–4.

31. The Osler Club, "Resolutions Put Before the Club," June 4, 1928.

32. A.W. Franklin, "The Osler Club of London: A Brief History," A brochure based on articles in *Medical Press,* 1949, p. 222, and *St. Barth. Hosp. J.,* 1961, 65, 53.

33. *Ibid.*

34. E. Ashley Underwood, "Charles Singer: A Biographical Note," p. vii. in E.A. Underwood, (ed), *Science, Medicine and History: Essays on the Evolution of Scientific Thought and Medical Practice written in Honour of Charles Singer*. London: Oxford University Press, 1953.

35. See: The Osler Club of London, *Geoffrey Keynes: Tributes on the Occasion of his Seventieth Birthday, with a bibliographical check list of his publications.* London: Rupert Hart-Davis Ltd., 1961. See also Geoffrey Keynes, *Gates of Memory.* London: Oxford University Press, 1981.

36. See: Fielding H. Garrison, *An Introduction to the History of Medicine.* Fourth Ed. Phil. Saunders Company, 1929, pp. 666, 885, 918.

37. His bibliography in 1931 included some 609 items. See: *Selected Writings,* London: Oxford University Press, 1931.

38. See: Garrison, *Op. cit.*, pp. 667, 747.

39. Harvey Cushing, *The Life of Sir William Osler.* Oxford: At The Clarendon Press, 1925. Vol. II, pp. 12, 672,673.

40. *Ibid.*, pp. 640, 648–649.

41. *Ibid.* The Almshouse of which the Regius Professor of Medicine was 'Master' was a residence for a number of elderly men. Osler took an active interest in the place and had discovered the muniments, a cache of 14th to 16th century documents in an old trunk. See: Harvey Cushing, *The Life of Sir William Osler.* Oxford: At The Clarendon Press, 1925. Vol. II, pp. 57–59.

42. 19 or 11 more than the 8 members, and 6 greater than the average attendence of 12 for 1928.

43. "The Osler Club," *The Lancet,* July 21, 1928, p. 144.

44. "The Osler Club," *British Medical Journal,* July 21, 1928, pp. 413–414(?).

45. Dr. Haseltine wrote up the even along with a broader account of his visit to England in: "The Osler Club: A Letter from Europe," *Clinical Medicine and Surgery,* October, 1928.

46. "The Osler Club," *British Medical Journal,* July 21, 1928, p. 414(?). Keynes and his friend Cosmo Gordon had became acquainted with Osler when as young surgeons they sought him out to explore their mutual interests in the bibliography of Sir Thomas Browne. Sir William nicknamed Gordon and Keynes St.'s Cosmas and Damian after traditional medical-chirurgical patron saints.

47. In 1928, five of the 6 initial members of the club ranged in age from 24 through 27 years of age. Five of the six would achieve membership in one

or the other of the Royal Colleges between 1927 and 1932. Franklin refers to them all as "ernest young medical students." A.W. Franklin, "The Osler Club of London," *The Medical Press.* Vol. CCXXII, No. 5749 (July 13, 1949), p. 5.

48. "In Memoriam: Sir D'Arcy Power, K.B.E., F.R.C.S., (1855–1941)," *The British Journal of Surgery*, 1955, p. 324.

49. Keynes autobiography, *Gates of Memory*, London: Oxford University Press, 1981, is almost an elegy on the beauty and value of the life of a "gentleman." It is noteworthy that Keynes declined a professorial position to free up more time for the private practice which would finance his growing family, and liberal pursuits— "I did not dislike teaching and enjoyed the company of students but I had many outside interests, among them a strong desire to form a library of original editions of English literature, science, and medical history. In addition I had a growing family of sons who had to be educated. All these things required a larger income than was awarded to a professor, and could only be provided by private practice; this had the additional advantage of fulfilling my desire to have human relations with a proportion of my patients, which one loses if they are all confined in hospital beds as 'cases.' " p. 219.

50. This information was generally culled from *The Medical Directory*, London: J. & A. Churchill, 1932 and 1933.

51. The list runs to four type-written pages and sixty eight separate citations including the following journals and periodicals:

British Medical Journal	New England Journal of Medicine
The Lancet	The Journal of the American
Deuts. med. Wachr.	Medical Association
The Clinical Journal	St. George's Hospital Gazette
St. Bartholomew's Hospital Journal	The London Hospital Gazette
St. Thomas's Hospital Gazette	British Journal of Surgery
British Journal of Tuberculosis	Wien. klin. Wschr
Medical Press	Canadian Medical Association Journal

52. A.W. Franklin, "The Osler Club of London: A Brief History." Reprint based on *M. Press*, 1949, 222, and *St. Barth. Hosp. J.x*, 1961, 65, 53.

53. Peterson, *Op. Cit.*, p. 88.

54. Later in life, he also wrote in a broader, liberal vein. See, George Pickering, *Creative Malady: Illness in the Lives and Minds of Charles Darwin, Florence Nightingale, Mary Baker Eddy, Sigmund Freud, Marcel Proust, Elizabeth Barrett Browning.* London: Oxford University Press, and Goerge Allen & Unwin, 1974.

55. A.W. Franklin, "In Praise of Walter Bett, 1903–1968: Remarks made at a meeting of The Osler Club on 5 June 1969," Privately Printed Pamphlet.

56. "John Fulton Number," *Journal of the History of Medicine and Allied Sciences*, Vol., XVII, No. 1, January 1963. An issue devoted entirely to Fulton's work.

57. It is perhaps worth noting that in the 1930's, consultants' incomes once they had achieved maturity were considerably higher than those of general practitioners. Stevens notes, "By the time both were in the 55–64 age group, the consultant was earning almost twice as much as the GP." (Rosemary Stevens, *Medical Practice in Modern England: The Impact of Specialization and State Medicine*, New Haven: Yale University Press, 1966, p. 58.) This despite a considerable improvement in the latters' circumstances in the early 20th century.

58. See: Peterson, *Op. Cit.*, passim.

59. "Presentation to Sir D'Arcy Power," Reprinted from the *British Medical Journal,* January 31st, 1931, p. 2.

60. Jack Morrell and Arnold Thackray, *Gentlemen of Science: Early Years of the British Association for the Advancement of Science,* Oxford: Clarendon Press, 1981, p. 25.

61. Philip M. Teigen, "William Osler as Medical Hero: An Essay Review of Jeremiah A. Barondess, John P. McGovern, and Charles G. Roland (eds.) *The Persisting Osler: Selected Transactions of the First Ten Years of the American Osler Society,* Baltimore: University Park Press, 1985." *Bull. Hist. Med.,* 1986, 60: p. 575.

62. See Stevens, *Op, Cit., passim.*

63. It was noted above that the Club met 72 times during the course of the period under study. During that time 113 presentations were named in the minutes. I was able to classify these as follows: 37 on individuals in medical history—largely clebratory of ' the greats;' 30 on diagnostic, therapeutic, or bio-medical clinical or scientific topics; 9 on books and or collections; 9 on Osler or Oslerian topics—largely on Osler's 'good qualities;' 11 on a medical or scientific dimension of a literary personage; 8 on a topic in general humanities; 5 on "places;" 4 uncertain.

64. A.W. Franklin, "Personal Note," *British Medical Journal,* 21 June 1975, 2, p. 682.

65. *Ibid.,* p. 684.

66. Coming closest perhaps is a talk by Dr. J.D. Rolleston, on "Osler as Epidemiologist," in which Sir William's battles for public health against tuberculosis and for sanitary conditions are most favorably described. See: "Osler as Epidemiologist," Note on J.D. Rolleston's Talk at Osler Club, *The British Medical Journal,* 5 January, 1929., p. 30.

67. A.W. Franklin, "Osler Transmitted: A Study in Humanism," *Medical History,* Vol. XVI, No. 2, April, 1972, pp. 103–104. Of course, Osler's early work on the prevention of infectious diseases in Baltimore, and his interest (continuing up to his death) in tuberculosis and its prevention make it impossible to say that he was uninterested in prevention. This interest can perhaps be justifiedly interpreted as a minor one in the broad spectrum of his other work.

68. *Ibid.*

69. See, for example: Franklin, Alfred White, *Widening Horizons of Child Health.* Lancaster, M.T.P. Press, 1976; Franklin, Alfred White (ed.), *Child Abuse: Prediction, Prevention and Follow Up.* N.Y.: Churchill Livingstone, 1978; *Family Matters: Perspectives on the Family and Social Policy: Proceedings of the Symposium on Priority for the Family.* Oxford: Pergamon Press, 1983.

70. Royal College of Physicians of London, *Lives of the Fellows of the Royal College of Physicians of London,* London, The College, 1984, pp. 166–167.

71. Anne Wilkinson, *Lions in the Way.* Toronto: Macmillan, 1956, p. 265.

72. Harvey Cushing, *The Life of Sir William Osler.* Oxford: At the Clarendon Press, Vol. I, 1925, p. 16.

73. *Ibid.,* p. 7.

74. *Ibid.,* pp. 27–69. Of course, these reflections on Sir William Osler"s heritage as British medical gentleman are meant to be suggestive of further study. A recent volume indicating how deeply embedded the British gentlemanly ideal was in the world in which Osler grew up and was educated is R.D. Gidney and W.P.J. Millar, *Professional Gentlemen: The Professions in Nineteenth Century Ontario.* Toronto: University of Toronto Press, 1994.

75. Roland, 1986, *Op. Cit.* p. 17, citing A.W. Franklin, "Osler Transmitted—A Study in Humanism," *Medical History,* Vol 16 (1972), pp. 99–112.

A Dinner for Dr. Osler

 John T. Truman, M.D., M.P.H.

On March 4, 1905 the Charaka Club of New York held a festive dinner to honor Dr. Osler prior to his departure for England. It is a pleasure to report that the Club, which was founded in 1898, is alive and well in the 21st century. Just as when Osler was a member the Club meets several times a year in a private dining room at the Century Club on West 43rd Street, its members in black tie, the candles guttering, the waiters serving and pouring discreetly. After coffee a member presents a paper of medico-historical interest as befits its original name, the Medico-Historical Club. One is impressed at how little has changed from one century to the next. Indeed, on October 20, 1998 the Club replicated the 1905 dinner that it held for Dr. Osler. In both instances the menu included a buffet a la Russe followed by crab bisque, mutton a l'anglaise, parfait noisette, cheese, fruit and coffee. A paper was delivered on the subject of Dr. Osler's attendance and membership in the Club, and toasts were made in his honor. In conclusion the Club sang 'Dr. Willie Osler', and it is easy to imagine Dr. Osler across the oblong table, announcing in his plummy southern Ontario accent that there is 'no doubt about it, eh?'

This was the third of six Charaka dinners that Osler was to attend, at which he made five formal presentations in 1902, 1904, 1906, 1907 and 1909. Of these he published two, one in both the Proceedings of the Charaka Club[1] and as a chapter in An Alabama Student[2], and the other as a monograph.[3] His name would be mentioned in the minutes of the Club an additional eight times. He, in turn, would mention the Club twice in his letters, and Lady Osler would mention it once. Cushing would mention the Club three time in his *Life of Sir William Osler*, and twice in *Consecratio Medici*.

What was it that made this small group so attractive to a man who would come all the way from Baltimore to attend three of these meetings and from Oxford to attend an additional three? Clearly, the members were men of many parts, physicians of significant accomplishment, yet humanists with a wide range of intellectual interest and expertise. They met regularly at the Manhattan home of one of the members, or at one of the comfortable men's

Presented at the American Osler Society, May 5, 1999, Montreal.

clubs such as the Metropolitan, University or Century Clubs. One or two of the members would be responsible, in alphabetical order, for presenting a topic of a non-medical or para-medical nature. The manuscripts would be collected by the secretary, and Volume I of the *Proceedings of the Charaka Club,* which consisted of eight papers, was published in 1902. The second volume was published in 1906, the third in 1910, the fourth in 1916, and the fifth in 1919, all in Dr. Osler's lifetime, and each consisting of 12 papers. Seven additional volumes up to 1985, to a total of twelve, have been published, together with a *History of the Charaka Club* in 1978. The Club is planning to publish a 13th volume.

A bibliophilic organization of this type was just the thing that would attract Osler. The fact that the members were eminent within the profession probably meant little to him, though the membership during Osler's lifetime would include John Shaw Billings, Weir Mitchell, Harvey Cushing, Thomas McCrae and Lewis Pilcher. Later it would include Fielding Garrison, Peyton Rous, Wilder Penfield and Alan Whipple amongst others. At no time has the membership exceeded 39, so the spirit of intimacy and camaraderie that Osler cherished was assured. Today the Club has 28 active and 6 emeritus members, all well placed in academic life, some very eminent, and all devoted to medicine as an art.

Osler's Third Dinner at the Charaka Club

Osler's third dinner with the Club was the gala farewell event of Mar. 4, 1905 bidding him *bon voyage* on his departure for Oxford. It was held at the University Club in New York, and is described in Volume II of the *Proceedings.*[4] An elegantly printed ten page pamphlet entitled "Folia of the Charaka Club to Dr. Osler" was prepared for each guest but was lost for 93 years until 1998 when it was discovered in the uncatalogued files of the Secretary of the Club at Columbia University.[5] Apparently it had not been felt worthy of inclusion in the club's archives that were given to the New York Academy of Medicine many years after the dinner.

However, as a document it tells us much about how Osler was regarded by his peers in 1905. In it are five pages of 'Things Once Said (And Not Regretted) by Dr. William Osler', which consist of 19 extended quotations from *Aequanimitas.* These fall into two categories: 7 extolling personal virtues and 12 being comments of a professional nature. The personal virtues include work (which is mentioned twice), stoicism, humility, sympathy, faith, and passion. The professional comments relate to science, learning, morality, politics, manners, commerce, the press, marriage, and women in medicine. Science is the dominant topic, and is the basis of 3 quotations: as a discipline, as a responsibility of the university, and as a laboratory adjunct to medical practice. It is thus that Osler seems to have been regarded by his contemporaries: as a scientist foremost and a humanist secondarily.

There are five pages of 'Things Put Before Him'. These include 'The Charaka Bedside Library' of two parts: 'The Osler First Ten', and 'The Charaka Second Ten, with Electives'. The former is the list Osler had published as the endpaper of *Aequanimitas*[6], (The Old and New Testament; Shakespeare; Montaigne; Plutarch; Marcus Aurelius; Epictetus; *Religio Medici; Don Quixote;* Emerson; Holmes—*Poet at the Breakfast Table*). The latter was prepared by the Charakans, perhaps as a rebuttal to the rather somber selections Osler favored. This includes:

1. Poets (Chaucer; Browning; Wordsworth)
2. 'Uitlanders' (Horace; Dante—*Vita Nuova;* Goethe— *Faust* and *Wilhelm Meister;* Moliere)
3. Thomas Carlyle—*Sartor Resartus* and *Heroes and Hero-Worship*
4. Matthew Arnold—*Essays*
5. Walter Pater—*Marcus, The Renaissance* and *Plato*
6. Herodotus
7. Robert Louis Stevenson
8. Samuel Johnson—*Lives of the Poets;* Boswell's *Life of Dr. Johnson*
9. Mark Twain
10. 'Any two new books'.

There then followed a listing of 'The Charaka Real Thing' identifying the most important scientific contribution of each of the 15 members of the club. Osler's was felt to be 'On Choleostoma of the Floor of the Third Ventricle'. John Shaw Billings's was *The Index Medicus,* vols. I to XII.

The penultimate page is the menu itself for the evening. In the finest Edwardian tradition there are 2 more courses than the modern-day Elizabethans were able to manage at the Club's centenary: shad preceding the mutton, and a duck casserole following it. One wonders how W.O., as he was always referred to in the Club's minutes, managed to stay as slim as he did.

The final page of the folio is an elegant engraving of Thomas Browne. This is the same engraving that was the frontispiece of Osler's boyhood copy of *Religio Medici,* and must have appealed greatly to him.

A bronze medallion was struck for the occasion and given to Osler and to each member of the Club. On one side was Osler's effigy and on the other side the words, 'The Charaka Club to Dr. William Osler, medico illustri, literarum cultori, socio gratissimo'.

Speeches were fulsome yet humorous. Dr. Charles Henry Dana presided, and noted that 'when a man stamped with such splendid achievements in science, in medical art and education, shows that he can also step a little aside and invoke the muse of history, of literature and art, the world admits it must be all right, and one may without being an outcast add literary cultivation to his career'.[7] Dr. Joseph Collins spoke of Osler's coming to the USA 'like John the Baptist, preaching in the wilderness of Judaea, teaching the gospel of bedside teaching to the exclusion of all other so far as possible'. He went on to say, 'The day when William Osler shall thrust his legs beneath our mahogany again, that will be a halcyon day for the Charaka Club, and great will be the happiness of its members'.[8]

Weir Mitchell read his own poem entitled 'Books and the Man' one verse of which said:

> 'Do you perchance recall when first we met-
> And gaily winged with thought the flying night
> And won with ease the friendship of the mind,-
> I like to call it friendship at first sight.'[9]

It had been Weir Mitchell who persuaded Osler to leave McGill for the University of Pennsylvania, and now Osler was leaving Johns Hopkins for Oxford.

The event was reported in the *British Medical Journal* on April 1, 1905 (April Fool's day) in an extensive review that described it with appropriate tongue-in-cheek humor, "The walls of the room were decorated with old prints and mezzotints of famous physicians of the past, most of them, it is stated, over 60, and all over 40."[10] This was a clear reference to Osler's widely misunderstood farewell address to the Johns Hopkins faculty on Feb. 22, which he called 'The

Fixed Period'.[11] The brouhaha that erupted over that, with headlines 'Osler Recommends Chloroform at Sixty' and the coining of the term 'Oslerize', hurt him deeply.[12] The Club put the appropriate emphasis on this by reading a fictitious telegram, allegedly from Pekin saying, 'TO CHALAKA CLUB, N.Y. BEST LEGARDS PLOFESSOR OSLER. FLAID WE GOT GO TOPSIDE NO CHLOLOFORM HEAD CHOP CHOP. GIN SENG. PHYSICIAN TO DOWAGER EMPRESS OF CHINA'. Similar bogus communications were read from 'Maxim Gorky' in St. Petersburg, 'HAVSKY READOFF OSLEROWICH FORTY SIXTY DAMSKY', and from the 'Geheimjustitsrath Zauberworst' of Jena, 'GELUNGEN. HABEN SCHON ZWEI HUNDERT DEUTSCHE AERTZE – BESONDERSNEUROLOGEN UND PATHOLOGEN-OSLERIZIERT. GLUCKLICHE IDEE!'[13] The levity of the occasion must have been a welcome relief.

But the highlight of the evening was the song, 'Willie, Willie Osler' written and sung by Dr. George Walton from Boston[14], with the diners all joining in on the choruses. It is a paraphrase of the 1893 music hall song 'Private Tommy Atkins' which itself is a paraphrase of one of Kipling's 'Barracks Room Ballads'. A trip to the New York Public Library found the sheet music that the words were set to [15], and it is very easy to play it on the piano [Fig. 1]. The words are as follows:

'Twas in Canada that Willie made his bow,
Then USA was added to his beat;
We put a little laurel on his brow,
And he landed in this country with both feet.
It didn't matter what he was before,
Or what McGill had fancied for his name,
We assumed that he was willing
To accept a little grilling,
And we called him Willie Osler just the same.

CHORUS (repeated after each verse)

O Willie, Willie Osler, you're a good 'un heart and hand;
You're a credit to your calling, not to say your native land;
May your luck be never failing, may your love be ever true,
God bless you, Willie Osler, here's Charaka's love to you.

In time of peace most famous of them all,
He practices upon the high and low-
And if microscope and test tube ever pall,
There is Aretaeus and Fracastoro.
It's open house he keeps in Franklin Street-
You can lunch with him at any time you say,-
Then back he goes to duty
Like the ancient Therapeutae,
And we hope he gets his thirteen pence a day.

Chorus

In strenuous times it's Willie at the front,
And it's absolutely sure he will be there.
We sit at home while Willie does the stunt
Which we read about upon our easy chair.
And whether he's in Paris or in Rome,
Or a-talking to the docs in Mattapan,
The standard he is raising
While admiring crowds are gazing,
Every inch of him philosopher and man.

Chorus

So, Willie dear, we'll back you 'gainst the world,
For pedagogy, frolic, or for work,
Where'er the flag of science is unfurled
You will do your best and never, never shirk.
We keep the warmest corner of our hearts
For you, old boy, wherever you may be,
Another flag will be above you,
But we're proud of you and love you,
God keep you, Willie, still by land and sea.

Chorus

Dr. Osler's comments are not recorded other than that 'his acknowledgement of the ovation given him was in the nature of a short story of his professional life, told simply and eloquently, and ending with warm appreciation of the friendship and good fellowship shown him.'[16]

The Dinner as Mentioned by Cushing and Osler

Cushing mentions the Charaka Club three times in his *Life of Sir William Osler*, and twice refers to the farewell dinner in *Consecratio Medici* in the chapter entitled William Osler, The Man. In the first of these Cushing writes, 'In a poem, Books and the Man, dedicated to Osler and read before the Charaka Club, March 4, 1905, Weir Mitchell recalls in these three verses their first meeting in London twenty years before'; these are given.[17] The second reference is to Osler's response at the dinner. 'Dr. Osler confessed, under the emotion of his reply to the tribute that had been paid him, that to few men had happiness come in so many forms as it had come to him; that his three personal ideals had been , to do the day's work well, to act the Golden Rule in so far as in him lay, and lastly to cultivate such a measure of equanimity as would enable him to bear success with humility, the affection of his friends without pride, and to be ready when the day of sorrow and grief came to meet it with the courage befitting a man.'[18]

Osler himself mentions the dinner in an unpublished letter in the Bibliotheca Osleriana. Returning home to Baltimore late at night after the farewell dinner, dated 'Sunday Eve. Mar 4+, 1905', he writes to Dana, 'I cannot go to bed without sending you a line of heartfelt thanks for that delightful evening. It was really a most memorable occasion, one which I shall cherish while "memory holds a seat" &c I enjoyed your remarks hugely & I hope to have a chance to read them. Mrs Osler is enchanted with the Medallion—indeed the whole affair was worthy of the club'.[19] However, there may have been a moment of concern in the months that followed. The likeness on the medallion had been copied from a plaque commissioned in 1903 in Paris by Dr. H.B. Jacobs, a colleague at Hopkins. On Oct. 11, 1905, Grace Osler would write to Charles Camac, a future Charakian, ' Dr. Osler wrote you I suppose that we always felt that Dr. Jacobs was not quite pleased at having the bronze distributed at the Charaka dinner—I did not feel that he would at all care for the general circulation.'[20] Both the medallion and the plaque are now in the Bibiotheca Osleriana.

Osler's membership in the Charaka Club may be seen as a metaphor for his life. It exemplified high conviviality, genuine medical accomplishment, and a profound level of humanistic scholarship. It centered around books, as objects of veneration and as living beings in the midst of being created. It spanned his Johns Hopkins years and Oxford years almost equally. Through it he exerted influence and gave pleasure, and this was reciprocated. Nearly a century later his spirit lives on around the Club's dining table as surely it lives when clinicians take students on bedside ward rounds, and the art and science of medicine meet.

References

1. Osler W, Fracastorius in *Proceedings of the Charaka Club*, Vol.II New York 1906, pp 278–294
2. Osler W, Fracastorius in *An Alabama Student and Other Historical Essays* London, OUP 1908, pp 278–294
3. Osler W, *Thomas Linacre* Cambridge, CUP 1908
4. *Proceedings of the Charaka Club*, Vol.II New York 1906, pp 142–152

5. Archives of The Charaka Club. Courtesy Dr. Andrew Frantz, Secretary-Treasurer, Columbia University College of Physicians & Surgeons
6. Osler W, Aequanimitas 2nd ed. Philadelphia, Blakiston 1906, p 451
7. *Proceedings of the Charaka Club,* Vol.II New York 1906, p 144
8. *Proceedings of the Charaka Club,* Vol.II New York 1906, pp 148–9
9. *Proceedings of the Charaka Club,* Vol.II New York 1906, pp FIRST PAPER
10. *British Medical Journal* 1905; i. 728–9
11. Osler W, *Aequanimitas* 2nd ed. Philadelphia, Blakiston 1906, pp 373–393
12. Cushing H, *The Life of Sir William Osler* Oxford, OUP 1925, vol. I p 669
13. *Proceedings of the Charaka Club,* Vol.II New York 1906, p 145
14. *Proceedings of the Charaka Club,* Vol.II New York 1906, pp 150–1
15. Hamilton H and Potter S, *Private Tommy Atkins* London, Hopwood & Crew ca.1893
16. *Proceedings of the Charaka Club,* Vol. II New York 1906, p 152
17. Cushing H, *Consecratio Medici* Boston, Little Brown 1940, p 99
18. Cushing H, *Consecratio Medici* Boston, Little Brown 1940, p 114–5
19. Archives, Bibliotheca Osleriana, McGill University, Montreal, Canada (courtesy Pamela Miller)
20. Osler GR, in Nation EF and McGovern JP, *Student and Chief* Pasadena, Castle Press 1980, p 57

SECTION V

 Varia

The Old Eugenics and the New Science

 Jeremiah A. Barondess, M.D.

William Osler's 1919 presidential address to the British Classical Association was entitled "The Old Humanities and the New Science."[1] In it he explored the separation of the humanities and science that had occurred despite their common origins and their continuing influence on each other.

Osler's talk was given immediately after the end of World War I. He viewed much of that demonstration of the new warfare as reflecting scientific advance. One could only imagine the difficulty he had in examining that issue, in light of the recent death of his son in an artillery barrage that reflected the new chemistry of explosives, and the newly refined science that allowed more accurate description of the trajectories of artillery shells. Adding the ghastly application of chemistry in the invention of poisonous gases used in the War, adding further the applied science of the new aeronautics, Osler found himself able to speak of "the final subjugation of nature," and raised, in an insight that continues to be dominant, the question of whether science can rule without invoking ruin. In further development of that thought, he said, "the extraordinary development of modern science may be her undoing . . . the workers lose all sense of proportion in a maze of minutiae."[1]

While it is presumptuous to paraphrase Osler's title, the old eugenics may be thought of as emblematic of the separation of science and humanism, and the new science, with its capacity to impact human welfare at the genetic level, will present challenges in managing this new frontier with awareness of its social implications, not least the threat of a resurgent and more powerful eugenics.

The international eugenics movement had its roots in the 19th century. In the early decades of the 20th it flourished and became a major social force, with linked objectives of improvement of the human gene pool and alleviation of complex and costly social problems. The central concept, that there was a hierarchy of human types, and that this hierarchy had biologic origins, had

Presented at the American Osler Society, May 6, 1998, Toronto.

Published in part in Trans Am Clin Climatol Assn, 1998; *109*:174–180. Reprinted with permission.

come under exploration previously. Morton, in 1839, for example, reported that the average Caucasian skull was 7 cubic inches larger in capacity than the average Negro skull, a finding thought to support the idea of the cultural superiority of whites[2]; and Cesar Lombroso, a 19th century Italian forensic pathologist, developed, through extensive morphometric and autopsy studies, a field that came to be called criminal anthropology; its basic tenet was that criminal behavior is inborn, physically determined, "an ineluctable product of (the criminal's) germ plasm."[3]

The power of these theorizations derived in considerable measure from Darwin's *Origin of Species,* published in 1859, and from the work of Francis Galton, a prominent British naturalist and mathematician and a cousin of Darwin, who in 1869 published a study of the accomplishments of children of eminent British judges in a volume entitled *Hereditary Genius: An Inquiry into its Laws and Consequences.*[4] This and other efforts led him to the conclusion that major accomplishment is largely the expression of inborn determinants. In 1883 he coined the term "eugenics," to embrace the concept of racial improvement through selective matings.

After the rediscovery of Mendel's experiments in 1900, a rapidly expanding social anthropology came to consider negative as well as positive human traits as reflecting inborn tendencies, transmitted hereditarily in fairly straightforward fashion. Retrospective studies of the pedigrees of prison populations, notably Dugdale's 1877 description of the family he called the Jukes,[5] appeared to demonstrate an extraordinary propensity for poverty, alcoholism and prostitution, as well as criminality, among the forebears of prison inmates, and Goddard's book on the Kallikak family in 1912 lent powerful support to the idea that social pathologies in individuals reflected Mendelian forces.[6] Further concerns emerged over studies that appeared to demonstrate that survival of the fittest through natural selection was at risk, since the fertility rates of the lower strata of society were outstripping those of the best stock, while at the same time social support systems and advances in medicine and public health were allowing more of the less fit to survive. Eugenic thinking coalesced early around these formulations.

A major force behind the growth of the American eugenics movement was Charles B. Davenport, an accomplished biologist, who, in 1904, founded the Station for Experimental Evolution, later the Cold Spring Harbor Biological Laboratory, and for a while the Department of Genetics of the Carnegie Institution of Washington. Leading American intellectuals, university presidents and philanthropists supported its work and the translation of its ideas into social policy. Studies at Cold Spring Harbor, based ultimately on nearly three quarters of a million family pedigrees, assembled retrospectively and without rigorous rules of evidence, were carefully analyzed by Davenport and his group. He concluded that hereditary patterns were evident in insanity, epilepsy, alcoholism, "pauperism," criminality and "feeblemindedness," and proselytized widely for efforts to contain the numbers of those affected by preventing them from reproducing. In 1923 the American Eugenics Society was formed; it contributed vigorously to an expanding welter of lectures, debates and popular publications that promulgated the eugenic viewpoint and argued for social action in response. Through the first third of this century, and especially in the 1920s and 1930s, eugenic rhetoric was very widespread; the country was subjected to exhortations concerning the selection of a mate, the obligation of the better classes to enhance the rate at which they were reproducing, and the continuing necessity of reducing the fertility of the genetically inferior. The latter were effectively demonized, seen as a major societal burden. These views led initially to efforts to segregate such individuals during their reproductive years, and later to a widespread involuntary sterilization movement that came ultimately to include some 60,000 individuals in this country, largely the criminal and feebleminded, mostly in state institutions. The state sterilization statutes came before the Supreme Court in 1924 in the landmark case of *Buck v Bell,* and were upheld.[7] Involuntary sterilization on eugenic grounds did not slacken until the eve of World War II. The procedure is still carried out on occasion.

Wide application of intelligence testing during and after World War I fed the view that feeblemindedness was widespread, that striking racial differences in intelligence obtained, and that those of low I.Q. were reproducing more rapidly than the better-endowed. In addition, the strong implication emerged that immigrants from Mediterranean and Southeastern European countries were major sources of divergence, intellectually, socially and with regard to undesirable behaviors, from the Nordic ideal, enhancing the xenophobia that led ultimately to the Immigration Restriction Act of 1924; the Act effectively excluded individuals from Southern and Eastern European countries, and was produced with the help, and to a substantial degree at the urging, of the Cold Spring Harbor group and the American Eugenics Society.

Behind the vigor of the eugenics movement was a widespread social receptivity to the idea that traditional, *laissez faire* approaches to social problems were inadequate, and that social and economic planning were required to manage problems produced by a series of late 19th century economic depressions, urban development, massive immigration, prostitution, crime, alcoholism and disease.[8] Cost concerns were prominent, and there was a rising sense of the importance of defending the qualities of the Nordic or Anglo-Saxon "race." The idea that Mendelian genetics might explain important social and behavioral problems was seized on, and eugenicists emerged as scientists with relevant expertise.

By the late 1930s support for eugenics was waning, and the movement atrophied rapidly thereafter, due in large measure to better science, an increasing realization of the impact of environmental factors on human development and behaviors, and gathering revulsion with the radicalization of the eugenics movement in Nazi Germany. Increasing resistance by the courts contributed to further erosion of eugenics in some of its more bizarre expressions, notably enforced sterilization of criminals and the feebleminded.

The power of the eugenics movement was such that, on the basis of relatively primitive genetic science, linked to social policies with strong racist and xenophobic overtones, violence was done to tens of thousands in this country and to millions in Europe. Now, a new, powerful genetics is emerging, although in a societal setting that is more sensitive to social issues and in a biomedical setting that includes an active and articulate bioethics community. Why then should we worry? The question revolves around our capacity as a society to manage wisely not only clinical application of the new knowledge, but derivative social complexities as well. We face the possibility of a new, more subtle eugenics, more powerful because science-based. We face the need to consider issues framed in contexts to some degree unfamiliar. Four constructs are offered here, each with eugenic implications, each requiring careful attention across our society, including, very importantly, those in medicine.

The first has to do with problems inherent in applying population-based predictions to individuals, and the dangers in acting on them. Even in the case of so-called single gene diseases, ascribing predictive causation to DNA sequence changes is to some extent problematic, since the expression of such mutations is in some degree dependent on other sequences in the genome. In genetically more complex morbidities, such as coronary artery disease, diabetes, cancer or Alzheimer's dementia, gene penetrance is usually low, multiple loci are involved, and processes of mutation and recombination make prediction at the individual level even more hazardous, and derivative reproductive and social choices more tenuous. With regard to so-called normal variation in attributes such as intelligence, aggressiveness, sexual orientation and social success, even greater ambiguity obtains, since, with relation to such traits and characteristics, biology is, at least to this point, not predictive at a level that would allow enhancement to be seriously contemplated. The idea, in fact the ideal, of the "normal" genotype is surely incorrect, as every individual carries some genetic load of mutations, expressed or not. Nevertheless, as attention is turned to normal variation in characteristics such as intelligence or social behaviors, the pursuit of the "normal," as well as the pursuit of enhancement, will result in eugenic pressures to respond.

In a second arena, population screening for predictive DNA sequences presents an additional set of issues. The World Health Organization has supported as preconditions for community carrier screening these criteria: The disease should be a major health problem; the course of the disease should be defined and severe; there should be a simple, cheap and accurate carrier test that is comprehensible to clinician and carrier; there should be a solution to the problem; and there should be educational and counseling backup in the community.[9] Almost certainly these will be insufficient, and screening will be less than discriminate. Screening tests will be increasingly commercialized, as is already happening with regard to BRCA I and II. Healthy women are being tested by private laboratories, even though the precise cancer risk for carriers detected in this way remains ambiguous and counseling is not necessarily linked to the testing process.

Genetic screening will also be applied increasingly by public health agencies, seeking high penetrance genes for specific disorders, and in order to assemble core genetic epidemiology collections.[10] While the promise of genetic testing with relation to public health lies in translating genetic technology into disease prevention, there is the prospect that genetic information about sub-populations will be disseminated, and, even if not linked to particular patients, will hold the potential of stirring new eugenic impulses.

A third area has to do with interactions of social pressures and the new genetic technologies. Such pressures may be experienced, for example, by women who refuse prenatal diagnosis for disorders implying ongoing costs, such as Down Syndrome;[11] managed care organizations and other payers could well increase co-payments and deductibles for expensive care implied as a consequence of enrollees deciding not to be tested or not to follow the least costly options after testing. Non-directiveness on the part of genetic counselors is likely to come under pressure as managed care organizations recognize that predictive genetic testing may save them money. An issue for consideration here is whether the motives of providers or the possible subtle resulting pressure on consumers should be viewed in a eugenic context.[12]

A fourth arena of concern is the threat of a resurgent, more powerful biological determinism, based on the belief that nature will be more manageable in light of new molecular genetic technology; but it appears that the more we learn about how various genotypes respond to various environments the more important the environment becomes at the individual level. The concern is that attention to environmental factors as forces in human health and welfare will erode, that opportunities for effective intervention will be blunted or lost, and that eugenic pressures will move us again toward categorizing individuals socially, based on genetic criteria. It is dangerous to assume that biology is destiny.[13]

Beyond these four sources of concern there is a broader set: genetically-based discrimination, for example in health insurance, is already an issue; further, there is at least reason to be concerned that, as mutant genes leading, for example, to schizophrenia or manic depressive disorder are isolated, or as genes and mutations determining high, medium or low intelligence are found, in the process these levels of intelligence as well as the phenotypes for schizophrenia and manic depression will be redefined. Muller-Hill has predicted that the frequency of mutations in such genes will be found to vary among ethnic groups, as has already been claimed for intelligence,[14] and social groups that appear to differ in the frequency of such mutations are likely to be stigmatized. In addition, a mutant gene on the X chromosome, thought to be identified with violent crime, but thus far identified only in a single Dutch family,[15] is capable of raising the same issue. We should imagine, as Muller-Hill suggests, what will happen if another crime gene is found where null mutations differ in frequency in various ethnic groups.[16] That scenario raises again for us some of the classic rhetoric of the early eugenicists.

Ultimately these issues will have special importance for physicians. They will call for more than technical expertise and genetic insights; they will call for wisdom, for efforts to raise the level of genetic literacy in the health professions and in the public, and for willingness to engage in the social and political discourse that will be required. They will challenge the moral integrity of medicine as a helping profession based in, but not identical with, the biological sciences. They will challenge us further to merge science not alone with the humanities, but with humanism and with humaneness. One is reminded of Osler's desired epitaph: "Write me as one who loved his fellow man."

References

1. Osler, W: The Old Humanities and the New Science. Brit Med J, ii 1919, 1–7.
2. Morton, SG: Crania Americana, Philadelphia, John Pennington, 1839.
3. Lombroso-Ferrero G.: Lombroso's Criminal Man. Montclair, Patterson-Smith, 1972.
4. Galton, F: Hereditary Genius: An Inquiry into its Laws and Consequences. London, Macmillan, 1869.
5. Dugdale, RL: The Jukes: A Study in Crime, Pauperism, Disease and Heredity. New York, GP Putnam & Sons, 1877.
6. Goddard, HH: The Kallikak family: A Study in the Heredity of Feeble-mindedness. New York, Macmillan, 1912.
7. Lombardo, PA: Medicine, eugenics and the Supreme Court: From coercive sterilization to reproductive freedom. J Contemp Health Law and Pol, 1996, *13:* 1–25.
8. Allen, GE: Eugenics and American social history. Genome 1989, *31:* 885–889.
9. World Health Organization Technical Report Series: Control of hereditary diseases. Geneva, World Health Organization, 1966.
10. McGee, G: Can there be a non-eugenic use of genetic screening? Suggestions for genetics and public health. Presented at: Eugenic Thought

and Practice, a Reappraisal Towards the End of the Twentieth Century. Jerusalem and Tel Aviv, May 26–29, 1997, to be published.

11. Holtzman, NA: Eugenics and genetic testing. Presented at: Eugenic Thought and Practice, *op cit,* to be published.

12. Paul, DB: Cost-benefit reasoning and eugenics. Presented at: Eugenic Thought and Practice, *op cit,* to be published.

13. Proctor, RN: Genonics and eugenics: How fair is the comparison? *in:* Annas, GJ, Elias, S (Eds): Gene Mapping Using Law and Ethics as Guides. New York and Oxford, Oxford University Press, 1992, pp. 57–93.

14. Hernnstein, R, Murray, C: The Bell Curve: Intelligence and Class Structure in American Life. New York, The Free Press, 1994.

15. Brunner, HG, Nelen, M, Breakefield, XO, Ropers, HH, van Ost, BA: Abnormal behavior associated with a point mutation in the structural gene for monoamine oxidase A. Science, 1993, *262:* 578–580.

16. Muller-Hill, B: The specter of kakogenics. Presented at: Eugenic Thought and Practice, *op cit,* to be published.

Benjamin Franklin, Mesmerism, and the Royal Commission of 1784

 Herbert M. Swick, M.D.

On November 21, 1783, Jean-Francois Pilatre de Rozier lifted off from a chateau near Paris in his aerostatic globe, and for the first time, man broke the bounds of earth. Hot air balloon flights quickly captured the public's imagination. The *Journal de Bruxelles,* on January 31, 1784, reported another balloon flight:

> It is impossible to describe that moment: the women in tears, the common people raising their hands toward the sky in deep silence. . . .The feeling of fright gives way to one of wonder. No one said anything but, 'Great God, how beautiful!' Grand military music began to play and firecrackers proclaimed their glory.[1]

In the 1780s, the French were captivated by the discoveries of science and awed by man's new ability to tame the forces of nature. Lavoisier had demonstrated that water was not one of the four basic elements but instead was composed of hydrogen and oxygen; Priestly and Cavendish had shown that air itself was made of several different elements. It was a time of "wonderful, invisible forces"—gravity had been described by Isaac Newton only a century earlier, Benjamin Franklin had explored the properties of electricity, and Luigi Galvani was experimenting with 'animal electricity'. As the historian Robert Darnton noted: "there were enough fluids, sponsored by enough philosophers, to make any eighteenth century reader's head swim."[2]

Into this fecund environment stepped Anton Mesmer. In his thesis for the doctor of medicine degree from the University of Vienna in 1766, titled *De planetarum influxu* (On the Influence of the Planets in the Cure of Diseases), Mesmer argued that celestial bodies acted upon living beings through a universal fluid that he called animal magnetism. In a memoir published in 1779, Mesmer wrote of his animal magnetism that

Based upon a paper presented at the American Osler Society, May 18, 2000, Bethesda, Maryland.

> it is capable of receiving, propagating and communicating all the
> impressions that are incident to motion. . . . The action and the virtue of
> the animal magnetism are capable of being communicated from one body
> to another, animated or inanimate. . .; this action is increased and reflected
> by mirrors; it is communicated, propagated by sound.[3]

Claims for animal magnetism's role in medicine were substantive:

> The animal magnetism is capable of curing immediately diseases of the
> nerves, and mediately other distempers; it improves the action of
> medicines; it forwards and directs the salutary crises so as to subject them
> totally to the government of the judgement; by means of it the physician
> becomes acquainted with the state of the health of each individual, and
> decides with certainty upon the causes, the nature and the progress of the
> most complicated distempers; it prevents their increase, and effects their
> extirpation, without at any time exposing the patient, whatever be his age,
> sex, or constitution, to alarming incidents or unpleasing consequences.[3]

Given these qualities, Mesmer developed a system for treating patients using
animal magnetism, but his approach was not well received in Vienna. Indeed,
he was expelled by the imperial court, so he went in search of more receptive
environments. Initially, neither Paris nor London welcomed him, but upon
his return to Paris in 1783, Mesmer and his animal magnetism quickly became
the vogue, and not only among the public: "struck with the clearness and accu-
racy of his reasonings, the magnificence of his pretensions, the extraordinary
and unquestionable cures he performed, some of the greatest physicians and
most enlightened philosophers of France became his converts."[4] During its
height in 1783–1784, mesmerism occupied more space than any other topic
in *Memoires Secrets* and *Journal de Paris*, at that time the only daily newspaper in
Paris[2]. Some predicted that mesmerism would soon become the sole universal
treatment for disease. Others were skeptical. M.-A. Thouret, a Regent Physician of the Faculty of Paris and member of the Royal Society of Medicine,
derided Mesmer's theories, tracing them back two centuries to the discarded
beliefs of Paracelsus, Kircher and others[5]. The Faculty of Medicine, in attack-
ing Mesmer and his techniques, sent the following letter to its members: "In
future no doctor will be allowed to write favorably of animal magnetism, or
practice the same, on penalty of losing his professional privileges."[6]

In the spring of 1784, two commissions began to investigate this phenomenon which had so quickly captured the attention of Paris. The Royal Society of
Medicine appointed a committee to examine Thouret's work and hence to
investigate Mesmer's system indirectly. And on March 12, 1784, Louis XVI
named a royal commission "to lay before him an account of the animal magnetism" (4, p. 19). The commission included four physicians of the faculty of
Paris, one of whom was Joseph Guillotin (who is better remembered for another
contribution), and five members of the Royal Academy of Sciences, including
Benjamin Franklin and Antoine Lavoisier. Franklin headed the commission.

Anton Mesmer refused to cooperate with the Royal Commission, but
Charles Deslon, one of his students and a member of the Royal Society of Medicine, agreed to demonstrate animal magnetism and reveal its methods:

> M. Deslon undertook to the commissioners, in the first place, to evince the
> existence of the animal magnetism; secondly, to communicate to them his
> knowledge respecting this discovery; and thirdly, to prove the utility of this
> discovery and of the animal magnetism in the cure of diseases. (4, p. 22)

The commission's report, issued on August 11, 1784, is a model of the experimental approach that had come to characterize the advance of science in the

late 18th century. It reflects the belief of the Enlightenment in the simplicity and rationality of the universe. It reflects the growing importance of science as a way to counter suppositions and belief in the occult. The commission's report offers insights into the state of scientific and experimental reasoning at that time, while quotes from the report reveal the care and detail with which the commissioner's approached their work.

The commissioners decided first to observe several public magnetism sessions, and the report describes the public setting in great detail. In the center of a large room sat the bucket, a circular box from which protruded several iron rods. The contents of the bucket—bottles of water and iron filings that were alleged to concentrate the magnetic fluid—"contained no substance either electric or magnetical" as measured by an electrometer or iron needle. (4, p. 24) The patients were arrayed around this bucket, each holding one of the iron rods. They were also connected by a cord passed around their bodies, and at times

> a second means of communication is introduced, by the insertion of the thumb of each patient between the forefinger and thumb of the patient next to him; the thumb thus inserted is pressed by the person holding it; the impression received by the left hand of the patient, communicates through his right, and thus passes through the whole circle. (4, p. 23)

A piano forte provided music, sometimes quiet and slow, sometimes faster and more lively. The music, the cord passed around the patients, the linked hands all helped transmit the animal magnetism. But perhaps most important was the fact that the mesmerist magnetized the patients by "the application of the hands, and by the pressure of the fingers upon the hypochonders and the regions of the lower belly; an application frequently continued for a long time, sometimes for several hours." (4, p. 25)

The report offers a detailed description of the effects of magnetism on the patients:

> In this situation the patients offer a spectacle extremely varied in proportion to their different habits of body. Some of them are calm, tranquil and unconscious of any sensation; others cough, spit, are affected with a slight degree of pain, a partial or a universal burning, and perspirations; a third class are agitated and tormented with convulsions. These convulsions are rendered extraordinary by their frequency, their violence and their duration. As soon as one person is convulsed, others presently are affected by that symptom. These convulsions are characterized by precipitate and involuntary motions of all the limbs or of the whole body, by a contraction of the throat, by sudden affections of the hypochonders and the epigastrium, by a distraction and wildness in the eyes, by shrieks, tears, hiccupings and immoderate laughter. (4, pp. 25–26)

Convulsions lasted as long as three hours, and were "either preceded or followed by a state of languor and reverie." (4, p. 26)

Having observed these rather dramatic responses during public sessions, the commission determined that the next step was to prove the existence of animal magnetism, recognizing that, "the animal magnetism may indeed exist without being useful, but it cannot be useful if it does not exist." (4, p. 29) Could it be detected by any of the five senses? The commissioners were soon convinced that

> this fluid was too subtle to be subjected to their observation. It is not, like the electrical fluid, luminous and visible; its action is not, like the attraction of the lodestone, the object of our sight; it has neither taste nor smell; its process is silent, and it surrounds you or penetrates your frame, without

your being informed of its presence by the sense of touch. If, therefore, it exist in and around us, it is after a manner perfectly insensible. (4, p. 30)

Since the presence of animal magnetism could not be detected directly, it would be necessary to study its effects under controlled circumstances:

They proposed to make experiments upon single subjects, who might be willing to submit to the various experiments which they should invent; and who, some of them by their simplicity, and others by their intelligence, should be capable of giving an exact and faithful account of their sensations. (4, pp. 38–39)

Further, the commissioners decided to determine magnetism's "momentary effects upon the animal economy and the perceptible changes there produced" rather than its effects on disease over time, since "nature, says the father of medical science, cures the diseased." (4, p. 33)

"The commissioners in the first place resolved to make their first experiments upon themselves, and personally to experience the action of the magnetism." (4, p. 39) Initially once a week, then on three successive days, Deslon magnetized the commissioners in private, at his home, using a separate bucket. "Dr. Franklin, though the weakness of his health hindered him from coming to Paris, and assisting at the experiments which were there made, was magnetified by M. Deslon at his own house at Passy." (4, p. 48) Those commissioners subject to "habitual derangements of health" and thought to be the most susceptible were magnetized more often than the others. The report does not reveal which of the nine commissioners were in this category. Nevertheless, none of the commissioners felt any effect.

The next step then was to "make experiments upon persons really diseased," (4, p. 44) The report describes a number of experiments in detail. Patients from the lower classes were identified by name, while those from the upper classes were identified simply as M. R_____ or madame de B_____. Nevertheless, identifying individual patients lent the report credibility and verisimilitude. Every experiment cannot be described; examples must suffice. The initial patients were chosen from the lower class. Seven such patients underwent the operation at Passy, Franklin's house outside Paris. Four of the seven felt nothing, while three had some response to being magnetized. The commissioners sought to better understand these observed responses, so they next studied patients from the upper classes, "selected from the polite world; such as could not be suspected of sinister views, and whose understanding made them capable of enquiring into and giving a faithful account of their sensations." (4, p. 56)

Some sick persons from the upper classes, who had come with Deslon to Passy responded to the effects of the magnetism, but others, including "Dr. Franklin, his two relations, his secretary, and an American officer, felt no sensation, though one of Franklin's relations was convalescent, and the American officer had at that time a regular fever." (4, p. 49)

After this sequence of experiments—beginning with observation of the public sessions, proceeding through attempts to detect directly the presence of animal magnetism, subjecting themselves to repeated trials, and finally mesmerizing "patients really diseased" from both the upper and lower classes—the commissioners felt that they could draw certain conclusions. They recognized the importance of two factors that we still recognize as important today, that patients have certain expectations about their treatment, and that they often want to please their doctor:

> Let us represent to ourselves the situation of a person of the lower class, and
> of consequence ignorant, attacked with a distemper and desirous of a cure,
> introduced with some degree of ceremony to a large company, partly
> composed of physicians, where an operation is performed upon him totally
> new, and from which he persuades himself before hand that he is about to
> experience prodigious effects. Let us add to this that he is paid for his
> compliance, and he thinks he shall contribute more to our satisfaction by
> professing to experience sensations of some kind; and we shall have definite
> causes to which to attribute these effects; we shall at least have reason to
> doubt whether their true cause be the magnetism. (4, pp. 52–53)

The commissioners were by this time somewhat skeptical of animal magnetism, and "having armed themselves with that philosophic doubt which ought
always to accompany enquiry" (4, p. 54) suspected that all the effects of magnetism were, in fact, "the fruits of anticipated persuasion" (4, p. 54), meaning
that they were caused by the patients' imagination. Their next logical step,
then, was to determine to what degree imagination might account for the
effects attributed to magnetism, so the commissioners designed another set of
experiments to address this question.

> The commissioners agreed to blindfold subjects who had already
> undergone the magnetical operation, for the most part not to magnetize
> them at all, but to put to them interrogations, so framed as to point out to
> them their answers. This mode of proceeding was not calculated to deceive
> them, it only misled their imagination. (4, p. 60)

The report describes the blindfold in detail (exemplifying the care with which
the report is written and the care with which the experiments were done):

> The bandage was made of two calottes of elastic gum, whose concavity was
> filled with edredon; the whole inclosed and sewn up in two pieces of stuff of
> a circular form. These pieces of stuff were then fastened to each other, and
> to two strings which were tied in a knot at the back part of the head. Placed
> over the eyes, they left in their interval room for the nose, and the entire
> liberty of respiration, without the person blindfolded being permitted to
> receive even the smallest partical of light, either through, or above, or
> below the bandage. (4, pp. 60–61)

Thus a woman who had shown sensitivity to magnetism was blindfolded and
magnetized. She did not feel any effects in the regions magnetized, but
instead "she felt only a heat in her head, a pain in both eyes and in the left
ear." (4, p. 56) The blindfold was then removed and the experiment repeated.
Once the mesmerist applied his hands to the abdomen, the woman felt a sensation of heat and in a few minutes, she fainted. When she had recovered, the
experiment was resumed. Again she was blindfolded, the mesmerist left the
room, and the woman was induced to believe that the operation was under-
way. "The effects were the same, though no operation, either near or distant
was performed; she felt the same heat, the same pain in her eyes and in her
ears; besides which she felt a heat in her back and loins." (4, p. 57) "It may be
observed," the report continues,

> that while the woman was permitted to see the operation, she placed her
> sensations precisely in the part towards which it was directed; that on the
> other hand when she did not see the operation, she placed them at hazard,
> and in parts very distant. (4, p. 58)

Following a large number of similar experiments, the commissioners were
convinced that imagination alone could produce various sensations, such as

pain and heat, in all parts of the body. But the effects of magnetism were frequently much more dramatic, with fainting and convulsions. Could imagination alone produce such profound effects?

The commissioners devised many experiments to answer this question. Mesmer had argued that all living things, including trees, were influenced by animal magnetism. Indeed, susceptible people had been known to swoon or even to have convulsions when they passed under a tree that had been magnetized. So Deslon agreed to magnetize a tree and choose an experimental subject who was extremely susceptible.

> M. Deslon therefore brought with him [to Passy] a boy of about twelve years of age; an apricot tree was fixed upon in the orchard of Dr. Franklin's garden, considerably distant from any other tree, and calculated for the preservation of the magnetical power which might be impressed upon it. (4, p. 66)

Deslon magnetized the tree while the boy was kept out of sight inside Franklin's house.

> The boy was then brought into the orchard, his eyes covered with the bandage, presented successively to four trees upon which the operation had not been performed, and caused to embrace each of them for the space of two minutes, the mode of communication which had been prescribed by M. Deslon himself." (4, p.67)

Trees ranged from 24 – 38 feet from the magnetized tree, yet at each the boy felt stupefaction and headache. At the fourth tree, at a distance of 24 feet from the apricot tree that Deslon had magnetized, he "fell into a crisis; he fainted away, his limbs stiffened, and he was carried to a neighboring grass-plot, where M. Deslon hastened to his assistance and recovered him." (4, p. 68)
The commissioners found that

> The result of this experiment is entirely contrary to the theory of the animal magnetism. . . . A person sensible to the power of the magnetism, could not hazard a walk in a garden without the risk of convulsions; an assertion confuted by the experience of everyday . . . The crisis was therefore the effect of no physical or exterior cause, but to be ascribed solely to the influence of imagination. (4, p. 69)

The commissioners conducted further experiments to determine whether imagination alone could produce a crisis. In one, a woman was seated facing a closed door and persuaded that Deslon was on the other side to perform the magnetical operation. Deslon, of course, was not anywhere in the house. In about a minute,

> she began to feel the symptoms of shuddering; in another minute she had a chattering of the teeth and an universal heat; in the third minute she fell into a regular crisis. Her respiration was quick, she stretched out both her arms behind her back, twisting them extremely, and bending her body forward: her whole body trembled; the chattering of her teeth became so loud that it might be heard in the open air; she bit her hand, and that with so much force, that the marks of the teeth remained perfectly visible." (4, p. 71)

Although the commissioners had by this time firmly concluded that the effects attributed to magnetism—no matter how dramatic—were due to imagination, they acknowledged that "the identity of the effects does not always prove an identity of the causes." (4, p. 78) Proponents of animal magnetism might argue that both magnetism and imagination could produce the same effects, so the commissioners decided to conduct additional experiments to determine the effect of magnetism in a setting where imagination could not possibly play a role. In one, for example, a lady who had previously been susceptible to magnetism was seated near a doorframe covered with paper. On the other side sat the mesmerist.

> Mademoiselle B_____ was accordingly magnetized during half an hour, at the distance of a foot and a half. . . .During the operation she conversed with much gaiety, and, in an answer to an enquiry concerning her health, she readily replied that she was perfectly well: at Passy she had fallen into a crisis in the course of three minutes; in the present instance she underwent the operation of the magnetism without any effect for thirty minutes. The only reason of this difference must be that here she was ignorant of the operation, and that at Passy she thought it had been performed. (4, p. 80)

The identical operation was then repeated with the patient's knowledge, and within twelve minutes she had a convulsive crisis, characterized by

> an interrupted hiccup, a chattering of the teeth, a contraction of the throat, and an extreme pain in her head; she was restless in her chair; she complained of a pain in her loins; now and then she struck her foot with extreme quickness on the floor; afterwards she stretched her arms behind her, twisting them extremely as at Passy; in a word, the convulsive crisis was complete and accompanied with all the symptoms. (4, p. 82)

The mesmerist then announced that it was time to stop the operation, "at the same time presenting to her his two forefingers in the form of a cross." (4, p. 83) In three minutes, the crisis resolved itself, and the patient declared that she no longer felt any sensation, but was perfectly restored to her normal state.

The commissioners concluded that animal magnetism did not exist, and that the observed effects were all due to imagination. They added:

> the history of medicine presents to us an infinity of examples of the power of imagination and the mental affections. . . .The action and reaction of the physical upon the moral system, and of the moral upon the physical, have been acknowledged ever since the phenomena of the medical science have been remarked, that is, ever since the origin of the science. (4, p. 89)

They acknowledged the importance of their systematic approach. Simply observing the public sessions was not sufficient. Instead it was necessary to conduct a sequence of investigations, in which the results of one set of experiments suggested the questions to be addressed by a subsequent set. "Such an examination," the report states, "demanded a sacrifice of time, and a number of systematical researches." (4, p. 99)

The effects of imagination, the commissioners realized, could be magnified and reinforced in public settings. And herein lies a fascinating subplot to the Royal Commission and to the use of science in public policy. Louis XVI had a genuine interest in the scientific basis of animal magnetism, perhaps especially because Marie Antoinette was a strong proponent, but there were also darker, subrosa reasons for his interest. The French revolution was still several years away, but storm clouds were forming, and some radicals tried to co-opt mesmerism for political purposes. Pamphlets portrayed Mesmer as a man who had come to Paris with a discovery that would end human suffering. Resistance and skepticism, lampoons and satires (there is even a satirical reference to Mesmerism in Mozart's opera *Cosi fan tutti*) led to the charge that the privileged classes, supported by the government, were attempting to suppress a movement that would improve the lot of the common man. Revolutionaries such as

Nicholas Bergasse tried to exploit the huge public interest in mesmerism: "The time has now come," Bergasse wrote, " for the revolution that France needs. But to attempt to produce one openly is to doom it to failure; to succeed it is necessary to wrap oneself in mystery, it is necessary to unite men under the pretext of experiments in physics, but, in reality, for the overthrow of despotism."[2] In May 1784, a few weeks after the commission had been appointed, the Paris police submitted a secret report to the king that "some mesmerists were mixing radical political ideas in their pseudoscientific discourses" [2]

Perhaps it was this political subtext that led the commissioners to write in their report that the effects of mesmerism could be likened to what happened when applause broke out in theaters, or to how soldiers responded to battle when "the drum, the sound of the military musical instruments, the noise of the cannon, the musquetry, the shouts of the army, and the general disorder" (4, p. 91) excited the imagination and hurried the soldiers to charge or to flee. More ominously,

> the same cause is deeply concerned in rebellions; the multitude are governed by the imagination; the individuals in a numerous assembly are more subjected to their senses, and less capable of submitting to the dictates of reason. . . . It has been useful to forbid numerous assemblies in seditious towns, as a means of stopping a contagion so easily communicated. (4, p. 93)

Politics is one thing, morality is quite another. When the Royal Commission submitted its report to Louis XVI in August 1784, it included a secret addendum, apparently never published, in which Franklin and his colleagues expressed serious concern about the moral impact of mesmerism, in which women were exposed to touching on the lower abdomen, sometimes for hours.

The Royal Society submitted its report on August 16, only five days after Franklin's report. Reaction to the reports was swift. Anton Mesmer challenged the conclusions and appealed to the parliament of Paris. In a letter to his grandson W. T. Franklin on September 8, 1784, Benjamin Franklin wrote:

> Mesmer has complained to the Parliament of our Report and requested that they would appoint Commissioners to whom he might submit the examination of the condition of his patients, not his theory and practice. . . . Many thought that Parliament would do nothing with it. But they have laid hold of it to clinch Mesmer and oblige him to expose all directly."[7]

The Franklin report had a profound effect on public opinion. Interest in Mesmer and animal magnetism ceased almost immediately, not only in Paris but also in the rest of Europe, though it was to reemerge several decades later. A bit of doggerel published in *Memoires secrets* on January 17, 1785, reflects the quick public reaction:

> That the charlatan Mesmer
> With another confrere
> Should cure many a female;
> That he should turn their heads,
> In touching them I know not where,
> It's crazy
> Very crazy
> And I don't believe in it at all. (8)

The work of the Royal Commission stands as a model of a thoughtful, well-designed sequence of experiments that attempted to validate through rational means a seemingly promising new therapeutic modality. In framing their hypotheses, then using a careful and well-controlled approach to testing those hypotheses, the commissioners relied on evidence not supposition. Certain observations led to further questions and further experiments. Conclusions grew from evidence, not from unsubstantiated testimony. Such was the stage of scientific reasoning during the Enlightenment in the late 18th century, a time when medicine was poised on the horizon of the many advances in knowledge that were to characterize the ensuing decades.

References

1. Journal de Bruxelles, January 31, 1784, pp. 226–227. Cited in Darnton R: (2).
2. Darnton R: Mesmerism and the End of the Enlightenment in France. Cambridge, Massachusetts: Harvard University Press, 1968.
3. Mesmer A: The Discovery of Animal Magnetism, 1779. Cited in Franklin B: (4).
4. Franklin B, et al.: Report of Dr. Benjamin Franklin and Other Commissioners, Charged by the King of France with the Examination of the Animal Magnetism, as now Practised at Paris. London: J. Johnson, 1785.
5. Thouret M-A: Recherches et doutes sur le magnetisme animal, 1784. Cited in Darnton R: (2)
6. Moll A: Hypnotism: including a Study of the Chief Points of Psycho-therapeutics and Occultism. New York: Charles Scribner's Sons, 1913.
7. Hale EE, Hale EE Jr.: Franklin in France. New York: Burt Franklin, 1887.
8. Memoires Secrets, January 17, 1785, pp. 45–46. Cited in Darnton R: (2).

Osler Usque Ad Mare: The S.S. *William Osler*

Charles S. Bryan, M.D.
Marilyn Fransiszyn, M.L.S.

Among the few facets of William Osler's life to escape extensive scrutiny has been his connection with the sea. Born in a country that proudly bears the motto *A mari usque ad mare* (From sea unto sea), Osler came from a long line of seafarers from the Cornish coast of England. His great-grandfather Edward may have been a merchant seaman—or even a pirate. One of his grandfathers, another Edward, was a Falmouth ship owner. A third Edward, Osler's uncle, joined the navy as a medical officer and wrote *The Voyage*, an epic poem that, along with his *Life of Lord Exmouth*, a biography of a Cornish admiral, was avidly read in the Osler home in Bond Head, Ontario. Osler's father, Featherstone, spent 10 years at sea in the Royal Navy, endured several maritime near-disasters, and was nearly shipwrecked on the voyage that brought him and his new bride to Canada. Such associations may have prompted William Osler, when made a Baronet in 1911, to choose waves for the field on his coat of arms.

Osler himself spent a great deal of time at sea. He crossed the Atlantic at least 32 times. Many of his extant correspondence bear the letterhead of ocean liners: the *Cedric*, the *Campania*, the *Coronia*, the *Teutonic*, the *Celtic*, the *Parisian*, the *Majestic*, the *Empress of Britain*, the *Empress of Ireland*, the *Empress of India*, the *Ems*, the *Furst Bismark*, and USMS *St. Louis*. In 1904, on a trans-Atlantic crossing aboard RMS *Campania*, Osler befriended the ship's surgeon, Francis Vernon, and together they organized the North Atlantic Medical Society, which met for tea in Vernon's cabin. The humorous proceedings included a prospectus for a 700-page volume, *Medico-Nautical Studies*, to be published by "The Utopian Press, Thos. More & Sons, Atlanta," and Osler's paper entitled "Sea, sleep, and obesity: a statistical inquiry."[1] In 1905 he attended the Cowes regatta aboard a palatial yacht, the *Kethailes*.[2] In 1911 Osler chose for his holiday a cruise in Egypt

Presented at the American Osler Society, May 7, 1999, Montreal.

Reprinted with permission from *Canadian Medical Association Journal, 161:* 849–852, 1999.

aboard Cook's Nile Service steamer, the S.S. *Seti*. As in his life ashore, while at sea Osler meticulously balanced his waking hours between reading, writing, and socializing with his fellow passengers.

Osler appreciated the seashore and enjoyed sea bathing. He spent many summer holidays by the sea in Canada, the United States, and England. He rented seaside cottages in Murray Bay, where the St. Lawrence River widens into the Gulf of St. Lawrence, on the coast of Cornwall and elsewhere. Letters from those places to his friends and colleagues often mention his having taken "a header off the rocks." The only known painting attributed to Osler shows a sailing ship on a stormy sea.[3]

Osler sometimes salted his inspirational addresses with nautical imagery. In "Books and Men,"[4] he wrote: "To study the phenomena of disease without books is to sail an uncharted sea" [page 210]. In "A Way of Life," an address written on a steamer and delivered to Yale students a year and 10 days after one of the most infamous disasters in maritime history, he urged students to live in "day-tight compartments"—presumably more secure than the water-tight compartments of the *Titanic*.[5] His remedy for alcoholism was to "throw all the beer and spirits into the Irish Channel, the English Channel, and the North Sea for a year."[6]

Osler's main hobby was book collecting. His huge library contained classics and lesser works of nautical medicine, such as James Lind's *Treatise on the Scurvy*, Sir Gilbert Blane's *Observations on the Diseases Incident to Seamen*, and Stephen Hale's *Descriptions of Ventilators: Whereby Great Quantities of Fresh Air May with Ease be Conveyed into Mines, Goals* [sic], *Hospitals, Work-Houses, and Ships*.[7] Osler was fascinated by the life of Thomas Dover (ca. 1660 to ca. 1742), an English physician who spent 3 years as a privateer in the South Seas during which he discovered the prototype for Robinson Crusoe in the person of one Alexander Selkirk, a shipwrecked Scot.[8] Also in Osler's library were the privately printed historical essays of Sylvanus P. Thompson, including an address on "Petrus Peregrinus and the Mariner's Compass in the Thirteenth Century," described by Osler in 1908 as "one of the best lectures I have ever heard"[page 117–8].[2]

Despite all of this, it would be an exaggeration to conclude that Osler had a deep, abiding interest in ships and the sea. His interest in medical history and his efforts in building his library were wide-ranging. His penchant for seaside holidays and his belief in the health benefits of sea bathing were shared by many people of his time. Considering his liking for fast automobiles, his enjoyment of an airplane show in Paris featuring the Wright brothers ("a great treat"), his obvious relief at the end of an ocean voyage, and his skill at time management,[2, 9–10] it seems probable that he would have preferred to travel between continents by airplane if given a choice. Posthumously, however, Osler came to have yet another connection with the sea, as described in a brief notice appearing one Saturday in March 1943 in the *Baltimore American* under the headline "Liberty ship named for Dr. Osler."[11]

The Liberty ships formed the backbone of a supply line that enabled the Allies to wage war against the Axis powers during World War II. In what has been called "the most stupendous building program the world will probably ever see" [page 4]"[12] some 2700 Liberty ships—making up nearly three-quarters of the 40 million dead-weight tons of shipbuilding in the United States during the war— were built at an average cost of US$1.6 million in 18 shipyards.[13] Baltimore's Bethlehem-Fairfield Shipyard was the largest and most efficient of its kind. It was there that the SS *William Osler*, one of 63 Liberty ships named for physicians, was built in a mere 28 days.

Like all of the Liberty ships, the *William Osler* was fitted with gun platforms and anti-aircraft guns and carried a naval gun crew as well as a regular crew. She was assigned the radio call and signal letters 343605 KKNN, was initially valued at US$1.75 million and was registered in Baltimore.[14] As was typical of the Liberty ships when finances permitted, her launching from the No. 14 way at the Bethlehem-Fairfield shipyard on March 6, 1943, occasioned a ceremony with music, speeches, and flowers for the person chosen to break a bottle of champagne over the bow. The ship's sponsor was Miss Beryl Scott Hobson, a Wren (a member of the Women's Royal Navy Service). Special guests included Dr. Thomas Cullen of Canada, a personal friend of Osler, members of the British consulates, and various dignitaries of the Royal Navy and the British Overseas airways.[11]

Immediately after her trials the *William Osler* was delivered by the War Shipping Administration to the States Maritime Corporation under the General Service Agreement. On March 24, 1943, she sailed by canal to Philadelphia where she picked up an armed guard and ammunition before proceeding to New York City. On April 7 she left New York with a cargo destined for the Persian Gulf; the nature of the cargo is not known. Her guns and ammunition were never needed, as she circumnavigated the globe without engaging the enemy. Her now-declassified secret log contains little of a secretive nature, most of the comments being about the conditions of the sea.[15] "Mountainous seas & swells" were no doubt significant to the crew, for Liberty ships were notoriously prone to "pitching, rolling, & laboring very heavily" to the extent that experienced navy gunners often asked to be transferred to another type of vessel. On the evening of September 29, 1943, she had her only potentially serious accident when, while steaming down the Río de la Plata between Uruguay and Argentina, a "bright red light [that] showed up directly ahead approx 300 yards" turned out to be the schooner *Favorita Maria*. The ships collided, with minor damage to both but no casualties. By November 13, 1943, the *William Osler* was back in New York.

To what extent did those aboard the *William Osler* appreciate her honoree? The existing logs contain no mention of Osler. It is known that many seamen had little or no idea about the persons for whom their Liberty ships were named. Unlike Navy destroyers, Liberty ships did not feature a memorial plate containing the honoree's biographical sketch. Name recognition for the *William Osler* was further complicated by the presence of 193 Liberty ships with *William* for their first names, 11 ships with either *William, Williams,* or *Williamson* for their last names, and one ship with both (the *William Williams*). After the maiden voyage, however, the question of Osler's recognition became moot. There would be no more wartime voyages under her original name.

The States Marine Corporation was notified on November 12, 1943, that the *William Osler* was to be delivered to the army for conversion into a hospital ship. She was one of 6 Liberty ships thus converted. The conversion took place at Bethlehem's, 27th Street, Brooklyn, New York shipyard between November 23, 1943, and July 15, 1944. The extensively rebuilt ship included a new superstructure with 23-meter masts and a funnel wide enough to display Red Cross symbols more than 3.7 meters in width (Figure 1). When completed, the ship had 44 wards with a total capacity of 595 patients, an operating room, a laboratory, radiology facilities, an autopsy room, and a morgue. There were quarters for a medical staff of 17 officers, 39 nurses and 159 attendants, as well as for chaplains, the signal corps and a crew of 123.[13] Because of a policy of the US Surgeon-General's Office to name army hospital ships after flowers, an order was issued on February 29, 1944, to rename the vessel the USHS *Wisteria*.[16] Thus, it is possible that neither patients, staff nor crew knew about the ship's association with the great physician-educator honoured at her christening.

Figure 1. Converted into an Army hospital ship, the *William Osler* was renamed the USHS *Wisteria*.

The *Wisteria's* voyages were largely uneventful except for a minor collision with a British destroyer. Starting on July 16, 1944, she made multiple round trips between the United States and England, Belgium, and the Mediterranean. After the war she made additional trips to Belgium, England, and Germany, carrying up to 611 patients at a time back to New York or to Charleston, South Carolina.[17] After the war, the *Wisteria* reverted to her original name, the *William Osler*. She was laid up in the reserve fleet in 1947 and apparently never saw service after that time. She was eventually scrapped in 1969 in Portland, Oregon. Dr. Ralph S. Crawshaw of Portland purchased the nameplate and later presented it to the Mütter Museum of the College of Physicians of Philadelphia, where it resides today (Figure 2).

Brief mention should be made of the fate of the *William Osler's* sister ships, for the *William Osler* was only 1 of 8 consecutive Liberty ships launched from Baltimore during March and April of 1943 and named for Johns Hopkins medical personages. Four of these ships honoured the founding giants of the Johns Hopkins Hospital depicted in John Singer Sargent's *The Four Doctors*: Osler, William H. Welch, Howard A. Kelly and William S. Halsted. The *William H. Welch* was shipwrecked off the coast of Scotland in 1944 with loss of all but

Figure 2. The nameplate is all that remains of the SS *William Osler*. Courtesy of the Mütter Museum, College of Physicians of Philadelphia.

12 of the 60 crewmen and navy gunners. The *Howard A. Kelly* narrowly escaped an explosion off the coast of Algiers. The *William S. Halsted* was 1 of 14 Liberty ships converted into mule carriers, in which capacity she retained her original name.[12] We can imagine that Sargent, who disliked Halsted to the extent that he allegedly did his portrait in pigments designed to fade over time, would have smiled at this disposition. The other Hopkins Liberty ships were the *Franklin P. Mall*, the *John Howland*, the *William H. Wilmer*, and the *John J. Abel*. Other Liberty ships named for persons dear to Osler included the *Oliver Wendell Holmes*, the *Silas Weir Mitchell*, the *Harvey Cushing*, and the *William S. Thayer*. Thus the playful perpetrator of the North Atlantic Medical Society was symbolically reunited with his friends in an undertaking crucial to the Allies' cause.

Acknowledgments

For records and information we thank Dr. Ralph S. Crawshaw of Portland, Oregon; Elaine Killam of the Mariners' Museum, Newport News, Virginia; Gregory J. Plunges, National Archives and Records Administration, Northeast Region (New York City); Gibson Bell Smith of the National Archives and Records Administration at College Park, Maryland; and Gretchen Worden of the College of Physicians of Philadelphia. We also thank Drs. George T. Harrell, Lawrence D. Longo, Alastair H. T. Robb-Smith, and Earl F. Nation for valuable suggestions, and Wayne Lebel of the Osler Library of the History of Medicine, McGill University, Montreal, for his assistance. This paper is dedicated to the memory of Nicholas Davies (1926–1991), who was working on a manuscript concerning the *William Osler* and her sister ships at the time of his unexpected death.

References

1. Malloch TA. *Scrapbook of Osleriana.* Accession no. 326/40/45–46. Montreal: Osler Library of the History of Medicine, McGill University.
2. Cushing H. *The life of Sir William Osler.* vol. 2. Oxford: Clarendon Press; 1925, vol. 2, p. 13, 76, 117–8.
3. William Osler, Artist? *Osler Library Newsletter* October 1997/February 1998; (86/87):. 7.
4. Osler W. Books and men. In: Osler W, *Aequanimitas, with other addresses to medical students, nurses and practitioners of medicine.* 3rd ed. Philadelphia: P. Blakiston's Son & Co.; 1932: p. 209–15.
5. Osler W. A Way of Life. In: *Selected writings of Sir William Osler, 12 July 1849 to 29 December 1919, with an introduction by G. L. Keynes, M.D., F.R.C.S.* London: Oxford University Press; 1951, p. 237–49.
6. Bean WB, editor. *Sir William Osler: aphorisms from his bedside teachings and writings. Collected by Robert Bennett Bean, M.D. (1874–1944).* New York: Henry Schuman; 1950, p. 66.
7. Osler W. *Bibliotheca Osleriana: a catalogue of books illustrating the history of medicine and science collected, arranged, and annotated by Sir William Osler, Bt. and bequeathed to McGill University.* Oxford: Clarendon Press; 1929, p. 111–2, 191, 288.
8. Osler W. Thomas Dover, physician and buccaneer. In: Osler W. *An Alabama Student and other biographical essays.* London: Oxford University Press; 1908, p. 19–36.

9. Bensley EH. The Oslers out for a drive. *Bull Hist Med* 1975; 49: 579.
10. Bryan CS. Manage time well: day-tight compartments. In: *Osler: inspirations from a great physician*. New York: Oxford University Press; 1997, p. 3–30.
11. Liberty ship named for Dr. Osler. *Baltimore American* 1943 Mar 6: 16.
12. Bunker JG. *Liberty ships: the ugly ducklings of World War II*. Annapolis (MD): Naval Institute Press; 1972, p. 4, 99–100, 119, 175.
13. Sawyer LA, Mitchell WH. *The Liberty ships: the history of the "emergency" type cargo ships constructed in the United States during the Second World War*. 2nd ed. London: Lloyd's of London Press, Ltd.; 1985, p. 18, 211–2.
14. *William Osler* (EX) *Wisteria* (US Army hospital ship) (EX) *William Osler* (vessel [MCE 954] [OFF 243065]). US Maritime Commission file No. 901–10023.
15. *Secret log* [now declassified) *for a United States merchant vessel. S.S.* William Osler. United States Fleet, 1943. Declassified NND project no. 917533. New York: National Archives—Northeast Region.
16. Grover DH. *U. S. army ships and watercraft of World War II*. Annapolis (MD): Naval Institute Press; 1987, p. 72.
17. Charles RW. *Troopships of World War II* . Washington (DC): Army Transportation Association; 1947, p. 351.

Author's Note

A rare photograph showing the SS *William Osler*, full-length, being launched at the Bethlehem Steel Fairfield Shipyard on 6 March 1943, from the Hagley Library and Museum in Wilmington, Delaware. Credit for the discovery of this photograph—the result of a lifetime project researching Liberty ships—must go to William F. Hultgren, self-described marine historian of Erie, Pennsylvania, who had not yet learned about this "treasure chest of maritime prints" when he was originally contacted by one of the authors in 1978. Last year, in a shipping enthusiast journal, he published an appeal for photographs of the remaining 25 Liberties for which he had not yet found illustrations: the SS *William Osler* was not in the list a clear indication that a photo of the *Osler* had been found at last. Over the years Mr. Hultgren has amassed the most comprehensive collection of Liberty Ship photographs in existence, over 2,500 prints. This photo was not available to us at the time the preceding article was published. Courtesy of the Hagley Museum and Library.

The Medical Repository—The First U.S. Medical Journal (1797–1824)

Richard J. Kahn
Patricia G. Kahn

July 1997 marked the 200th anniversary of the founding of the Medical Repository, the first medical journal indigenous to the United States (Figure 1). It was printed by T. & J. Swords, Printers to the Faculty of Physic of Columbia College in New York City.[1,2,3,4,5] The journal, originally edited by Samuel Latham Mitchill, Elihu Hubbard Smith, and Edward Miller, was published quarterly from 1797 to 1824. Why was the Medical Repository founded, who was responsible, and what was the proposed subject matter?[6,7] Finally, who read it, and why did publication cease in 1824?

The British blockade during the American Revolution (1775 to 1783) created shortages of European medical periodicals and books as well as of drugs and medicines. Physicians who normally relied on Britain for information felt isolated. Dr. Benjamin Rush of Philadelphia, an elite physician, scientist, and signer of the Declaration of Independence, wrote to Dr. William Cullen, one of his teachers in Edinburgh, on September 16, 1783: "What has physic to do with taxation or independence? . . . One of the severest taxes paid by our profession during the war was occasioned by the want of a regular supply of books from Europe. . . . "[8] If Rush in Philadelphia had difficulty obtaining European medical literature, what was it like for the average physician?

In our present state of information glut, it is hard to imagine the isolation of the 18th-century physician faced with a medical quandary. Where did he turn for information on the theory and practice of medicine? Excerpts from a manuscript by Dr. Jeremiah Barker of Gorham, Maine, describe a labo-

Reprinted by permission from: The New England Journal of Medicine—1997, Vol. 337, No. 26

Presented at the American Osler Society, 4/4/97, Williamsburgh.

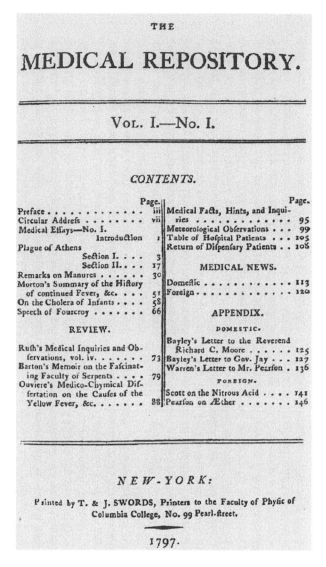

Figure 1.   Title Page of the *Medical Respository*, Volume 1, Number 1.
Courtesy of the Francis A. Countway Library of Medicine.

rious process of consulting local colleagues and writing to "several aged and experienced physicians in different parts of Mass. for advice" during an outbreak of puerperal fever in 1784 and 1785.[9]

Barker's search was probably not unusual. Much of the medical information physicians acquired came from sources other than books and medical journals. Letters, one of the main channels of medical communication, often contained the original observations of the writers as well as excerpts from hard-to-find books, laboriously hand-copied. Popular magazines and newspapers were also major sources of medical information for practitioners and for the public.[10] William and Virginia Beatty write that "between 1704 . . . and 1785, 200 different newspapers had appeared in the colonies; of 250,000 pages, there were 10,000 articles of medical interest, many aimed at the practitioner."[11]

Until the appearance of the Medical Repository there was no medical journal in the United States. As a specialized form of publication, the medical journal brought "a new element of timeliness to the dissemination of medical information," writes historian James Cassedy, "one that invigorated and greatly accelerated the processes of medical change . . . [and] became a locus of medical influence and authority as well as a measure of medical professionalism."[5,12] There were many reasons to begin an American medical journal. Chief among them were the desire for cultural independence and the medical and economic impact of major epidemics in the coastal cities. Even before the British colonies in America became independent, there were those who encouraged the writing and publication of the "American medical experience." In 1769 Peter Middleton, Professor of the Theory and Practice of Physic at the new Medical School at King's College, in New York, wrote: "The physicians of this country have still more forcible reasons, for imparting to the World, such Medical Remarks as may seem instructive or uncommon: For our Climate, Way of Living, and other Circumstances, which ought always to be regarded in the Treatment of Diseases, are so very different from those of the Countries. . . ."[13] In 1791 Benjamin Waterhouse delivered a discourse entitled "The Rise, Progress, and Present State of Medicine" to the Middlesex Medical Association of Boston, stating that "A country so completely independent in other respects as the United States, however ready to receive information in the higher grades of science . . . should blush to be indebted to foreign seminaries for the first principles of professional instruction."[14]

In New York on October 31, 1795, Noah Webster, a layman, published a circular that included the following appeal: "To the Physicians of Philadelphia, New-York, Baltimore, Norfolk and Newhaven. . . . As malignant fever has, for three summers past, raged in different parts of the United States, and proved fatal to great numbers of our fellow-citizens, and extremely prejudicial to the Commerce of the Country. . . . To decide on the origin and nature of the Yellow Fever, we want the evidence of facts [about] epidemics in the United States. . . ."[15]

The papers Webster sought in that circular were edited and published by him in 1796 as A Collection of Papers on the Subject of Bilious Fevers, prevalent in the United States for a few years past.[15] Webster did not receive as many communications as he had hoped. Asked in July 1796 to advertise for more papers for another edition, he wrote: " . . . I have neither inclination nor leisure to devote much time to this object: nor am I convinced that the object itself will reward a continuance of my labors. . . . "[15]

Webster's decision to abandon this project proved crucial to the creation of the Medical Repository. Six weeks later, on August 11, 1796, a young New York City physician named Elihu Hubbard Smith wrote in his diary: " . . . I think, as Mr. Webster has relinquished his plan of continuing his collection, of taking it up myself . . . & publishing an annual volume; the principal object of which will be the preserving & collecting of the materials for a History of the Diseases of America, as they appear in the several seasons. . . . "[16] The Medical Repository was conceived.

Born in Litchfield, Connecticut, in 1771, Smith entered Yale College at the age of 11, graduated in 1786, and studied medicine both under the direction of his father and in Philadelphia. In 1793 he moved to New York City, where he practiced medicine, read voraciously, wrote poetry, and proposed and helped found the Medical Repository.[17,18] Webster had graduated from Yale eight years before Smith, but they were members of the same literary club, the Brothers in Unity. The fact that they were in close communication probably accounts for the short time between Webster's comment that he would "relinquish his collection" of data on epidemics and Smith's diary entry.[19]

A proposal for Smith's new medical journal is found in his diary entry of August 17, 1796:

> Circular: To the Physicians, of the United States . . . this is no other than an endeavor to obtain an accurate & annual account of those general diseases which reign each season, over every part of the United States. [Subjects to include] The State of the Atmosphere . . . Accurate & succinct accounts of General Diseases that have heretofore appeared in any part of the United States . . . Useful Histories of particular Cases . . . New Methods of curing Diseases . . . Accounts of new discovered & applied remedies—either in the cure of common or of rather & hitherto incurable diseases . . . American Medical Biography . . . Accounts of former Medical Publications in America . . . Accounts of New Medical Publications in America . . . [and] Medical News. . . . It is intended to issue the first volume of the Collection in the month of May 1797, under the title of the Medical Repository.[20]

On November 10, 1796, Smith's diary reads: "Drs. Mitchill and Miller came in. They stayed an hour; & we agreed to unite in the prosecution of the plan for a Medical Repository, as projected by me last Summer."[21] An altered version of Smith's August circular was published as a "Circular Address," dated November 15, 1796, and signed by Samuel Latham Mitchill, Edward Miller, and E.H. Smith.

Samuel Latham Mitchill was born in North Hempstead, Long Island, in 1764. Having apprenticed under his uncle, Dr. Samuel Latham, from 1781 to 1783 and under Dr. Samuel Bard from 1783 to 1786, Mitchill received the M.D. degree with honors from the University of Edinburgh in 1787. He became Professor of Chemistry and Natural History at Columbia College, and later held the Professorship of Botany and Materia Medica at the College of Physicians and Surgeons. Of particular note is his interest in teaching and writing about the new French chemistry of Lavoisier, with its application to medicine.[22,23] Debates on the changing theories of medicine and chemistry found a home in the Medical Repository, which would be edited by Mitchill until 1821.

The last of the triumvirate of founders was Dr. Edward Miller, born in 1760, a native of Delaware who graduated from the Medical Department of the University of Pennsylvania in 1785. Miller moved to New York in 1796 and later became chair of the Practice of Physic in the College of Physicians and Surgeons and a physician at New York Hospital.[3,18,24]

The first issue of the Medical Repository, a quarterly, came off the press on July 26, 1797. It was edited by Mitchill, Miller, and Smith until Smith's death in 1798. In 1801 the title was changed to The Medical Repository and Review of American Publications on Medicine, Surgery, and the Auxiliary branches of Philosophy. After Miller's death in 1812, the title was changed to the Medical Repository of Original Essays and Intelligence, which it remained until the journal ceased publication in 1824.[25] Samuel Latham Mitchill, last of the original editors, disappeared from the title page after 1821.

Subscribers to the Medical Repository of 1797–1798 (volume 1) represented 14 states, with a disproportionately high number, relative to the population, coming from the states associated with the editors: New York, Connecticut, and Delaware (Figure 2). Of the 266 subscribers, 73 percent were physicians, 11 percent merchants, 10 percent lawyers or judges, 3 percent ministers, and 2 percent booksellers. The booksellers ordered a total of 119 copies, with Philadelphia (50 copies) and Boston (36 copies) leading the sales. We have been unable to locate later subscription lists or business records. The cost, as published in the journal itself in 1800, was ". . . a dollar to be paid on receipt of the first number, and a half a dollar on delivery of each succeeding number. . . . copies shall be

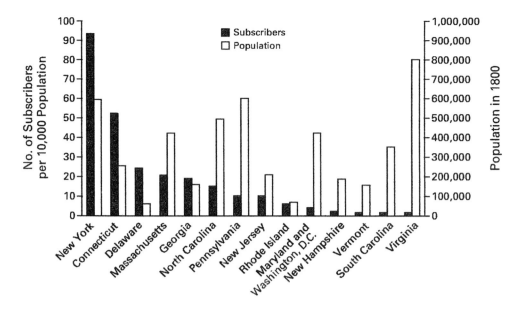

Figure 2. Subscribers to the *Medical Repository* According to State, 1797–1798.

sent, regularly, to Subscribers, by any conveyance they shall point out, they being at any charge which may so arise." There were occasional advertisements in the Medical Repository, mainly for other books and journals, but we have no information about whether advertising was used to recover costs.

The content of the Medical Repository was as outlined in the circular of 1796. It emphasized epidemics, contagious disease, and fevers, as well as climate and meteorology and their effect on disease in America. Joseph Priestley, Samuel Mitchill, and others wrote on various aspects of chemistry. Early issues regularly included tables listing patients admitted to New York Hospital and New York Dispensary, with information on diagnoses and results. Published articles originated from nearly all the states, although New York was disproportionately represented. Two hundred nineteen articles, on contagious disease, sepsis, fever, tuberculosis, climate and disease, meteorology, and chemistry, were published in the Medical Repository between 1797 and 1824. Fifty-eight of those articles came from New York, 15 from Virginia, 12 from Maine, and 12 from Maryland and Washington, D.C. Three hundred twenty-five books were reviewed in the Medical Repository; of these, 262, or 81 percent, were written by Americans. It was an American medical journal.

Smith's diary gives scant evidence of true peer review of the Medical Repository, although many entries suggest that the three editors read and discussed papers submitted for publication. For example, on June 3, 1797, Smith wrote that he was at Dr. Mitchill's: "Read there, letters of Dr. Barker of Portland, Maine, on Alkaline practice in Fevers. . . ."[26] The only explicit reference to rejection of a paper was on November 7, 1797, when Smith and Miller agreed to persuade Mitchill not to publish an "Inquiry into the nature and composition of Nitric and Nitrous Acid. . . ."[27] Of the 34 articles Mitchill published during his years as editor, only 1 can be considered an editorial in the modern sense of an article that puts other work in perspective, interpreting, explaining, and advising. Book reviews were frequently long extracts from books, or summaries, rather than critical reviews. Medical and philosophical news included information on lectures, publications, and medical schools, both foreign and domestic.

In the United States, as in Europe, medical journals in the first third of the 19th century had a short life expectancy (Figure 3).[28] Seven New York medical journals began publication between 1797 and 1822, and 31 U.S. medical journals began between 1820 and 1829.[4,28] The proliferation of medical journals accompanied the proliferation of medical schools, influenced, as Cassedy notes, by "the jealousies, aspirations, and loyalties of every region and state, all of which demanded medical journals to go along with other institutions rising in their capitals or principal cities."[5]

The Medical Repository ceased publication in 1824 after 27 years, at a time when the average life span of a U.S. medical journal was 5.4 years. Competition, printing costs, postage, loss of institutional support, and loss of enthusiastic editors were probably all factors in the fate of the journal. Most editors of medical journals in the first half of the 19th century "did not remain editors long enough to achieve any particular journalistic reputation, either for their periodicals or themselves."[5] Miller (editor of the Medical Repository for 15 years) and Mitchill (editor for more than 20 years) were an exception. The final volumes of the Medical Repository, volumes 7 and 8, are dated 1822 and 1824 and were edited by James R. Manley and Charles Drake. Though Manley was president of the New York Medical Society from 1825 to 1826, he did not have Mitchill's reputation. The publisher, E. Bliss and E. White, was by this time also producing the New-York Medical and Physical Journal (1822 to 1830). The Medical Repository may have failed for medical, scientific, philosophical, or economic reasons, or for a combination of them.

The Medical Repository was the first serious attempt in this country to present the relation between science and practice in a serial format that allowed response and communication. It introduced new theory, such as the chemistry of Lavoisier and Priestley as it related to medicine, and allowed nonelite physicians from small towns to describe what they saw and how they tried to apply emerging theories to their practice. It became a publication in which physicians and others could find the latest thoughts on subjects as diverse as manure, meteorology, and medical practice, paving the way for a tradition of medical journalism that has grown in rigor and influence to the present day.

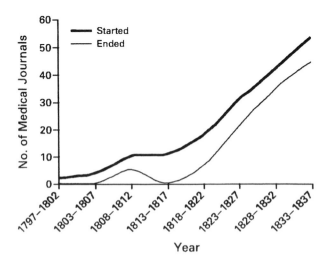

Figure 3.   Number of U.S. Medical Journals Started and Ended, 1797–1837.
Data are from Billings.[28]

Richard J. Kahn, M.D.
Patricia G. Kahn, M.L.S.
Penobscot Bay Medical Center
Rockport, ME 04856

We are indebted to Mr. Richard J. Wolfe (Boston Medical Library) for years of help on this and many other projects, and to Ms. Lucretia McClure (Boston Medical Library), Mr. Tom Horrocks (Library of the College of Physicians of Philadelphia), Ms. Toby Appel (Cushing-Whitney Medical Library, Yale University), Ms. Georgia B. Barnhill (American Antiquarian Society), and Dr. Robert H. Jones (Duke University Medical Center).

Source Information

Address reprint requests to Ms. Kahn at the Niles Perkins Health Science Library, Penobscot Bay Medical Center, 6 Glen Cove Dr., Rockport, ME 04856.

Presented to the American Osler Society meeting, Williamsburg, Va., April 4, 1997, and to the College of Physicians of Philadelphia as the Samuel X. Radbill Lecture, Philadelphia, October 7, 1997.

References

1. Robinson V. The early medical journals of America founded during the quarter-century 1797–1822. Medical Life 1929;36:552–85.
2. Garrison FH. An introduction to the history of medicine. Philadelphia: W.B. Saunders, 1929.
3. Billings JS. Literature and institutions. In: Clarke EH, Bigelow HJ, Gross SD, Thomas TG, Billings JS, eds. A century of American medicine, 1776–1876. Philadelphia: Henry C Lea, 1876:291–366.
4. Ebert M. The rise and development of the American medical periodical, 1797–1850. Bull Med Libr Assoc 1952;40:243–76.
5. Cassedy JH. The flourishing and character of early American medical journalism, 1797–1860. J Hist Med Allied Sci 1983;38:135–50.
6. Kronick DA. A history of scientific & technical periodicals/the origins and development of the scientific and technical press, 1665–1790. Metuchen, N.J.: Scarecrow Press, 1976.
7. Porter R. The rise of medical journalism in Britain to 1800. In: Bynum WF, Lock S, Porter R, eds. Medical journals and medical knowledge: historical essays. London: Routledge, 1992:6–28.
8. Butterfield LH, ed. Letters of Benjamin Rush. Vol. 1: 1761–1792. Princeton, N.J.: Princeton University Press, 1951:310.
9. Barker J. A history of diseases in the District of Maine, commencing in 1772 and continued to the present time. Vol. 1. Manuscript Collection 13. Portland: Maine Historical Society, 1797–1831.
10. Coggins CC. Medical articles in eighteenth century American magazines. Bull Med Libr Assoc 1965;53:426–37.
11. Beatty WK, Beatty VL. Sources of medical information. JAMA 1976;236: 78–82.

12. Cassedy JH. American medicine and statistical thinking, 1800–1860. Cambridge, Mass.: Harvard University Press, 1984:1–24.

13. Middleton P. A medical discourse or an historical inquiry into the ancient and present state of medicine: the substance of which was delivered at opening the Medical School in the City of New York. New York: Hugh Gaine, 1769:68.

14. Waterhouse B. The rise, progress, and present state of medicine: a discourse. Boston: Thomas and John Fleet, 1792:28.

15. Webster N. A collection of papers on the subject of bilious fevers, prevalent in the United States for a few years past. New York: Hopkins, Webb, 1796.

16. Cronin JE, ed. The diary of Elihu Hubbard Smith (1771–1798). Philadelphia: American Philosophical Society, 1973:201.

17. Thacher J. American medical biography: or memoirs of eminent physicians who have flourished in America: to which is prefixed a succinct history of medical science in the United States from the First Settlement of the Country. Vol. 2. Boston: Richardson & Lord and Cottons & Barnard, 1828:88–95.

18. Kelly HA, Burrage WL. American medical biographies. Baltimore: Norman, Remington, 1920.

19. Cronin JE, ed. The diary of Elihu Hubbard Smith (1771–1798). Philadelphia: American Philosophical Society, 1973:3.

20. Cronin JE, ed. The diary of Elihu Hubbard Smith (1771–1798). Philadelphia: American Philosophical Society, 1973:204–6.

21. Cronin JE, ed. The diary of Elihu Hubbard Smith (1771–1798). Philadelphia: American Philosophical Society, 1973:245.

22. Mitchill SL. Remarks on the gaseous oxyd of azote or of nitrogene, and on the effects it produces when generated in the stomach, inhaled into the lungs, and applied to the skin: being and attempt to ascertain the true nature of contagion, and to explain thereupon the phenomena of fever. . . . New York: T. and J. Swords, 1795:43.

23. Mitchill SL. Nomenclature of the new chemistry. New York: T. and J. Swords, 1794.

24. Miller S. The medical works of Edward Miller, M.D., collected, and accompanied with a biographical sketch of the author. New York: Collins, 1814.

25. Weinstein RJ. Index to the Medical Repository, 1797–1824. (Master's thesis. New York: Pratt Institute, July 1952.)

26. Cronin JE, ed. The diary of Elihu Hubbard Smith (1771–1798). Philadelphia: American Philosophical Society, 1973:320.

27. Cronin JE, ed. The diary of Elihu Hubbard Smith (1771–1798). Philadelphia: American Philosophical Society, 1973:388.

28. Billings JS. The medical journals of the United States. Boston Med Surg J 1879;100:1–14.

 # Index